Praise for *Seafood Cooking For Dummies*

"This book removes the mystery surrounding seafood and proves that cooking fish and shellfish is easy and enjoyable. *Seafood Cooking For Dummies* is filled with tips for using seafood in everyday dinners or for special occasion celebrations. It's a must-have addition to your cookbook library."

— John Fiorillo, editor-in-chief, *Seafood Business* magazine

"When you are ready to feast on fish or throw a festive party, *Seafood Cooking For Dummies* offers a wide range of recipes for the novice or the experienced seafood chef. Exciting and fun, this reference book will become a culinary collectors staple — indispensable for seafood lovers. Remember, everything that swims can sustain you, whether for your body or your soul. And that's no fish tail."

— Rich Catanzaro, director of Seafood Marketing and
Procurement, HEB Grocery Company, San Antonio, Texas

"The talented authors have assembled a masterful collection of conscientiously tested recipes and useful tips and techniques for cooking and enjoying seafoods of all stripes and varieties. Their sparkling ideas for entertaining will put pizzazz on party tables and pepper daily suppers with pleasure."

— Irena Chalmers, president, Chalmers Food Publications, Inc.

"If knowledge is power, then even the most tentative fish cook will find culinary muscle when armed with a copy of *Seafood Cooking For Dummies*. Great recipes with clear-cut directions are supported by informative tips and interesting information. This is the seafood book that will actually get you into the kitchen."

— Marcel Desaulniers, author of *Death by Chocolate Cookies* and
Salad Days: Main-Course Salads for a First-Class Meal

"If you feel like a fish out of water when it comes to cooking them, fear no more. At last, a user-friendly cookbook that will forever end the mysteries of the deep, written with style and jam-packed with creative, downright delicious recipes guaranteed to please. Truly a fish lover's bible!"

— Sharon Tyler Herbst, author of *Food Lover's Companion* and
The Ultimate A-to-Z Bar Guide

"*Seafood Cooking For Dummies* takes the fear out of cooking seafood. It contains a wealth of information on fish and shellfish that you can't find any place else under one cover. Best of all, the recipes are great, require few ingredients, and are quick to prepare. Leslie Beal Bloom and Marcie Ver Ploeg can make you look like an expert while getting you in and out of the supermarket and the kitchen really fast."

> — Shirley A. Estes, executive director, Virginia Marine Products Board

"*Seafood Cooking For Dummies* is a one-of-a-kind book and a must-read for anyone interested in seafood. Far from just a cookbook, this book offers a variety of seafood information cleverly put together for easy reference. It's written with that personal touch with real people sharing seafood knowledge and recipes. It will be difficult not to eat seafood every day after you read this book."

> — Carol A. Haltaman, president, National Fisheries Institute

"The best place for a fish out of water to land is *Seafood Cooking For Dummies*. It will receive very special treatment. Far more than just a recipe book, [the authors'] expertise covers identification, handling, seafood shippers, even Web sites on the subject. I've always wondered how to make that elusive Old Bay seasoning for boiled crab, but no longer. Now I know where to look for temptingly simple recipes, plus the latest information on American seafood. I'm hooked!"

> — Anne Willan, founder and president of La Varenne Cooking School, author of *Look and Cook Classic Fish,* and host of the 26-part PBS series *Look and Cook*

Open Season for Seafood

Simple seasonings give "Wow!" power to your seafood. Try these helpful hints:

- Meaty fish, such as swordfish, tuna, grouper, catfish, and mahimahi, stand up to hearty seasonings — flip to Chapter 12.
- Tender, more fragile fish, such as cod, flounder, and whitefish, prefer more delicate seasonings. Check out Chapter 12 for further details.
- Save your leftover fresh herbs and mix 'n' match in flavored butters, as we do in Chapter 12.
- Season fish with rubs or dry herb mixtures for 15 minutes to 1½ hours (refrigerated) before cooking to best let the rubs absorb moisture and flavor the fish.
- Marinades that have more fat than acid work best on fish — the flesh won't get soft.
- Marinate seafood from 15 minutes to one hour (refrigerated) to pick up yummy flavors.
- Partner shrimp, crabs, and crawfish with regional seasonings, such as Chesapeake Bay-Style Seasoning or Louisiana Crab and Shrimp Boil (both in Chapter 7).
- Keep sassy sauces and salsas on hand to superbly season fish — see Chapter 15.
- Puree fresh herbs, such as dill, basil, and cilantro with garlic and olive oil to make a snappy puree, like pesto. Keep puree on hand to stir into sour cream, yogurt, or mayonnaise for a quick fish topper.

"Grate" Grilling Tips

Grilling is an easy, fun way to cook seafood. Get fired up with these tips!

- Allow about 10 minutes to heat a gas grill before cooking; 35 to 40 minutes to ready a charcoal fire.
- Use a grill topper to grill tender, flaky fish (such as cod) or small shellfish (such as scallops). When you use a grill topper, heat it on the grill before cooking.
- Brush the grill grid or topper with oil before heating to let you shift fish more easily.
- If you're new to grilling, start grilling with the lid up so that you can see what the fish looks like as it cooks. When you've mastered grilling with the lid up, close the lid to capture the smoke and add flavor.
- Take the advice of a New Orleans fish seller and try a mayonnaise marinade. Don't use lowfat, though — the fat in regular mayo keeps fish from sticking.
- For kebabs, cut vegetables small so that they cook as fast as the seafood. Soak bamboo skewers in water for 30 minutes before threading fish on them to prevent the skewers from disintegrating (they always char anyway).
- Use a spatula to lift fish, rather than a fork, which may break apart the fish flesh.
- Always bring cooked seafood from the grill inside on a clean plate, not the same one that carried the raw fish.
- To lessen the chance of fish sticking to the grill, clean the racks with a stiff wire brush or cleaning pad after each use (while the grill is warm).

Coming Out of Their Shells

The shell is the key for keeping shellfish alive when you buy and bring them home — and for determining when they are cooked. Here are some shellfish lovin' care tips:

- Even out of the water, clams, mussels, oysters, and scallops breathe by opening and closing their shells. When the shell is tightly closed, the animal inside is alive.

- When you buy live mussels, hardshell clams, or scallops (when you're lucky enough to find them), look for shells that are free of cracks or chips, and are closed (or not gaping wide open).

- If a shell is slightly open, you can check to see if the clam, mussel, or scallop is still alive: tap the shell (a spoon works just fine) or press the two shells quickly together several times with your fingers. If the shells close, the critter is still alive, and "clamming up." Discard any that remain open.

- A soft-shell clam never fully closes, because its neck gets in the way. To ensure that soft-shells are alive, touch or tap one of the shells; the clam should quickly pull its shells closer together.

- For oysters in the shell, we suggest buying only those that are tightly closed.

Life of the Seafood Party

Need to liven up your next party? Showcase seafood and your next bash will be a big hit. Here's how:

- Go beyond shrimp cocktail — try Macho Nachos; Mediterranean Shrimp Pizza; Fiesta Shrimp Salsa; Remoulade Sauce; Marinated Shrimp in a Mustard Duet; or Shrimp with Lemon, Sun-Dried Tomato, and Goat Cheese Dip (all in Chapter 5); and Texas-Style Bacon-Wrapped Barbecue Shrimp (Chapter 11).

- Celebrate the bounty of U.S. coastal regions with a Backyard Lobster-and-Clam Bake (see Chapter 17), a Chesapeake Bay crab feast, a low-country shrimp boil, or a Louisiana Crab and Shrimp Boil (all in Chapter 7).

- Gather friends and dive into a big-dipping Coastal Fondue — see recipe in Chapter 17.

- Create a wrap 'n' roll sushi party at home — without raw fish, as described in Chapter 18.

- Savor seafood at a southwest seafood fiesta.

- Welcome the New Year by nibbling and noshing on seafood.

- Score big with a Super Bowl bash.

- Throw a memorable Mardi Gras party.

- Order smoked salmon or shellfish, lobster and clam bakes, or crab legs and claws for a seafood extravaganza.

...For Dummies®: Bestselling Book Series for Beginners

TM

References for the Rest of Us!™

BESTSELLING BOOK SERIES

Do you find that traditional reference books are overloaded with technical details and advice you'll never use? Do you postpone important life decisions because you just don't want to deal with them? Then our *...For Dummies*® business and general reference book series is for you.

...For Dummies business and general reference books are written for those frustrated and hard-working souls who know they aren't dumb, but find that the myriad of personal and business issues and the accompanying horror stories make them feel helpless. *...For Dummies* books use a lighthearted approach, a down-to-earth style, and even cartoons and humorous icons to dispel fears and build confidence. Lighthearted but not lightweight, these books are perfect survival guides to solve your everyday personal and business problems.

> "More than a publishing phenomenon, 'Dummies' is a sign of the times."
>
> — The New York Times

> "A world of detailed and authoritative information is packed into them..."
>
> — U.S. News and World Report

> "...you won't go wrong buying them."
>
> — Walter Mossberg, Wall Street Journal, on IDG Books' ...For Dummies books

Already, millions of satisfied readers agree. They have made *...For Dummies* the #1 introductory level computer book series and a best-selling business book series. They have written asking for more. So, if you're looking for the best and easiest way to learn about business and other general reference topics, look to *...For Dummies* to give you a helping hand.

1/99

SEAFOOD COOKING

FOR

DUMMIES®

SEAFOOD COOKING FOR DUMMIES®

by Leslie Beal Bloom and Marcie Ver Ploeg

IDG BOOKS WORLDWIDE

IDG Books Worldwide, Inc.
An International Data Group Company

Foster City, CA ◆ Chicago, IL ◆ Indianapolis, IN ◆ New York, NY

Seafood Cooking For Dummies®

Published by
IDG Books Worldwide, Inc.
An International Data Group Company
919 E. Hillsdale Blvd.
Suite 400
Foster City, CA 94404
www.idgbooks.com (IDG Books Worldwide Web site)
www.dummies.com (Dummies Press Web site)

Library of Congress Catalog Card No.: 99-65843

ISBN: 0-7645-5177-9

Printed in the United States of America

10 9 8 7 6 5 4 3 2 1

1B/SX/QY/ZZ/IN

Distributed in the United States by IDG Books Worldwide, Inc.

Distributed by CDG Books Canada Inc. for Canada; by Transworld Publishers Limited in the United Kingdom; by IDG Norge Books for Norway; by IDG Sweden Books for Sweden; by IDG Books Australia Publishing Corporation Pty. Ltd. for Australia and New Zealand; by TransQuest Publishers Pte Ltd. for Singapore, Malaysia, Thailand, Indonesia, and Hong Kong; by Gotop Information Inc. for Taiwan; by ICG Muse, Inc. for Japan; by Norma Comunicaciones S.A. for Colombia; by Intersoft for South Africa; by Eyrolles for France; by International Thomson Publishing for Germany, Austria and Switzerland; by Distribuidora Cuspide for Argentina; by LR International for Brazil; by Galileo Libros for Chile; by Ediciones ZETA S.C.R. Ltda. for Peru; by WS Computer Publishing Corporation, Inc., for the Philippines; by Contemporanea de Ediciones for Venezuela; by Express Computer Distributors for the Caribbean and West Indies; by Micronesia Media Distributor, Inc. for Micronesia; by Grupo Editorial Norma S.A. for Guatemala; by Chips Computadoras S.A. de C.V. for Mexico; by Editorial Norma de Panama S.A. for Panama; by American Bookshops for Finland. Authorized Sales Agent: Anthony Rudkin Associates for the Middle East and North Africa.

For general information on IDG Books Worldwide's books in the U.S., please call our Consumer Customer Service department at 800-762-2974. For reseller information, including discounts and premium sales, please call our Reseller Customer Service department at 800-434-3422.

For information on where to purchase IDG Books Worldwide's books outside the U.S., please contact our International Sales department at 317-596-5530 or fax 317-596-5692.

For consumer information on foreign language translations, please contact our Customer Service department at 1-800-434-3422, fax 317-596-5692, or e-mail rights@idgbooks.com.

For information on licensing foreign or domestic rights, please phone +1-650-655-3109.

For sales inquiries and special prices for bulk quantities, please contact our Sales department at 650-655-3200 or write to the address above.

For information on using IDG Books Worldwide's books in the classroom or for ordering examination copies, please contact our Educational Sales department at 800-434-2086 or fax 317-596-5499.

For press review copies, author interviews, or other publicity information, please contact our Public Relations department at 650-655-3000 or fax 650-655-3299.

For authorization to photocopy items for corporate, personal, or educational use, please contact Copyright Clearance Center, 222 Rosewood Drive, Danvers, MA 01923, or fax 978-750-4470.

About the Authors

Leslie Beal Bloom is the author of *Barbeque: Sizzling Fireside Know-How* and *Chicken on the Run*. She has published articles in *The Washington Post*, *The New York Times*, *Bon Appétit*, *Gourmet*, *Food & Wine*, and elsewhere. Leslie consults, designs recipes, and teaches for companies and associations, and has worked with Ocean Garden Products, the Smithsonian, the National Fisheries Institute, the Alaska Seafood Marketing Institute, the National Pasta Association, and Time-Life Books. She is a past president of the International Association of Culinary Professionals and holds a Bachelor of Science in Nutrition.

Marcie (Marcena Christian) Ver Ploeg grew up on an Iowa farm where living off the land was a way of life, but never insular. Her fascination with the global food chain began early and she now embraces both *turf* and *surf*. As founder and partner (with her husband, Don) of VP Communications in Pittsford, New York, she offers food clients a broad spectrum of marketing services. Besides co-authoring this cookbook, Marcie oversaw the photography for the center photo section and served as food stylist. Her previous cookbooks include *Chicken Soup — 75 World-Class Recipes to Warm Your Heart and Soul* and *The Buckwheat Cookbook*.

Dedications

Dedicated with love to Betty and Bill Beal (Mom and Dad) for instilling in me a love for food and the passion to strive for the best, and to Joe Bloom, my other Dad and a good friend, who believed I could accomplish anything I set my heart and mind to.

Leslie Beal Bloom

To all the men and women throughout the world who devote their lives and careers to bringing quality, safe seafood to our tables — from those who brave the elements on fishing vessels in pursuit of the wild harvest to scientists who fine-tune technologies for farm-raising ecologically sound, healthful seafood to the employee behind the counter where you shop, whose job is one of the most demanding in retailing today.

Marcie Ver Ploeg

About the Photography

The award-winning photo team at Buschner Studios in Rochester, New York, is acclaimed for its ability to add maximum visual character to their food photography. "Our tools are very simple, but by carefully controlling the propping, backgrounds, lighting, and composition, we create beautiful pictures," said Ken Buschner, the owner/photographer (far right in photo), when coaxed to emerge from beneath his black Zorro-like cape. "To be successful, our food shots must be appetizing as well as visually exciting."

Our kudos and thanks to this talented, accommodating team which also includes stylist Shawn Milne (center) and associates Rich Brainerd (left) and Ryan Stein. Rounding out the team to produce the 25 photos featuring 37 recipes for the center spread and the cover of this book were June Gullace, stylist/designer, and Marcie Ver Ploeg, food stylist.

Special Acknowledgment

Behind these pages is a creative, sustaining force without equal. June Gullace's multi-faceted roles in helping to bring this project to fruition went way above and beyond what could be expected from her affiliation with VP Communications. A day-by-day partner from start to finish, June also assumed major design responsibility for the overall "look" of the center photo section and the hands-on art direction of each photo. You, indeed, are an incredible guardian angel, June, and so much more.

Authors' Acknowledgments

To our seafood colleagues — A to K for helping us wade through who's who and what's what in the world of fish and shellfish: Scott Allmendinger, Takeout Business; Susan Barber, Maine Lobster Promotion Council; Rich Catanzaro, H.E.B. Grocery Company; Jack Donlan, The Fish House; Ken and Sue Drenth; Shirley Estes, Virginia Marine Products Board; John Fiorillo, Seafood Business; Peter Jarvis, Francesca's Favorites; Chef Robert Kinkead, Kinkead's; and Chef Chuck Kline, CMR.

And from H to Z: Doris Hicks, University of Delaware Sea Grant College Program; Bill Milne, FreshFish4U.com; Lynn Nelson, The Provincial Kitchen; Diane Pleschner, California Seafood Council, Jon Rowley, Jon Rowley & Associates; Chef Jamie Shannon, Commander's Palace; Paula Sexton, Sexton's Seafood; Anne Sterling; Karl Turner, formerly with the Louisiana Seafood Promotion and Marketing Board; and Dave Veach, Perishable Distributors of Iowa.

To our seafood suppliers for giving us fabulous fish for our photo shoot in addition to species assistance: Chad Ballard and Tim Parsons, Cherrystone Aqua Farms; Dixie Blake, Ocean Garden Products; Peter Gati, Storm Seafood; and Russell Turner, Maine Lobster Direct.

To our friend Sharon Tyler Herbst, whose acclaimed culinary reference, *Food Lover's Companion,* came to the rescue wherever pronunciation and de'fin'itive help was needed, from fahn-DOO to tuh-LAH-pee-uh.

To our fish masters: chefs, fish farmers, seafood sellers, scientists, and educators near and far for sharing their recipes, species knowledge, safety tips, and cooking expertise. A special salute to Kim Gorton and Slade Gorton & Co., for their dynamite *Slade Gorton CD-ROM Interactive Seafood Guide.*

To our fabulous recipe testers: Ann (and Ernie) Norris; and Mary (and Mike) Landsman, and daughter Caitlin; and Becky Weickel and family. They enthusiastically dived into testing and, at the end of it all, told us that they appreciate seafood in a new way.

To our of"fish"ial technical reviewer: Cynthia Nims, formerly the food editor of *Simply Seafood* magazine, whose extensive knowledge of seafood (particularly northwest fish) and what the home cook finds useful helped immeasurably to focus our book's approach and content.

To our e-mail fish bites buddies: Gail Bellamy, Restaurant Hospitality; Paula Disbrowe, Restaurant Business; Des FitzGerald, Ducktrap River Fish Farm; Brent Frei, CHEF; Joan Lang, MasterWorks; and all of our respondents.

To the team at IDG Books: Project Editor Tere Drenth redefines multi-tasking with her tremendous ability to see the big picture amid myriad details, to satisfy the demands of both authors and publishers, and to offer encouragement at just the right times and places. Illustrator Liz Kurtzman simultaneously gave birth to another bundle of joyful and insightful ...*For Dummies* illustrations — and a real bundle of joy of her own (a baby girl). Our special appreciation to Holly McGuire, acquisitions editor; Jonathan Malysiak, Maureen Kelly, and Heather Prince, acquisitions coordinators; and Michelle Vukas, editorial administrator.

To our literary agent, Carol Susan Roth, for believing in us from the beginning and connecting us with the team at IDG Books. To dear friend Merle Ellis for making the initial match.

To our fearless fish pals: Lila Gault, Sue Z. Zelickson, Shirley King, and Pat Vacca who tagged along, and sometimes led the way, to new seafood tastes — at out-of-the-way places at any hour of the day or night, on both full or empty stomachs.

In addition, Leslie wishes to acknowledge: Barbara Howard, my indefatigable assistant for her incredibly inventive mind and creative culinary touches. Treasured friends who are a major part of my support system: Irena Chalmers, Charles Chu, Phillip Cooke, Lisa Ekus, Anne Fishman, Sharon Tyler Herbst, Daniel Maye, Chan Patterson, and Anne Willan.

My bloomin' family: Ruth, Allison (my spirited 7-year-old niece who eats anything with me), Jamie, Kate, Nora, Liza, Lennie, Margie, Steve, and Jenni — for the laughter. The Ottawa Valley gang: Deb and Rose Doran, Janey and Janet Garrow, Megan and Dorothy Reid; Barbara, Noel, Chantal, Chris, and Angie Dupuis. The Midland crew: Deb and Jim Bonthron, Gisela and Ken St. Amant, Deenie and John Stewart, and Joyce Roberts.

David Bloom, my best friend, for his love and encouragement, and for helping me stay the course!

Publisher's Acknowledgments

We're proud of this book; please register your comments through our IDG Books Worldwide Online Registration Form located at `http://my2cents.dummies.com`.

Some of the people who helped bring this book to market include the following:

Acquisitions and Editorial

Project Editor: Tere Drenth

Acquisitions Editor: Holly McGuire

Technical Reviewer: Cynthia Nims

Recipe Testers: Mary Landsman, Ann Norris

Editorial Coordinator: Maureen Kelly

Editorial Director: Kristin A. Cocks

Production

Project Coordinator: Regina Snyder

Layout and Graphics: Angela F. Hunckler, Brent Savage, Jacque Schneider, Janet Seib, Michael A. Sullivan, Brian Torwelle, Mary Jo Weis, Dan Whetstine

Special Art: Elizabeth Kurtzman

Proofreaders: Betty Kish, Marianne Santy, Rebecca Senninger

Indexer: Cynthia D. Bertelsen

Special Help
Jill Alexander, John Hislop, Jonathon Malysiak, Heather Prince, Michelle Vukas

General and Administrative

IDG Books Worldwide, Inc.: John Kilcullen, CEO; Steven Berkowitz, President and Publisher

IDG Books Technology Publishing Group: Richard Swadley, Senior Vice President and Publisher; Walter Bruce III, Vice President and Associate Publisher; Steven Sayre, Associate Publisher; Joseph Wikert, Associate Publisher; Mary Bednarek, Branded Product Development Director; Mary Corder, Editorial Director

IDG Books Consumer Publishing Group: Roland Elgey, Senior Vice President and Publisher; Kathleen A. Welton, Vice President and Publisher; Kevin Thornton, Acquisitions Manager; Kristin A. Cocks, Editorial Director

IDG Books Internet Publishing Group: Brenda McLaughlin, Senior Vice President and Publisher; Diane Graves Steele, Vice President and Associate Publisher; Sofia Marchant, Online Marketing Manager

IDG Books Production for Dummies Press: Michael R. Britton, Vice President of Production; Debbie Stailey, Associate Director of Production; Cindy L. Phipps, Manager of Project Coordination, Production Proofreading, and Indexing; Tony Augsburger, Manager of Prepress, Reprints, and Systems; Laura Carpenter, Production Control Manager; Shelley Lea, Supervisor of Graphics and Design; Debbie J. Gates, Production Systems Specialist; Robert Springer, Supervisor of Proofreading; Kathie Schutte, Production Supervisor

Dummies Packaging and Book Design: Patty Page, Manager, Promotions Marketing

◆

The publisher would like to give special thanks to Patrick J. McGovern, without whom this book would not have been possible.

◆

ABOUT IDG BOOKS WORLDWIDE

Welcome to the world of IDG Books Worldwide.

IDG Books Worldwide, Inc., is a subsidiary of International Data Group, the world's largest publisher of computer-related information and the leading global provider of information services on information technology. IDG was founded more than 30 years ago by Patrick J. McGovern and now employs more than 9,000 people worldwide. IDG publishes more than 290 computer publications in over 75 countries. More than 90 million people read one or more IDG publications each month.

Launched in 1990, IDG Books Worldwide is today the #1 publisher of best-selling computer books in the United States. We are proud to have received eight awards from the Computer Press Association in recognition of editorial excellence and three from Computer Currents' First Annual Readers' Choice Awards. Our best-selling ...*For Dummies*® series has more than 50 million copies in print with translations in 31 languages. IDG Books Worldwide, through a joint venture with IDG's Hi-Tech Beijing, became the first U.S. publisher to publish a computer book in the People's Republic of China. In record time, IDG Books Worldwide has become the first choice for millions of readers around the world who want to learn how to better manage their businesses.

Our mission is simple: Every one of our books is designed to bring extra value and skill-building instructions to the reader. Our books are written by experts who understand and care about our readers. The knowledge base of our editorial staff comes from years of experience in publishing, education, and journalism — experience we use to produce books to carry us into the new millennium. In short, we care about books, so we attract the best people. We devote special attention to details such as audience, interior design, use of icons, and illustrations. And because we use an efficient process of authoring, editing, and desktop publishing our books electronically, we can spend more time ensuring superior content and less time on the technicalities of making books.

You can count on our commitment to deliver high-quality books at competitive prices on topics you want to read about. At IDG Books Worldwide, we continue in the IDG tradition of delivering quality for more than 30 years. You'll find no better book on a subject than one from IDG Books Worldwide.

John Kilcullen
Chairman and CEO
IDG Books Worldwide, Inc.

Steven Berkowitz
President and Publisher
IDG Books Worldwide, Inc.

IDG is the world's leading IT media, research and exposition company. Founded in 1964, IDG had 1997 revenues of $2.05 billion and has more than 9,000 employees worldwide. IDG offers the widest range of media options that reach IT buyers in 75 countries representing 95% of worldwide IT spending. IDG's diverse product and services portfolio spans six key areas including print publishing, online publishing, expositions and conferences, market research, education and training, and global marketing services. More than 90 million people read one or more of IDG's 290 magazines and newspapers, including IDG's leading global brands — Computerworld, PC World, Network World, Macworld and the Channel World family of publications. IDG Books Worldwide is one of the fastest-growing computer book publishers in the world, with more than 700 titles in 36 languages. The "...For Dummies®" series alone has more than 50 million copies in print. IDG offers online users the largest network of technology-specific Web sites around the world through IDG.net (http://www.idg.net), which comprises more than 225 targeted Web sites in 55 countries worldwide. International Data Corporation (IDC) is the world's largest provider of information technology data, analysis and consulting, with research centers in over 41 countries and more than 400 research analysts worldwide. IDG World Expo is a leading producer of more than 168 globally branded conferences and expositions in 35 countries including E3 (Electronic Entertainment Expo), Macworld Expo, ComNet, Windows World Expo, ICE (Internet Commerce Expo), Agenda, DEMO, and Spotlight. IDG's training subsidiary, ExecuTrain, is the world's largest computer training company, with more than 230 locations worldwide and 785 training courses. IDG Marketing Services helps industry-leading IT companies build international brand recognition by developing global integrated marketing programs via IDG's print, online and exposition products worldwide. Further information about the company can be found at www.idg.com.   1/24/99

Contents at a Glance

Cartoons at a Glance

By Rich Tennant

page 169

page 45

page 285

page 7

page 103

page 303

Fax: 978-546-7747 • E-mail: the5wave@tiac.net

Recipes at a Glance

Sandwiches and Wraps

Sauces, Salsas, and Condiments

Seasonings, Rubs, and Butters

Soups

Miscellaneous

Table of Contents

Introduction

∙ ∙

Give a man a fish and you feed him for a day.
Teach a man to fish and you feed him for a lifetime.

— Confucius

*O*ur philosophy? Give a man a fish *cookbook,* and you double his eating pleasure.

Sure, seafood is an incredibly healthful food. In fact, the health factor may be your prime motive for reading this book. But we didn't set out to write a healthy cookbook. We're just unabashed seafood lovers, eager to share our enthusiasm. So if you're an adventuresome cook, but shy away from cooking seafood, we want to tip the scales and entice you into your kitchen.

How to Use This Book

Seafood, as we use the word, refers to any and all matter of flavorful, edible, living things that move about (mostly by swimming) in the underwater world. Under that broad umbrella, we split seafood into two groups: shellfish and finfish (or simply *fish,* for short).

Delve into each category throughout this book as much or as little as you like. You don't have to start at the beginning and read to the end of *Seafood Cooking For Dummies* before you don your apron. Swim freely from one part to another. If you're not a very strong swimmer, however, we recommend that you first build your confidence with the basics in Part I.

You also don't need to digest every word of this book in order to become a confident, creative seafood cook. Through our recipes and tips, we aim to show you that cooking seafood is simple, sensational, smart, and scrumptious.

How This Book Is Organized

Dividing the diverse world of seafood into parts, as is the custom with
...*For Dummies* books, was nearly as difficult as damming off a rushing river.
We discarded the A-to-Z approach of listing fish alphabetically and instead
"schooled" them by popularity and where in the meal we like to eat them.

Shrimp and salmon are at the head of the class. We put our two seafood
superstars near the front — with fabulous, user-friendly recipes for each.
Then, after an intensive swim with seafood from lobsters to caviar, you reach
the heart of this book's extensive recipe section.

Part I: Hooked on Seafood Cooking

You could call this part the alpha and omega of seafood. Except when talking
about seafood, omega comes before alpha. We start off singing the praises of
seafood, including the healthy ways of omega-3s, the good-for-you fatty acids
that seafood is so noted for. We then shop for seafood tools, from the essential to the exotic. Our next shopping stop is to buy seafood, get it home in
prime condition, and cook it perfectly.

Part II: Seafood Superstars

Try naming two popular seafoods that top the list of worldwide favorites,
based on tons consumed. Did you guess shrimp? The other is salmon. If they
rank at the top of your list, too, you may be pleased to know that each super-
star solos in its own chapter. Follow our comprehensive tips, illustrations,
and your pick of the recipes in Chapter 5 (shrimp) or Chapter 6 (salmon) — and
you'll be well on your way to becoming well schooled in the world of seafood.

Part III: Sea Fare

If shrimp is at the head of the class, lobster can't be far behind. We begin this
part with a look at lobster and its crusty cousins. Even non-cooks find guid-
ance here with our step-by-step illustrations of how to eat a whole lobster
without missing a single, tasty morsel. Get the scoop on clams, mussels, oysters, finfish — even caviar — in the rest of this part. Don't clam up — we've
only just begun to slurp.

Part IV: Making the Most of Your Catch

Tie on your apron and grab your whisk. Fire up the grill or the broiler. You're cookin' now. In this part, we organize recipes primarily by the customary categories: snacks and appetizers; main courses; and soups, salads, and sandwiches. A bonus chapter features yummy kids' fare with recipes that kids love to eat, as well as some that they may love to cook. If your idea of saucing the fish is store-bought tartar sauce, this part may change your life forever. Make waves with condiments, salsas, and flavored butters that will play to rave reviews.

Part V: Serving Seafood from A to Z

This part is all about how easy seafood is for entertaining. Our party ideas include a backyard clambake (with lobsters, too), a seafood fondue that will make you wish for your retired fondue pot, and a wrap 'n' roll sushi party — without any raw fish.

Part VI: The Part of Tens

While we devote the majority of this cookbook to enticing you to eat seafood at home, in this part we encourage you to eat it away from home — at our favorite seafood restaurants, both upscale and down-home. Are you an oyster lover? If so, check out our top ten oyster bars. We also point you to some of the freshest, best-tasting seafood served up at regional festivals.

In this part, we take "take-out" to a higher dimension: We took seriously our difficult but delicious assignment of sleuthing out the best vendors who ship spectacular seafood right to your door. Finally, when you want to cast your net for more information, connect with the seaworthy Web sites that we cite in this part.

Recipe locators

Don't miss the Recipes at a Glance in the front of the book. Recipes are grouped into user-friendly clusters — from appetizers to party fare. Or use the index in the back of the book to locate a recipe either by key ingredients or by name.

Photo inspirations

Take advantage of the eight-page color photo section near the center of the book for a visual idea of how several recipes look. In total, we feature 37 of the over 100 recipes in the book.

Icons Used in This Book

In nautical vernacular, we include buoys — or icons — as navigational aids and alerts. The following icons guide you to safe harbors and ensure a smooth voyage from start to finish:

When you need to get dinner on the table faster, look for this icon. Pick up ready-made pestos, salsas, olive spreads, or guacamole to top your catch of the day.

This icon highlights tips and techniques, based on our seafood experiences, to make you seafood savvy. Sometimes we use this icon to mark a tidbit you don't absolutely need to know, but will surely impress your friends. In an instant, you can sound like a seafood guru.

This icon points you to helpful information about ingredients and seasonings that work well with seafood — from toasting mustard seeds to working with fresh cilantro to savoring chipotle chiles.

We've asked our friends who love to cook seafood to share their cooking tips. Some are colleagues in the seafood industry, some are friends who catch their own fish, and some are fabulous professional chefs, known for their fish-cooking talents.

Take note of these alerts for keeping your seafood safe from the moment you place the package in your shopping cart until you're ready to eat. This icon, for example, pops up when we want to make sure that you discard any left-over marinade after you marinate raw seafood.

This icon offers reminders about cooking or equipment information that we offer elsewhere in the book.In addition to these icons, we offer another way to add pizzazz, vary, and expand the use of recipes in this book. Look for this at the end of many recipes:

In addition to these icons, we offer another way to add pizazz, vary, and expand the use of reciped in this book. Look for this at the end of many recipes:

Vary It! When you cook seafood, you have lots of choices that work equally as well in a given recipe. We offer you a selection of fish and shellfish that you can substitute in each recipe and still get great taste.

A Few Guidelines before You Begin

SOPs — standard operating procedures — are the buzzword for many industries these days. Cooks and cookbooks need them, too. Here are the SOPs we use in *Seafood Cooking For Dummies:*

- ✔ The terms "seafood" and "fish" are occasionally used interchangeably. Usually, but not always, we use seafood as the umbrella designation, and then differentiate between shellfish and fish (finfish).

- ✔ Temperatures are always based on the Fahrenheit scale. Whether an oven temperature of 350° or a refrigerator temperature of 38°, we mean 350 degrees Fahrenheit (350° F) or 38° F.

- ✔ If a recipe calls for a non-reactive container, use something other than an aluminum pan, which could interact with a highly acidic ingredient, such as a pickling brine or tomato sauce.

- ✔ All butter is unsalted (also called *sweet*). Salted butter can make a big difference in desserts. It doesn't make that much difference in savory seafood recipes, but we like to control the salt levels ourselves. If you use salted butter, season accordingly.

- ✔ All salt is kosher. We prefer the clean flavor of kosher salt that usually doesn't contain additives. We also like the larger crystals, which are easier to pick up and sprinkle.

- ✔ Many of our recipes call for fresh herbs. When you won't use the entire bunch for a specific recipe or other foods you serve within a few days, we recommend freezing herbs to pop into future soups and sauces.

  To freeze herbs, simply chop the washed and dried herbs, wrap them air-tight in small freezer-weight bags, and then freeze. Or we pack them into ice cube trays with just enough water to fill the empty spaces, freeze, and then store the frozen cubes in a larger bag.

- ✔ When a recipe calls for a dried herb or spice that you're unfamiliar with, you may not want to buy a full-size container until you're certain that you like the flavor. Look for a source that sells herbs in bulk. Health food stores, food cooperatives, and some supermarkets are possibilities. Buy only what you need.

Part I
Hooked on Seafood Cooking

The 5th Wave   By Rich Tennant

"Let's see, what've we got here? Eel, squid, octopus... I knew they made nice stocking-stuffers, but I never thought of cooking with them."

In this part . . .

*W*e're totally immersed in fish and hope we can get you to dive in, too! In this part, we offer you tasty and healthy tips for choosing your catch and for cooking it to perfection. This part also talks about making seafood cooking easy with suggestions for adapting basic kitchen equipment that you have on hand, and tips for special tools that can simplify the job.

Chapter 1

Seafood Serendipity

. . . .

In This Chapter

▶ Riding the wave of seafood popularity

▶ Exploring the benefits of seafood

. . . .

*F*rom sea to shining sea — and everywhere in between — seafood is getting a thumbs-up from cooks, chefs, doctors, dietitians, medical researchers, and us.

Seafood is naturally:

- ✔ **Lean:** Nothing to trim.
- ✔ **Quick:** It cooks fast and easy.
- ✔ **Scrumptious:** Naturally tasty.
- ✔ **Healthy:** Seafood needs no help to be a smart or functional food. In its natural state, seafood wards off ailments and more.

No wonder we exuberantly sing seafood's praises. And we hope you will, too. Just in case you belong to that school of fish lovers who order fish when you eat out but rarely cook it at home, this book is especially for you.

Catch the Wave

The undulating wave that swaying fans send pulsating around the Ohio State football stadium during the Buckeye's Big Ten football games isn't the only wave in landlocked Columbus, Ohio, these days. Seafood lovers there catch the wave and get hooked on seafood at the Columbus Fish Market, a recently opened, upscale seafood restaurant that includes a retail seafood department.

Columbus exemplifies a growing trend. About as far inland as you can go — Minneapolis, Minnesota, and Des Moines, Iowa, are other landlocked examples — seafood retailers and seafood-focused restaurants offer sparkling, fresh seafood that customers rave about and crave. Catching the wave is de"fin"itely not exclusively a coastal tradition.

At the Columbus Fish Market, Chef Kevin Jones and Mary Beth Zakany, retail market manager, serve up seafood cooking classes to sellout crowds. A wine expert joins each class to help pair the fruits of the sea with the fruits of the vine. The two following sections answer the basic questions that students ask Mary Beth and Kevin.

How much do I need to buy?

If you study the nutrition facts on seafood package labels, you may discover that the serving size listed on the label is skimpy compared to what the fish lovers in your family like to see on their plates. For most seafood, the U.S. government-specified serving size is 3.5 ounces (or 100 grams) of raw fish. Imagine a deck of cards: That comes pretty close to the size of the standard portion after it's cooked.

Because seafood tastes so good and is so good for you, we fish-fanciers want you to eat more. We confess that most of the time your yield from the recipes in this book will exceed that deck of cards per serving. Use the label serving size (as we do) to compare products — and as a prudent, but not rigid, guide to portions.

Check the recipe that you plan to prepare for the amount you need to buy. When you aren't following a specific recipe, here are general guidelines for the amount per person for main-course servings:

- ✔ **Cleaned whole fish (head and tail on):** ¾ to 1 pound
- ✔ **Fillets or steaks:** ⅓ to ½ pound
- ✔ **Shrimp (shell-on, raw headless):** ½ pound
- ✔ **Shrimp or scallops (shell-off, raw):** ⅓ pound
- ✔ **Mussels or clams (live, shell-on):** 2 to 3 pounds
- ✔ **Lobsters or crabs (live):** 1¼ to 1½ pounds
- ✔ **Shellfish (cooked, shell-off):** ⅓ to ½ pound

If I'm not a big seafood fan, what type of fish should I try?

Table 1-1 helps you zoom in on the flavor and texture combination of your choice. Whether you're picking fish to order from a restaurant menu or selecting fish to cook at home, you may find these groupings useful. This chart is based on one from *Simply Seafood* magazine (unfortunately no longer in publication). Flip to Chapter 9 for details about many of these fish.

DINNER TONIGHT

A quick and easy weekday meal

By Marge Perry

The sweet and slight licorice flavor of fennel is a natural partner with rich salmon.

Salmon With Fennel

2 tablespoons flour
$\frac{1}{2}$ teaspoon salt
$\frac{1}{4}$ teaspoon black pepper
$\frac{1}{2}$ teaspoon fennel seeds
4 (6-ounce) pieces salmon fillet
1 tablespoon olive oil
1 fennel bulb, in $\frac{1}{4}$-inch dice
1$\frac{1}{2}$ pounds tomatoes, diced
$\frac{1}{2}$ cup white wine

1. Combine the flour, salt, pepper and fennel seeds on a plate. Dredge the salmon pieces thoroughly in the mixture.

2. Heat oil in a large, deep skillet, preferably nonstick. Add salmon, skin-side up, and cook 5 minutes until surface is golden. Turn salmon and add fennel to pan all around (but not under or on top of) the fish. Cook, stirring fennel occasionally, until it is slightly softened, about 3 minutes.

Fish Selection Guide

Moderate	Full-Flavored
Delicate Texture	
Arctic char	Smelt
Catfish	
Pink salmon	
Walleye	
Medium Texture	
Atlantic pollock	Amberjack
Black sea bass	Atlantic salmon
Chum salmon	Bluefish
Drum	Escolar
Mahimahi	King salmon
Ocean perch	Mackerel
Opah	Sablefish
Pacific rockfish	Shad
Perch	Sockeye salmon
Pompano	
Porgy	
Rainbow trout	
Sheepshead	
Steelhead	
Striped bass	
Firm Texture	
Shark	Chilean sea bass
Sturgeon	Cobia
	Swordfish
	Tuna

...thy Benefits

...mercial that hypes a revolutionary new miracle drug that, with one or two doses per week, can cut your risk of sudden cardiac death in half. Suppose the new miracle drug also improves your mood or your memory and helps your creaking knee joints. And what if it boosts your resistance to certain cancers? Would you rush right to the phone to call the toll-free number to place your order? Or would you say "that's too good to be true"?

Believe it. One landmark medical study after another confirms these healthful benefits derived from the *omega-3 essential fatty acids* found in fish, especially oily fish such as mackerel, herring, salmon, sardines, and sablefish. All types of fish contain some omega-3s, but oily, cold-water varieties have about twice as much as fish from warm water. Table 1-2 shows the best sources.

Table 1-2	Omega-3 Fatty Acid Content*
Most (more than 1.0 gram)	*Moderate (0.5 to 0.9 grams)*
Anchovy	Arctic char
Atlantic bluefish	Chum salmon
Atlantic salmon	Pompano
Bluefin tuna	Rainbow trout
Chilean sea bass	Shark
Coho salmon	Smelt
Herring	Spot
King salmon	Striped bass
Mackerel	Swordfish
Pink salmon	Yellowfin and other tunas
Sablefish	Pacific oysters
Sardines	Squid (calamari)
Sockeye salmon	
Spiny dogfish	
Whitefish	

*In 3.5 ounces of raw edible portion   Source: U.S. Department of Agriculture

Even without accounting for its omega-3 benefits, fish has a lean profile, is easily digested, and is nutritionally dense. Fish are an excellent source of high quality protein, B vitamins, iron, zinc, and other minerals. And just look at their infinite variety, flavor, and value.

Chapter 2

Seafood Cooking Tools

∙ ∙

In This Chapter

▶ Identifying basic, useful, and esoteric seafood cooking equipment

▶ Transforming everyday household equipment into fish-cooking tools

▶ Sizing up fish masters' tricks

∙ ∙

*O*ur fondest seafood memories revolve around cooking and eating seafood with friends — and without fancy equipment. Leslie recalls cooking mounds of head-on shrimp in old, tin camping pots filled with seawater — the shrimp plucked fresh from Svalbard's coastal waters (the big island due east of northern Greenland). Marcie remembers sparkling tastes of sailboat-baked red snapper, scantily wrapped in the galley's last foil — the fish from a local fisherman as friends anchored in a secluded British Virgin Island bay. So in our opinion, a paring knife, pot, skillet, and foil can suffice.

But the right tools can make cooking seafood more fun. We devote this chapter to basic kitchen equipment that helps you more easily cook fish; useful equipment, often specialized, for cooking and eating seafood; and esoteric equipment for uncommon seafood tasks.

Many pieces of equipment relate to specific seafood cooking techniques. Take a look in Chapter 4 for tips and techniques that make your fish cooking more efficient and fun.

A Fine Kettle for Your Fish — Basic Equipment

You're sure to have much of the following equipment in your kitchen, but we've added a few fishy twists to transform everyday basics into fish-cooking tools.

✔ **Aluminum foil:** Baking fish or shellfish in an individual foil package is one answer when you want to prepare seafood simply, entertain with ease, or avoid clean-up chores. (Check out Chapters 5 and 6 for our shrimp and salmon foil-packet recipes.) Use foil for baking a whole fish, for grilling a gorgeous whole fillet of fresh salmon, or for creating foil boats to contain all the juices when you grill delicate freshwater fillets.

Rich Catanzaro, a friend of ours who's been purchasing fish for supermarkets for more than twenty years, uses strips of foil to help flip whole fish when he grills. Depending on the size of the fish, cut two or three pieces of foil, 3 feet long and 4 inches wide. Fold the strips in thirds lengthwise to make a strong, narrow strip. Lay strips equally spaced across a tray and spray strips with vegetable oil. Place marinated or oiled fish on top of the strips and loosely twist each strip together near the body of the fish to create handles. During grilling, lift the strips to flip the fish within the strips as needed. When the fish is cooked, lift the strips and the fish to a platter.

On a restaurant menu, when you see fish *en papillote* (ahn pah-pee-YOHT), expect your fish to be served in a foil or parchment paper package. Parchment paper is a nonstick paper that comes in rolls, sheets, or triangles. When you're ready to wrap, look no further than the following trio of recipes — edible evidence that deliciously good things do come in small packages: Caribbean Shrimp Packets (Chapter 5), Salmon Sealed in Silver (Chapter 6), and Big Fish Swallows the Little Fish (Chapter 15).

✔ **Brushes:** We like to buy inexpensive, natural-bristle paint brushes to use when grilling seafood: one for basting seafood while you cook it and one for brushing the grill rack with oil to lessen the chance of fish sticking. Spending less on a brush allows you to frequently replace your brushes — even when you wash a brush after each use with hot, soapy water, the bristles get sticky. Look for a brush that has 2-inch or longer bristles, and is 1½ inches wide. A slender wire-capped brush with stiff bristles can be useful for thin sauces, while a basting mop works well with thick sauces. Figure 2-1 shows several brush options.

✔ **Cake cooling rack:** You can improvise a broiler pan by using a cake cooling rack and a jellyroll pan, as shown in Figure 2-2. We find that this offers good heat circulation and flexibility when you want to cook fish at a specific distance from the broiler. For instance, if you want to cook fish closer to the broiler, simply slip a pan under the jelly roll pan to move the fish higher.

What started out as a makeshift grill topper has turned into standard equipment for us: two large, nonstick cooling racks to help you when grilling large fish fillets, steaks, or a whole fish. Place one rack on the grill with the seafood on top. When it's time to turn the fish, place the second rack on top to sandwich the fish. Grip the ends of both racks using hot pads, and flip the racks and fish together. Remove the top rack and finish grilling.

Figure 2-1:
Long handles, from 12 to 16 inches, let you easily baste fish while grilling.

basting brushes

✔ **Grill cleaning brush:** A stiff wire brush is essential for keeping your grill racks spotless, because fish easily sticks to the grill grid. Burn off any bits of food stuck to the grill grid after each use by heating the grill for a short time after you remove seafood. Loosening the charred bits with the brush is a snap.

✔ **Grill topper:** Nothing makes grilling fish easier than a *grill topper*. Toppers eliminate the chance of fish falling through the grill grid and help you grill delicate fillets, shrimp and scallops, or whole fish with ease. Toppers are available in aluminum and porcelain enamel, and have varying sizes of grids or holes. We prefer an aluminum topper that has a fine mesh pattern, as shown in Figure 2-3. When you grill seafood, the fish sticks less. Perforated porcelain enamel toppers usually have more surface area between the holes (to which fish can stick), and are more costly.

Figure 2-2:
Set a cake cooling rack on a jellyroll pan for an effective broiler pan.

cake cooling rack + jellyroll pan

improvise!

Figure 2-3:
A grill topper helps you grill delicate fish and shellfish.

To use a grill topper, simply place the topper on top of your grill grid. Lightly oil the topper just before cooking seafood to keep the oil from burning off. Toppers may be round, square, or rectangular, and range in size from 12 inches in diameter to 12 by 16 inches. A lip along one long edge is useful for leverage when you turn seafood with a spatula. Avoid a two-lipped topper; it is difficult to slip the fish on and off the rack.

✔ **Oyster knife:** If you love eating oysters on the half shell at home, an *oyster knife* is essential for shucking them. (If you don't care for oysters, send the oyster knife to the bottom of your equipment list.) People who shuck oysters have definite knife-style preferences. Often an oyster knife has a short blade and a guard to protect your fingers — see Figure 2-4. You use the blade both to pry apart the shell and to cut the oyster meat from the shell. An oyster knife may also have a more slender blade, with a sharp cutting edge on one side. You may find an oyster glove helpful (see Figure 2-4) if you're prone to ramming your hand with the knife while shucking. (A folded dishtowel also works well.) Check out Chapter 8 for more oyster shucking information, or Chapter 22 for our list of great oyster bars.

✔ **Fish tweezers:** Similar in design to tongs, you use these stainless steel tweezers to pull bones out of fish. The arms are 4 to 6 inches long and ½-inch wide, and curve inward to give you extra spring and strength when grabbing the bones. See Figure 2-5.

Figure 2-4:
Shuck oysters with ease using an oyster knife and glove.

✔ **Paper towels:** Paper towels keep fish from slip-sliding away. When you need to skin a fish fillet, place a paper towel, either dry or damp, on a cutting board. Lay the fish skin-side down on the towel to secure it. If your cutting board shifts around, place a damp paper towel under the cutting board to keep it in place.

When cooking, we recommend using disposable paper towels, rather than fabric towels. Cross-contamination is a common food safety concern.

✔ **Paring knife:** This short little knife, with its 2- to 4-inch blade, can be the ultimate kitchen tool. (See Figure 2-6.) Use a paring knife for numerous tasks, from deveining shrimp or opening clams to filleting and skinning fish in a pinch. Keep your knives sharp to prevent them from tearing tender seafood flesh as you cut.

✔ **Scissors:** Small scissors with short, slender blades and sharp, pointed tips are great for a variety of tasks, from cutting through shrimp shells before deveining to snipping fresh herbs.

✔ **Shears:** When you need to cut through lobster or crab shells, look no further than your local gardening store. Chef Jasper White, in his book *Lobster at Home,* says straight-edged garden shears are perfect for the job. We find that curved pruners also work well for this task and for trimming fins or gills from fish.

✔ **Skewers:** Seafood makes wonderful kebabs, both for grilling and for broiling. Simply thread a skewer through the center of the fish or shellfish — or use a double set of skewers, as shown in Figure 2-7. You can find a variety of bamboo and metal skewers available in varying lengths: short skewers for appetizer kebabs and longer ones for main course servings.

- Bamboo skewers are inexpensive and disposable. They vary in length from 6 to 12 inches and should be soaked in water for 30 minutes or longer before using. Soaking reduces the chances of the skewers disintegrating in flames, but even with soaking, the skewers will char.

- Metal skewers are more expensive than bamboo, but are durable and reusable. Square, flat, or twisted skewers keep food from spinning on a skewer better than round skewers do, and let you more easily turn seafood. Metal skewers range from 7 to 14 inches long, and some, like *hâtelets,* the French cousin of skewers (shown in Figure 2-7), have decorative figures on top.

- Disposable wooden chopsticks also are fun for making seafood fingers. Soak chopsticks in water for 30 minutes before using to lessen the chances of burning. Choose firm-fleshed fish such as catfish, grouper, or tilapia, and thread the chopstick lengthwise through the fillet. Flip to Chapter 12 for the Middle Eastern Grilled Catfish Fingers recipe — we show an example in the color photo section near the middle of this book.

metal skewers

Use two wooden skewers to prevent spinning!

hâtelets

Figure 2-7:
Skewers
and seafood
are made
for each
other.

✔ **Skillet:** A large, shallow skillet with sloping sides works best for pan-frying or sautéing seafood. Fish cooks fast, sticks to the pan more readily than meat or poultry, and its flesh is more fragile. To make sautéing fish as easy and worry-free as possible, we suggest using a non-stick skillet — or a good old-fashioned, well-seasoned, cast-iron skillet. Large skillets work best, from 10 to 12 inches in diameter, to make flipping fish easy. Large pans also give the fish lots of room to sizzle and brown. Plus, for sautéing you want a skillet that has a smooth surface to evenly cook fish — save rib-bottomed skillets for grill-style recipes. For slower, stove-top recipes that cook fish and vegetables together, you need a heavier skillet than you do for quick-cooking sautés.

✔ **Spatula:** A long-handled, rectangular-bladed spatula is ideal for grilling. Look for a spatula that's 15 to 18 inches long with a blade about 3 inches wide, as shown in Figure 2-8. For sautéing or pan-frying, a shorter spatula works best. For specialty fish lifters, see the "More Fish to Fry — Optional Equipment" section, later in this chapter.

spatula

Figure 2-8:
A well-insulated handle keeps you from cooking along with the seafood.

✔ **Steamer:** Steamers may be simple or elaborate, depending on your needs. To steam seafood successfully, your steamer needs a tight-fitting lid to prevent steam from escaping during cooking. See Figure 2-9.

- For clams and mussels, turn a pot into a steamer by placing a vegetable steamer rack in the pot. Add shellfish, and top pot with a tight-fitting lid.

- Steaming fish fillets or whole fish on a plate works well. To improvise a rack, place an upside-down metal bowl, upside-down colander, or tuna cans (with ends removed) into a tall pot. Top with a heatproof plate (the plate should be about 1 inch smaller in diameter than the pot to allow steam to circulate). Place fish in a single layer on the plate for best steaming results.

Figure 2-9:
Fish cooks
beautifully
in any
steamer.

steamer

- Chinese steamers, with several stacking layers, also work well over a pot or a wok. The bottom of each layer of a bamboo steamer has widely spaced overlapping strips to allow the steam to rise. Steamers may also be stainless steel or aluminum.

- A traditional crab or clam steamer consists of two stacked pots. The upper pot is perforated on the bottom to allow the steam to rise. Styles differ, and the upper pot may be set on top of the lower pot or nested inside. The pots are usually porcelain coated and may have a spigot near the bottom to draw off juices.

✔ **Timer:** Give yourself an edge when cooking fish and shellfish, and keep a timer nearby. Family, friends, and pets can easily distract you during cooking — as you probably know, fish cooks fast.

✔ **Tongs:** Tongs, shown in Figure 2-10, are handy for lifting and turning seafood during cooking. We prefer tongs that aren't spring-loaded because you can better handle and feel a piece of fish as you pick it up. Tongs work best with sturdy, firm fish, such as swordfish and salmon, or shellfish, such as shrimp. Shorter tongs, around 9 inches long, work well for stove-top cooking, and tongs that are 12 inches and longer are perfect for baking, broiling, and grilling. Small bamboo tongs from southeast Asia are lovely for serving shellfish.

Figure 2-10:
Tongs that
are not
spring-
loaded let
you handle
tender
seafood
easily.

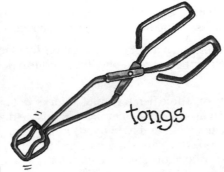

tongs

More Fish to Fry — Optional Equipment

The tools that we suggest in this section are primarily used for cooking and eating seafood. Use them when you have a specific technique that you want to accomplish or for a delicious dining experience ahead.

- **Clam knife:** A *clam knife,* shown in Figure 2-11, looks similar to an oyster knife, but often has a more rounded tip and a longer, thinner blade. Occasionally, one side of the blade will have a sharp cutting edge. Check out Chapter 8 for more information about shucking clams.

clam knife

Figure 2-11: Shuck clams efficiently with a clam knife.

- **Crab and lobster crackers:** Cracking crab and lobster shells is tough work. Good old-fashioned, hinged nutcrackers work like a charm, but you can find specialty and decorative shellfish crackers that are based on the same principle. (Flip to Chapter 7 for more on cracking crabs and lobsters.)

  A small hammer or a Chinese cleaver is a good substitute, but duck as the shellfish juices fly with each whack.

- **Crab forks and picks:** This short fork with two or three slender prongs or tines is perfect for prying out succulent bits of crab and lobster meat from hard-to-reach claws and legs — and for plucking an oyster from its shell when you prefer not to slurp. Slender metal picks work well to extract every last morsel from tiny legs. (Jump over to Chapter 7 for more on eating crab.)

- **Fillet knife:** You use this specialized knife to fillet and skin fish. A *fillet knife* has a narrow, slender blade, about 6 to 7 inches long — see Figure 2-12. When filleting fish, the pointed, flexible blade easily follows the contours of the fish bones.

Figure 2-12:
A fillet knife
makes easy
work of
filleting fish.

✔ **Fish-cooking guide:** A *fish-cooking guide* is a device to help you determine the cooking time needed for fish based on the measurement of its depth. The guide may be a ruler variation, but keep in mind that the guide is simply a guide — not a sure and fast doneness rule. Check out Chapter 4 for techniques for determining the doneness of fish.

✔ **Fish lifter:** A *fish lifter* is a flexible, slotted metal spatula for lifting and turning portions of sautéed, grilled, or poached fish. A fish lifter may have a lip for slipping under the edge of the fish, or a slight curve down its length to cradle the fish. See Figure 2-13. Lifters also are designed with the handle attached at the center of the lifter (at a 90-degree angle) to make easier work of lifting small whole fish or large pieces of fish.

Figure 2-13:
The slots in
a lifter let
liquid drain
off quickly.

✔ **Fish poacher:** This is a long, narrow pan with straight sides that you use to cook or poach a whole fish (or fillets) in liquid — see Figure 2-14. Look for a poacher that includes a two-handled, perforated inset rack to hold the fish during cooking. Poachers range from 16 to 40 inches long and 5 to 7 inches wide, and are made from stainless steel, aluminum, or copper. Unless you poach fish often, save your pennies and improvise: Nest a couple of heavy-duty disposable foil pans together and line with a double layer of cheesecloth to hold the fish.

Figure 2-14: A poacher works well for whole fish or fillets.

fish poacher

✓ **Fish grill basket:** A *fish grill basket* is a wire fish-shaped basket that holds a whole fish during grilling. You flip the entire basket to turn the fish. We find fish baskets cumbersome and prefer to use a grill topper (discussed in the "A Fine Kettle for Your Fish — Basic Equipment" section, earlier in this chapter) and two long spatulas to turn fish. You can also use two cake cooling racks or several long, narrow foil strips.

✓ **Mallet:** A hammer-like mallet, made of wood, steel, or aluminum, is great for cracking crab and lobster shells.

✓ **Scallop shells:** These pretty shells follow a scallop's natural shell shape and are traditionally used to bake scallops and other seafood dishes. Made from genuine scallop shells or ovenproof materials, the shells range from 2 to 5 inches in diameter. Use the shells also to serve salsas, sauces, crab dip, or antipasto.

Nancy Pollard, a friend of ours who owns La Cuisine cookware in Alexandria, Virginia, bakes pastry shells for fish in scallop shells.

✓ **Shrimp deveiner:** A slender metal or plastic tool, a *shrimp deveiner* has a gently curving blade that mimics the curved back of the shrimp, and a pointed tip. You can use a deveiner to remove both the shrimp shell and the digestive vein that runs down its back. A deveiner may rip the shrimp flesh, though, so we prefer to slip the shell off with our fingers and remove the vein with a paring knife. See Chapter 5 for more on deveining shrimp.

✓ **Thermometer:** Take the guesswork out of determining when a thick piece of fish or a whole fish is sufficiently cooked by using one of the new-style thermometers with skinny temperature-sensing probes. We have two favorites: an instant-read thermometer with a digital dial, and a new-fangled combination digital timer-thermometer with a long, flexible cable that's ovenproof (both shown in Figure 2-15). The combination device allows you to monitor temperature changes degree by degree, without peeking in the oven or opening the grill lid. Plus, it sounds an alarm when the fish reaches the temperature that you select. The instant-read thermometer doesn't stay in the fish during cooking. You slip the thermometer into the thickest part of the fish for a few seconds and read the temperature on the dial. For information about fish-cooking temperatures, flip to Chapter 4.

✔ **Wok:** A Chinese wok, with its narrow circular bottom and steeply sloping sides, is ideal for stir-frying or deep-frying seafood, and for steaming fish. Check out Chapter 12 for the Cantonese Whole Steamed Fish recipe.

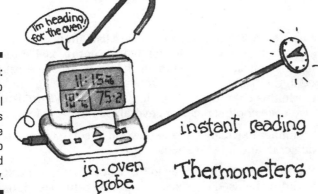

Figure 2-15: Cook fish to an internal doneness the same way you do meat and poultry.

Not Your Usual Tool — Esoteric, But Fun

The specialized seafood cooking equipment in this section, shown in Figure 2-16, is pretty exotic, but one man's unusual equipment is another man's useful cooking tool.

✔ **Crawfish boiling rig:** You can't have a crawfish party for a crowd without one of these gigantic pots. The pot often is fitted with a wire basket insert so that crawfish can be easily pulled out and drained without having to dump out hot water, which you may want to reserve for the next batch. The pot sits on a sturdy, adjustable gas burner that's usually fired by a butane tank.

Frances Williams, a friend of ours, says that the 100-quart pot works well for a party. Frances should know — she and her sister Christine own Ecrevisse Acadienne in Louisiana.

✔ **Fish cutters:** Shaped like miniature shrimp, lobster, and crab, you can use these sharp metal cutters to create whimsical garnishes from vegetables (such as carrots) or pastry dough.

Figure 2-16:
Exotic tools
are fun,
but not
essential.

✔ **Fish molds:** These large, metal molds are ideal for a pretty salmon mousse. If miniatures are more your style, flip to the color photo section near the center of this book to see our bite-sized fish and shellfish shapes — in chocolate. You can find plastic molds impressed with these shapes — they're perfect for shaping single servings of flavored butter to serve with seafood.

✔ **Sardine grill:** This circular wire frame features a sunburst of fish-shaped forms for grilling fresh sardines or small fish. Each form radiates from the center and can house one 5-inch sardine.

✔ **Sea urchin scissors:** With short, slender blades, long handles, and sharp, pointed tips, sea urchin scissors offer the precise cutting ability and leverage for tackling crusty sea urchins. You can also use the scissors to snip shrimp shells for deveining.

✔ **Japanese bonito shaver:** Japanese seafood cooking may require using this totally unique piece of equipment. The rectangular box has an inset metal shaving blade on top and is set on a base with a drawer. To use, rub a chunk of dried *bonito* (a type of tuna) against the blade to produce fine flakes of fish. You use dried bonito for making classic Japanese dashi or stock. For more information on tuna, see Chapter 9.

Chapter 3

Choosing and Handling Seafood

· ·

In This Chapter

▶ Finding the best user-friendly seafood

▶ Maintaining the quality of fresh seafood

▶ Playing it safe with your seafood choices

· ·

"*W*hat's for dinner?" Not tonight's dinner — instead, fast-forward one hundred years. Martha Stewart answered this question in *The New York Times Sunday Magazine* centennial edition (September 29, 1996), which focused on lifestyles in 2096. Yes, Martha's house-of-the-future still has a kitchen. For dinner, she envisions a succulent, steamed red snapper that you conveniently pluck from its home — the saltwater aquarium in your kitchen. Genetically improved, the snapper is extra meaty with bones that pull out without fussing. For supper tomorrow? Vary your menu — choose your catch from your matching freshwater aquarium.

Now that's a short food chain. Back here in real-time, our food chain from ocean to oven or pond to plate joins multiple links and spans the globe. Swimming in our giant global aquarium are hundreds upon hundreds of seafood selections. Quite a varied menu! And you're the final link in this vast seafood chain.

In this chapter, we shop for seafood and help you keep its tiptop quality until you're ready to cook. Going beyond the A–to–Z approach of "how-to" check-lists, we weave in thought-provoking perspectives about your position in this ever-evolving food chain.

No longer can we take seafood — such a rich resource — for granted. Over 50,000 years have elapsed since humankind first became hunter-gatherers. Seafood hunted in the wild may be the one remaining vestige of authentic hunter-gathering in the world today. Every day, dedicated fishermen brave stormy weather, high seas, icy temperatures, and quota limits to bring the ocean bounty to your table. Elsewhere, on sea ranches and aquatic farms around the world, modern-day aquaculture pioneers are rushing to produce protein to feed the burgeoning world population.

The whole truth

The latest answer to the question "What's for dinner?" at four o'clock may still be swimming at five. Martha Stewart's prediction for The Age of Aquariums may not be so far-fetched. The modern hunter-gatherers have been gathering at international meetings and seminars on this very subject: capturing fish alive for the live market. Going beyond the familiar lobster holding tank, this "wet market" is rapidly growing in more ways than one. If you live in or near a large city, check out what's swimming in the aquariums in shops catering to the Asian market in your corner of the world. You may find, as we did, the perfect striped bass for our Cantonese Whole Steamed Fish recipe in Chapter 12. Grab a jar of fermented black beans for the recipe while you're there.

Your Quest for the Best

You've probably heard the saying "A chain is no stronger than its weakest link." Fish becomes the best food in the world when everyone involved delivers fish in the best possible condition to the next person in the chain. When we asked vendors to identify the weak links in the seafood chain, we expected them to cite problems with uncertain supplies, find flaws in the transportation system, or bemoan their labor woes. Needless to say, we were unprepared for their stern response. More than one point their finger at *us,* the shoppers. Talk about a wake-up call!

While we don't fully agree, we took their admonitions to heart. We plead guilty — both to sins of commission (goofs that we've made when choosing or using seafood) and sins of omission (things that we've failed to do in handling seafood). Live and learn. As a result, the seafood on our plates is better, too. Now we want the same for you.

Six super signs of a savvy shopper

If you don't know a fin from a flipper, you're not alone. In this chapter and throughout this book, we coach you to increase your savviness, whatever your starting point.

The savvy seafood shopper:

- Knows where to go.
- Asks the right questions.
- Substitutes a fresher but similar fish when necessary.

✔ Stays flexible — is open to new options.

✔ Protects the purchases all the way to the plate.

✔ Praises and complains appropriately.

Start by connecting with the link closest to you on the seafood chain. Where do you go to find the quality you want? Who do you buy from?

Finding your favorite fishmonger(s)

When was the last time you asked someone "Where's the nearest fishmonger?" A friend reading our rough draft asked, "What's all this fishmonger stuff?"

Long before Sweet Molly Malone rambled down the street chanting "cockles and mussels, alive, alive oh," the British were using *fishmonger* to describe those mongering (selling or trading) in fish. (If you visit Dublin, don't miss the statue of this 18th-century fishmonger pushing her wheelbarrow at the end of Grafton Street.) At ports around the world where the H.M.S. fleet docked in its heyday, you're apt to hear the word "fishmonger" in everyday usage.

Until fairly recently, we may have been inclined to steer you to a fishmonger in a specialty seafood shop, where most are outstanding — we give them high marks for quality and personal service. And we may have been less than enthusiastic about buying from big supermarkets. But we've changed our tune. A supermarket's reputation rests on total quality throughout the store and beyond. It understands that safe, topnotch-quality seafood sells. Overall, you're on the receiving end of consistently better than ever seafood.

A good fishmonger:

✔ Displays raw seafood separately from cooked products.

✔ Clearly indicates if products are previously frozen.

✔ Strives to keep display cases around 29° to 32°.

✔ Arranges fish fillets or steaks so that the flesh doesn't sit directly on the ice; instead, keeps cut fish in trays or on plastic liners above the ice.

✔ Follows a HACCP plan to control defined risks (see the "State-of-the-art seafood safety" sidebar for more information on HACCP).

✔ Welcomes your questions.

If your quest for a good local fishmonger is futile, consider overnight delivery of fabulous, pristine seafood as a viable alternative. See Chapter 24 for a list of our favorite shore-to-door suppliers.

State-of-the-art seafood safety

Have you heard of HACCP? Hazard Analysis and Critical Control Point is an industry process to anticipate food safety risks and prevent them before they happen. HACCP (pronounced HAS-sip) became mandatory for seafood processors in December 1997. HACCP replaced an antiquated inspection program focused on the end of the line, after damage may have already been done. Now each processor keeps detailed monitoring records and follows rigorous sanitation standards.

✔ Wegmans Food Markets, with stores in New York, Pennsylvania, and New Jersey, take pride in their pioneering initiative that extends the HACCP concept from the processing level (mandatory) to retail (voluntary).

Carl Salamone, director of seafood, champions their system-wide checkpoints from the loading dock until you put your purchase into your shopping cart.

✔ Hy-Vee Supermarkets, headquartered in West Des Moines, Iowa, was one of the first chains to launch a pilot program with an on-site federal inspector at its seafood distribution facility. We watched Tom Toguchi, the chain's resident United States Department of Commerce inspector, analyze incoming seafood for color, odor, texture, temperature, and flavor. Customers from Hy-Vee's 180 stores can call Tom toll-free for direct answers to their seafood questions or problems.

Finding your favorite forms

Seafood embraces a much, much wider variety than red meats and poultry do:

✔ Shellfish or finfish

✔ Freshwater or saltwater

✔ Farm-raised or wild-caught

✔ Alive or dead

✔ Shell-on or shell-off

✔ Raw, cooked, or ready-to-cook (pan-ready)

✔ Fresh or frozen, or previously frozen and "refreshed"

✔ Whole or pre-cut

Mesmerized by all these choices? If so, use the tips and recipes in Parts II, III, and IV to celebrate this rich and amazing diversity.

Also celebrate the fact that, unless you want to, you don't have to begin by buying and tackling a whole fish. When's the last time you plucked a chicken? Grab-and-go cooks go for serving-size portions. See Figure 3-1 for a clearer picture of where these cuts were attached to the fish.

Figure 3-1:
Cutting
up —
Fish
Anatomy
101.

Six super signs — fresh fish

You've heard this advice over and over: Choose the freshest fish that you can find. Short of catching the fish yourself, how can you judge how fresh it really is?

Ask the person behind the counter which fish he or she plans to cook tonight. Expect a more straightforward reply than when you merely ask, "Is this fish fresh?" Even better, ask "Which day(s) does your fresh fish come in?" Plan your future shopping trips to catch the freshest fish!

Don't hesitate to ask the fishmonger to show you, up-close and personal, how he or she evaluates fresh fish. Chances are, the pointers will include these:

- ✔ Smells fresh, not "fishy" — briny and clean, like an ocean breeze. Give it the sniff test, if you can.

- ✔ Looks resilient and elastic. Doesn't leave an indentation if you poke it.

- ✔ Shines with a moist, translucent sheen. Surface isn't tacky.

- ✔ Doesn't look dried out or mottled with yellowing. Reddish muscle swirls in swordfish and similar fish are bright, not dull brown.

- ✔ Glistens and sparkles: Whole fish have clear eyes, bright gills, shiny (not slimy) scales and skin. Exception: Very fresh fish may have a clean-smelling, slick (slimy) coating on their skin.

- ✔ No bruises or separations (technically called *gaping*) in the flesh. Tell-tale signs of mishandling.

Gaping occurs when trauma triggers enzymes to break down the thin, delicate, connective tissues that separate the narrow strands of fish muscle fibers. Select fish pieces without any of these gapes or splits.

John French, head of Pegasus Enterprises in Seward, Alaska, phrases the issue of fresh fish this way: "You can't make bad fish better or old fish fresher." The clock begins ticking the moment the fish comes out of the water. The two key elements are time and temperature. The less you have of each in the fish, the better it's likely to be. Depending on how a fish is handled from the minute it comes out of the water until it reaches you can mean a difference of maintaining high quality for 16 days or longer — or as short as two or three days when handled carelessly anywhere along the way.

Flip to Chapter 6 for specific information on choosing salmon and Chapter 9 for more information about other types of finfish.

Six super signs — frozen fish

We think it's time to get over any bias that you may cling to that fresh is the only way to go. For our money, frozen fish can be superior in quality to fresh. Fresh and frozen are not opposites: Factory-freezer ships travel alongside many fishing fleets. On ship or shore, flash freezers using cryogenic or blast-freezing technologies plummet fish to frigid temperatures in seconds. Freshness is locked in with little or no damage to delicate cells.

When you plan to serve fish the day you buy it or the next day, previously frozen fish that's "thawed for your convenience" is fine, assuming the seller defrosted the fish slowly and gently. (Use the same criteria we list in the "Six super signs — fresh fish" section to select your fish.) When you plan to freeze your fish anyway or don't intend to cook it for a few days, consider buying still-frozen fish. If you don't see what you want, ask your fish seller if any is available.

When you buy frozen fish, here's what to look for:

- No signs of freezer burn or loose ice crystals. No "cottony," dry edges.
- Frozen rock solid.
- Snug packaging, preferably vacuum-sealed.
- *IQF* (individually quick frozen) pieces that are loose and distinct, not clumped.
- Packages that don't protrude above or in front of the load lines in self-service freezers.
- Dated packages showing date of production (preferably no older than 6 months).

Six super signs — shellfish

Shellfish stars in many places in this book: Shrimp solos in Chapter 5 — look there for specifics on selecting the best shrimp, fresh or frozen; find buying hints for lobsters and their crusty cousins in Chapter 7; go to Chapter 8 to unlock the secrets of clams, mussels, and other mollusks who hide their treasures inside hinged shells; and seek out calamari tips in Chapter 10.

In general, here's how to select shellfish:

- ✔ Exposed raw flesh on uncooked shellfish has a translucent sheen.

- ✔ Cooked shellfish looks moist.

- ✔ Aromas are pleasant. Ask to sniff and whiff.

- ✔ Live lobsters, crabs, and crawfish act lively.

- ✔ Live clams and mussels should have tightly closed shells — or shells that close when tapped or squeezed. The exception is soft-shell clams with their long-necks that can't close completely.

Getting Your Precious Cargo Home

After you purchase seafood, you become the key link in the food chain. You may be surprised how important your next steps can be in ensuring a lip-smacking result. Follow these pertinent pointers to protect both the quality and safety of what you purchase:

- ✔ Shop for seafood last. Or ask for a bag of ice to keep seafood super-cool.

- ✔ When you buy a gorgeous, large fillet or whole fish, tell the person who waits on you not to fold the end under to make the bundle more compact. Any bend can create a soft spot that may cook up mushy.

- ✔ Carefully keep packages of cooked seafood away from packages of raw seafood, poultry, or meat in your shopping cart.

- ✔ At the check-out, make sure other groceries aren't bagged on top of seafood: It bruises easily.

- ✔ Carry a cooler in your car to use when you're not headed straight home.

- ✔ When the weather is hot and you don't have a cooler with you, don't put fish in the trunk. Keep seafood packages inside your vehicle, near an air-conditioning vent.

✔ When you buy ready-to-eat, hot seafood:

- Keep these hot, home-meal replacements separate from raw seafood or meat in your shopping cart.

- Plan to eat these hot foods within one hour.

- Buy an insulated bag designed to keep hot foods hot (similar to what pizza deliverers use). Look in the housewares' department or in mail-order catalogs.

- If you can't eat these hot foods within an hour, refrigerate them and reheat thoroughly before serving.

Safe at Home

You bought fresh fish for its freshness. Now enjoy it. The sooner you use it, the less likely you lose it.

"Hot foods hot" and "cold foods cold" are wise adages for all foods, but especially important for seafood. Fish is a bit more finicky than meat or even poultry.

✔ Find the cold spot in your refrigerator and check the temperature with an appliance thermometer. Seafood holds best between 32° and 38°.

Ken Hildebrand, a Seafood Processing Specialist with Oregon State University's Sea Grant Program, gives the following caution: "Watch those extended door openings. Don't be surprised if the current setting in your refrigerator tops 40° or dangerously higher, especially if anyone at your house dallies in front of the open refrigerator trying to figure out what he or she wants for a snack."

✔ If you're not cooking fresh fish the same day you bring it home, rinse it under cold running water and pat it dry with paper towels. Place it in a clean, resealable plastic bag. Store the bag inside a pan, with a bag of ice cubes or a freezer gel pack under the fish. Set the pan in the coldest part of your refrigerator.

✔ Don't suffocate live shellfish by sealing them in a plastic bag. They need to breathe.

✔ Defrost frozen seafood slowly to retain its moisture. While freezing fish in a flash keeps more cell walls intact, the opposite is true for thawing:

- Thawing overnight in the refrigerator is best.

- Running cold tap water over seafood in a resealable plastic bag for about 30 minutes is second best. Place the bag in a large bowl, positioned so that a steady trickle of water circulates and spills out of the bowl.

- Thawing seafood in the microwave on the lowest defrost setting (10 to 30 percent power), rotating the package once or twice, is another alternative. Stop short of complete thawing; instead remove the package from the microwave when it's pliable but still icy.

✔ When you can't use fresh seafood within two days, freeze it as soon as possible. The key to successful freezing is to create a barrier to air. Here are some other tips:

- Don't refreeze thawed fish.

- Double-wrap seafood, first in a freezer-weight plastic bag or plastic wrap, then overwrapped with heavy-duty foil. Make packages as airtight as possible.

- Set your freezer temperature to 0° or colder. As close to a frigid –20° is best.

- Date all packages. Practice FIFO: first in, first out. For best eating quality, use home-frozen fish as soon as possible, preferably within six months.

Doris Hicks, seafood specialist with the University of Delaware's Sea Grant College Program, recommends a quick guide for the maximum length of time to keep fish you buy and then freeze at home: It's based on the color of the flesh. Darker flesh fish tend to have a higher percentage of fat, which may cause "off" flavors to develop in the freezer. So freeze bluefish, for example, no more than three months. Don't freeze lighter (and usually leaner) fish such as flounder for more than six months.

✔ Despite your care, when you encounter a result that disappoints, don't blame yourself. Simply decide that you won't buy *that* again, and complain to your fishmonger — some quality problems aren't detected until you cook the fish or seafood. Bottom line: Let the fish retailer know!

Don't get bugged

Add to your adages: "When in doubt, toss it out." You can't always see, smell, or taste bacteria that cause food-borne illness. "If you don't know, give food the heave ho," advises Alice Henneman, a registered dietitian and extension educator with the University of Nebraska Cooperative Extension. "And just because food safety is serious stuff doesn't mean that learning about it has to be." She proves her point with a jazzy, award-winning game, "Don't Get Bugged by a Foodborne Illness," and a clever, concise, monthly e-mail newsletter. Subscribe to FOOD REFLECTIONS online at http://www.lanco.unl.edu/food.

Chapter 4

Cooking Tips and Techniques

· ·

In This Chapter

▶ Banishing your *phishy-phobias* — including fishy odors and fear of frying

▶ Cooking your catch to perfection every time

▶ Brushing up on techniques old and new

· ·

"Un-dish-cover the fish, or dishcover the riddle."

—*Through the Looking Glass,* Lewis Carroll

*W*here did the notion that cooking seafood is difficult or daunting come from? Let's unravel the riddle and reclaim the joy in en-*joy*-ing seafood. Quite simply, cooking sensational seafood is simple. Faster than you can say "Freddy fried five flavorful flounders Friday," you'll be ready to tackle the basics and serve up net results that are "shore" to please everyone at your table.

Nice and Easy Does It

You have plenty of reasons to hum a happy tune when you cook seafood. Here are some of the ways Mother Nature makes it easy:

✔ You don't have to worry about making seafood tender — it's naturally tender.

✔ You don't have to spend a lot of time cooking. Seafood cooks faster than any meat.

✔ You don't have to cope with one part taking longer to cook than another part. Unlike tender chicken breasts versus tougher thighs or tender beef rib eye versus tougher, chewier round steak, fish muscles tend to be uniform from head to tailfin, whether you're talking about a 300-pound-tuna or a 1-pound perch.

Cooked to a "T"

If there's a riddle to cooking seafood, it's this: When is it cooked — but not overcooked? Cooking is part art, part science, and part common sense. We consider all three, beginning with common sense.

Cooking is a *process*. Like the Energizer Bunny, cooking keeps going, and going, and going. . . . It doesn't come to a screeching halt when you turn off the burner. Even after you remove food from the heat, cooking continues. And when you remove food from the hot cooking pan, cooking doesn't stop immediately. You expect this when you roast something big, such as your Thanksgiving turkey or a 6-pound standing rib roast. What surprises us is how many degrees a small, thin piece of fish continues to go up after we take it off the burner and transfer it to a plate. For perfectly cooked seafood, count on this carry-over cooking time.

Testing, testing 1-2-3

Get ready to poke, press, peek, peer, pierce, prod, and practice the arbitrary art of eyeballing when finfish is done. (For help on cooking shrimp, see Chapter 5. For other shellfish, flip to Chapters 7, 8, and 10.)

Here's our assessment of telltale clues commonly used for finfish. We begin the list with two tests that we favor (both shown in Figure 4-1) and finish with three methods that others recommend but that we find too imprecise.

- ✔ **Nudge 'n' judge:** Our favorite test is to remove fish from the heat when its flesh begins to flake at the nudge of a fork. Using a regular table fork, insert the tines about halfway into the depth of the fish and give the tines a slight twist — you should be able to see flakes separating at the upper surface of the fish. Where the fork tines penetrate deeper into the fish, you should feel some resistance. In addition, if you try to gently push the fork through the fish, it won't glide easily all the way to the bottom. Voilà! With a few minutes of standing time, the fish will be perfectly cooked.

- ✔ **The cling thing:** If you're cooking fish with bones, gauge its doneness by looking at how the flesh clings to the bone. Stick the tip of a paring knife beside or into a bone to see if the bone wiggles. If the flesh clings firmly to the bone (no wiggle), cook it longer. Look for the moment that the flesh still clings slightly to the bone, but just starts to pull away. Don't cook the fish until the flesh falls off the bones — that's overdone.

- ✔ **Not glassy is classy:** Most raw fish flesh is translucent with a glassy sheen. Cooking turns it opaque. Use a knife or fork to open a space that's wide enough so that you can peek into the middle of the thickest part.

For medium-rare tuna, look for a ribbon of translucency still showing in the middle (about a ½-inch center strip in a 1-inch thick tuna steak). Remove salmon from the heat when it's cooked through except for a ¼-inch translucent band at its midpoint. Otherwise, cook fish until only a tinge of translucency remains.

✔ **Im-*press*-ive touch:** Some cooking authorities take a touchy-feely approach. This technique is best when the fish is cooked simply — without a thick glaze or coating — on the grill, in the oven, or in the skillet. Proponents say fish is done when you press the fish and it feels like what you feel when you press the end of your nose. You're right on if both are wiggly, yet firm. Others say that fish is perfectly done when the feel of the fish matches a spot on your lightly-clenched fist where your thumb and index finger connect. Are they both semi-rigid, but bouncy? Are you im-*press*-ed? Did you burn your finger?

✔ **Flakes are flaky:** Forget the age-old flaky test. If your fish flakes, it's probably overdone. Plus, some meaty fish (swordfish is the best example) separate into thin strands, not flakes.

Figure 4-1: Testing finfish for doneness.

The ten-minute guide

Bewildered by too much variability in the ways to evaluate doneness? Food scientists grappled for years to find an easy way to estimate how long fish needs to cook. Maybe you've heard of the Canadian timing theory that came to be known as *the ten-minute guide*. First promoted over twenty years ago by Canada's Department of Fisheries test kitchen, the theory is simple:

1. **Measure the thickness of fish at its thickest point.**

2. **Cook for 10 minutes per inch.**

This guideline applies to baking in a 450° oven, frying, broiling, poaching, steaming, or grilling — but not to microwaving.

The late James Beard, who wrote a number of definitive books on cooking seafood, proclaimed this technique "foolproof" and called it "probably the most important announcement in fish cookery of the last century."

Today, many cooks show less enthusiasm for this theory, finding that the cooking is generally too long for best eating quality and doesn't take into account all the variations in fish and cooking equipment. And we tend to agree. But we still suggest it as a helpful, but not absolute, guide.

You rarely need more time than the ten-minute guide. Start checking for doneness at least a minute or two before the estimated cooking time has elapsed. Additional time can always be added, but never subtracted.

Keep in mind the following exceptions to the ten-minute guide:

✔ Double the estimated cooking time for solidly frozen fish that you haven't thawed first (for a total of 20 minutes per inch).

✔ Allow five extra minutes per inch for foil-wrapped fish.

✔ When you bake at temperatures lower than 400°, figure an extra five minutes per inch as well.

Temperature targets

Instead of poking and piercing, why not probe with precision? Take the temperature of seafood to accurately tell when it's done. With a handy digital thermometer/timer, you can even monitor the cooking process in real time. Insert the thin probe at the end of the long, ovenproof cable into the thick part of any fish (except for thin fillets) and set the temperature alert to beep you. We use ours in the grill, in the skillet, and in the oven. Check it out in Chapter 2, along with information about the instant-read thin-probe stem thermometer. You may discover, as we have, that fish cooks faster than you imagine — fish is done before you know it.

✔ **For optimum eating quality:** For most finfish, we remove the fish from the heat when the temperature reaches 140°, expecting it to climb a few more degrees off the heat.

If you prefer salmon or tuna on the rare side, remove tuna from the heat when the temperature reaches 125°; remove salmon when its temperature reaches 130°. Expect their final temperatures to rise 5 or more degrees after removing from heat. Don't hesitate to cook the fish a bit more to your taste. Refer to Chapter 6 for some cautions if you're cooking wild-caught salmon.

✔ **For optimum safety:** Follow the Food and Drug Administration specification, which states that cooked fish sold commercially should be cooked until all parts are heated to 145° for 15 seconds. For shellfish, 165° is generally a safe target to use.

Overcooking fish may create fishy odors. Volatile oils in fish burn off and become sulfurous or acrid when fish gets too hot. Don't overcook fish — you'll prevent most, if not all, fishy odors. Our favorite ways to eliminate or mask fishy odors is to simmer water with thin slices of ginger and lemon, allspice, or pickling spices in an open pan.

Cooking Options from A to Z

Seafood takes swimmingly to almost any way you want to cook. Whiz through this alphabetical overview of familiar cooking techniques. We're impressed — and hope you are, too — with seafood's versatility. Get out of that "same-old, same old" rut and try a new technique or two. (For techniques that apply solely to shellfish, see Chapters 5 and 7.)

Baking or roasting

What used to be called "baking" may now be called "roasting." Fish is *roasted* when you bake it uncovered and relatively unadorned. From our perspective, everything else cooked in the oven is baked. Roasted or baked, we — and your fish — like a high temperature; 450° is fine. Estimate time with the guidelines in "The ten–minute guide" section, earlier in this chapter. Lower the heat only when other ingredients in the recipe are sensitive to high temperatures or take longer to cook. Preheat the oven for best cooking.

Broiling

Spoil yourself — broil. It's easy and straightforward to keep things under control when you cook seafood under the intense, direct heat from the broiler. Pamper yourself a step more by using disposable foil broiler pans. Once upon a time, we turned inch-thick fish steaks or fillets when half the estimated cooking time had elapsed. Now we don't.

1. **Before turning on the broiler, place the broiler pan that you plan to use in position under the heating element.**

   Adjust the distance so that the top surface of thick fish will be about 5 to 6 inches from the heat; for thin fillets, 2 to 3 inches.

2. **Preheat the broiler.**

   If the fish is thicker than ½ inch, also preheat the broiler pan.

3. **Lightly oil the pan. Place marinated or lightly oiled fish in a single layer.**

   Be careful if the pan was preheated; don't burn yourself.

4. **Estimate time with the guidelines in "The ten-minute guide" section, earlier in this chapter, basting once or twice. Test early for doneness.**

Adopt our secret for keeping thick steaks or fillets extra juicy: Steam-broil by pouring ½-cup hot water into the bottom pan of a typical two-piece broiler pan with perforated top rack before broiling.

Frying

Why add fat calories to something as skinny and healthy as seafood? For incomparable flavor, that's why! Frying seafood runs the gamut from a skinny sauté in a nonstick skillet with a mere trickle of healthful olive oil to a big pot of hot oil for deep-frying. Midway between the extremes of skimpy and indulgent, we love to start with our cast-iron skillet and real butter.

Deep-frying

If you're going to deep-fry, do it right. Don't skimp on the equipment. Either use a fryer with a thermostat or buy a high-quality thermometer that's designed for frying. Maintain the oil temperature at 375° by frying in small batches. Otherwise, when the oil cools down, you end up with greasy, soggy tidbits instead of incredibly crunchy crusts that envelop juicy, perfectly cooked seafood morsels.

Do yourself a big favor if you love fried foods — find out how to do it right from our friend Rick Rodgers, who wrote the book *Fried and True*. Here are a couple of his secrets:

✔ **Use enough oil.** As Rick says, "it's not called 'deep' frying for nothing." Start with fresh oil. The hassle of filtering, storing, and reusing oil isn't worth it.

✔ **Forget about draining fried foods on paper towels or, heaven forbid, newspapers or brown paper bags.** Steam collects under the surface and makes the crusts soggy. Instead, drain the food on wire cake racks set in rimmed baking sheets.

Pan-frying, sautéing, or searing

Technically, these are different names for the same technique — cooking seafood with fat in a skillet. By using a nonstick skillet and spray oil, you can nearly eliminate added fat and still achieve a crispy result. Or use your old cast-iron skillet with a light float of oil or butter.

We recommend using a medium-high heat. Also be sure that the seafood is dry, either by patting it with a paper towel or applying a light dusting of flour or some other coating. Check Chapter 2 for information on why we prefer a flat-bottomed skillet to one with ridged grids.

Stir-frying

Choose firm-textured seafood for this quick-cooking technique. A wok works best, but a big skillet is fine.

1. **Get the wok hot, add a swirl of oil, and then toss bite-sized pieces of seafood for a few seconds.**

2. **Remove the seafood from wok, and stir-fry veggies until crisp-tender.**

3. **Return seafood to the wok for a final flourish — and savor the vivid flavors.**

Grilling

Grilling is one of our favorite ways to cook seafood. The only thing fish needs for successful grilling is a clean *grill grid* (the rungs, that is), so that the fish flips easily without sticking. (To clean a grill, turn the heat up high, close the lid, and come back 10 minutes later. Turn off the grill and scrape the grid clean.)

We like to grill seafood on medium-high heat, so fire up your charcoal grill 35 to 40 minutes in advance or light a gas grill about 10 minutes before you start cooking.

1. **Drizzle the fish with olive oil and season or marinate.**

2. **Set the seafood on the grill, and leave it alone without moving it for 2 to 3 minutes to firm the flesh.**

3. **Lift the seafood, flip, and finish cooking, 3 to 6 minutes more, depending on the fish and its thickness.**

   Flip fish once more during longer cooking. To grill fragile fish, such as cod, use a grill topper. (See Chapter 2 for grilling tool tips.)

 If you're new to grilling seafood, grill with the cover left open — so that you can see what's going on. When you get the timing down pat, put the lid down to capture smoky tastes. For extra smoked flavor, use aromatic chips, not hardwood chunks, because fish cooks so fast.

Microwaving

Advocates of microwaving seafood, including cookbook author and culinary authority Barbara Kafka, believe that microwaves are the answer for consistently moist, delicate fish. In addition, we find the process fast and easy. Prove it to yourself by trying our speedy recipe for Three, Two, D-one Salmon Pockets with Shortcut Emerald Sauce in Chapter 6.

When microwaving fish, use its total weight, not its thickness, for your time guide. Figure three minutes per pound as a minimum.

1. **Arrange portions in a single layer with thicker edges toward the outside.**
2. **Cover with plastic wrap, leaving one corner vented open.**
3. **Cook on high power, rotating the dish a couple times.**

Don't forget that seafood continues to cook for a few minutes after it's removed from the heat. With microwave cooking, always allow for this *standing time,* or *carry-over cooking time,* before indulging.

Poaching

Poaching has nothing to do with snitching fish from your neighbor's pond — that's unforgivable. *Poaching* fish in warm liquid, however, is a forgiving technique. You just submerge fish in gently simmering liquid — water, wine, or fish stock that's enlivened with herbs, spices, lemon, or garlic. During poaching, the bubbles in the liquid shouldn't break the surface; a low heat guarantees a gentle poach and tender fish. Although poaching is a forgiving technique that yields moist results, timing still counts. Estimate time using "The ten-minute guide" section, earlier in this chapter: Poach a 1-inch fillet for about 10 minutes; a ¾-inch piece, 8 minutes; and so on.

After removing the cooked fish, we like to boil the liquid until reduced (to intensify the flavors) for a tasty sauce or to freeze for future soups. If you want more flavor and color, combine sautéing and poaching. Simply sauté fish golden brown on one side before poaching.

Steaming

S-s-s-steaming is one of the best-kept secrets of chefs specializing in seafood. They love this method because it captures the intensity of the flavors, especially when seafood is steamed on a solid plate or platter and not on a perforated steamer rack. See Chapter 2 for details on fashioning and using a makeshift steamer. Time by the guidelines discussed in "The ten-minute guide" section, earlier in this chapter.

Part II

Seafood Superstars

In this part . . .

Shrimp and salmon are at the head of the class when it comes to everyone's favorite seafoods. This part introduces you to the major players for each species, from those that roam the wilds to those raised down-on-the-farm. We give you a variety of recipes that use techniques — from familiar to fast — to showcase each. And we share some fishmasters' tips with you.

Chapter 5

Shrimpology 101

· ·

In This Chapter

▶ Selecting and storing shrimp

▶ Identifying shrimp types and sizes

▶ Discovering how to cook shrimp

▶ Making sumptuous shrimp recipes

· ·

Sweet and succulent shrimp is festive, fun, and it's America's favorite shellfish. Serve shrimp, and you're guaranteed a "wow!" reaction. Shrimp stars on menus around the world — from white-tablecloth elegance to down-home barbecues; with shells on or off; and grilled, broiled, steamed, stir-fried, baked, sautéed, or deep-fried. Use these cooking techniques to bring shrimp to your table as party fare, snacks, appetizers, soups, salads, sandwiches, and main courses.

In this chapter, we show you how to partner shrimp with seasonings such as garlic, ginger, cilantro, curry, dill, and mustard for dynamic tastes to delight your taste buds.

Although shrimp is rich in cholesterol, recent scientific studies reveal that most people need to watch the amount and type of fat in food, not the cholesterol content alone. Shrimp is lowfat and lean — it has a skinny 80 calories per serving and only 9 calories (1 gram) of that is fat. Shrimp's fat is a good kind of fat — unsaturated — and includes omega-3s, the type of fats that are known to improve heart health (see Chapter 1).

The Wonderful World of Shrimp

Precooked shrimp are popping up in seafood departments everywhere, but your favorite shrimp dishes taste lots better when you cook the shrimp yourself. Home-cooked shrimp have a bigger, fuller flavor than precooked shrimp — and a firmer, less-watery texture. However, when unexpected guests arrive, precooked shrimp are a handy solution. And they're a fast way to jumpstart salads, sandwiches, and salsas. Even if you use precooked shrimp, you can make shrimp cocktail taste tons better by quickly concocting your own scrumptious sauce and avoiding the often gluey-tasting bottled cocktail sauce. See the "Dressing (shrimp) for success" sidebar, later in this chapter, for more cocktail ideas.

Over the years, we've tasted and evaluated a lot of shrimp from all over the world. The ones that we prefer have a full, sweet taste and firm, toothsome texture. Some of our favorites are regional specialties. (To help you pick the best in your area, take a look at the Appendix.) Shrimp is both wild-caught and farm-raised, and if you conduct a side-by-side taste test of both varieties, you notice that they differ in taste and texture.

Nobody knows more about shrimp than Ocean Garden's Dixie Blake, the "shrimp lady," as her friends in the seafood industry affectionately call her. Dixie's repertoire includes identifying taste nuances of shrimp that feed on specific seaweeds in different bodies of water, understanding technologies of raising shrimp, and determining global influences on which country buys which type of shrimp, among other things. Dixie compares wild-caught and farm-raised shrimp to athletes and couch potatoes:

- **Wild-caught shrimp** have a rich, sweet taste and firm, dense flesh. They freely swim the oceans and develop strong muscles, just like a well-toned athlete. Shrimp in the wild eat a diet rich in shellfish and seaweeds, which enhance their taste and strengthen their shells.

- **Farm-raised shrimp** grow in slightly less roomy habitats and eat a more utilitarian diet. They develop fewer muscles, have a softer, less dense texture, and a milder taste.

Seldom do you find shrimp with their anatomy (head and tail) intact; most likely, you can only find headless shrimp. But don't despair, this definitely isn't a case of "heads, you win." A shrimp's head is nearly 40 percent of its total body weight. Because most people aren't aficionados of shrimp heads (adventurous foodies, however, do find delectable morsels and juices inside them), you won't pay for something you don't want to use. Further, the heady stuff is more prone to rapid spoilage. Heads-on shrimp, if you buy them, need to be handled with utmost care and consumed quickly.

Dressing (shrimp) for success

The following figure gives you a quick recipe to make your own cocktail sauce:

1. **Start with bottled chili sauce or ketchup.**

2. **Perk it up with prepared horseradish and lemon juice, tasting as you go.**

3. **Splash with Tabasco sauce, Worcestershire sauce, or both for added zestiness (optional).**

4. **Add minced green onions for texture and flavor (optional).**

Flip to Chapter 15 for a bevy of quick-mixin', quick-fixin' sauces to update your shrimp cocktails. The Remoulade Sauce in this chapter also makes a dynamite shrimp cocktail.

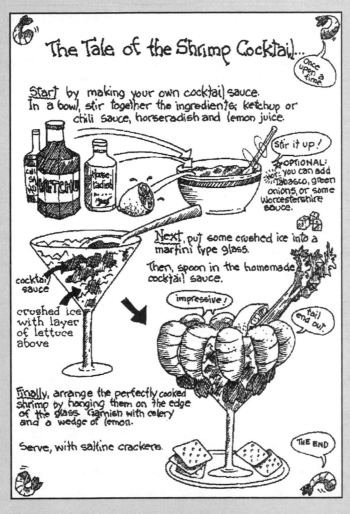

Shrimp is sold by size in two ways: by the number of shrimp in a pound or by size designation as small, medium, large, or jumbo. Unfortunately, one store's "jumbo" may be someone else's "large." Look at the numbers on the counter sign or package label — the bigger the number, the smaller the shrimp. For example, shrimp labeled 26/30 count equal 26 to 30 shrimp per pound. Really big shrimp may be labeled U-10s or U-15s (Under-15 shrimp per pound), while tiny shrimp may run 70/100 or smaller.

When buying shrimp, look both at the dish that you want to prepare and the shrimp size that's the best buy. You always have choices, so don't get locked into the one size a recipe calls for. For example, the Marinated Shrimp in a Mustard Duet recipe calls for 31/35 count shrimp. If you're serving four people, that's seven or more shrimp each, a generous appetizer. But if you'd like to serve eight, that's only four shrimp each. (Math alert: If you count only 31 shrimp when you're serving dinner, as host you have to make do with one less shrimp than your guests.)

So look at the next smaller size, 41/50s, which are less pricey. Now for eight guests, you have five to six shrimp per person, and they're still a good size to pick up and pop into your mouth. It may seem that a larger shrimp, say 26/30, would be more dramatic, and it would, but it's too large for most people to eat in one bite. Plus, the 26/30s are more costly, so you save your money for another dish.

Shrimp buying strategies: Fresh options

Rarely do you find fresh, never-frozen shrimp, unless you live near shrimping boats. Today's flash-freezing technologies often mean that quickly frozen, fresh shrimp are better quality than shrimp that may have stayed at sea several days before they came to shore — to be sold as fresh, never-frozen shrimp.

What's the difference between a shrimp and a prawn?

The terms *shrimp* and *prawn* have no exact zoological definition — they're often used interchangeably. When you eat in your favorite restaurant, a "prawn" is often the largest shrimp at any given moment. If you live in the eastern and southern United States, a shrimp is typically called a shrimp. In California, the Pacific northwest, and the state of Alaska, *spot prawns* are a prized regional shrimp.

In Europe, most people refer to shrimp as prawns. To further confuse the issue, if you order prawns when you're in Britain, you may be served a member of the lobster family (miniature pale pink look-alikes) that Dublin Bay fishermen catch — which in France are called *langoustines.* No matter what you call shrimp, though, you'll always enjoy!

When you buy shrimp from the seafood counter, it's usually already defrosted for you. Keep the following shopping tips in mind:

✔ **Take a good look at the shrimp.**

- If the shells are on, select shrimp with shells snugly attached, with no cracks or breaks, and with most of their little legs intact. Look for clean shrimp, with no muddy yellowing on the shell or at the head end. The shells should be spotless, with no black spots on them — just as you have enzymes in your digestive system, so do shrimp. If shrimp aren't quickly rinsed and iced at harvest, the enzymes react and cause black spots. Generally this isn't harmful, but it does indicate less-than-careful handling, so pass on those shrimp.

- If the shells are off, select shrimp that are whole (not broken into pieces), with a clean and bright sheen, and no yellowing at the head end.

✔ **Look for well-toned biceps.** Top quality shrimp is firm (not flabby) when you press it between your fingers. If you can handle the raised eyebrows when you ask your fish seller for a squeeze (the shrimp, that is), you have a good experience for your memory bank. After you feel a soft, mushy shrimp, you can better determine firmness from a distance.

✔ **Your nose knows.** Thawed, raw shrimp has a briny, oceany, nonammonia smell. Of course, it's pretty hard to determine this if the shrimp are packaged or in a case, but if you can find a fish seller to give you a sniff, go for it.

✔ **Size up your selection.** Whether you buy shell-on or peeled shrimp, look for shrimp that are a uniform size. For example, at $17.99 for a pound of U-15s, you're paying a premium for a big, special size. Occasionally, smaller shrimp slip into the batch — you're still paying dearly, but not for the extra-special size.

Here's an a-"peeling" statistic: Naked (shell-off) raw shrimp weigh in at 25 percent less than their shell-on buddies. So if a recipe calls for 1 pound of shell-on shrimp, simply buy ¾ pound (12 ounces) of peeled shrimp.

Make buying seafood the final stop on your shopping trip. If you have to stop somewhere, ask your fish seller for a bag of ice to keep your shrimp cold all the way home. At home, quickly rinse uncooked shrimp under cold water, drain, and repack in a container or resealable plastic bag, cover tightly, and refrigerate for no more than two days. After you cook the shrimp, you can keep them refrigerated up to four days.

The tale of shrimp cocktail

In trying to verify who "invented" the shrimp cocktail, we solicited all of the international food sleuths we know and still came up empty-handed: No one's sure. Based on their and our best evidence, here's the most likely scenario:

✔ Shrimp cocktail is a United States invention.

✔ The sauce itself probably is a spin-off of the sauce a bartender first concocted for oysters during the California Gold Rush.

✔ Shrimp cocktail was solidly entrenched as a sophisticated first course during the Victorian era. Lavish accoutrements included sterling cocktail forks and double-bowled crystal goblets (to hold ice in the base).

Few other dishes enjoy such sustained popularity as *the* party dish to impress.

Shrimp buying strategies: Frozen assets

Buy frozen shrimp and extend your dining and entertaining options by always having shrimp on hand. Most frozen shrimp is *IQF* (individually quick frozen), which means that each fresh shrimp is coated with a quick icy glaze to hold in its quality. Not as common, but still widely available, are shrimp frozen in blocks (around five pounds) that are packed in boxes.

When you buy IQF, keep these pointers in mind:

✔ Good quality IQF shrimp is pristine — no crunchy ice crystals surrounding the shrimp or dry white spots on the shell or flesh. These telltale signs indicate poor handling.

✔ Frozen shrimp shouldn't clump. Reject any package in which the shrimp clump together — a sure sign they've defrosted and refrozen somewhere along the way.

✔ Fancy, colorful packages sometimes have only a tiny see-through window for you to look for these quality signs, so you may have to look closely. The captivating photo on the package may or may not accurately reflect the size of the shrimp inside.

Make sure that the shrimp don't defrost on the rest of their journey. Ask for ice, and don't dally on your way home.

You may already have discovered the advantages of IQF — removing a handful of shrimp as you need them. Well-sealed IQF packages keep their quality in a home freezer, at 0° for up to four months.

Using your block

If you shop at warehouses or wholesale clubs, you may be able to buy a box of rock-hard frozen shrimp (usually 4.4 or 5 pounds).

✔ For a big party, when you plan to use the whole box, defrost the shrimp (set the box in a leakproof pan) for 24- to 48-hours, in the refrigerator.

✔ To use part of the box and refreeze the rest, remove the block of shrimp from the box and place it under cold — never hot — running water. Concentrate the flow on the sections of solid ice — these melt quite rapidly. Using a cooking fork or other sturdy utensil, carefully pry the block into smaller portions, trying not to break individual shrimp. Refrigerate any shrimp that have completely thawed and cook within two days. Place the still-frozen portions in freezer bags or wrap in heavyweight foil and refreeze immediately. Use within 3 months.

When defrosted slowly, shrimp retain their juicy succulence. You may find package directions on individually quick-frozen shrimp that suggest adding frozen shrimp directly to boiling water to cook. But our side-by-side tests favor thawing shrimp first. The best way to defrost is to thaw shrimp overnight in the refrigerator.

Avoid the temptation to run hot water over rock-hard shrimp. That's pouring juices — and money — down the drain. If you need to speed up the thaw, here's how to do it safely:

1. **Put frozen shrimp into a resealable plastic bag and seal well.**

2. **Fill a large bowl with half water and half ice.**

3. **Put the sealed bag of shrimp into the ice water.**

4. **Turn the bag occasionally.**

Depending upon the size and quantity, defrosting takes 30 to 45 minutes.

Cooking in Concert: Raw Shrimp Is the Key Ingredient

When you cook shrimp in a soup or pasta sauce, or mixed with a recipe's other ingredients, you gain flavor and save time. Because the shrimp don't need to be precooked for the six recipes in this section, you can be sure that your dish retains shrimp's succulent juices.

Caribbean Shrimp Packets

Cooking shrimp in foil packets gives you moist, juicy tastes with no cleanup. The tangy, sweet sauce, lively with fresh ginger, garlic, and bits of coconut, partners beautifully with shrimp. Check out the snazzy shrimp packet photo in the color photo section near the center of the book.

Preparation time: *20 minutes*

Cooking time: *12 minutes*

Yield: *4 main course servings*

1 pound raw, shell-on, medium shrimp (41/50 per pound)

½ cup apricot preserves or mango chutney

½ cup flaked, sweetened coconut

¼ cup fresh lime juice

2 teaspoons minced garlic

1 tablespoon peeled and minced fresh ginger

1 teaspoon kosher salt

½ to 1 teaspoon red pepper flakes

4 slices pineapple (fresh or canned)

1 green bell pepper, cored, seeded, cut into thin strips

1 medium red onion, peeled, halved, and thinly sliced

1½ cups long-grain rice

1 Preheat oven to 450°. Peel shrimp; devein, if desired (see Figure 5-1). For the apricot sauce, in a small bowl combine apricot preserves, coconut, lime juice, garlic, ginger, salt, and red pepper flakes.

2 Cut four sheets of foil, each 1-foot square. Place a pineapple slice on each piece of foil. Top each portion with ¼ of the green pepper, onion, and shrimp. Spoon ¼ cup of the apricot sauce over each portion. For each serving, lift two corners of the foil to form a triangular packet. Double-fold open edges tightly so that no steam escapes, leaving as much air space around the shrimp as possible.

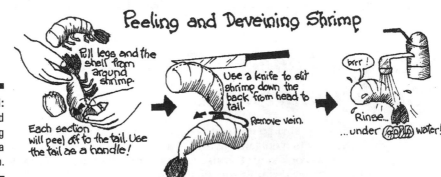

Peeling and Deveining Shrimp

Pull legs and the shell from around shrimp.

Each section will peel off to the tail. Use the tail as a handle!

Use a knife to slit shrimp down the back from head to tail.

Remove vein.

brrr!

Rinse... ...under COLD water!

Figure 5-1: Peeling and deveining shrimp is a cinch.

To devein or not to devein

Ever wonder what that black vein is that runs down the back of a shrimp? It's simply the shrimp's digestive track. Digestive tracks are harmless, but occasionally sandy, so whether or not to *devein* (remove the vein from the shrimp) is your choice. Depending on what a shrimp eats for its last meal, and how much time elapses before it is harvested, the vein may be black and highly visible, or clear and almost invisible. (Personally, if the vein is clear, we don't ever bother removing it.)

Look for easy-to-peel shrimp with the shell split down the middle. The vein has already been removed for you.

3 Cook rice according to package directions.

4 Place packets on a metal baking sheet and bake for 12 minutes. Remove the baking sheet from the oven and let packets stand, without opening, for 5 minutes. Place each packet on a dinner plate and let everyone carefully open his or her own. Serve with rice.

Vary It! Scallops, squid, crab, crawfish, whitefish, snapper, grouper, and surimi all work well as substitutes for shrimp.

Many of our recipes call for medium shrimp (41/50 shrimp per pound), because this size is often a good buy in your supermarket. Larger shrimp work well in almost any recipe. Just remember that as you increase the size of the shrimp, increase the shrimp cooking time by a minute or two.

1-2-3 Crispy Shrimp Bake

This is *the* recipe for non-cooks of any age to show off their culinary prowess. It's simple enough for kids to make for a quick weeknight dinner or elegant enough to serve for a dinner party.

Preparation time: 20 minutes

Cooking time: 6 minutes

Yield: 4 main course or 8 appetizer servings

(continued)

1 to 1½ pounds raw, shell-on, large (31/35 per pound) or extra large shrimp (26/30 count)

3 cups fat-free seasoned croutons

⅓ cup fat-free classic herb vinaigrette (or lowfat Italian dressing)

⅛ teaspoon Tabasco sauce (optional)

Lemon wedges

1 Preheat oven to 450°. Peel shrimp. To butterfly the shrimp, slit along the vein almost to the tail; discard vein. (See Figure 5-2.) Open shrimp, cut side up, like a book; flatten slightly. Repeat with remaining shrimp. Pat dry with paper towels. Arrange shrimp in a single layer in a large ovenproof dish or 4 individual casseroles.

2 Pour croutons into a resealable plastic bag; close bag and crush croutons to form somewhat chunky crumbs.

3 Combine vinaigrette and Tabasco sauce, if desired. Spoon vinaigrette over shrimp, coating evenly. Sprinkle with crumbs and pat slightly, so crumbs stick.

4 Bake for 5 minutes, and then check a shrimp in the middle of the dish. If it's almost white in the center, shrimp are done. If not, continue to bake for 1 to 3 minutes more. Garnish with lemon wedges and serve.

Vary It! Equally successful combos are Caesar croutons with Caesar salad dressing, Thai peanut sauce with plain croutons and a tablespoon of toasted sesame seeds (or use sesame breadsticks instead of croutons), or honey mustard salad dressing with garlic croutons.

Lemon Shrimp with Curly Pasta

This is one of our favorite weekday dinners — fast, easy, and scrumptious. The brown sugar mellows out fresh lemon's zing, but still leaves a bright taste. Use any curly or short pasta for this dish. These types of pasta catch the chunky sauce better than long, thin spaghetti strands. We're big on salads, so serve the pasta with mixed greens and watercress tossed with marinated artichoke hearts.

Preparation time: *15 minutes*

Cooking time: *10 minutes*

Yield: *4 main course servings*

(continued)

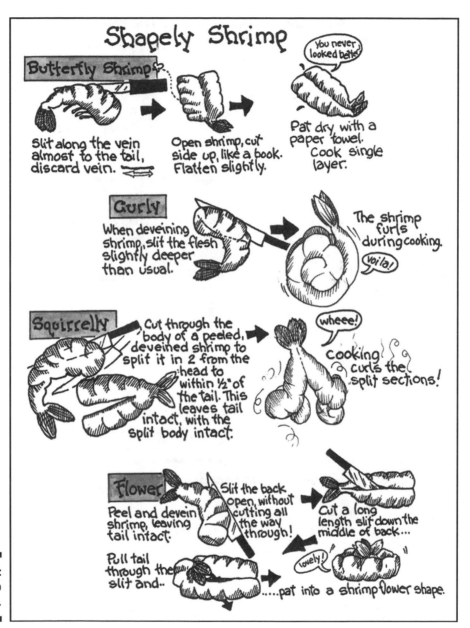

Figure 5-2:
Shape up
your shrimp.

*1 pound raw, shell-on, medium shrimp
(41/50 per pound)*

¾ pound corkscrew pasta

1 tablespoon grated lemon zest

½ cup fresh lemon juice

2 tablespoons minced garlic

2 tablespoons brown sugar

1½ teaspoons kosher salt

1 teaspoon freshly ground black pepper

½ teaspoon red pepper flakes

*1½ cups minced green onions, including
tops*

¼ cup olive oil

1 Peel shrimp, devein, if desired. Cook pasta in a large pot of boiling water
according to package directions.

2 In a large bowl, stir together lemon zest and juice, garlic, sugar, salt, pepper, red pepper
flakes, green onions, and olive oil. Add shrimp and toss to coat.

3 Heat a large, heavy skillet on medium-low heat until hot, about 4 minutes. Add shrimp
mixture, cover, and cook until center of shrimp turns almost white, 3 to 4 minutes.
Makes 3 cups sauce.

4 Divide warm pasta among 4 bowls and top with shrimp and sauce.

Vary It! Toasted pine nuts, roasted red peppers, and asparagus tips are tantalizing
additions to the pasta.

Southwest Shrimp and Corn Soup

A chunky and piquant soup with the flair of the southwest. Crisp tortilla chips and an
avocado and Boston lettuce salad are enticing accompaniments. Try rock shrimp for a
colorful and tasty change. For more information about rock shrimp, refer to the
Appendix.

Preparation time: *20 minutes*

Cooking time: *25 minutes*

Yield: *6 servings (about 8 cups)*

*1 pound raw, shell-on, medium shrimp
(41/50 per pound), peeled, or ¾ pound
peeled rock shrimp*

2 teaspoons corn oil

2 tablespoons minced garlic

1¼ cups clam juice or chicken broth

1 cup vegetable or tomato juice

1¼ cups minced green onions

3 cups cooked corn or thawed, frozen corn

1 to 2 fresh or canned jalapeño peppers, seeded and minced

2 cans (14.5 ounces each) chopped tomatoes with liquid

1 teaspoon kosher salt

1 teaspoon freshly ground black pepper

8 queen-size pimento-stuffed olives, sliced

1 can (4 ounces) chopped, mild green chiles undrained

½ cup chopped fresh cilantro

1½ cups sour cream (optional)

1 If desired, cut shrimp into squirrelly shapes. (Refer to Figure 5-2, which demonstrates transforming shrimp into a variety of shapes.) In a heavy 5-quart pot over medium heat, stir garlic in oil until garlic is softened, about 3 minutes. Add clam juice, vegetable juice, onions, corn, jalapeños, tomatoes, salt, and pepper. Bring to a boil, uncovered, over high heat. Reduce heat to medium and simmer to blend flavors, about 5 minutes.

2 Stir in olives, green chiles, and shrimp; simmer, uncovered, until center of shrimp turns almost white, about 2 minutes. Don't overcook, because the shrimp continues to cook as the soup stands. Ladle soup into bowls and sprinkle with cilantro. Serve with sour cream.

Vary It! Try crab, squid, clams, mussels, haddock, salmon, scallops, cod, grouper, or snapper instead of the shrimp.

Peel 'n' Eat Steamed Spiced Shrimp

In the Chesapeake Bay region, when we steam blue crabs, we often make a dipping sauce with vinegar and Old Bay Seasoning. Make a similar sauce for these shrimp, but use barbecue seasoning instead. Lots of ice cold beer is a must.

Preparation time: *5 minutes*

Cooking time: *2 to 4 minutes*

Yield: *4 main course servings*

1½ cups cider vinegar, divided

¾ cup barbecue, shrimp, or crab boil seasoning, divided

1½ cups water

1½ pounds raw, shell-on, medium (41/50 per pound) or small shrimp (51/60 count)

(continued)

1 Make a dipping sauce in a separate bowl for each person. For each serving, combine ¼ cup vinegar and 1 tablespoon barbecue seasoning.

2 To steam the shrimp, place a steamer rack in a large pot and pour in water and ½ cup vinegar. Make sure that the liquid is just below the rack. Reserve 2 tablespoons barbecue seasoning. Place the shrimp on the steamer in layers, sprinkling each layer with remaining barbecue seasoning. Bring liquid to a boil, cover pot, and steam until center of shrimp turns almost white, 2 to 3 minutes.

3 Transfer hot shrimp to a large bowl and sprinkle with reserved barbecue seasoning. Peel as you eat and dip in.

Use ground shrimp- or crab-boil seasoning for the best flavor, instead of the Louisiana and Shrimp Boil Seasoning that's made with whole spices.

Mardi Gras Shrimp

Messy, but fun — and a great excuse for a party. Shell-on shrimp, swimming in garlic butter spiked with barbecue spices, are a favorite New Orleans appetizer. And there's no better way to kick off Mardi Gras, the celebration of Fat Tuesday that precedes Lent, than with this decadent dish. (Revel in the dish today, repent later.) Serve the shrimp with lots of crusty bread to mop up the hearty sauce.

Preparation time: *20 minutes*

Cooking time: *15 minutes*

Yield: *4 main course servings*

1½ pounds raw, shell-on, jumbo (20/25 per pound) or extra large shrimp (26/30 count)

½ cup butter

4 teaspoons minced garlic

2 bay leaves

2 teaspoons minced fresh rosemary or parsley

4 teaspoons paprika

2 teaspoons coarsely ground black pepper

4 teaspoons fresh lemon juice

1 teaspoon dried basil leaves

1 teaspoon dried oregano leaves

2 tablespoons brown sugar

¼ cup Worcestershire sauce

½ teaspoon cayenne pepper

6 ounces beer, preferably dark

1 French baguette, heated

1 Preheat oven to 450°. Slit the shrimp shell down the back, leaving the shell intact, so the shrimp absorb more flavor from the garlic butter; devein, if desired.

2 In a large, heavy, ovenproof skillet, melt butter over low heat. Add garlic, bay leaves, rosemary, paprika, pepper, lemon juice, basil, oregano, sugar, Worcestershire sauce, and cayenne. Cook, uncovered, until fragrant, 3 to 4 minutes. Add shrimp and toss to coat with seasoning mixture.

3 Place pan in oven, and bake, uncovered, for 8 to 10 minutes. Heat the beer while the shrimp cook. Pour beer into a 2-cup measuring cup, cover, and microwave until hot, about 2 minutes, set aside. Pour in warm beer, shake pan to mix, and bake until shrimp are firm, but still tender, 1 to 2 minutes. Serve shrimp in bowls with bread to dunk into the sauce.

Vary It! Crawfish tails, scallops, langoustines, mussels, clams, or chunks of monkfish or grouper swim well in this garlicky sauce.

Cooking in Concert: Cooked Shrimp Stars

We cook our own shrimp instead of buying precooked shrimp, even in recipes that call for cooked shrimp as an ingredient. The flavor and texture differences between shrimp that you cook and shrimp that you buy already cooked are significant. In this section, we share tips and techniques for cooking shrimp perfectly for every day and party fare.

Great performances begin with your perfectly cooked shrimp

You can easily master our techniques for knowing when shrimp is cooked and how to stop it from overcooking. You get perfectly cooked shrimp every time.

Knowing when shrimp is done

Changes in color and texture are the keys to knowing when shrimp is done. Watching shrimp cook is like magic — it happens quickly and you're not quite sure how it got there — but practice watching, and you soon understand the process.

✔ **Look at the color** of the shrimp's shell and flesh before you begin cooking, and then observe changes as you cook. Cooking shrimp with the shell on is the easiest way to start. Watch the color. When the shell changes from muted gray, clear, or light pink to vivid pinky-red or coral, take the pan off the heat. (When you cook shrimp without the shell, its surface also turns pinky-red but less vividly than with the shell on.)

✔ **Look at the color** of the flesh at the *head end* (the fatter end) of the shrimp. When properly cooked, it changes from glassy and translucent to opaque white. Compare it to cooking an egg: As you watch an egg cook, the egg white also changes from clear and shiny to white. You can no longer see through a cooked egg white — or through a cooked shrimp.

✔ **Quickly check the texture.** Cool a shrimp under cold running water until you can comfortably squeeze the head end between your thumb and finger. A perfectly cooked shrimp feels firm, but still is somewhat resilient and springy. An undercooked shrimp is softer and more tender with less spring. An overcooked shrimp is stiff as a board and doesn't spring back.

One of Leslie's favorite fish sellers, Mr. Malik of Cameron's Fish Market in Silver Spring, Maryland, shares his doneness tips for steamed or boiled shrimp. Carefully squeeze the fat end of a just-cooked shell-on shrimp and look at the following:

- **The amount of moisture that you squeeze from the shrimp flesh.** If there is a fair bit, the shrimp is undercooked; drop it back into the pot to finish cooking.

- **The amount of space between the shell and the cooked meat:** There should be only a tiny space for perfectly cooked shrimp. If the shell separates around the flesh leaving a big gap, you know the shrimp is overcooked.

Customers flock to Cameron's for their sensational steamed shrimp — every day the staff steams over 90 pounds of shrimp. But when July's sizzling heat hits and families are ready to picnic, the number soars to 300 pounds — every Friday and Saturday. Now we know why Mr. Malik has his shrimp cooking techniques down pat.

✔ **Time your shrimp.** When you're cooking shrimp in water or seasoned liquid, begin to time cooking as soon as you toss the shrimp into the liquid. *Never* wait to start to time until the liquid returns to a boil. You end up with tough, overcooked shrimp.

Stopping the cooking

Keep in mind that shrimp continues to cook after it's removed from the heat and for as long as it remains in hot cooking liquid.

To stop shrimp from overcooking in its hot liquid, drain shrimp and plunge into an ice water bath, as shown in Figure 5-3. We like to take shrimp out of cooking liquid when its center is a tiny bit translucent, because the shrimp finishes cooking when it's standing.

Create an Icy Bath

1. Fill a large bowl half with cold water and half with ice cubes and place bowl in sink.

2. Immediately drain shrimp in a colander (or remove shrimp with a slotted spoon) and stir into ice water bath. Let stand for 2 minutes!

3. Drain shrimp, cover, and refrigerate if not using IMMEDIATELY!

Figure 5-3: Quick-chill shrimp to stop cooking.

Shrimp takes center stage

In the recipes in this section, you first cook shrimp simply — in water. Then, they're ready for you to toss onto pizza or nachos, slip into marinades or salsas, or dunk into a sensational dip. So get ready for your standing ovation when you give star billing to our high-stepping party fare. Bravo!

Super Bowl Baguettes with Shrimp and Artichoke Melt

You'll score big with sports fans of all ages when you pass this dish for halftime snacks or dinner. For dinner, serve 2 baguette boats per person. For the big game, cut the boats into 1-inch wide slices.

Preparation time: *35 minutes*

Cooking time: *15 minutes*

(continued)

Yield: *12 baguette boats; 6 main course or 12 appetizer servings*

1 pound raw, shell-on, small shrimp (51/60 per pound) or ¾ pound peeled rock shrimp

Three 9-inch baguettes

½ medium white onion, peeled and quartered

4 canned or thawed, frozen artichoke hearts, quartered

1 cup plain, nonfat yogurt

1 cup grated Provolone cheese

3 tablespoons sweet sherry or apple juice

1 tablespoon paprika

1 teaspoon kosher salt

1 teaspoon freshly ground black pepper

½ teaspoon Tabasco sauce

2 tablespoons minced fresh oregano or parsley

1 Bring a large pot of water to a boil. Place a large bowl with water and ice in sink. Add shrimp to pot and cook until center of shrimp turns almost white, about 1 minute. Drain shrimp and plunge into ice water to stop cooking. Shell shrimp.

2 Heat oven to 425°. Cut baguettes in half lengthwise and crosswise. Scoop centers of baguettes, leaving a ½-inch rim. Put the scooped bread into a food processor and process until you have fine crumbs. Remove bread crumbs and measure 1 cup to use and freeze the remaining crumbs for future use.

3 With the food processor running, add onion and artichoke hearts; pulse until finely chopped. Add 1 cup shrimp and pulse 3 times, until shrimp is coarsely chopped. Reserve the remaining shrimp to garnish baguette boats. Add 1 cup of breadcrumbs, yogurt, cheese, sherry, paprika, salt, pepper, and Tabasco sauce; pulse 5 to 6 times to blend. Makes about 3 cups. Toss the remaining shrimp with oregano.

4 Spoon about ¼ cup filling into each baguette boat; spread filling over the rim to the edges to prevent drying. Bake, uncovered, on a baking sheet 12 to 14 minutes, or until hot. Remove from oven.

5 Turn on broiler; arrange oregano-covered shrimp on top of baguettes and broil until warm, about 1 minute.

Substitute 12 ounces of cooked salad shrimp for raw shrimp. Make the filling a day ahead and refrigerate, so that you have more time to play.

Mediterranean Shrimp Pizza

Who needs to call out for pizza when you can make a lip-smacking, gourmet pizza on a moment's notice? Capture all the bright flavors and vivid colors of the sunny Mediterranean — just like an uptown bistro does. If you precook the shrimp a day ahead, you shave the last-minute prep time in half.

Preparation time: *18 minutes*

Cooking time: *8 minutes*

Yield: *1 12-inch pizza*

¾ pound raw, shell-on, medium shrimp (41/50 per pound)

One 12-inch prebaked thin pizza crust

¼ cup pesto

1 tablespoon plain, nonfat yogurt

½ cup sliced, pitted kalamata or other black olives

¾ cup thinly sliced roasted red bell pepper

2 ounces feta cheese, thinly shaved or crumbled

Optional toppers: balsamic vinegar, extra virgin olive oil, fresh basil

1 Bring a large pot of water to a boil. Place a large bowl with water and ice in sink. Add shrimp to pot and cook until center of shrimp turns almost white, about 2 minutes. Drain shrimp and plunge into ice water to stop cooking. Shell shrimp. Carefully halve shrimp lengthwise, removing veins. Pat dry with paper towels.

2 Preheat oven to 450°. Place pizza crust on large baking sheet. Combine pesto and yogurt until well mixed. Spread pesto on crust, leaving a one-inch rim.

3 Top pesto with olives, roasted peppers, shrimp (cut-sides down), and feta.

4 Bake for 7 to 8 minutes or until cheese is softened and crust is crisp.

5 Before serving, if desired, splash with a teaspoon of balsamic vinegar, a thin drizzle of olive oil (about a teaspoon), and garnish with fresh basil cut into narrow ribbons.

When small shrimp are your best buy, you don't need to halve them. If you use large or jumbo shrimp, dice them into bite-size morsels.

Macho Nachos

These shrimp nachos will be a macho hit at your next gathering. The photo crew found them irresistible (see the photo in the color photo section near the center of this book) and especially liked the rainbow array of colorful and flavorful flour tortillas. We remember when, not too long ago, we had to travel to a specialty market to find plain white flour tortillas — now they're everywhere. You can also find flavored tortillas — the green (spinach), gold (southwest seasonings), and red (sun-dried tomato) are our favorites.

Preparation time: *20 minutes*

Cooking time: *5 minutes*

Yield: *4 lunch or 6 to 8 snack servings*

¾ pound raw, shell-on, medium shrimp (41/50 per pound)

½ cup thinly sliced green onions, including tops

Two 10- to 12-inch flour tortillas (preferably flavored) or eight 6-inch corn tortillas

4 fresh or pickled jalapeño peppers, thinly sliced

Vegetable spray (butter- or olive oil-flavored)

6 ounces fontina or Mexican-style cheese, shredded (about 1½ cups shredded)

2 cups refried beans

1 cup sour cream

½ cup sliced black olives

1 cup guacamole (optional)

1 Bring a large pot of water to a boil. Place a large bowl with water and ice in sink. Add shrimp to pot and cook until center of shrimp turns almost white, about 2 minutes. Drain shrimp and plunge into ice water to stop cooking. Shell shrimp. Carefully halve shrimp lengthwise, removing veins. Pat dry with paper towels.

2 Preheat oven to 450°. Cut each flour tortilla into quarters. To crisp tortillas, lightly spray both sides of each tortilla with vegetable spray. Arrange on baking sheets and bake until crisp, turning once, about 3 minutes per side.

3 Spread each tortilla with beans, leaving a ¼-inch border. Top with shrimp (cut-sides down), olives, onions, peppers, and cheese.

4 Bake until cheese melts, about 3 to 5 minutes. Serve warm. Let everyone add sour cream and guacamole, if desired.

Fiesta Shrimp Salsa

This jewel-toned, zesty salsa is a great way to stretch shrimp for a party. See how it sparkles in the color photo section near the center of this book. Your guests will likely fight for the last smidgen, but make an extra batch (and hide it) for lunch. Fill fresh flour tortillas with the salsa, shredded lettuce, and a dollop of Dill Pesto with Asian Notes (see Chapter 15) for a treat tomorrow.

Preparation time: *35 minutes*

Cooking time: *1 to 2 minutes*

Yield: *8 appetizer servings (5 cups)*

1 pound raw, shell-on, medium (41/50 per pound) or small shrimp (51/60 count)

1 cup finely diced yellow bell pepper

1 cup finely diced red bell pepper

⅓ cup minced green onions, divided

2 to 3 jalapeño or serrano chiles, seeded and minced

6 tablespoons fresh lime juice

1 teaspoon kosher salt

1 teaspoon sugar

1 cup finely diced avocado

2 teaspoons olive oil

1 teaspoon minced garlic

Two 10-ounce bags tortilla chips

1 Bring a large pot of water to a boil. Place a large bowl with water and ice in sink. Add shrimp to pot and cook until center of shrimp turns almost white, 1 to 2 minutes. Drain shrimp and plunge into ice water to stop cooking. Shell and devein shrimp. Slice shrimp crosswise, ¼ inch thick.

2 In a large bowl, mix shrimp, yellow and red peppers, all of the onion except 1 teaspoon, and the chiles.

3 In a small bowl, stir lime juice, salt, and sugar together to dissolve the salt and sugar. Add lime juice mixture, avocado, olive oil, and garlic to the shrimp mixture. Stir gently to avoid mashing the avocado.

4 Garnish salsa with reserved green onions. Refrigerate until ready to serve. Serve salsa with tortilla chips.

Vary It! For a different taste, substitute mango or nectarine for the avocado, and green pepper for yellow pepper to brighten the color contrast. Rock shrimp (see the Appendix for a description) are great in the salsa.

Marinated Shrimp in a Mustard Duet

This subtle, silky marinade lets shrimp's sweet flavor shine through for a dynamite first course or appetizer. Use the marinade as a tasty topper for steamed mussels or clams on the half shell, or as a dipper for stone crab or snow crab claws.

Preparation time: *30 minutes*

Cooking time: *2 minutes*

Yield: *6 to 8 first course or appetizer servings*

½ cup cider vinegar

½ cup water

1 tablespoon kosher salt, divided

1½ cups thinly sliced white onion rings (1 medium white onion, peeled, halved, sliced)

2 tablespoons brown or yellow mustard seeds

½ cup fat-free mango or raspberry vinaigrette

¼ cup Dijon mustard

¼ cup minced fresh flat-leaf parsley

¼ cup olive oil1 pound raw, shell-on, medium (41/50 per pound) or large shrimp (31/35 count), peeled

1 In a small pot, bring the vinegar, water, and 1 teaspoon salt to a boil. Stir the onions into the vinegar mixture and remove the pot from the heat. Let stand 15 minutes to soften onion and lightly pickle; drain and set onions aside.

2 To toast mustard seeds, heat seeds in a heavy dry skillet on medium heat until seeds turn brownish-gray and become fragrant, 6 to 8 minutes, shaking pan occasionally. When seeds begin to pop, shake pan for about 1 minute to prevent burning. Remove pan from the heat; pour seeds into a dish to cool.

3 For the marinade, in a medium bowl, whisk together the mustard seeds, vinaigrette, mustard, 1 to 2 teaspoons salt, and parsley to blend. Whisk in oil. If desired, make marinade a day in advance. Makes 1 cup.

4 Slit the shrimp through the shell down the back and devein. Slit the shrimp flesh slightly deeper than usual, so the shrimp will furl up during cooking and catch more of sauce when marinating. Refer to Figure 5-2, earlier in this chapter, for instructions on making that deep cut.

5 Bring a large pot of water to a boil. Add shrimp to pot and cook until center of shrimp turns almost white, 1½ to 2 minutes. Drain shrimp; don't quick chill in an ice water bath. Shell shrimp.

6 Immediately add the warm shrimp to the marinade. Serve at once or refrigerate, covered, 4 to 6 hours. To serve as a first course, divide onions evenly between small plates; top with shrimp and marinade. For a more casual appetizer, stir onions into marinated shrimp shortly before serving and serve with toothpicks — messy but delicious.

Shrimp with Lemon, Sun-Dried Tomato, and Goat Cheese Dip

You don't need to take extra time to rehydrate these sun-dried tomatoes. They transform themselves into tender bites as they soak up the dip. For a dramatic presentation, arrange the shrimp on a midnight blue platter with the sauce bowl at one edge. Anything nautical is equally dramatic, like the lucite shell shown in the color photo section near the center of this book.

Preparation time: *30 minutes*

Cooking time: *2 minutes*

Yield: *6 to 8 appetizer servings*

4 to 5 sun-dried tomatoes, not marinated	*½ teaspoon kosher salt*
1 lemon	*2 tablespoons mayonnaise*
3 ounces goat cheese	*½ cup sour cream*
1 teaspoon Worcestershire sauce	*1 pound raw, shell-on, large shrimp (31/35 per pound)*
1 tablespoon finely chopped fresh basil plus basil leaves to garnish	

1 For the dip, with a pair of kitchen scissors, cut tomatoes into fine slivers (the slivers are easier to chew than the larger tomato bits that you can buy). You need about 1 tablespoon for the dip; set aside 1 teaspoon for a garnish. Grate or zest lemon; set aside ½ teaspoon of zest for a garnish. Halve lemon and squeeze 2 teaspoons juice; reserve remaining half lemon for future use.

2 In a medium bowl with a fork, mash together the goat cheese, sun-dried tomatoes, lemon zest, lemon juice, Worcestershire sauce, chopped basil, and salt. Blend in mayonnaise and sour cream. Let stand for 30 minutes to soften tomatoes. Makes about 1 cup. Spoon the dip into a bowl and garnish with lemon zest, sun-dried tomatoes, and basil leaves; serve at room temperature.

(continued)

3 If desired, slit shrimp shell down the back and devein before cooking. Bring a large pot of water to a boil. Place a large bowl with water and ice in sink. Add shrimp to pot and cook until center of shrimp turns almost white, 2 to 2½ minutes. Drain shrimp and plunge into ice water to stop cooking. Shell shrimp and arrange on a serving dish and serve with dip.

If you buy 26/30 shrimp per pound or larger, your guests will want to double dip their second bite — and heaven forbid, the germ patrol comes out in force. Conversely, 41/50 per pound are too small for dipping into this chunky sauce.

Sensational Shrimp Secrets Revealed

Fish masters — professional seafood chefs — know how to bring out the best in shrimp. In this section, our good friends share their shrimp secrets with you.

Is there a best way to cook shrimp?

Like sex, everyone has an opinion about what works best. Our colleague Shirley Corriher features this technique in her award-winning book, *CookWise.* Shirley super-seasons shrimp by cooking and chilling it in seasoned liquid. In addition, she cooks the shrimp at a lower temperature, so that it simmers, rather than boils. The theory is that lower-temperature cooking causes the shrimp to retain more moisture than cooking at a higher temperature.

Here's how it works: Heat causes the strands of shrimp protein to join together and take up less space — like your fingers, when you clasp them. The pressure tightens the strands and pushes out the moisture trapped between them. Higher temperatures produce increased tightening, water loss, and shrinkage — and this can lead to dry, tough shrimp.

So take your pick. Cook the shrimp recipes throughout the book using our suggested techniques or try Shirley's for equally delicious results.

Shirley's Seasoned Shrimp

Show off Shirley's Seasoned Shrimp with the jazzy Remoulade Sauce that follows this recipe. Serve the shrimp as an appetizer and dip into the Remoulade Sauce, or make a popular New Orleans first course, called *shrimp remoulade:* For each serving, place shredded lettuce on a small plate and top with shrimp, as shown in the color photo section near the center of this book. Spoon on the Remoulade Sauce to taste and pass extra.

Preparation time: *30 minutes*

Cooking time: *2½ to 4½ minutes*

Yield: *8 appetizer or 6 first course servings*

12 cups water, divided	*1 medium onion, skin-on, quartered*
1 tablespoon Herbes de Provence	*1 lemon, quartered*
2 bay leaves	*30 ice cubes*
1 teaspoon red pepper flakes	*1 to 1½ pounds raw, shell-on, medium-large (36/40 per pound), large (31/35 count), or extra large shrimp (26/30 count)*
1½ tablespoons kosher salt	

1 In a large pot, bring 6 cups water to a boil, uncovered, with the Herbes de Provence, bay leaves, pepper flakes, salt, onion, and lemon. Reduce heat and simmer about 5 minutes.

2 Remove 2 cups seasoned liquid and add it to a medium bowl along with the ice cubes. Let stand and cool.

3 Add remaining 6 cups water to seasoned liquid in pot and bring back to a boil. Add shrimp and stir. When water comes back to a simmer, immediately reduce heat to medium-low and begin to time cooking. For 26/30 shrimp, simmer 4½ minutes until the center of shrimp turns almost white. Remove shrimp with a slotted spoon or strainer and place in cool seasoned liquid, adding more ice if all ice has melted. Stir and let shrimp stand for about 5 minutes. Drain, peel, and devein. Cover and refrigerate until serving.

For 31/35 count shrimp, simmer about 4 minutes before removing; for 36/40s, simmer about 2½ minutes.

Rather than discarding the cooking liquid, we like to strain it and boil it for several minutes, and then chill and freeze. It's great to have on hand for the next time you cook shrimp or poach fish.

Remoulade Sauce

We dare you to limit yourself to dipping only shrimp into this creamy, tart sauce. Bursting with crunchy pickles and olives, Remoulade Sauce is the perfect partner for seafood, from tuna to tilapia to clams on the half-shell.

Preparation time: *25 minutes*

Yield: *2 cups*

1 lemon

⅔ cup mayonnaise

½ cup sour cream

1 teaspoon grainy or Creole mustard

4 green onions, including tops, finely chopped

¼ cup finely chopped gherkins or baby dill pickles

¼ cup queen-size pimento-stuffed olives, finely chopped

4 teaspoons drained capers, finely chopped

2 teaspoons dried tarragon

3 tablespoons minced fresh parsley or dill

½ teaspoon celery seeds

Tabasco sauce to taste

1 Grate lemon zest and reserve 2 teaspoons; juice lemon. In a medium bowl, combine the mayonnaise, sour cream, and mustard until smooth. Stir in the lemon zest, lemon juice, green onions, gherkins, olives, capers, tarragon, parsley, celery seeds, and Tabasco sauce.

2 Let stand 30 minutes to blend flavors before serving. Use as a dip for shrimp or as a sauce for seafood cakes and wraps.

Vary It! Try shrimp tarts remoulade, one of Leslie's popular catering party foods. Simply fill ready-made miniature tart shells with the Remoulade Sauce and top with a tiny shrimp. Yummy.

Is there a best way to fry shrimp?

One bite of this crispy, fried shrimp from our friend Chef Joe Simone, and we knew he was doing something special. This creative chef from Boston learned his technique from Cesare Benelli, the chef/owner of Al Covo in Venice, Italy. Their secret: Let the shrimp rest in an icy, saltwater bath until just seconds before frying them. The result: the most delicate crispy crust that's never greasy, and a shrimp center that's divinely succulent and juicy. Incidentally, Chef Joe chose his teacher wisely: Chef Benelli's *ristorante* was voted best seafood restaurant in all of Italy by *La Stampa* (a major Italian newspaper) in 1997.

The routes of remoulade sauce

Remoulade and its kissing cousin, tartar sauce, find their roots in France. Both start life as mayonnaise — often homemade — but there are as many variations for each as there are fish in the ocean. You can find mustard, cornichons or gherkins, herbs, and often anchovies in remoulade sauce. When the French sailed into New World ports, such as New Orleans and Mobile, they brought their recipes with them — including remoulade sauce. When you're eating remoulade in the south, it may be jazzed up with ingredients such as paprika, cayenne, ketchup, or celery leaves.

Joe Simone's Crostini with Shrimp and Sicilian Mint Sauce

Don't want to deep-fry? Do as Chef Joe Simone often does. He serves this same preparation with wood-fired grilled shrimp, instead of fried, and accompanies the dish with mesclun salad greens. Some Sicilians call this sparkling sauce a *bread salad;* other Italians call it *minted olive oil.* We call it delicious! Any leftover sauce adds a bright note to grilled fish or chicken. Contemporary menus give new meaning to the literal translation of *crostini* — "little toasts." In this recipe, the toasts are big slices of crusty country bread.

Preparation time: *30 minutes*

Cooking time: *10 minutes*

Yield: *4 generous appetizer or lunch servings*

Sicilian Mint Sauce

Yield: *½ cup*

1 slice stale rustic country bread	*1 canned anchovy, rinsed and patted dry*
1½ teaspoons red wine vinegar	*1 teaspoon capers, rinsed and drained*
½ cup water	*¼ cup extra virgin olive oil*
2 tablespoons minced fresh mint leaves	*Salt and freshly ground black pepper*
2 tablespoons minced fresh flat-leaf parsley	

1 Remove and discard the crust from the bread. Tear the bread into small pieces (makes about ¼ cup). In a glass or other non-reactive bowl, combine vinegar and water; stir in bread and allow it to soak for about 10 minutes for bread to fully absorb the liquid.

(continued)

2 Add the mint, parsley, anchovy, and capers to the bowl of a food processor that's fitted with the steel blade. Pulse to finely chop.

3 Squeeze the soaked bread, discarding excess liquid. Add bread and olive oil to herb mixture and pulse to combine. Don't puree. Season to taste with salt and pepper. ***Note:*** You can make the sauce ahead of time and refrigerate it for up to one day before serving.

Shrimp and Crostini

1 pound raw, shell-on, jumbo or larger shrimp (under 20 per pound)

Lightly salted ice water

4 slices rustic country bread, cut ½-inch thick

1 tablespoon olive oil

3 to 6 cups vegetable oil (for deep-frying)

½ cup flour

1 Peel and devein shrimp. Place them in a bowl of lightly salted ice water.

2 Brush both sides of the bread with olive oil and grill, bake, or broil until golden brown.

3 In a deep fryer or other large pan over medium-high heat, add vegetable oil to a depth of 2 to 3 inches. When oil reaches 350°, remove shrimp from ice bath and dredge or dip them in flour. Shake off excess flour and carefully fry 4 to 5 shrimp at a time until golden brown, about 3 minutes. Keep shrimp warm until all are cooked.

4 Toss the hot shrimp with ¼ cup mint sauce. Arrange shrimp on top of crostini. Pass the remaining sauce for those who want an extra dollop — or two.

Chapter 6

Salmon Tales

· ·

In This Chapter

▶ Singing salmon's praises

▶ Clarifying the array of salmon choices

▶ Getting smarter about a smart food choice

▶ Partnering salmon with great flavors

▶ Transforming salmon with salt — a metamorphosis

· ·

*L*ove salmon? You're in good company. You and millions of other salmon lovers, both at home and in restaurants, have sent salmon soaring to the top of the popularity charts, giving it seafood super-star status.

You've made this majestic fish the preferred fresh finfish. Overall, tuna consumption outranks that of salmon, but most tuna is canned, not fresh.

Salmon is consistently in the limelight, week in and week out, at the fresh fish counter where you shop. With few exceptions, you can count on salmon year 'round. Its meteoric rise to the top of marine cuisine is a pretty big fish story, so we've given it a chapter to itself. In this chapter, we give you bits and pieces of this fascinating salmon story, along with all you need to know to eliminate any confusion about what to buy, how to get it home safely, and how to jazz up your purchase with easy, delicious recipes.

Salmon Superstars: Who are the Players?

Before we take you shopping for salmon, here's a pop quiz:

Question: Where does Atlantic salmon come from?

   a. Off the Atlantic coast of Maine (U.S.A.) and Canada's Bay of Fundy

   b. In the southern Pacific along Chile's slender coastline

   c. In the North Sea between the United Kingdom and Norway

   d. Off the Pacific coast of British Columbia, Canada

Answer: All of the above and more!

Did you logically pick the Atlantic coast? It would make sense that Atlantic salmon swim in the Atlantic Ocean and Pacific salmon swim in the Pacific Ocean, wouldn't it? Not so anymore because of salmon farming.

What's growing down in the farm?

Atlantic salmon (or *salmo salor* to be precise) is growing down in the farm. Tons of it. Around the world, elaborate, scientifically monitored salmon farms are flourishing, trying to keep up with the insatiable demand for this succulent seafood. When the wild catch of Atlantic salmon from its native waters of eastern North America and Europe dwindled to a few thousand pounds a year, Norwegians pioneered Atlantic salmon farming in the 1960s, creating a worldwide market for this salmon.

In 1980, farm-raised Atlantic salmon accounted for a mere one percent of the world's salmon supply. Today it's more than 50 percent and still climbing. In the United States alone, farm-raised salmon consumption has skyrocketed from under 7 million pounds per year in the early '80s to over 240 million pounds today!

All Atlantic salmon sold commercially is farm raised — wild Atlantic salmon supplies are virtually depleted. In addition, even though it may not be labeled as such, some coho salmon, steelhead, and king salmon you buy may be farm raised, too. Expect to pay a premium when you find farm-raised kings (also called *chinooks*) on the menu or in your specialty markets. Compared to Atlantic salmon, these pampered nobility take twice the feed and time to reach market size.

From farm to fork

Leslie toured the salmon farms on the northwest coast of Norway where the cold North Sea wraps into the fjords. And just as land farmers raise their herds, so salmon farmers raise their *schools* in submerged pens, under careful, scrutinized supervision. Whether the salmon farms repose in breath-taking, quiet fjords or battle the elements in choppy seas (sometimes an hour-long, flat-out boat ride from the coast), sophisticated technology is the name of the game. Salmon farms around the world — in the United Kingdom, Canada, the United States, and Chile — are run in a similar fashion.

Salmon is *caught* (scooped from the pens) on a daily basis and transported in sea water-filled ship holds to nearby processing plants onshore. Stainless steel equipment, workers in lab-like garb with waterproof footwear, and a pristine environment prevail. The salmon is readied for fresh and frozen markets, from France to Japan and beyond. A mere four hours may elapse from swimming fish to blast frozen (a frigid −40°), skinless, boneless portions — vacuum-packed and ready for shipping.

But how do they cut all those salmon into neat and tidy portions? The cutting looks like magic, but it's hi-tech science: Computer-guided laser beams or high-pressure jets of water sleekly slice the fillets into weight-specific portions. A computer program calculates the exact place on a whole salmon fillet for each precise cut, customizing the pattern based on its shape and weight. Pretty amazing!

What's harvested from the wild?

Perhaps you had a school-age fascination for salmon with their unerring, but fatal homing instinct. We were mesmerized by the stories of these fish travelling thousands of miles back from the ocean, swimming upstream to their freshwater birthplace to spawn, and then dying. Those, however, are the wild Pacific salmon. (They belong to the scientific genus *Oncorhynchus*, a name formed by combining two Greek words: *onco* meaning hook or barb, and *rhyno*, nose.) As a salmon gets closer to spawning, its jaw takes on a hooked shape. Pacific salmon come in the following varieties:

✔ **King (or Chinook) salmon** is literally the king — the biggest and most highly valued of all Pacific salmon. The raw flesh is a bright red and cooks up bright, deep-orange. King salmon has the highest fat content of the wild Pacifics, which imparts a buttery texture complementing its rich, earthy taste, and chewy, big flake. Kings are perfect for grilling and for smoking. They *run* (head back to their birthplace to spawn) from May through October. Copper River kings and their Yukon River counterparts are becoming national celebrities. See "Copper River cache" sidebar, later in this chapter, for this Cinderella story.

- **Sockeye (or Red) salmon** is renowned for its vivid red flesh, which turns intense deep-orange when cooked. Its distinct, complex flavor is described in nonfishy terms, such as "woodsy," "wild mushrooms," and "herbal." Grilling or smoking intensifies these flavors. The meat is firm and slightly chewy, with a finer flake than king salmon. The United States exports huge quantities of sockeye to Japan, where it is highly prized for sushi and sashimi. Sockeye runs in parts of Alaska in mid-May and during the summer months. It is the premium canned salmon species.

- **Coho (or Silver) salmon** is leaner than king or sockeye with a milder taste and finer-textured flesh. The flesh also can be brightly colored, ranging from dark orange-red to light pink — the color lightens when cooked. Coho has a medium oil content and is more delicate than king or sockeye, so it's best when grilled skin-on or whole. Wild coho runs from July through early October, and range from 5 to 15 pounds.

- **Chum (or Keta) salmon** is the meatiest and firmest of all Pacific salmon, with flesh ranging from pale orange to pink. The leanest of the Pacific salmon, chum can be grilled without fear of fat flare-ups. It is best when grilled skin-on or whole (using a grill topper), or baked, poached, or sautéed. Chum is often canned, smoked, or harvested for its bright orange eggs (salmon caviar), much of which is exported to Japan. Chum salmon run from July through October, and weigh in the 8-pound range.

Copper River cache

Out of the can and into the limelight. This is a modern day Cinderella story orchestrated in no small part by one of our favorite fish masters — Jon Rowley from Seattle, Washington. Fifteen years ago, the Copper River king salmon was just another salmon that found its way into a can. Jon and others decided that this salmon deserved better and proceeded to catapult the Copper River salmon to celebrity status.

Weeks before the first salmon of the fishing season are caught at Alaska's Copper River, retailers and restaurateurs around the northwest begin stirring up the excitement, counting down to the day that they'll have the first of these prized salmon available. After the long, cold winter, these highly anticipated salmon remind locals that summer (along with an abundance of locally caught wild salmon) is just around the corner. But the Copper River salmon (both king and sockeye) are also among the most flavorful salmon available all year. The reason is their higher levels of fat, which the fish develop for extra fuel to make it up the long river, leaving the flesh richly marbled and full of flavor. (Compare it to a well-marbled steak.) It's a short season on the Copper River — just a few weeks — which emphasizes the special quality of these fish. In the northwest, home cooks and diners can try to get their fill, but outside the region you have to look for Copper River salmon as a special attraction on upscale seafood menus or in specialty fish shops. It's worth the hunt, though — a great reward for the effort!

✔ **Pink (or Humpy) salmon** has flesh that ranges from light to deep pink. Pink salmon is low in fat, and is best pan-fried, poached, or baked. The flesh dries out if it's grilled or broiled. Available only in the fall, pink salmon is the smallest of the wild salmon. A lot of pink salmon is canned.

Some unexpected members of the salmon family include Arctic char, rainbow trout, and steelhead. Refer to Chapter 9 for details about their special traits and habitats.

What's the difference?

Gather three or more salmon-lovers around the same table, and you're likely to hear them debate which is better — wild-harvested or farm-raised salmon. We don't take sides; we love both!

What we like about farm-raised salmon:

✔ Available fresh all year

✔ Quick to fix portions

✔ Consistent quality

✔ Appealing rich, mild flavor

✔ Affordable

What we like about wild-caught salmon:

✔ Firm texture

✔ Complexity of flavor

✔ Color and texture nuances that vary with the type of salmon, what it eats, where and at what time of year it's caught

✔ Sides and whole salmon great for summer barbecues

Scoping Out Your Buying Options

Want salmon tonight? Whisk into almost any supermarket on your way home from work, and you can count on finding salmon any which way you like it. In this section, we offer you tips for buying salmon in the forms that suit you and your family best — from fillets, steaks, and single-serving portions to whole fish or sides — as well as fresh and frozen options.

Sizing up salmon shapes

In addition to finding familiar salmon fillets, steaks, and whole fish, you can find single-serving size fillets (or *portions*). The majority of these portions are skinless and boneless, so they are ready to grab-and-go when you're on the run. So look over your options and take your choice:

- ✔ **Portions cut at the factory:** Fillets portioned before they leave the processing plant are revolutionizing the way salmon is sold. Available in sizes from 4- to 8-ounces, you can buy them fresh or frozen — even boneless. (For more information on how portions are cut, see the "From farm to fork" sidebar, earlier in this chapter.)

  Whole salmon fillets have a row of bones, called *pin bones,* that run down the center of the fillet about one-third of its length. The bones start at the wide (or head) end of the fillet. Many processing plants now use state-of-the art, pin-bone removing devices. Should pin bones remain in what you buy, they are easy to pull out. Use a pair of needle-nose pliers or fish tweezers. See Chapter 2 for tips on removing pin bones.

  - • **Skin-off fillets:** Ready to cook. The fish world's user-friendly equivalent of boneless, skinless chicken breasts.

  - • **Skin-on fillets:** Usually priced less per pound than skin-off fillets. Flip to the tip on using skin-on fillets in the Avocado Chipotle-Glazed Salmon recipe, later in this chapter.

- ✔ **Whole fillets (also called *sides*):** Great to grill or poach for company.

- ✔ **Steaks:** Pretty presentation. Some don't like the bone. Others claim the tastes next to the bone are the best bites.

- ✔ **Roasts:** Usually 1- to 2-pound cross-sections from the center of the whole fish, bone-in and skin-on. Uniform shape cooks evenly. Wonderful filled with your favorite stuffing. Great grilled: The skin encircling the roast prevents the juices from escaping and the flesh from drying out.

- ✔ **Whole fish — head-off or head-on:** Poached salmon always one-ups anything else on the buffet table. Great oven-roasted, too, for a fix-and-forget elegant entrée.

Choosing fresh or frozen

Are you insistent that fresh is always better than frozen? You may want to reconsider. Flip to Chapter 3 for more about the hi-tech innovations that may change your mind about what is really fresher: never-frozen fish or frozen-at-sea. Jack Amon, a top chef at an upscale Anchorage restaurant, admits he prefers the quality of frozen salmon for his stunning, signature dish: king salmon crusted with king crab. And he's in Alaska, where some of the greatest fresh salmon resources in the world are at his doorstep.

If you eat salmon rare or medium-rare (as we often prefer it) or make your own *gravlax* (a Scandinavian specialty of salmon cured with salt, pepper, fresh dill, and other spices), you may be doubly interested in the frozen option. The U.S. Food and Drug Administration (FDA) Food Code (adopted by some, but not all, states and local jurisdictions) specifies that fish served raw in commercial establishments (including sushi bars) must have been kept frozen at −4° or colder for 7 days or −31° or colder for 15 hours in a blast freezer. Like other critters who roam the woods and waters, wild salmon carry a slight risk of harboring tiny roundworm parasites that may escape detection during the inspection process. Prolonged freezing or cooking to 140° for one minute kills them. If you have concerns, play it safe and take your cue from the FDA guideline. When you don't plan to cook salmon thoroughly, look for wild salmon that's commercially frozen. (Don't rely on your home freezer to do the job — temperatures are not frigid enough.) Or choose farm-raised salmon — food safety experts agree that a parasite problem with farm-raised salmon is highly unlikely.

When you buy fresh

You can't look a boneless, skinless fillet in the eye to size up its freshness. To help you buy the best fresh salmon, here's a review of some general quality and freshness signs to look for, plus hints to maintain those qualities:

- ✔ Be wary of a display of salmon fillets or steaks stacked sky-high. The fish on top may not be cold enough, and the one on the bottom of the stack gets squished.

- ✔ Look for arrangements where any salmon in direct contact with ice is positioned so exposed flesh isn't on ice. When ice and fish flesh meet, the contact makes the fish soggy and leeches out its good juices. Except for whole salmon on ice, we like display set-ups with either a tray or plastic film that keeps cut salmon off the ice.

- ✔ Choose flesh that looks firm, has a nice sheen, and has no dried out spots. Avoid flesh that has slits or gaps (someone's not handled the salmon carefully along the way).

- ✔ Ask for a sniff — you shouldn't smell any detectable "off" odors.

- ✔ Avoid jagged cut edges in the visible skin and residual scales clinging to the surface of the flesh.

- ✔ Buy fish last when you shop, ask your fish seller for a bag of ice, and don't leave your purchase in a hot car while you complete other errands. Because salmon is a cold-water fish, spoilage can get started at lower temperatures than for meat, poultry, and fish from warmer waters.

- ✔ Refrigerate wrapped salmon in the coldest part of your refrigerator, nestled with a frozen ice pack (either a gel pack or ice cubes in a plastic bag).

- ✔ Cook fresh salmon within two days. If you can't use it that quickly, double-wrap it as airtight as possible and freeze it quickly. Even when stored at home-freezer temperatures, salmon oils oxidize and become rancid when poorly packaged and held longer than two or three months. Refer to the freezing instructions in Chapter 3.

Eau de salmone, perchance?

Sniff, sniff. Do we detect a note of salmon in your fragrance? Indeed, your perfume, hand cream, and some medicines may soon contain salmon. A chemical compound found in the cartilage of salmon heads, *chondroitin sulfuric acid,* is an essential ingredient in the manufacture of many cosmetics and drugs. Non-salmon sources of these compounds used in the past are in short supply and are costly. It's a good thing that the scent of good fish isn't fishy!

Captain Jack Donlan of The Fish House in Grand Blanc, Michigan, isn't happy when some sellers call fish "fresh" when it actually has been frozen and thawed — and charge you fresh-fish prices. His test: Try to gently fold a fillet in half, end-to-end, with skin side out (or what was the skin side if it's skinless). A previously frozen fillet will ooze moisture from the midpoint. A fresh one won't drip, because its cell walls haven't been ruptured by freezing and thawing.

When you buy frozen

The trend in frozen food packaging is to cover the contents with an opaque package; thank goodness this isn't typical for frozen salmon. As you look at your frozen salmon options, follow these clues to finding high quality:

- Look for vacuum-packed portions for the best-sealed protection. Avoid packages with pinhole punctures.

- Don't buy packages that look suspiciously like someone simply tossed unsold fresh packages past their "sell-by" date into the store's freezer. Complain to the manager!

- Reject packages with loose ice crystals or uneven icy coating (symptoms of poor handling and possible thawing and refreezing).

- Pass on packages with signs of freezer burn: white, cottony patches and dry edges.

- Avoid products extending above the top of open freezer cases. Salmon, especially, needs frigid freezer temperatures.

- Thaw overnight in the refrigerator, if you have time. To defrost quickly, seal salmon in a plastic bag and submerge the bag in a bowl of cold water for 15 to 20 minutes. Or carefully defrost in microwave using a defrost or low-power level, rotating the package several times to assure even thawing.

We like to keep a stash of vacuum-packed, boneless, skinless salmon fillets in the freezer for quick, healthy, convenient meals anytime. We buy 6- or 8-ounce portions from a wholesale seafood distributor — most club stores carry a similar product. Also try phoning salmon wholesalers listed in your yellow pages; some may sell directly to consumers.

Smart food — good fats

Salmon has more going for it than good taste, wide availability, consistent quality, and affordable prices. Besides all that, it's good for you, too.

Read the fine print on the nutrition label, and you may be surprised by the amount of fat listed: About half of the calories are fat in most king salmon and in some farm-raised salmon. But that's more good than bad! Salmon oils are the good fats, with very little saturated fat. Most importantly, salmon contains high levels of fatty acids, especially the omega-3s. Medical research continues to validate the role of omega-3s in protecting against coronary heart disease, high blood pressure, rheumatoid arthritis, and other childhood and adult disorders. Flip to Chapter 1 for more facts about heart-healthy fats.

Center-of-the-Plate Salmon Sensations

Talk about versatile: Salmon responds to almost any cooking technique. Take your pick. In this section, we offer you a bevy of choices: grilling, baking, pan-searing, sautéing, steaming, poaching, microwaving, slow-roasting, and pickling. Or try them all!

Besides the recipes in this chapter, you can also find salmon swimming in recipes in Chapters 11, 14, and 16. And don't overlook the sauces and condiments in Chapter 15 that partner perfectly with any simply cooked salmon. Check out the "What to drink with salmon" sidebar, later in this chapter, for hints on recommended wines.

Grilled

A member of the Lewis and Clark expedition to the northwest in the early 1800s described salmon as "superior to any fish I ever tasted. I find them best when cooked Indian 'stile,' . . . by roasting a number of them together on a wooden spit."

Two hundred years later, we agree that Lewis and Clark had the right idea. Head outdoors to grill kebabs or capture the woodsy aromas in our easy supper salad with grilled salmon and couscous.

Before you fire up the grill, you may want to look in Chapter 2 for grilling tools and in Chapter 4 for grilling techniques and tips.

What to drink with salmon

Tom Douglas, the chef/owner of three of Seattle's most popular restaurants, is credited with helping to create what has come to be known as *northwest cuisine.* No question that he knows a thing or two about pairing salmon and other great regional foods with wine. When Tom and his staff help diners at Dahlia Lounge, Etta's Seafood, and Palace Kitchen choose a wine to sip alongside salmon, they often turn to white wines that have spent little or no time in wood barrels. Among their favorites are Semillon, Sauvignon Blanc (also known as Fumé Blanc) and Pinot Gris.

But the surprise to many is that many Pacific northwesterners prefer a red wine — Pinot Noir — with salmon. Here, Tom points out, a little woodiness is okay, enhancing the overall balance of flavors, rather than overwhelming as an oaky white wine would. The exception? Farmed Atlantic salmon. He finds that the pronounced richness and unique flavor of this species simply doesn't pair as well with red wine, so he suggests sticking with the white options for these salmon.

Tarragon Salmon Kebabs

This is one of the prettiest, easiest, and most versatile dishes we know. Bright red peppers and dark green zucchini highlight pale pink salmon. If you're having a party, you can assemble the kebabs a day ahead and refrigerate them overnight. Plus, you can substitute almost any firm-fleshed fish or shellfish for the salmon: mahimahi, swordfish, grouper, snapper, sea bass, scallops, or shrimp. (Check out the kebabs in the color photo section near the middle of this book.)

Preparation time: 30 minutes

Cooking time: 8 minutes

Yield: 4 main course servings

Sour Cream Sauce (see the following recipe)

Tarragon Basting Sauce (see the following recipe)

1¾ pounds salmon fillet, skin-off, pin bones removed, cut into 1-inch cubes

Eight 12-inch skewers (soak wooden skewers 30 minutes)

1 red bell pepper, seeded, cored, and cut into 1-inch squares, or 12 cherry tomatoes

1 medium zucchini, sliced ⅛-inch circles

16 medium mushrooms, cleaned

¼ teaspoon kosher salt

¼ teaspoon freshly ground black pepper

1 Prepare a medium-hot fire in a charcoal or gas grill. As the grill heats, alternate pieces of the salmon, red pepper or tomatoes, zucchini, and mushrooms on skewers, allowing 2 skewers per person. Completely brush the kebabs with Tarragon Basting Sauce. Sprinkle kebabs with salt and pepper just before grilling.

2 Brush grill with oil. Grill kebabs, with grill lid closed, until golden brown and a bit crispy, 6 to 8 minutes, turning every 2 minutes. Serve hot, passing Sour Cream Sauce separately.

Sour Cream Sauce

½ cup sour cream

¼ cup plain, nonfat yogurt

3 tablespoons minced fresh tarragon or 2 teaspoons dried tarragon leaves

1 tablespoon white wine vinegar

¼ teaspoon kosher salt

¼ teaspoon freshly ground black pepper

In a small bowl, mix the sour cream, yogurt, tarragon, vinegar, salt, and pepper.

Tarragon Basting Sauce

¼ cup olive oil

2 tablespoons fresh lemon juice

2 tablespoons minced fresh tarragon or 2 teaspoons dried tarragon leaves

In a small bowl, mix the olive oil, lemon juice, and tarragon.

For a party appetizer, make mini-kebabs and wow your friends: Tuck one cube of salmon between two vegetables on a short skewer.

Volcano Salmon and Couscous Salad

This energizing salad is a great excuse to eat grilled salmon and is ideal for a summer evening. Quick-cooking couscous and salmon are the perfect foils for the fiery flavors from eastern Asia. (See "The fire of sambal oelek" sidebar, later in the chapter, for hot tips.) For an up-close look at this combo, check out the color photo section of this book.

Instead of salmon, try snapper, mahimahi, swordfish, shrimp, or mussels; smoked mackerel, trout, or bluefish; sardines or canned salmon. Serve the salad with warm, crusty bread and ample cold beer.

Preparation time: *20 minutes*

Cooking time: *8 minutes*

Yield: *4 main course servings*

(continued)

1½ cups couscous

1⅓ cups water

1 tablespoon kosher salt, divided

¾ to 1 pound salmon fillet, skin-off, pin bones removed

1 tablespoon plus 1 teaspoon olive oil

¼ cup fresh lemon juice

2 to 3 teaspoons ground Asian chili paste, such as sambal oelek, or 1 teaspoon red pepper flakes

½ bunch watercress, washed, dried, sprigs separated, or 2 cups washed, torn fresh spinach

18 cherry tomatoes, halved

1 cup finely chopped fresh flat-leaf parsley or cilantro

½ cup finely chopped green onions

1 Prepare a medium-hot fire in a charcoal or gas grill. As the grill heats, cook the couscous: Bring the water and 1 teaspoon salt to a boil. Stir in the couscous, cover, and remove from the heat; let stand for 5 minutes. Fluff couscous with a chopstick or fork and set aside.

2 Rub ½ teaspoon olive oil into each side of salmon. Brush grill with oil. Grill salmon with grill lid closed, and cook for 3 minutes. Gently flip salmon, cover the grill, and cook 3 minutes more. Turn salmon again and cook about 2 minutes, or until the flesh of the salmon just begins to flake with the nudge of a fork.

3 For the dressing, in a small bowl, stir together the lemon juice, 1 to 2 teaspoons salt, chili paste, and remaining 1 tablespoon oil. In a large bowl, toss couscous, watercress, tomatoes, parsley, and green onions. Pour the dressing over couscous and toss to coat. Spoon couscous mixture onto 4 serving plates. Break salmon into large chunks and place on top of couscous.

Baked

Turn on the oven for the tantalizing trio of recipes in this section. To entice you even more, flip to the color photo section near the center of this book and see for yourself what eye-appealing results are in store for you. Turn up the heat a notch with two kinds of chiles in our creamy avocado topper, accent salmon with the oh-so-popular flavors of Provence with a tapenade, and serve everyone a shiny silver package (aluminum foil!) and let them discover for themselves the meal-in-one inside with warming Asian flavors.

Avocado Chipotle-Glazed Salmon

This velvety avocado glaze plays two roles: It seals moisture in the salmon and makes a zesty serving sauce. *Chipotle chiles,* often shortened to just *chipotles* (chee-POHT-lehz), are smoked and dried jalapeño peppers that are sold two ways: simply dried or canned in a seasoned tomato sauce called *adobo* (ah-DOH-boh). Chipotles add bold, smoky flavor and energize almost any sauce for fish (they're one of our favorite ways to perk up dishes). If you can't find chipotles, substitute 2 teaspoons of chili powder and a drop of liquid smoke in the avocado glaze.

Preparation time: *40 minutes*

Cooking time: *8 minutes*

Yield: *4 main course servings*

1 medium ripe avocado	*½ teaspoon kosher salt*
¾ cup plain, nonfat yogurt	*Pinch white pepper*
1 can (4 ounces) chopped, mild green chiles, undrained	*4 skin-on salmon fillets or steaks, 6 to 7 ounces each, about 1-inch thick, pin bones removed*
1 teaspoon fresh lime juice	
1 teaspoon ground cumin	*¼ cup minced fresh cilantro*
1 chipotle chile (canned in adobo sauce), undrained, minced	

1 Preheat oven to 450° or prepare a medium-hot fire in a charcoal or gas grill. Peel and pit avocado; remove pulp and mash. Measure ½ cup pulp. If you have extra pulp, use it to replace some of the yogurt and reduce yogurt by the same amount.

2 For the avocado glaze, mix together the avocado, yogurt, green chiles, lime juice, cumin, chipotle, salt, and pepper. Set aside one cup of the glaze to use for the sauce. Place salmon skin side down on a jellyroll pan (lightly oiled if you're using steaks) and spread about 2 tablespoons of the glaze over each piece of salmon. For the serving sauce, stir cilantro into the remaining glaze.

3 Bake salmon for about 10 minutes until the flesh of the salmon just begins to flake at the nudge of a fork. Or grill salmon, fillets preferably, with grill lid down, without turning for 8 to 10 minutes. Serve salmon with avocado sauce.

Vary It! Tuna, catfish, snapper, Arctic char, cod, or grouper also work well instead of the salmon.

(continued)

Look for ready-made guacamole in the deli case or freezer section of your supermarket (you need about ½ cup of guacamole to replace 1 avocado).

Here's why this recipe calls for skin-on salmon. When you bake this dish, either skin-off or skin-on salmon gives a fine result. Grilling, however, is another story. Because you don't turn the salmon in this recipe (if you did, the topping would fall off), the skin protects the salmon flesh from overcooking or sticking to the grill. The salmon skin also adheres to the grill to help you easily remove the salmon — simply slip your spatula between the salmon and the skin, and then serve the salmon.

 ### *Black Olive Tapenade-Topped Salmon*

Olive trees abound in Provence in southern France, and everyone has a favorite recipe for the popular olive spread, called *tapenade*. The French make tapenade with either green or black olives and spread the zesty sauce onto rounds of bread for an appetizer. Visually, black olives are stunning; check their showy appeal in the photo of this dish near the center of this book. We love this recipe, which tops salmon with tapenade, adapted from our good friend Anne Willan. Anne is an acclaimed international cookbook author and the founder of La Varenne Cooking School in Burgundy, France.

Preparation time: *20 minutes*

Cooking time: *12 minutes*

Yield: *4 main course servings*

¼ cup cold water	¼ cup sliced almonds
1 slice white bread	2 tablespoons drained, rinsed capers
4 salmon fillets, skin-off and pin bones removed, or steaks, 6 to 7 ounces each, about 1-inch thick	2 garlic cloves, peeled
	2 anchovy fillets
1 lemon	¼ cup olive oil
¾ cup pitted oil-cured black olives, such as kalamata (10 ounces with pits)	½ to 1 teaspoon freshly ground black pepper

1 Preheat the oven to 375°. Pour ¼ cup cold water over bread and set aside to soak. Place salmon in a single layer in a lightly oiled baking dish. Cut 4 thin slices from lemon and set the rest aside.

2 For the tapenade, in a food processor, add olives, almonds, capers, garlic, and anchovies. Squeeze bread in your hands to extract the water, tear in thirds, and add to processor. Using the pulse button, coarsely chop the ingredients. With the machine running, slowly add oil until tapenade is a slightly chunky, stiff sauce. Add the juice from the remaining lemon and pepper to taste. Spread 2 tablespoons of tapenade over the top of each piece of fish and top with a lemon slice. You can refrigerate leftover tapenade up to a week.

3 Bake salmon, uncovered, for 10 to 12 minutes until the flesh of the salmon just begins to flake at the nudge of a fork.

You can substitute ready-made green or black olive spread for this tapenade. You need about ½ cup.

Microwave the salmon, if desired. Use a microwaveable dish; cover with plastic wrap, leaving one corner open to vent. Cook 3 minutes on high, rotate dish, and cook for an additional 2 to 3 minutes. For dinner for one, cook a single portion for 2 minutes.

Salmon Sealed in Silver

Entertaining is a snap with this foil-packet baking method — and there's no cleanup. Serve this pretty medley with small, boiled potatoes and a spinach salad tossed with a sesame-orange dressing. For Foil-Packet Folding 101, turn to the photo of the shrimp packets, the cousin of this dish, in the color photo section near the middle of this book. To ensure squeaky, clean leeks, see the recipe for Sicilian-Style Swordfish with Capers in Chapter 12.

Preparation time: 10 minutes

Cooking time: 10 to 12 minutes

Yield: 4 main course servings

4 teaspoons butter

½ cup mango chutney or apricot preserves, pureed

1 tablespoon minced fresh ginger or pickled ginger

1 tablespoon cider vinegar

2 teaspoons minced garlic

¼ to ½ teaspoon crushed red pepper flakes

2 cups slivered leeks or green onions

4 skin-off salmon fillets, 6 to 7 ounces each, about 1-inch thick, pin bones removed

1 to 2 teaspoons kosher salt

1½ teaspoons freshly ground black pepper

1 red bell pepper, seeded, cored, and cut into ⅛- by 2-inch matchsticks

1 small zucchini, sliced ⅛-inch thick and then cut into matchsticks

28 snow peas, slivered lengthwise

(continued)

1 Preheat oven to 500°. For the sauce, place butter in a measuring cup, cover, and microwave on high for about 1 minute to melt, or melt butter in a small saucepan. Stir in chutney, ginger, vinegar, garlic, and red pepper flakes.

2 Cut four sheets of foil, each one-foot square. Place ½ cup of the leeks in the center of each piece of foil. Season both sides of salmon with half of the salt and pepper. Place salmon on leeks and spoon 3 tablespoons of the chutney sauce over each portion. Top each portion of salmon with ¼ of the red peppers, zucchini, and snow peas. Season with remaining salt and pepper.

3 For each serving, lift two corners of the foil to form a triangular packet. Double-fold open edges tightly, so that no steam escapes, leaving as much air space around the salmon as possible. Preheat a metal baking sheet in the oven for 2 minutes until very hot. Set packets on baking sheet and bake for 12 minutes. Remove baking sheet from oven and let packets stand, without opening, for 5 minutes. Place each packet on a dinner plate and let everyone carefully open his or her own.

Vary It! You can substitute mahimahi, swordfish, snapper, or whitefish for the salmon.

Measure the thickness of the salmon before cooking. A 1-inch thick piece will take about 12 minutes, with 5 minutes standing; a ½-inch piece, about 10 minutes, plus 3 minutes of standing time.

Steamed, microwaved, and poached

Do a double-take with our next two recipes: They are the quick and quicker versions of the same idea. We layer salmon fillets with a vivid herb stripe that integrates the zesty flavors in a unique way. You're also guaranteed a big splash when you serve the Asian Noodle Bowl with Salmon, bursting with fragrant flavors that infuse poached salmon for a heart-warming meal.

The fire of sambal oelek

Spicy condiments, called *sambals*, are popular in Indonesia and Malaysia. One of our favorites is a *sambal oelek* (SAHM-bahl OH-lek), a fiery red mixture of dried or fresh ground chiles, vinegar, and salt. Sambal oelek adds a rich, zesty zing to Asian Noodle Bowl with Salmon, Volcano Salmon and Couscous Salad, salsas, and sauces. If you can't find sambal oelek in your supermarket, look in Asian or Indian markets.

Steamed Salmon Pockets with Emerald Sauce

Layered with a ribbon of zingy emerald puree, this pretty salmon is a colorful way to welcome spring (or to pretend then it's just around the corner). Flip to the color photo section near the center of this book to see the layered effect. Transform some of the puree into a silky serving sauce. To guarantee a smooth sauce, check out the squeeze-dry tip that follows this recipe. Serve with fresh asparagus and crisp, baked potatoes.

Preparation time: *40 minutes*

Cooking time: *9 minutes*

Yield: *4 main course servings*

Emerald Puree

One 2½-inch piece fresh ginger, peeled

3 green onions

1 jalapeño pepper, seeded and cored

1½ cups washed, well-dried fresh parsley leaves (about 1 bunch)

1½ cups washed, well-dried fresh cilantro leaves (about 1 bunch)

3 cloves garlic, peeled

3 tablespoons vegetable oil

1½ tablespoons fresh lime juice

1½ teaspoons sugar

½ teaspoon kosher salt

Cut the ginger, green onions, and jalapeño into ½-inch pieces. Place the parsley and cilantro in the workbowl of a food processor and process until minced. With the machine running, add the ginger and garlic; pulse until minced. Repeat with green onions and jalapeño. With the machine running, add the oil, lime juice, sugar, and salt; process until pureed, scraping as needed. Or place all ingredients into a blender and puree. Makes 1 cup. You can make this puree 1 to 2 days in advance, and it freezes beautifully.

Salmon Pockets

4 skin-off salmon fillets, 6 to 7 ounces each, about 1-inch thick, pin bones removed

⅔ cup plain, nonfat yogurt

1 Slit each portion of salmon and open (see Figure 6-1); set aside.

2 Set aside 10 tablespoons of puree for Emerald Sauce. Spread the cut surfaces of each salmon portion with 1½ tablespoons of the remaining puree. Refold the salmon to its original shape, gently pressing to seal in the puree.

3 Place a steaming rack in a wok or 10-inch pot and steam salmon, covered, for about 9 minutes until the flesh of the salmon just begins to flake at the nudge of a fork. Flip to Chapter 4 for more information about steaming techniques.

(continued)

4 Stir yogurt into the remaining puree. Spoon ½ tablespoon of this Emerald Sauce across each fillet. Pass remaining sauce.

Vary It! You can use halibut, cod, sea bass, or striped bass instead of salmon.

Figure 6-1:
One step
to open
salmon like
a book.

 The parsley and cilantro need to be completely dry after you wash them or the Emerald Sauce consistency won't be as smooth as it should be. To start, pick the leaves from the parsley and rinse in a strainer. Place parsley on several thicknesses of paper towels, roll jelly-roll-style, and tightly squeeze to remove excess moisture. Repeat with cilantro.

Three, Two, D-one Salmon Pockets

Zappity-do-dah! This speedy microwave recipe was inspired by our Steamed Salmon Pockets with Emerald Sauce and takes advantage of the increasingly popular precut salmon portions. Knock minutes off your meal prep with little effort, and without compromising delicious flavors.

Look for versatile coriander chutney in the Indian section of your supermarket or in an Asian specialty food store. This bright green, pesto-like condiment is a pleasantly zesty combination of fresh coriander (cilantro), green chiles, vinegar, and other seasonings. An opened bottle keeps refrigerated for months. Also try its cousin, mint chutney, an equally refreshing, convenient flavor-builder with a minty note. We enjoy both — straight or muted with mayo or drained yogurt. *Note:* Because these condiments contain some salt, the salmon doesn't require additional salt or pepper.

Preparation time: 3 minutes

Cooking time: 3 to 4 minutes

Yield: 2 main course servings

One 8-ounce skin-off salmon fillet, about 1-inch thick, pin bones removed

1 teaspoon bottled coriander chutney

Shortcut Emerald Sauce (optional — see the following recipe)

1 Divide salmon into 2 equal pieces. Cut each portion horizontally (refer to Figure 6-1).

2 Using a small, flexible spatula, spread ½ teaspoon coriander chutney on the "open book" surface of each portion. Refold salmon to its original shape, gently pressing to seal in the chutney.

3 Place salmon in a microwaveable container; cover with plastic wrap, leaving one corner open to vent. Microwave on high for 2 minutes. Let stand 1 minute, and then test for doneness. Salmon should just begin to flake at the nudge of a fork. (Refer to Chapter 4 for more information about microwaving and testing for doneness.) If it is necessary to cook longer (microwave's wattage varies), add time in 30 second increments to avoid overcooking.

4 Serve hot with Shortcut Emerald Sauce, if desired.

Shortcut Emerald Sauce

1 tablespoon mayonnaise

1 teaspoon bottled coriander chutney

¼ to ½ teaspoon water (optional)

In small bowl, whisk together mayonnaise and coriander chutney. Stir in water for a thinner consistency, if desired.

Vary It! If your quest for coriander chutney is unsuccessful, this recipe is equally delicious and fast when made with bottled pesto. Or when time permits, prepare a batch of authentic Emerald Puree that accompanies the Steamed Salmon Pockets (see previous recipe); freeze for this recipe and other uses.

For accuracy, insert a thin-probe, instant-read thermometer into the middle of one portion. Salmon is thoroughly cooked at 140°. High quality, commercially frozen salmon or farm-raised salmon may be eaten less well done without undue concerns about food safety (we prefer 135°). Refer to Chapter 4 for more information about using a thermometer as a cooking aid for all seafood.

Asian Noodle Bowl with Salmon

Big bowls of noodles and broth are the rage in trendy restaurants. But our Asian noodle bowl, brimming with ginger and fragrant sesame oil, spells comfort any season of the year. (And it's not impolite to slurp when eating this dish!) Serve the soup with a salad of cucumber slices tossed with rice vinegar and crunchy toasted sesame seeds.

Preparation time: *30 minutes*

Cooking time: *15 minutes*

Yield: *4 servings*

4 ounces dried cappellini or soba (buckwheat) noodles

1 carrot, peeled

6 cups clam juice, chicken stock, or fish stock

8 quarter-size slices unpeeled fresh ginger

¾ cup (7-ounce jar or can) drained straw mushrooms

1 teaspoon grated lemon zest

1 to 2 teaspoons ground Asian chili paste, such as sambal oelek, or crushed red pepper flakes

2 green onions, including tops, slivered on the diagonal

1 tablespoon minced garlic

½ to 1 teaspoon kosher salt

1 pound skin-off salmon fillet, pin bones removed, divided into four portions

2½ cups finely shredded napa or Chinese cabbage

2 tablespoons finely chopped fresh cilantro or dill

2 teaspoons Asian toasted sesame oil (optional)

1 Cook noodles according to package directions. Drain and rinse under cold water to stop the cooking; set aside. Cut carrot into an Oriental flower shape or slice very thinly on the diagonal. Take a look at the carrot flowers in the color photo section near the center of this book.

2 In a 5- to 6-quart pot, bring clam juice, carrot, and ginger to a boil. Loosely cover and cook 4 minutes. Stir in mushrooms, lemon zest, and chili paste.

3 Add cooked noodles. Reduce heat to medium-low, cover, and simmer until hot, stirring occasionally, about 3 minutes. Stir in green onions, garlic, and salt to taste.

4 Immerse the salmon in the broth. Cover and simmer until the flesh of the salmon just begins to flake at the nudge of a fork, about 5 minutes. Using a slotted spoon or spatula, gently transfer salmon from the pot to a warm platter, cover, and keep warm. Remove and discard the ginger.

5 Divide cabbage evenly among four large, deep soup bowls. Ladle the noodles and broth into the bowls, place salmon on top, and sprinkle with cilantro. Drizzle with sesame oil, if desired.

Vary It! Pink-fleshed fish or shellfish are the prettiest fish for this soup, so try trout, Arctic char, shrimp, crab, crawfish, or surimi. Grouper, catfish, tilapia, orange roughy, whitefish, or cod are also tasty.

To craft Oriental carrot flowers, firmly hold a 3- to 4-inch long section of carrot flat on a cutting board. Using a sharp knife, carefully remove V-shaped grooves, cutting about ⅛-inch into the carrot. Repeat until you have removed 3 to 5 evenly spaced skinny wedges. Next slice carrot into thin, crosswise coins. If carrot is slender, make crosswise cuts on the diagonal to form larger flowers.

Pan-seared and sautéed

From the sublime (Morocco) to the ridiculous (cartoon-land) describes the inspirations for the tempting recipes in this section. Wield your skillet and preside at the stovetop.

Salmon Tagine

Executive Chef Bader Ali's Salmon Tagine is as elegant as it is quick and easy to make. Chef Ali serves his version of the salmon with saffron couscous and a roasted lobster claw at Le Tarbouche restaurant in Washington, D.C.

Preparation time: *30 minutes*

Cooking time: *12 minutes*

Yield: *4 main course servings*

2 tablespoons five-spice powder

½ teaspoon ground cumin

½ teaspoon ground cardamom

½ teaspoon turmeric

4 skin-off salmon fillets, 6 to 7 ounces each, about 1-inch thick, pin bones removed

3 tablespoons olive oil

1 tablespoon thinly sliced garlic

½ teaspoon saffron threads, slightly crumbled

½ teaspoon kosher salt

1 cup diced peeled, seeded tomatoes (8-ounce tomato)

(continued)

1 For the spice blend, mix the five-spice powder, cumin, cardamom, and turmeric in a small bowl. Rub both sides of each fillet with the mixture until completely coated.

2 Using a one-quart saucepan, heat 1 tablespoon olive oil over medium heat. When hot, add the garlic, cook until the garlic just starts to brown, then add the saffron, salt, and tomatoes. Cook for 1 minute and cover; turn heat off and let pan stand on burner while salmon cooks.

3 Heat remaining 2 tablespoons olive oil in a large, heavy skillet over medium-high heat. Add salmon and sauté 2 minutes per side until browned. Turn fillets again and cook 2 to 3 minutes more for medium-rare doneness. If you prefer your salmon more fully cooked, turn and cook 1 to 2 minutes more until the flesh of the salmon just begins to flake at the nudge of a fork.

4 To serve, top each salmon fillet with about 2 tablespoons of the saffron tomato sauce.

Vary It! The saffron tomato sauce is also a colorful accent for white-fleshed fish, particularly halibut, Chilean sea bass, or sablefish.

If fresh tomatoes aren't in season, substitute canned diced or seasoned, stewed tomatoes (drained and chopped).

Saffron adds a tart, pungent flavor to the tomato sauce and cuts the richness of the salmon. Saffron is the world's most expensive spice — but a little goes a long way. You can buy saffron as a powder or as whole yellow, orange, or red short crinkly threads. The threads are better quality than the powder. To best maintain saffron's taste and color, we store it tightly sealed in the freezer.

Popeye's Salmon Cakes

Offer your family a knock-out supper when you pair Popeye's favorite vegetable with sensational salmon. To better visualize how far we've come from old-fashioned canned salmon patties, check the photo of these colorful cakes in the color section near the center of this book.

For a pretty appetizer, serve mini-salmon cakes atop tiny pitas or pita wedges with arugula and Catalan Romesco Sauce in Chapter 15, thinned with a bit of sour cream.

Preparation time: *40 minutes*

Cooking time: *12 minutes*

Yield: *4 main course servings*

¾ cup thawed, frozen, chopped spinach squeezed-dry

1¼ cups cooked salmon (10-ounce fillet with skin, cooked)

¾ cup shredded, cooked potato (5-ounce potato, cooked)

2 tablespoons well-beaten egg, about ½ a large egg

2 tablespoons plain, nonfat yogurt

2 teaspoons finely chopped chives or green onion

½ teaspoon dried tarragon

½ teaspoon Dijon mustard

¼ teaspoon freshly ground nutmeg or pinch ground nutmeg

½ teaspoon kosher salt

¼ teaspoon freshly ground black pepper

1 to 1½ tablespoons vegetable oil

Spray vegetable oil (optional)

1 In a medium bowl, place the spinach and pull apart with two forks. (Don't be tempted to super-charge the cakes and use the whole package of spinach. You'll add too much moisture and the cakes will fall apart.) Add salmon and finely flake. Add potato and toss with spinach and salmon to blend well.

2 In a small bowl, combine egg, yogurt, chives, tarragon, mustard, nutmeg, salt, and pepper until mixed.

3 Pour egg mixture over salmon and toss until well blended. Moisten hands with water or spray with oil; form salmon mixture into four 3-inch cakes. If desired, make eight 2-inch cakes instead. Cook cakes or refrigerate up to 24-hours. (We've even frozen Popeye's Cakes, and they're still tasty.)

4 Add 1 tablespoon oil to a large, heavy skillet and heat on medium-high heat for about 4 minutes, until a drop of water sizzles when added to the oil. Add salmon cakes to skillet, reduce heat to medium and cook 3 minutes until the bottom is browned; loosen cakes part way through cooking. If necessary, add extra oil. Turn cakes and cook 3 more minutes. Flip again and cook 2 minutes more, until cakes are hot all the way through. For 2-inch cakes, cook 2 to 3 minutes per side. Serve 1 large or 2 small cakes per person.

Vary It! Offer guests a smoky taste instead by substituting hot-smoked salmon or trout for cooked salmon (you must omit the salt). You can find more information about smoked salmon later in this chapter and in Chapter 10.

 If you don't have leftover, cooked potato to use as a binder, microwave a potato on high for 5 minutes. Place the potato in the freezer for 1½ hours to chill thoroughly. Peel potato and shred on the largest hole of a grater.

Salmon and Salt Serendipity

Do you notice that salt and salmon begin with the same three letters? Through the ages, the combination of salt and salmon marked the beginning of several salmon delicacies, and still does today: smoked salmon, pickled salmon, salmon jerky, and even salmon caviar. All begin with salmon and salt spending some uninterrupted time together.

Sometimes salt is a rub; other times, a *brine*, a solution of salt and water. Sometimes it's the sole means of preparing the salmon; in other instances, it's a first step to prepare the salmon for smoking. In both cases, salting removes some moisture from the flesh and leaves it receptive to absorbing flavors. Herbs and spices, sugar, spirits, and *woods* (the woods used in the smoking process) contribute to the personality of the fish. Refer to Chapter 10 for descriptions of most of the following salmon specialties where salt plays an integral role:

- Cold-smoked salmon
- Hot-smoked salmon
- Hard-smoked salmon
- Kippered salmon
- Lox
- Nova lox
- Gravlax
- Pickled salmon
- Salmon jerky
- Indian-cure salmon
- Salmon chews
- Salmon bacon-bits
- Salmon caviar

Norwegian Pickled Salmon

In a pickle as to how to get the non-fisheaters in your family to boost their omega-3 intake? Forget about swallowing oil-filled gel caps! Nibble instead on this enticing sweet-and-sour Norwegian smorgasbord specialty shared by the chefs at Restaurant Akershus located in the Norway Pavilion, at EPCOT, Disney World. Whether you serve it as a casual snack (as pictured in the color photo section near the center of this book) or for your elegant, black-tie New Year's Eve buffet (see the festive menus described in Chapter 17), your guests will devour this dish with gusto.

Preparation time: 25 minutes (plus 90 unattended minutes)

Pickling time: 24 hours

Yield: 6 to 8 appetizer servings

1 pound skin-off salmon fillet, pin bones removed

⅓ cup kosher salt

1 medium onion

Brine

2 cups water

1½ cups sugar

1¼ cups plain white vinegar (5% acidity)

2 tablespoons mixed pickling spices

1 bay leaf (optional)

1 Rinse and then dry salmon with paper towels. Cut fish into strips about ¾-inch by ¾-inch by 2 inches. Place strips in bowl, sprinkle with salt, and blend gently until salt is evenly dispersed. Refrigerate for 1½ hours.

2 In a large non-reactive pot, combine all brine ingredients and bring to a boil, stirring to dissolve sugar. (May be microwaved in a large, 2-quart glass measuring pitcher.)

3 Meanwhile, slice onion into ¼-inch circles and separate into rings. Remove brine from heat and cool slightly. While brine is still warm, stir in onion rings and transfer to a glass container.

4 Put salmon strips in strainer and rinse off salt with cold running water. When brine is cool, add salmon strips; gently stir to mix. Cover and refrigerate at least 24 hours before serving.

5 To serve, use a slotted spoon to remove salmon and onions from the brine. Serve as an appetizer or snack along with thinly sliced rye bread. Pickled salmon may be kept refrigerated for up to 1 week.

(continued)

Vary It! If you don't have pickling spices, substitute 2 teaspoons white or black peppercorns, 2 teaspoons whole cloves, and 2 teaspoons mustard seeds.

You can't stand the heat? This salmon "cooks" without any. It's the acidic brine that cooks the salmon. After the salmon has been in the brine about an hour, you can observe the texture changing from soft to firm, and the color transforming from vivid orange to muted pinkish-orange. Be assured that the acidic content will also render harmless any unfriendly bacteria.

Like the Scandinavians, we both love this year 'round. Elsewhere, pickled salmon is a traditional food served as part of the Seder feast during the Jewish celebration of Passover.

Slow-Roasted Salmon Bruschetta

When we judged last year's Chef of the Year competition for *Simply Seafood* magazine, we loved this recipe from Chef Charles Dale of Renaissance restaurant in Aspen. Other judges clearly agreed, because Chef Dale won the contest. The recipe is lengthy, but it's great for entertaining because you can make four of the parts one day ahead: the Salmon Marinade, the Tomato Jam, the Bruschetta, and the Salad Dressing.

Before slow-roasting salmon, Chef Dale recommends curing it in a salty-sweet marinade that helps to firm the salmon flesh and infuse it with aromatic Mediterranean flavors of lemon, oregano, and ouzo — the classic anise-flavored Greek liqueur. Notice that the oven temperature is unusually low, but 220° is correct. Slow roasting this cured salmon gives it a firm but moist texture.

Slow-Roasted Salmon

Preparation time: 10 minutes

Marinating time: 2 to 3 hours

Cooking time: 25 minutes

Yield: 4 main course servings

4 skin-on salmon fillets, 6 to 7 ounces each, about 1-inch thick, pin bones removed

4 slices hearty country or sourdough bread

2 teaspoons extra virgin olive oil

Salmon Marinade (see the following recipe)

Tomato Jam (see the following recipe)

Arugula Salad (see the following recipe)

1 Prepare the Salmon Marinade. Place salmon skin side up, on top of the marinade, cover tightly, and refrigerate for 2 to 3 hours.

2 Make the Tomato Jam while salmon is marinating.

3 Brush both sides of bread with olive oil and toast under a broiler to brown both sides.

4 Preheat oven to 220°. Lift salmon from marinade and place it skin side down, on an ungreased jellyroll pan. Do not spoon marinade over salmon or it will be too salty. Roast salmon for 25 to 35 minutes until the flesh of the salmon just begins to flake at the nudge of a fork.

5 To serve, make the bruschetta; spread Tomato Jam on the toasts and set each in the center of a plate. With a spatula, carefully lift salmon from skin (the skin conveniently sticks to the baking pan) and place on top of each bruschetta.

6 Prepare the Arugula Salad. Pile the salad over the salmon and wait for the "wows" from your guests.

Salmon Marinade

1 lemon

3 tablespoons kosher salt

2 tablespoons ouzo or Pernod

2 tablespoons vodka, lemon-flavor preferred

2 tablespoons raw coarse sugar or brown sugar

1 tablespoon chopped fresh oregano

Remove lemon zest, juice the lemon, and reserve juice for salad dressing. In a shallow glass or ceramic dish just large enough to fit the salmon fillets, stir together the zest, salt, ouzo, vodka, sugar, and oregano.

Tomato Jam

Preparation time: *15 minutes*

Cooking time: *2 hours*

Yield: *1¼ cups*

6 large tomatoes, peeled, seeded, chopped

¼ cup red wine vinegar

¼ cup sugar

2 cloves garlic, chopped

Pinch kosher salt

Combine the tomatoes, red wine vinegar, sugar, garlic, and salt in a small, non-reactive saucepan and simmer, uncovered, until thick, about 2 hours, stirring often. Keep warm.

(continued)

Arugula Salad

Preparation time: *10 minutes*

6 ounces arugula or watercress or 4 ounces mixed baby greens

Lemon juice (reserved from salmon marinade)

⅓ cup extra-virgin olive oil

2 tablespoons large capers

One 3-ounce chunk Parmesan cheese, preferably Parmigiano-Reggiano

Remove stems from the arugula; wash leaves and dry well. Whisk together the lemon juice and olive oil; add capers. Create Parmesan shavings with a vegetable peeler. Just before serving, toss the arugula with the dressing and the shavings.

Part III
Sea Fare

The 5th Wave   By Rich Tennant

FISHING TACKLE

"What kind of line do I use when I go fishing? Usually, 'I'm only doing this to save money on our food budget, Honey'."

In this part . . .

Granted, there are a lot of fish swimming out there, but in this part we offer you tips for identifying your catch, whether it's an everyday favorite or exotic fare. We help you master techniques for shucking, cooking, cracking, twisting, and eating shellfish so as not to miss a succulent bite. This part also takes you on a tour of coastal seafood feasts and suggests how you can make your own at home.

Chapter 7

Crabs, Lobsters, and Crawfish

● ●

In This Chapter

▶ Cracking up with crabs

▶ Lusting after lobsters

▶ Twisting away with crawfish

▶ Feasting with crabs, lobsters, and crawfish

● ●

*F*or us, feasting on crabs, lobsters, or crawfish and gathering family and friends to share in the fun are the essence of enjoying shellfish. We've discovered that where you live clearly shapes your shellfish experience. In the United States, for example, the eastern shore of the Chesapeake Bay conjures up images of spicy, steamed blue crabs; further north, lobsters are the catch of the season. Dungeness, snow, and king crabs reign in the Pacific northwest; in Florida, stone crabs and spiny lobsters are the name of the game; in Louisiana, crawfish rules.

Walk a beach or seashore anywhere and you see an amazing array of sea shell designs. Scientists group (and we identify) shellfish, such as crabs and clams, by their style of shell. Crabs, lobsters, crawfish, and shrimp belong to one big family, the *crustaceans,* which have a hard, crusty shell that protects them, like a suit of armor. Like armor, the shell is divided into sections for ease of movement. Clams, mussels, scallops, and oysters belong to a second group of shellfish, the *mollusks,* and have two hinged shells that open and close for feeding and movement (see Chapter 8).

In this chapter, we offer you tips for choosing, storing, cooking, and eating shellfish to your heart's content, as well as species information. Plus, we showcase regional shellfish feasts for you to enjoy.

Get a jumpstart on your dining pleasure and flip to the dynamite shellfish photos near the center of the book. When your shellfish choices are limited or you want to send some as a gift, check out Chapter 24 for our favorite flying fish vendors.

From Kickin' Alive to Cracking Delight

Expect lots of smiles from friends when you mention a feed of crabs, lobsters, or crawfish. These crusty cousins are fun, with their colorful personalities and exquisite tastes. When cooked, these shellfish burst into color, ranging from bright red-orange to brilliant cardinal red. Their sweet, succulent white meat, in flakes, chunks, or fine shreds, is often tinged red. Here are tips for keeping your live shellfish alive and healthy, and frozen shellfish well chilled and tasty.

✔ **Staying alive:** When you buy live crabs, lobsters, and crawfish, look for lively action: crabs scuttling around (or trying to), and lobster and crawfish tails flapping. Also look for lobster claws that are closed with rubber bands or pegs — no pinching allowed.

✔ **Keep cool:** Take a cooler when you pick up live shellfish, and make this the last stop on your trip home. We prefer to cook live shellfish the day that we buy it, but you can refrigerate it for one day. Create a moist environment for the shellfish, using wet seaweed or damp newspapers to line a disposable foil pan, box, or paper bag. Live shellfish need to breathe, so don't seal them in plastic or drop them into your bathtub (a salt water bath doesn't work!). Shellfish must be alive before cooking — dead shellfish spoil quickly — so check their action and discard any that don't move.

✔ **Take the plunge**: Choose your cooking method, from steaming to boiling or grilling. See our regional shellfish feasts in the "Creating Lobster, Crab, and Crawfish Feasts" section, later in the chapter, for cooking suggestions, as well as for lobster and crawfish species listings. And for more information, check out the shellfish recipes in Chapters 11, 13, 14, 16, and 17, and cooking tips and techniques in Chapter 4.

Why do crab, lobster, and crawfish shells turn red when cooked? Many color pigments combine to give live shellfish their various colors, from blues to greens to tans. Cooking disguises all the colors except for the pigment *astaxanthin,* the background red pigment. Many farm-raised salmon get their pink flesh color from the astaxanthin that the farmers add to their feed.

✔ **Dig in:** Digging into whole cooked shellfish is the most fun. And we hope we've made it easy with cracking and eating tips for extracting every last little delectable morsel of meat from the nooks and crannies. See figures in this chapter for visual instructions.

✔ **Chill out:** Even if you don't live by the shore, there's plenty of shellfish for you to crack. Shellfish that needs to travel the distance is often cooked and frozen. Some of it is even available picked from the shell, perfect for jazzing up fajitas, tacos, pasta, or salads. Technology and transportation give us tastes that we'd otherwise rarely get the chance to try, from the whole family of crabs to lobster tails, langostinos, and crawfish. Here's the quality checklist:

- Look for clean, tightly wrapped packages with no frosty ice crystals. Examine the exposed meat of a crab leg or body, or a lobster tail. Raw flesh should be translucent white with no dark spots. Shells should be intact with no cracks or holes, which indicate poor handling and potential moisture loss. For cooked crab legs, look at the space between the meat and the shell; it should be pretty tight, with the meat filling up most of the space.

- Keep frozen shellfish on hand, but don't keep it forever in your home freezer (up to 6 months is fine). Thaw shellfish slowly, to retain the most moisture within the cell walls. Thawing overnight in the refrigerator is best, but when your time is tight, place frozen shellfish in a resealable plastic bag in a bowl of ice water. Depending on the package size and shellfish, thawing takes from 30 minutes to an hour; turn the bag several times for even thawing.

- Serve most thawed, cooked shellfish room temperature to avoid toughening through heating. But if you prefer to serve shellfish warm, steam for just a minute or two.

✔ **Pretty cool:** You can store cooked shellfish for 2 or 3 days if you keep it well chilled. We find that a freezer pack or a bag of ice cubes works well. Place the pack on the bottom refrigerator shelf and place the shellfish on top of the pack.

Crab: Taking Your Pick

The crab family is a tasty group. Some crabs, like the blue crab and Dungeness, have bodies that are laden with meat, claws that offer a bite, and little legs to suck on. Others, like king and snow crab, have legs brimming with meat; stone crab and Jonahs are known for their big meaty claws; red, golden, and rock crabs have bite-size cocktail claws. See Figure 7-1 for a glimpse at some popular crabs and Table 7-1 for who's who in the crab world.

Table 7-1	Who's Who in the World of Crabs
Variety	*Description*
Blue crab	**Meat:** Delicate, sweet-tasting firm, tender flake; white
	Best parts: Body (2 jumbo lumps), claws, tiny legs
	How sold: Live, cooked hard shell; live or frozen soft-shell (after crab sheds its hard shell); picked meat

(continued)

Table 7-1 *(continued)*

Variety	Description
	Tidbits and trivia: The only crab eaten as soft-shell (see "The soft-shell story: no hammers needed!" sidebar, later in this chapter). Name means "beautiful swimmer" (from the Latin); blue tinges on shell and blue patches on leg
	Source: Cape Cod to Gulf of Mexico (May to mid-November)
Dungeness crab	**Meat:** Rich, tender flake; bright white; red streaks on legs and claws
	Best parts: Big body, claws, and legs
	How sold: Live, cooked; cooked, frozen; picked meat
	Tidbits and trivia: First crab fished in the Pacific northwest
	Source: California through Alaska (November through the summer)
Jonah crab and Rock crab	**Meat:** Firm, short flake; moister than stone crab; white
	Best parts: Big claws
	How sold: Live, cooked; cooked, frozen claws; picked meat
	Tidbits and trivia: Related to Dungeness, stone-crab-type claw; rock crab is half the size of Jonah
	Source: Both northeast U.S. coast, rock also U.S. west coast
King crab	**Meat:** Creamy white; red tinges; slightly salty; moist, long strands
	Best parts: Big, long legs; one "killer" claw
	How sold: Cooked, frozen legs and claws
	Tidbits and trivia: Steel traps for king and snow crab (see following entry) weigh 700 pounds
	Source: North Pacific and the Bering Sea (and boy, is it cold!)
Snow crab	**Meat:** Slightly salty; snow-white, red-pink tinges; long strands
	Best parts: Claws; long, slender legs
	How sold: Cooked; frozen sections of legs, claws, and body
	Tidbits and trivia: Similar to king crab, but only 3 feet across
	Source: North Pacific and the east coast of Canada

Variety	Description
Stone crab	**Meat:** Rich, firm, dense, short flake; white
	Best part: Claws
	How sold: Cooked; cooked, frozen
	Tidbits and trivia: Stone-hard, black-tip claws; only the claw is removed from live crab; claw regenerates
	Source: Primarily in Florida (mid-October to mid-May)
Golden crab	**Meat:** Delicate, extremely moist flake; white with red flecks
	Best part: Claws
	How sold: Cooked; cooked, frozen cocktail claws; picked meat
	Tidbits and trivia: 2,000 feet down in Gulf of Mexico and the south Atlantic; first commercially caught in the early 1980s; golden-tan cooked shell with red tinges; New England red crab is closely related

Figure 7-1: The crab world.

Crabmeat that's picked from the blue crab is named by where the meat comes from in the crab. The meat may be fresh, in season, or pasteurized. Use fresh crab meat within 3 days. Unopened, pasteurized crabmeat has a refrigerated shelf life of up to 6 months, but we suggest checking the date on the container when you buy it. After it's opened, use as fresh crabmeat.

> ✔ *Jumbo* or *lump* crabmeat consists of the largest, unbroken pieces of white meat from the crab body (there are only two lumps per crab), so it's truly expensive; ideal for salads or crab Imperial, a rich Chesapeake Bay-area dish that bakes crab in a creamy sauce.
>
> ✔ *Backfin* includes smaller pieces of body meat and a bit of broken lump meat; perfect for crab cakes.
>
> ✔ *Special* is still smaller pieces of body meat, ideal for dips and spreads.
>
> ✔ *Cocktail claws* for nibbling or picked claw meat for cakes or dips.

There's no question about it. If you're new to crabs, figuring out where and how to start can be perplexing. Look at the parts of a crab for some clues. For blue and Dungeness crabs, the body has the most meat, and the claws (and legs) offer tasty bites; for stone and Jonah crabs, it's the claws.

To clean the body, pull off the tab on the crab bottom, as shown in Figure 7-2. Pry off the top shell, and scrape off ribbed gills and spongy innards. Break the crab in half to see the meat tucked inside. Cut the crab horizontally to further expose the meat. Twist off the claws and crack with a mallet. Remove the meat with picks, forks, and for the most fun, your fingers.

Lobster Reigns

Few foods generate the excitement and enthusiasm of lobster. Whether you boil, steam, or grill lobster, this rich-tasting shellfish is the king of crustaceans. If you're new to cooking or eating lobsters, in this section, we identify who's who in the lobster world, and show you how to cook and eat lobster to your heart's content. Lobster is one good-for-you-food, especially when you go light on the butter.

Who's who in the lobster clan

Lobsters range the oceans worldwide, from the cold waters of the northeastern United States to sunny areas like the Caribbean, Brazil, and Australia. Whether lobsters have big claws, no claws, or tiny little tails (like the langostino), lobsters give you luxurious seafood tastes.

American lobster

The northeast waters of Maine, Massachusetts, and Canada's Maritime provinces are home to the famed delicacy — the *American lobster*. The lobster's drab, dark-greenish-brown shell cooks to a brilliant cardinal red. The cooked meat is creamy white (not translucent) with a speckled red surface. It has a buttery-rich, sweet taste, and a tender, but chewy texture. Lobster meat, unlike fish, doesn't flake, but cuts into firm, dense pieces.

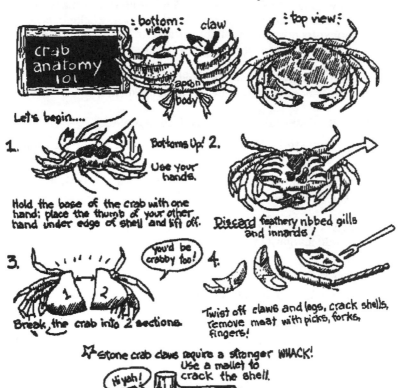

Figure 7-2:
Clues to
cracking
and eating
crab.

 Lobster is high in fat, right? No way. A typical serving of lobster has 98 calories, 72 milligrams of cholesterol and 0.6 grams fat. Compare that to the same serving of light chicken meat, with 173 calories, 85 milligrams of cholesterol, and 4.5 grams fat.

Spiny lobster

The *spiny lobster* somewhat resembles the American lobster, but it has no claws — it's the meaty tail that we enjoy. The cooked white meat is rich and sweet with red-orange tinges on the outside. The meat is moist and dense, but can be a bit softer and less chewy than the American lobster. We prefer to grill, broil, or bake the tails because they are somewhat moist, but you can also steam or boil them.

Also called *rock lobster,* the tails range in size from mini 2-ounce varieties to 8 ounces and larger, and have mottled shells decorated with polka dots and stripes. Warmwater spiny lobsters come from California waters and from Florida to Brazil; coldwater, from Australia, New Zealand, and South Africa. Spiny lobsters are most available as frozen, raw tails (unless you're lucky enough to enjoy the local catch in your area).

Here's an easy and scrumptious recipe for grilled lobster tails from Peter Jarvis of Francesca's Favorites Seafood in Florida.

1. **Split lobster tails lengthwise into two pieces**.

2. **Marinate the tails in three parts olive oil to one part lemon juice, mixed with thyme, garlic powder, and crushed red pepper.**

3. **For an 8-ounce tail, grill meat side down for 3 minutes, and then shell side down for 3 minutes; flip back to the meat and grill 2 minutes.**

Because Peter is close to fresh seafood and citrus, he serves stone crabs with homemade margaritas to round out the menu. We've got our bags packed!

Langostino

The *langostino* is a miniature member of the lobster family. It has a small body, 4 to 5 inches long, and slender, dainty-looking claws about the same length. The langostino yields a tasty bite-size morsel of meat from the tail. The meat is snow white tinged with reddish orange, and has a mild, slightly sweet flavor and firm texture. Langostinos are caught off the coast of Chile.

They are most often available as cooked, frozen tail meat. Use langostinos as you would cooked shrimp.

Langoustine is the French term for the Dublin Bay prawn and the Norway lobster (or lobsterette). *Langouste* and *langosta* are the French and Spanish words for spiny lobsters and shouldn't be confused with the langostino we're talking about here.

Taking the plunge

The best way to cook a whole lobster is an ongoing debate among lobster lovers. Is boiling or steaming better? When you're cooking a bunch of lobsters, boiling gives you even, fast cooking. And if you have good, salty ocean water, boiling can't be beat. But we like the pure lobster flavor that steaming gives you. Plus, if you're a first time lobster cooker, steaming is easier — you don't have to worry about a big pot of boiling water, and you have less dripping water to contend with.

✔ **To steam:** Take one large pot, place a steamer rack inside the pot, and fill with about 2 inches of water. Bring to a rolling boil, add the lobsters head first (be careful of the flapping tail), cover, and steam. See Chapter 2 for more steaming tips and Chapter 17 for grill-steaming ideas.

✔ **To boil:** Fill a large pot ⅔ full of water; add 1 to 2 tablespoons salt per quart, unless you're using briny ocean water. Bring water to a rolling boil, add lobsters, and bring water back to a boil. Reduce heat and simmer lobsters.

Whichever way you cook lobster, choose a pot that has lots of room. Use a 3-gallon pot to cook two lobsters. If you want to cook four or more lobsters, cook them in batches, using a couple of pots (or a larger pot, if you have one). Carefully add the lobsters to the pot. The tails may flap, so grasp the body firmly behind the front legs and lower them head-first. To remove cooked lobsters from the pot, lift with tongs and set in a large bowl for 5 to 10 minutes to cool slightly before cracking, twisting, sucking, and slurping your way to a blissful experience.

Check out Table 7-2 for approximate cooking times.

Table 7-2	Boiling or Steaming Whole Lobsters
Weight	*Cooking Time*
1 to 1¼ pounds	10 to 12 minutes
1¼ to 1½ pounds	12 to 15 minutes
1½ to 2 pounds	15 to 20 minutes

What is all that stuff inside a lobster?

Delicious — that's what. Other than the small sand sack behind the head, the ribbed white gills, and the soft green liver (the tomalley), everything else is fair game. The red stuff is the *coral,* or tiny lobster eggs (they are jet black when uncooked). The coral has a slightly nutty taste and grainy texture. The white stuff that looks like cooked egg whites is the lobster blood (uncooked, it's clear), and it's tasty, too. Be aware that although lobster lovers adore the rich-as-butter tomalley, the Maine Lobster Council advises you to discard it. As with other animals, contaminants may settle in the liver, so its best to be on the safe side.

One of the easiest parties Leslie ever threw was a lobster-cracking bash — but her fishseller cooked the lobsters for her. She called in advance and picked up the warm lobsters shortly before guests arrived — an instant feast. (Now that's the way to throw a party!)

Digging into lobster

Digging into a lobster is messy, but fun. The tail and claws have huge pieces of meat, and the body and legs hide morsels just waiting for you to discover. Break the lobster apart as shown in Figure 7-3. Break off the front legs where they attach to the body, and snap off the claws. Crack claws and legs with a nutcracker or mallet, and pull out the meat.

Grab the body in one hand and tail in the other; twist to separate. Break off the tail flippers and pull out meat with a pick. To get the tail meat in one gigantic piece, push meat from the flipper end, and then pull the wide end (or cut through the shell and flip tail out).

For some people, the body is the most fun. Grasp the body and crack apart the shell. Discard the gray-black stomach just behind the eyes, the ribbed gills, and the green *tomalley* or liver. Twist off the legs with attached meat; crack and suck legs like a straw. Don't miss the red lobster coral (or *roe*).

Lobsters love a variety of seasonings and partners. So says Chef Jasper White, author of *Lobster at Home*. Pair lobster with sensuous tarragon and chervil, robust chiles and garlic, silky avocados, or luscious, red ripe tomatoes.

Crawfish Tales

Crawfish look like tiny American lobsters, in the 3- to 4-inch range, but with slender pincers instead of lobster's meaty claws. Crawfish give you a meaty little morsel from the tail. The meat is sweet, firm, and chewy, white on the inside, bright red on the outside. Live crawfish are the most fun to cook for a crawfish party boil. (See the Louisiana Crab and Shrimp Boil recipe, later in the chapter, for spicy cooking tips.) If live crawfish aren't available (they're exorbitant to ship), look for fresh, cooked whole crawfish straight from Louisiana at your fish store. Pick up a few buckets and you're ready to throw a party. You can also find cooked, peeled crawfish tail meat (often frozen), that are great for gumbo, étouffée, jambalaya, deep-frying, or any way you use shrimp (see Chapter 5).

In Louisiana, nothing beats a Cajun crawfish feast for frolicking fun. (Some restaurants that specialize in crawfish boils have a dance floor so you can take a break between your first and second courses of crawfish.)

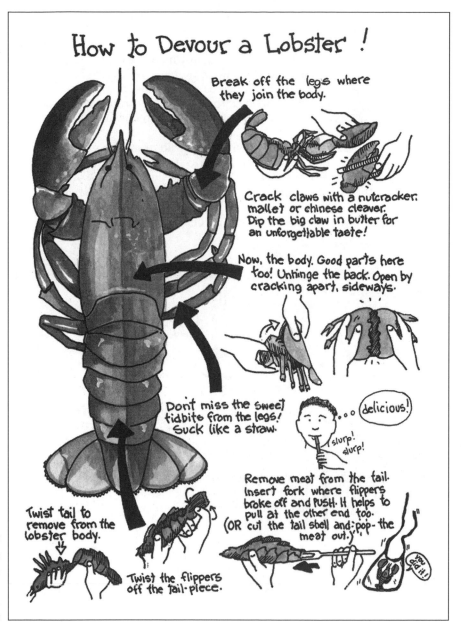

Figure 7-3:
Steps to
eating
lobster.

So roll up your sleeves, heap the crawfish on a tray, and have plenty of napkins on hand. As shown in Figure 7-4, twist the crawfish in half and pull the tail from the head. Experts remove the meat from the shell by pinching the tail between their fingers, biting down on the meat that extends past the shell, and pulling the shell away. We have yet to master this trick, and suggest that you crack the shell open to pop out the meat. The crawfish head has tasty juices and fat, so suck the heads, as is tradition, or spoon out the goodies with your fingers or a knife so as not to miss great tastes.

In the United States, crawfish grow wild or are farm-raised, primarily in the freshwater swamps, rivers, and rice fields of Louisiana, with some in Texas, Washington, Oregon, and California. Crawfish crawl — and so goes the legend of the crawfish name. But shellfish names, as with fish names, are generally a matter of location, location, location. So you may eat *crawfish, crayfish, crawdad,* or *mudbugs,* but they're all delicious.

Cracking and Eating Crawfish

Figure 7-4: Cracking and eating crawfish (shown larger than actual size).

Grasp the head and body.

Twist to break apart Put the head to your lips and give it a good suck to get out all the juices!

Place tail, curved side down.

To peel, grasp each side of the shell with your thumbs.....and crack open!

Lift out the meat and devein it...

YUM!

Pop the crawfish tail into your mouth..... ..... ENJOY!

Crawfish are most plentiful from March through May. Much of Louisiana's whole crawfish go to Scandinavia, where crawfish festivals are a popular pastime. When you pick up a package of cooked, peeled crawfish tails, don't be surprised to see China as the source — the Chinese farm a lot of crawfish.

Creating Lobster, Crab, and Crawfish Feasts

Make-at-home seafood feasts around the country highlight the local catch — from New England's lobsters and clams to the Chesapeake Bay's blue crabs, from shrimp of the Carolinas to Louisiana's crafty crawfish. Here are tastes that you can savor to celebrate seafood around the country — and you don't have to travel.

New England shore dinner or lobster bake

Lobster bakes or shore dinners are a summer tradition in New England. Cooked on a sandy beach in the fresh salt air, lobsters steamed in seaweed capture the essence of the season. Potatoes, onions, mussels, hard-and-soft-shell clams, corn on the cob, and eggs (it's true) complete the authentic picture. Stacking each food in the right order in the seaweed (everyone's traditions differ) ensures perfect cooking. Start with slow-cooking potatoes and onions on the bottom, and move up to the lobsters on top. Putting each food into mesh bags makes handling a breeze and lets the flavors blend.

Dig a steaming pit on the beach (build a fireplace or use a clean 30-gallon metal barrel). Add driftwood, burn down to coals, and top the coals with moist seaweed. Add your food in layers with seaweed tucked into each layer to create the steam. Top with a damp tarp, steam (45 minutes to an hour), and wait for the fun to begin. Flip to Chapter 17 for our version, the Backyard Lobster-and-Clam Bake, on the grill.

Chesapeake Bay crab feast

Blue crabs abound in the Bay, and come hot, humid summer days, locals head to a crab house or gear up to feast at home. Rather than boil the crabs, we steam them over equal amounts of vinegar and beer (or water). Some folks swear you must first chill the crabs in ice water to help seasonings stick to the shell. Either way, layer the crabs (two dozen) in a steamer, and sprinkle each layer with 1 to 2 tablespoons of Old Bay Seasoning. Cover and steam for 20 minutes. Serve the picked crab hot with vinegar for dipping (our local choice), and platters of fresh eastern shore corn-on-the-cob and sliced tomatoes. See Chapter 5 for more spicy steaming tips.

Low-country shrimp boil

Summer traditions along the South Carolina coast center around shrimp. And like the Chesapeake's crab feast, this low-country tradition highlights their catch of the season. Our friends Ginger and Dick Howell have been offering a transplanted version of the boil for years to students at their cooking school, The Seasonal Kitchen, near Rochester, New York.

1. **Cook spicy summer sausage in beer and water, seasoned with Louisiana Crab and Shrimp Boil.**

   See the Louisian Crab and Shrimp Boil recipe, later in this chapter.

2. Add just-picked corn (cut into bite-size chunks), a nice, fat julienne of zucchini to brighten the boil, and big shell-on shrimp. Simmer until just cooked through.

3. Pass lots of napkins and serve with pots of grainy mustard for the sausage, along with juicy, ripe, local tomatoes.

Louisiana crawfish and shrimp boils

For a grand feed, count on about 3 pounds live crawfish (or 1½ pounds head-on shrimp) for every adult; wash the crawfish thoroughly to remove mud. Cook in well-seasoned liquid in a crawfish cooking rig or a 30-gallon metal garbage can. Get the most out of your crawfish experience with the crawfish twistin' tips (refer to Figure 7- 4) and don't miss those succulent heads.

1. Fill the rig ⅓ full of water.

2. Add about a dozen each onions, lemons, and green onions, sliced; 4 heads of garlic, chopped; 2 to 3 cups salt; a half-dozen 3-ounce packets shrimp boil spices; and cayenne to taste. Bring to a boil and cook 30 minutes.

3. Add the crawfish and 5 pounds of small new potatoes, if desired, and bring to a boil. Cook 10 to 15 minutes, taste, and turn off the heat.

4. Add 2 to 3 pounds of ice to the pot to prevent overcooking, and let crawfish stand in the liquid to suck up more of the spice (to taste).

Dungeness crab feeds

For classic Pacific northwest simplicity, grab a whole bunch of Dungeness when the season peaks and prices are low, and boil in a big pot of salted water (about 20 minutes), just as you would lobster or shrimp. Crack, pick, and savor the pure, sweet taste of crab. Serve simply with bread, salad, and white wine or beer — plus melted butter and lemon for dipping the crab.

Dueling Seafood Spices

Distinctive seasonings characterize regional shellfish cooking, including Louisiana's Crab and Shrimp Boil (also popular on the southeastern coast of the United States) and Old Bay Seasoning from the Chesapeake Bay.

Louisiana Crab and Shrimp Boil

Customize your own version of this classic combination that Louisianans have used for centuries to impart snappy flavor to the steaming liquid used to cook crabs, shrimp, and crawfish. Their original seasonings were sold in cheesecloth or muslin bags, while the ones you buy today are in teabag-like pouches. No cheesecloth? Inventive cooks sometimes knot the spices in a short length cut from a discarded, clean, sheer pantyhose. In any case, encase the seasonings for easy removal — you don't want anyone to choke on a bay leaf.

Preparation time: *8 minutes*

Yield: *Enough seasoning for 2 quarts water*

2 to 3 bay leaves

1 teaspoon black peppercorns

1 teaspoon brown or yellow mustard seeds

1 teaspoon coriander seeds

½ teaspoon whole allspice

½ teaspoon dill seeds

¼ teaspoon dried red pepper flakes (optional)

2 whole cloves (optional)

Securely wrap the ingredients in cheesecloth or other mesh fabric. Bring to a boil in 2 quarts water in a large pot, reduce heat and simmer, covered, for 5 minutes before adding seafood.

Chesapeake Bay-Style Seasoning

This spicy mixture gives prepared shellfish from the Chesapeake Bay region its distinctive taste. (Different varieties are known commercially as Old Bay, Chesapeake Bay Seasoning, and Chesapeake Bay-Style Seasoning.) The chunky blend contains celery salt and spices, including mustard, pepper, laurel leaves, cloves, pimento, ginger, mace, cardamom, cassia, and paprika. Developed by Gustav Brunn, a German immigrant who sold spices in the early 1940s to local Baltimore fishmongers, Old Bay Seasoning was named after the Old Bay Steam Packet, a steamship line that carried people to Norfolk, Richmond, and other cities along the eastern U.S. shore.

(continued)

Those who live in the Chesapeake Bay area sprinkle this seasoning in generous quantities over layers of Maryland blue crabs before steaming them. Add it to steamed shrimp, crab cakes, or corn-on-the-cob; sprinkle over fish before broiling or baking; or mix with cornmeal for a crunchy, zesty coating for panfried fish.

Preparation time: *5 minutes*

Yield: *¼ cup*

2 tablespoons celery salt	*1 teaspoon freshly ground black pepper*
1 tablespoon celery seed	*½ teaspoon mace*
2 teaspoons paprika	*¼ teaspoon ground cloves*
2 teaspoons dry mustard	*Pinch cinnamon*
1½ teaspoons powdered ginger	

In a glass container with a tightly fitting lid, combine all ingredients. Store in a dark, dry area. Use within 6 months for top quality.

Vary It! For a cornmeal coating, mix 3 tablespoons of Chesapeake Bay-Style Seasoning with ¼ cup cornmeal, coat fish, and panfry. See Chapter 12 for panfried fish.

Sprinkle 1 to 2 teaspoons of this seasoning on a pound of fish before baking or broiling. A drizzle of melted butter or high quality olive oil is the only additional flavoring you need.

Check out your vitamins for *chitin,* a shell-hardening substance. Before molting, a shellfish saves the calcium and chitin from its old shell. At the end of its growth period after molting, the crab redeposits both of these in the new shell to harden it. For years, chitin has been used in dietary supplements and for agricultural and medicinal purposes (and may be cropping up in clothing fibers). One more great shellfish attribute.

The soft-shell story: No hammers needed!

Just as people discard clothes that they've outgrown, so a crab, lobster, crawfish, or shrimp casts away its shell (a process known as *molting*) when it grows. Each crusty shellfish sheds its shell many times from birth through adulthood.

At the start of molting, each shellfish shrugs off the old shell. Before the new shell hardens, it takes in water and air to stretch the wrinkled new skin to the next larger size, and then grows into the space between molts. At that point, the crab, lobster, crawfish, or shrimp is back to its old hard-shell self.

For blue-crab fishermen, determining when a crab is going to shed its shell is a practiced art that allows you to savor an exquisite taste treat — soft-shell crabs. See Chapter 13 for a great soft-shelled crab recipe, as well as some cleaning tips.

Likewise, lobsters shed as the summer waters warm, so from summer through early fall, you can find new-shell lobsters — no crackers or hammers needed. You can cut the cooked shell with scissors and easily pull out the meat.

Soft-shell crawfish, deep-fried to a crispy, decadent bite, are an extraordinary eating experience. A fiery Cajun martini is a must to cut the richness.

Chapter 8

Clams, Mussels, Scallops, and Oysters

....

In This Chapter

▶ Digging in for clams

▶ Shaping up with mussels

▶ Diving in for scallops

▶ Slurping up oysters

....

*H*ere's a riddle: What's bite size, comes in its own protective package, may not need cooking, and is simply delicious? Mother Nature's take on the perfect convenience food — clams, mussels, scallops, and oysters.

In this chapter, we offer you tips for selecting live shellfish and its shelled counterparts; guidelines for storing, shucking, cooking, and eating shellfish to your heart's content; and information on species, sex, and safety. For party inspiration, flip to a photo of the exuberant Backyard Lobster-and-Clam Bake in Chapter 17 in the color photo section near the center of the book — also check out Pam's Sting Ray Bloody Marys for a "clam"-dunk taste of the sea.

Stayin' Alive: The Shell Game

Clams, mussel, scallops, and oysters belong to a huge family — the *bivalves* — whose two shells make up a sturdy "suit of armor." The shells hinge at one side and open and close so that clams, mussels, and their cousins can filter food from the water.

Clams, mussels, scallops, and oysters are members of the mollusk group, one of two main categories of shellfish. *Mollusks* take their name from the Latin *mollis* or soft, which refers to their soft, tender flesh. Snails, abalone, and squid are also members of this huge, popular group of shellfish. In addition to food, mollusks provide shells that have long been used as a source for currency, dyes, tools, mother-of-pearl, and fishing hooks. (*Crustaceans* are the second major group of shellfish, and include crabs, lobsters, shrimp, and crawfish — see Chapter 7.)

The shell is the key for keeping shellfish alive when you buy and bring them home — and for determining when they are cooked. (Most sea and bay scallops are shucked after they're caught.) Here are some shellfish loving-care tips:

- ✔ **Zip up:** When you buy live mussels, hardshell clams, or scallops, look for shells that are free of cracks or chips and are closed (or not gaping wide open). Even out of the water, shellfish breathe by opening and closing their shells. When the shells are tightly closed, the animal inside is alive. If the shells are slightly open, you can check to see if the clam, mussel, or scallop is still alive: tap one of the shells (a spoon works just fine) or press the two shells quickly together several times with your fingers. If the shell closes, the critter is still alive, and clamming up.

  Look over the entire shellfish display: If only a few mussels or clams have slightly open shells, it's likely a lively batch; if many are gaping, it's best not to purchase them.

  A soft-shell clam never fully closes, because its neck gets in the way. To ensure that soft-shells are alive, touch or tap the shell — the clam should pull its shell closer together. For oysters in the shell, buy only those that are tightly closed. Oysters in the shell are hardy creatures, and can live a week or so out of the water when carefully handled. But a gaping oyster, even if alive, has lost its precious liquor and lots of flavor — it's past its prime.

  All live mollusks that your fish seller buys are accompanied by a shellfish shipping tag. This tag indicates the harvest date and harvest location. Don't hesitate to ask to see the tag, which the shellfish farmer or company that catches the shellfish is required by U.S. law to attach. If the tag isn't available (although retailers, also by law, are required to keep all tags for at least 90 days), don't buy the shellfish. This is sound advice from Tim Parsons, our respected colleague and clam guru from Cherrystone Aqua Farms on the Chesapeake Bay.

- ✔ **Keep cool:** Take a cooler when you pick up live shellfish, and make this the last stop on your trip home. Ask you fish seller for ice or frozen gel packs for the homeward journey.

- ✔ **Store with care:** Remove shellfish from nonbreathable bags or packages and refrigerate in an open, shallow container. Keep mussels, oysters, or scallops in the shell moist by covering loosely with damp paper towels to allow shellfish to breathe (keep towels damp). Store the container on freezer packs, or on a bag of ice cubes.

Clams don't like it quite as cold as mussels, so simply refrigerate in a bowl or open container. Loosely cover clams with dry paper towels. According to Cherrystone's Tim Parsons, "Clams sense moisture and begin to open and close, probing around for water."

You can refrigerate live mussels, clams, and scallops for 2 days — oysters for up to a week. Place shucked scallops in a tightly sealed container and refrigerate for up to 2 days.

✔ **Scrub up:** Wash and scrub shellfish (in the shell) shortly before using. Check to make sure they're alive, and discard any whose shells don't close. See Figure 8-1 for mussel-cleaning tips.

Figure 8-1:
Cleaning
mussels.

✔ **Shuck on:** Shucking clams and oysters is a lot more fun when you have a buddy to work with. See Figures 8-2 and 8-3 for shucking tips. (When you chuck an oyster, you may prefer to shuck it cupped side down.) Flip to Chapter 2 for tools to start you on the right track (a screwdriver or bottle opener can suffice in a pinch). Shuck shellfish shortly before eating, and place half shells on plates in a single layer to save all of those delectable juices. Tightly wrap the plate with plastic wrap to prevent drying out, and refrigerate no longer than 30 minutes for the best flavor.

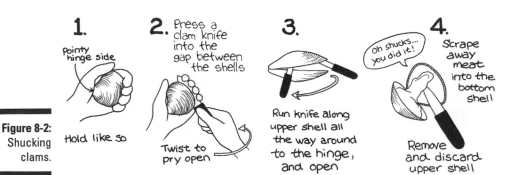

Figure 8-2:
Shucking
clams.

Shucking Oysters

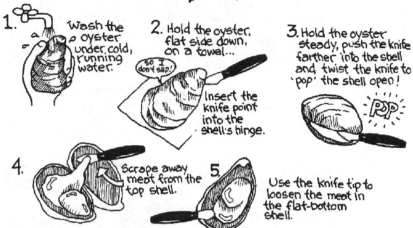

1. Wash the oyster under cold, running water.

2. Hold the oyster, flat side down, on a towel... *(so I don't slip!)* Insert the knife point into the shell's hinge.

3. Hold the oyster steady, push the knife farther into the shell and twist the knife to 'pop' the shell open! *POP*

4. Scrape away meat from the top shell.

5. Use the knife tip to loosen the meat in the flat-bottom shell.

Figure 8-3:
Shucking
oysters.

- ✔ **Take the plunge**: Choose your cooking method: steaming, frying, baking, or grilling.

  - Steamed clams are done when their shells open and the meat firms, 5 to 8 minutes; mussels, oysters, and scallops cook in 3 to 5 minutes.

  - Cook shucked sea or weathervane scallops 4 to 5 minutes; bay scallops or oysters, 1 to 2 minutes.

  For shellfish recipes, see Chapters 7, 11, 13, 14, 16, and 17; for cooking tips and techniques, flip to Chapter 4.

  Look for shucked, raw shellfish — either oysters in their liquor in glass jars or in the seafood case (the liquor or juices should be clear, not murky) or chopped, raw clams in containers (may be frozen). Use as you do fresh shellfish. You can also find ready-to-eat shellfish: cooked and marinated mussels; frozen oysters, mussels, bay scallops, and clams in the shell; and green mussels on the half shell. See Chapter 7 for thawing tips.

- ✔ **Pretty cool:** You can store cooked shellfish for a day or two, and an opened container of clams and oysters for three to four days, if you keep them well-chilled.

Clamology 101

Eating clams has been an American pastime since early colonial days when clam shells were *wampum*, the currency between colonists and Native Americans. Four of our main clams are native to the east coast — the hard-shell, soft-shell, surf, and ocean clam, while the Manila, geoduck, and most razors hail from the Pacific northwest. Clam shells vary from tan with white splotches to off-white, with ridges and swirls; they can be rock hard or thin and brittle.

Some of our favorite clams belong to one big happy family, the hardshell clam. The hardshell clam is widely known by its Native name, *quahog*, pronounced KWAH-hog. Each clam in this family is named by its size, the bay or creek it originally grew in, or how it is most often prepared:

- **Littleneck clams:** 10 to 12 per pound. Named after Little Neck Bay, Long Island, New York.
- **Topneck clams:** 6 to 8 per pound.
- **Cherrystone clams:** 3 to 5 per pound. Named after Cherrystone Creek on Virginia's eastern shore.
- **Chowder clams:** 1 to 2 per pound.

See Table 8-1 for a rundown of the most popular types of clams. (Also be sure to try our recipe for Classic Steamed Clams in Chapter 13.)

Table 8-1	Who's Who in the World of Clams
Variety	*Description*
Hardshell clam	**Tidbits:** One big, happy family: See familiar names earlier in this section
	Shell: Tan to brown; nearly oval; thick and hard with concentric rings around shell
	Meat: Briny, salty, melon-orange, chewy-tender, resilient
	Best to eat: On half shell, steamed, grilled, baked, or in chowder
Soft-shell clam	**Tidbits:** Also called steamer, mud, or Ipswich clam
	Shell: Long oval, off-white; thin and brittle with long neck that keeps shell from completely closing; 3-inch range
	Meat: Pale golden, tender, and delicate; neck chewy
	Best to eat: Deep fried or steamed
	Tip: Before eating, slip leathery skin off neck

(continued)

Table 8-1 *(continued)*

Variety	Description
Surf clam	**Tidbits:** Newly hatched clam carried inshore on surf; also called chowder clam
	Shell: 5 to 6 inches across; 1 to 1½ pounds
	Meat: Bright golden beige; tough
	Best to eat: In chowder, as clam strips, canned, or as minced clams
Ocean quahog	**Tidbits:** Deep sea clam
	Shell: 2 to 4 inches across
	Meat: Dark orangy-beige; chewy; strongest tasting clam
	Best to eat: Chopped for chowder, canned; small ocean quahogs (30 per pound) called mahogany clam; steamed
Manila clams	**Tidbits:** Popular in Japan; hitchhiked across to Pacific northwest on shipments of Asian oysters
	Shell: Light brown, fine concurrent ridges radiating in sunburst from hinge; 20 per pound
	Meat: Tan with orange; mild, chewy; softer; less solid flesh than Atlantic
	Best to eat: On half shell, steamed
Geoduck (GOO-ee-duck)	**Tidbits:** Up to 2-feet long, 3 pounds, resembles giant soft-shell clam with thick, protruding neck; respected in Asian cuisine
	Shell: Oval, ridged
	Meat: Body is tender, chewy, and richly flavored; raw neck crunchy; makes good sushi
	Best to eat: Body fried as steaks; neck used in chowder
Razor clam	**Tidbits:** Looks like an old-fashioned straight razor
	Shell: Narrow brown, rectangular shell, brittle, like soft-shell clams; 8 to 12 per pound
	Meat: Sweet, tender, and chewy; tan to beige
	Best to eat: Steam, sauté, or deep fry

Pam's sting ray bloody marys

Clam and tomato juices are long-time partners, but spike the duo with Chesapeake Bay-Style Seasoning (see Chapter 7), and transform them into Pam Barefoot's award-winning Sting Ray Bloody Marys. Pam stirs up her Sting Ray (plus seafood soups and seasonings) at her company, the Blue Crab Bay, a stone's throw from the Chesapeake Bay. When you can't find the mix locally, try the following recipe, which Pam shared with us.

1. Stir together 2¼ cups tomato juice, ¾ cup clam juice, 2 tablespoons horseradish, 2 tablespoons each fresh lemon juice and Chesapeake Bay-Style Seasoning, 4 teaspoons Worcestershire sauce, 1½ teaspoons celery seed, ¾ teaspoon each onion powder and black pepper, and hot pepper sauce to taste.

2. Let flavors blend 1 hour before serving with the spirit of your choice.

Soft-shell clams usually contain sand (they can't close their shells completely because their necks stick out). Russell Turner of Maine Lobster Direct says he soaks freshly dug soft-shell clams or *mud clams* in salt water (just to cover) for 24 hours (about ¼ cup salt per gallon). At home, soaking soft-shells for several hours should rid them of remaining sand.

Shape Up with Mussels

Mussels grow in waters around the world, and you can easily recognize the two main types by their midnight blue-black or green-tinged shell. Mussels literally "hang around" in groups. The clump of silky, curly threads (or beard) that you see sticking out of the edge of the mussel shell is the anchor that mussels use to attach themselves to rocks and grasses (when growing wild) or ropes suspended from rafts (when farm-raised). Mussels have been farmed in France since the thirteenth century, with Spain, the Netherlands, France, and Italy now the largest producers. In the United States, some mussels are farmed, but most are harvested wild (raked from coastal beds and scrubbed before sorting).

Refer to Figure 8-1 for mussel-cleaning strategy.

Blue mussels

Mussels are the best value of the shellfish game and are a great way to feed a crowd. There are two types of blue mussels, the northern blue and the Mediterranean mussel. The northern blue mussel is the most prevalent mussel, and varieties of it grow on both coasts of the United States, in the Canadian Maritimes, and in northern European waters. Its dark blue-black shell is tear-drop shaped, has concentric rings around the shell, and is about 3 inches long. The cooked meat has a smooth, slightly chewy texture and oceany taste, and ranges from creamy beige (in the males) to deep peach-orange (in the females).

The Mediterranean mussel, native to the Mediterranean, is now farmed in the Pacific northwest and in California. It resembles the northern blue mussel, but is about 50 percent larger and wider, and has a gold band near the hinge. The big, plump, tender meat fills the shell, and ranges from white (in the males) to orange (in the females) when cooked.

Green mussels

Native to New Zealand, *green-lipped* or *green shell* mussels are large, like Mediterranean mussels (see the previous section). The deep apricot flesh is mild and slightly chewy. You can sometimes find green mussels live, shell-on, but usually you fiind them cooked and frozen on the half shell (after steam-cooking, the top mussel shell is removed and the mussel is frozen in the bottom shell for protection).

Buy precooked mussels to make quick work of salads, pasta, paella, soups, and starters. Top green mussels on the half shell with salsa or check out sassy sauces in Chapter 15.

Sizing Up Scallops

You can find scallops in varying sizes, from jumbo sea scallops to tiny calicos. On occasion, you may see a scallop with its orange roe attached. Knowing the difference between scallops can help you pick the ideal cooking technique. For instance, meaty sea scallops lend themselves to grilling and sautéing, while little bays cook quickly when stir-fried, broiled, or slipped into soups and chowders. See Figure 8-4 for ways to identify scallops.

In France, scallops are called *coquilles St. Jacques* — "seashells of St. James." Legend has it that, as the patron saint of fishermen, the apostle St. James adopted the scallop shell as his symbol. Today, the shell marks the trails to his shrine in Santiago de Compostela in Galicia, Spain.

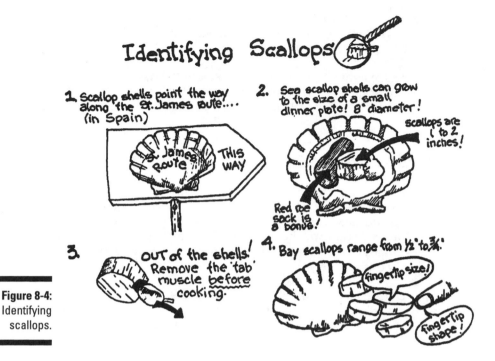

Figure 8-4:
Identifying
scallops.

Sea scallops

The voluptuous New England sea scallop is one of Mother's Nature's finest designs. Its big, thick morsel of meat is shiny, opaque, and creamy white or lightly tinged with pink. Raw sea scallops lack surface moisture and tend to stick together when raw (that's okay, though). You may want to remove the little tab-like (tough) muscle on the side of the scallop before cooking (refer to Figure 8-4). Cooked scallops turn white and have a sweet, rich taste and firm, luxurious texture. Sauté, grill, broil, bake, or smoke.

A *diver scallop* is a jumbo-size sea scallop that's hand-plucked from the ocean floor, unlike the majority of scallops, which are dredged by boat. Divers, outfitted in sturdy drysuits, brave cold, dark waters, snatch the jet-propelled, elusive scallop, and send it quickly to shore.

Bay scallops (and calicos, too)

Bite-size bay scallops are pearly white (raw and cooked), have a delicate, sweet taste, and a fine, tender texture. Bay scallops (also called *bays*) run forty or more scallops per pound, and are ideal for sautéing or stir-frying.

Harvested from New England to the Gulf of Mexico, bays are similar to another scallop, the *calico,* which is smaller, and is caught from North Carolina south through the Gulf of Mexico.

China began farming bay scallops in the early 1980s, and the first time around, only a few scallops survived. Today, China exports tons of frozen bays. Generally, the American bay scallop has a sweeter taste than the Chinese variety.

West-coast scallops

The weathervane and pink (or singing) scallops are two Pacific northwest specialties. They usually remain in the local market. Weathervane scallops are large and meaty, similar to sea scallops. They are commonly shucked and frozen immediately. Weathervanes can be compared in taste and quality to highly prized east coast diver scallops (covered in the "Sea scallops" section, earlier in this chapter).

Pink scallops have beautiful fluted pink shells (about 2 inches across) and are usually sold and served in the shell. The delicate, sweet meat is about the size of bay scallops. Steam them as you would clams or mussels.

Don't get soaked

Rather than being sold shell on, scallops are usually shucked because they are highly perishable. Scallops lose moisture easily, so to increase shelf life and to reduce moisture loss, most scallops are treated by soaking in water mixed with sodium tripolyphosphate. Soaked scallops may be referred to as *treated* or *wet*; unsoaked scallops, *natural* or *dry.* When phosphates are used correctly, treated scallops can be tasty.

Unless you see treated and natural scallops side-by-side, it's hard to tell the difference. Treated, raw scallops are shinier, more slippery, and stay more separate than natural scallops. Untreated scallops have a less shiny, duller look and naturally stick together. Both scallops may have liquid in the pan they are sold in, so unfortunately that's not a definitive indicator.

Always rinse scallops and pat dry before cooking. When scallops are oversoaked, they contain huge amounts of water (which is why it's impossible sometimes to get crispy, golden-brown scallops). Treated scallops have a mild, less sweet taste (due to the extra water) than natural scallops, and remain translucent when cooked (or over-cooked), instead of turning opaque the way that natural scallops do.

If you want to know whether scallops are treated, ask your fish seller; if he's not sure, ask to see the container (usually a white plastic tub) that he buys them in. When treated with tripolyphosphate, the FDA requires that, on the ingredient label, scallops must be listed as containing water, with the name of the specific phosphate used. When buying frozen scallops, check the package label.

A Love Affair with Oysters

We both adore oysters — including all of the myths, clichés, and literary joy that surround this much-rhapsodized creature. In spite of growing up inland, in Canada's lumbering Ottawa Valley, Leslie's seafood heritage includes oysters. December always brought a case of Malpeque oysters (nestled in seaweed and a healthy coating of mud) shipped by train from friends in Prince Edward Island. Stored in the shed (covered with a blanket and Dad's winter coat), the oysters lasted until Christmas Eve, when the final feast was Mom's silky oyster stew.

There are a half dozen or so species of oysters worldwide that we treasure for eating, and five are available in North America: Eastern oyster, Pacific oyster, Kumamoto, Olympia, and European flat oyster. Oysters grow in east coast waters from the Canadian Maritimes through the Gulf coast, and in the Pacific northwest from northern California to Washington State, British Columbia, and up to Alaska.

Don't be fooled by all those names you see on an oyster bar menu — it's simply a matter of geography. When the same species, such as the Eastern oyster, grows in different places, the oyster takes its name from each place it grows. For example, Wellfleet oysters hail from Wellfleet, Massachusetts; Chincoteague oysters from the island of the same name in the Chesapeake Bay; and so on. (In the following sections, we mention each oyster species' Latin name simply because you may see them listed on an oyster bar menu.)

Raw oysters are usually served on the half shell (the meat is loosened from both the top and bottom shell and presented in the cupped lower shell to hold the juices).

What to drink with oysters

Choose wine or beer, depending on your mood. Tom Meyer, who oversees The Old Ebbitt Oyster Bar in Washington, D.C., prefers a classic Chablis, one that "sees no oak" during aging. "You can taste the Chardonnay grape, but it has a short, crisp, clean finish that leaves your palate ready for the next oyster." Tom also enjoys a Sauvignon Blanc because the austere, flinty, grassy quality is delightful with oysters (and grilled fish).

Last year's Old Ebbitt Grill Wines for Oysters Competition (similar to the Pacific Coast Oyster Wine Competition) produced intriguing results. The ten winning wines were evenly split between New Zealand and France. Eight of the ten were Sauvignon Blancs, and five of those were from the Marlborough area of New Zealand. Among those, the Cloudy Bay has been a winner for years, and the Nobilo was the best value among the five. Most of the winning French wines were from the Loire Valley (three Sancerres and a Muscadet), with one from Chablis. Will these flavor trends continue? You have to wait for this year's results.

Fired-up martini oyster

If you prefer your oysters spirited, fire-up a batch of martini oyster shooters to launch your next party, and watch your guests eyes light up.

Jalapeño peppers add provocative sensations to these simple spirited sippers. But don't hesitate to experiment with your favorite fiery peppers. So sip and enjoy this Big Easy embrace from the New Orleans' Emporium restaurant, as we first did.

✔ Pop a single oyster or clam into a shot glass, topped with just enough peppered vodka (homemade or purchased) to make the shellfish tipsy — or to your taste. Add a squeeze of lemon juice and pinch of salt and pepper.

✔ To make your own spicy peppered vodka mix, in a jar, shake together 1¾ cup vodka; ¾ ounce dry white vermouth; and 1 fresh jalapeño pepper, seeded and quartered. Let stand 1 to 2 days, refrigerated, to kick-up the heat level; remove peppers and use to garnish shooters.

Eating raw oysters that grow in different coastal waters offers a range of flavors, just like tasting your favorite coffees or wines from around the world. Oysters develop their personalities from the bays and estuaries in which they grow. The salinity of the water, minerals in the water, temperatures — and even yesterday's rainfall — all play a role.

Cooking transforms oysters into plump, luxurious bites. So look for gumbo, fried oysters, and other enticing oyster recipes throughout the book.

Eastern oyster (Crassostrea virginica)

You know these beauties as Malpeque, Blue Point, Wellfleet, Chesapeake, Apalachicola, and Louisiana oysters, among other names. Eastern oysters grow in waters from Prince Edward Island, down the east coast, and through the Gulf of Mexico. The flavors range from delicate, crisp, briny, and salty to lightly salty-sweet. On the half shell, the oyster is tender and silky with a clean aftertaste. The oyster averages 3 to 4 inches long, with a tear-drop to gentle half-moon shape.

A naturally occurring bacteria, *Vibrio vulnificus,* may be present in warm waters (such as those in the Gulf of Mexico). The bacteria often exists in oysters because oysters filter food from surrounding waters, especially during the summer months. Harmless to most people, *Vibrio* can be deadly to persons with chronic liver disease or any illness that compromises the immune system — if they eat oysters raw. Thorough cooking kills the bacteria.

Pacific oyster (Crassostrea gigas)

Take a northwest and Pacific Ocean oyster-lovers' tour and slurp on Pacific oysters from Wescott Bay, Hood Canal, Samish Bay, Hog Island, and Fanny Bay, among others. The Pacific oyster has a moderately deep lower shell that cups the oyster's creamy, plump flesh. Flavors range from mild and lightly salty to full, rich and briny; length, 3 inches and longer, with ruffled edges and swirling ridges running around the shell. The Pacific oyster is native to Japan and also grows well in the United Kingdom, Europe, Asia, Australia New Zealand, and South America.

Kumamoto oyster (Crassostrea sikamea)

The Kumamoto is smaller than the Eastern or Pacific oyster (about 2 inches long) and is characterized by a deep shell with frilly edges and fluted ridges that spread like a sunburst from the hinged end. The meat is mildly salty, sweet, nutty, and buttery with a pleasantly flinty or metallic aftertaste. Once native to — and now extinct in — Japan, the Kumamoto is farmed in Pacific northwest waters.

Eating oysters during hot summer months is a question of sex — and refrigeration. Oysters spawn when the weather warms and lose their natural sweetness (what can we say, it's sex without touching). The flesh loses its firm succulence and oyster eating is not at its peak. In the past, poor refrigeration didn't help, so it made sense to wait to eat oysters during cold weather months. Oyster-raising technology is expanding the oyster's availability by developing oysters that don't spawn, so you can slurp flavorful oysters all year long. But keep in mind that oysters from October through April still offer the best eating.

Olympia oyster (Ostrea lurida)

The tiny Olympia is the native jewel of the Pacific northwest. Its quarter-size meat is delicate and tender; the flavor sweet, and briny with a mild coppery aftertaste. Olympias were the Gold Rush oyster, popular in bars and saloons, but they fell to the brink of extinction in the 1930s. Olympias are back, thanks to the rebuilding efforts of dedicated northwest oyster visionaries.

European flat oyster (Ostrea edulis)

European flats are know as the Belon oyster in France, where the Belon River estuary in Brittany is their original home. The oyster is big, round, and flat, like a pancake. The meat is firm, and somewhat chewy, with a strong briny or metallic coppery taste. The flats are farmed in the United States on the northeast coast and in the Pacific northwest, with names like Spinney Creek and Wescott Bay Flats.

Chapter 9

Fish with Fins

· ·

In This Chapter

▶ Identifying favorite fish

▶ Recognizing new fish on the block

▶ Tracking down regional fish

▶ Finding fascinating fringe fish

· ·

*W*e both grew up inland, far removed from the ocean's briny bounty. But the rivers and lakes offered us fine fin fare. Marcie's dad, an Iowa farmer, proudly brought home walleyes from his trips to central Canada's pristine lakes. On sunny, spring mornings when the pickerel were running, Leslie and her dad played hooky from church to head to the Ottawa River to fish. Her mom fried mounds of onions in bacon drippings until tender with their edges crisped black, then gently fried the freshly caught fish. As the sweet, seductive scents of onions caramelizing mingled with the smoky aromas of bacon and the catch, the family knew breakfast was ready.

Whether you cook freshwater fish or the ocean's saltwater catch, you can find plenty of fish from which to choose. Consider that over 2,500 species of catfish, 350 species of grouper, and 700 species of tilapia swim the waters worldwide. And that's just a start.

Scientists group fish by their habitat, into freshwater and saltwater fish. Fish can be further grouped by the temperature of the water they live in: warmwater or coldwater. Warmwater fish include grouper, mahimahi, and snapper. Coldwater fish include salmon, halibut, monkfish, and cod, to name a few. Others, such as tuna, swim in both warm and cold waters.

Choosing the fish to feature in this chapter was a challenge, and we acknowledge our list is not the de"fin"itive one. While the categories we arrange the fish in are totally subjective, we hope that they help you figure out where the fish swim. For each fish, we describe its taste, color, and texture to better help you pick a fish you'd like to try; suggest cooking techniques for the fish; and add fun tips.

You can find recipes featuring fish with fins in Chapters 6, 11, 12, 14, 15, 16, and 17.

Schooling in the Mainstream

You can usually find the fish in this section at your local fish counter. Cod, salmon, flounder, and sole are long-time favorites. Other popular mainstream fish include trout, catfish, and swordfish.

Atlantic salmon

Atlantic salmon has a bright-orange flesh; mild, rich flavor; and luscious, silky texture. Cook it any way you like: grill, bake, sauté, or steam for equally superb tastes. You can count on getting fresh Atlantic salmon year 'round, because the fish is farm-raised all around the world. Fish farming brought the Atlantic salmon back into the mainstream when the wild catch dwindled. Norway, Chile, the United Kingdom, Canada, and the United States farm Atlantic salmon — and it's all the same species, no matter where the salmon grows. Flip to Chapter 6 for more shopping and cooking tips for this seafood superstar.

Both Atlantic and Pacific salmon are members of one huge family (the *Salmonidae* family), and they have lots of relatives, including trout, Arctic char, and steelhead. Folk etymology derives the word "salmon" from the Latin *salire,* "to leap." Also derived from *salire* are energetic words such as somersault, resilient, and exultant, which aptly describe salmon's antics (well, maybe not full somersaults).

Catfish

Those living in the southern United States love their catfish, and homegrown wild catfish has long been a staple of fish fries, served with hush puppies (deep-fried cornmeal dumplings), of course. Farm-raised catfish arrived on the scene in the early 1970s, and the fish has gained national popularity. Americans now eat the same amount of catfish as cod. Farmed catfish has a consistently mild taste; the ivory flesh turns white when cooked and the fine-grained meat is firm and springy. Grill, fry, broil, blacken, or stir-fry catfish, or add it to gumbo or stews. The U.S. is the prime producer of farmed catfish in the world, and catfish tops the list of fish that are farm-raised in the States. Wild catfish remains popular, as are catfish festivals, featuring both wild and farmed catfish. Check out Chapter 19 for the information about the World Catfish Festival.

When you want a taste of the real thing, head to Middendorff's, the 66-year-old restaurant that specializes in fried wild catfish from the Atchafalaya Basin. When Leslie was writing a piece about down-home restaurants in New Orleans, Chef Jamie Shannon of Commander's Palace insisted that she taste Middendorff's catfish. Middendorff's hand-cuts their catfish fillets into thin slices before deep-frying in yellow cornmeal to a clean, crispy taste. And they serve them with hush puppies. With glimpses of soaring egrets, pelicans, and ducks along the way, the 30-minute drive from New Orleans to Pass Manchac for this catfish is worth it.

Cod and its cousins

With so many varieties widely available, cod is one of the most important food fish in the world. Some varieties are known simply as *cod.* Cousins of cod go by names like *haddock, hake,* and *pollock,* among others.

The Pacific and Atlantic cod (sometimes called *true cod* to differentiate them from their cousins) are nearly identical.

- **Cusk** refers to a cousin with a larger, firmer flake and moister texture than cod and haddock. Makes for a soggier sauté, but a good broiling and frying fish.

- **Haddock** is an Atlantic cod that's favored for a more distinctive flavor and texture.

- **Hake** (HAYK) or **whiting** tends to get less respect than true cod, with flesh that is often blander and softer. Like pollock, hake is often used in commercial processing.

- **Pollock** is a quiet hero in the seafood business — you may not know it by name, however, because a good percentage of pollock is processed and frozen for convenience food (such as fish sandwiches at fast-food places). Pollock also is made into a flavored mixture called surimi, which is formed into imitation crab-like flakes or chunks. See our recipe for Layered Southwestern Dip with Surimi in Chapter 11.

- **Scrod** (SKRAHD) is a term used on the U.S. east coast, primarily for small cod.

Cod flesh is usually pearly white, flaky, and delicate, with a mild sweet flavor that makes the fish versatile and widely popular. Lean towards light-handed cooking methods for cod, with flavorings that won't overwhelm its mildness. Bake, panfry, sauté, deep-fry (great for fish 'n' chips), poach, or add to chowders and stews. You can grill delicate cod if you use a grill topper (discussed in Chapter 2), which keeps the cod from falling through the rungs.

Unrelated to cod are other fish with cod in their names, such as lingcod (from another family) and black cod (sablefish). See the "West coast" section, later in this chapter, for the delicious scoop on sablefish.

Flounder and sole

Whoever coined the phrase "42nd cousin" must have had the flounder and sole family in mind. Flounder, sole, and their unfathomable number of relations are collectively called *flatfish* because of their distinctive flat body and shape. Flatfish also include *plaice, turbot,* and the granddaddy of them all, *monster halibut.* (We list halibut separately because its large size provides meaty steaks and fillets.)

In general, flounder, sole, and their relatives have delicate, thin fillets (about ½-inch thick) with a translucent, creamy white flesh. The fillets cook up white, with tender to firm meat that has a light, delicate flavor and a small flake. Flatfish cook quickly and are ideal for sautéing, panfrying, or broiling for a weekday dinner. Steaming, poaching, or baking in individual foil packets nicely preserves the fish's natural moisture. (See Chapters 5 and 6 for foil packet recipes.) Plus, the slender, skinless fillets lend themselves to stuffing and rolling, or topping and baking, especially with shellfish such as crab and shrimp.

Flatfish swim in Pacific and Atlantic waters, in the Gulf of Mexico, and in waters worldwide. Whether you call the fish a "flounder" or a "sole" depends on your habit and your location. In the United States, a New Englander's flounder is a Pacific northwesterner's sole. You can find Pacific flatfish commonly sold as *petrale, rex, rock, U.S. Dover sole,* and *Pacific sand dab.* Common Atlantic flatfish names include *yellowtail flounder, fluke (summer flounder), lemon sole (winter flounder),* and *gray sole.* The original, true Dover sole swims only in European waters, as do plaice and turbot. Greenland turbot hails from the North Atlantic and the North Pacific.

The eyes have it

Flatfish are interesting creatures and undergo a bizarre metamorphosis as they mature into ocean-bottom dwellers. When young, the fish's eyes are in a normal position, one on either side of the head, but as the fish matures, one eye travels over the top of the head and comes to rest beside the other. The head twists, the mouth adjusts, and the fish flips on its side to now glide through the water as a sleek, flat fish. Picture an oval-shaped Frisbee with eyes perched at one end, the tail at the other, and ripply fringes along the sides — and that's the shape of your basic flatfish. With its camouflaged, mottled brown-gray top, flatfish are all the better prepared to snuggle into a sandy bottom to hide from predators.

Swordfish

Like tuna and other long-distance swimmers, swordfish slips comfortably into ethnic garb, from Mediterranean herbs, capers, and olive oil, to Caribbean reggae gear. Swordfish has a mild, sweet, rich flavor that unfolds with grilling, broiling, sautéing, or baking. Its raw, translucent flesh is pinky-beige to creamy white; cooking turns it off-white. The meaty, dense fish is moist and succulent. The texture of swordfish is a cross between pork and chicken. When you cut swordfish meat, it breaks into slender shreds rather than into big flakes, the way salmon and cod do.

Swordfish has a big, reddish swirl in the cross-section of a steak. And like tuna, mahimahi, and shark (also fast-moving, migratory fish), this specialized tissue fuels the long journey of the swordfish. If the line is dark brown, the fish is getting old, so choose something else.

Trout

The rainbow trout, a freshwater fish native to western U.S. and Canada, is a member of the salmon family. Rainbow trout is the hallmark of aquaculture around the world, and is one of the top farmed species. The farmed fish consistently range from ¾- to 1-pound, making them ideal for single-serving portions, whether in fillets or whole on the bone. Farmed trout have a white to pink to orange flesh, depending on their diet; the meat cooks up creamy white with a mild flavor. Wild trout have flesh that ranges from pale pinky-orange to deep salmon red, with varying degrees of flavor intensity.

Virtually all trout that you find in your fish store come from fish farms, although there are areas in the U.S. where wild trout — such as lake trout or speckled trout — are available. It is best to cook trout skin on, to hold the delicate, flaky flesh together. The thin skin is edible and tasty, though you can remove it before serving if you like. Panfry, broil, bake, poach, grill, or smoke trout. For information about lake trout, flip to the "Inland lakes — great and small" section, later in this chapter.

The New Kids on the Block

Real estate agents achieve success through location, location, location. In the fish business, the motto could be "transportation, transportation, transportation." The new fish on the block are arriving from everywhere: sea bass from Chile (and other Polar waters); fresh halibut from the Alaska and the Pacific northwest; mahimahi from the Gulf of Mexico, Hawaii, and Ecuador; farm-raised tilapia from Costa Rica and Columbia; and tuna from Chile, Hawaii, the Gulf of Mexico, and California.

Chilean sea bass

Chileans call sea bass *cod-of-the-depths* (sea bass live as deep as 3,000 feet in coastal Polar seas). Like cod, Chilean sea bass has snow-white flesh that cooks up whiter than white. But unlike lean-fleshed cod, sea bass has a rich, mild flavor and silky texture. The meat is firm and dense, and when cooked, has a huge, moist, tender flake. Sea bass is forgiving in the kitchen: It's virtually impossible to overcook, whether you grill, bake, broil, or sauté it. Plus, Chilean sea bass is high in omega-3s (see Chapter 1). Like salmon or sablefish, it also smokes beautifully (it's all that luscious good fat). Chilean sea bass is unrelated to any basses; its real name is *Patagonia toothfish,* but savvy marketers realized that name wouldn't sell much fish.

Fish that live in frigid polar and Arctic waters make their own antifreeze. Seriously! Although icy seawater can infiltrate a fish's blood, its antifreeze stops ice crystals from growing.

Halibut

Halibut's Latin family name *hippoglossus* translates to "hippo of the sea," so it shouldn't be much of a surprise that the fish can attain sizes of 500 pounds or more. Halibut is a member of the flounder family, all of which are flatfish with both eyes on top of their head (see the "Flounder and sole" section, earlier in this chapter, for more information on flatfish).

The flesh of halibut is translucent, pearly-white when raw and turns a beautiful snowy white when cooked; it's firm with large flakes. Because the fish is lean, it's particularly important to not overcook halibut because you'll lose its moist texture. Halibut's a great candidate for virtually all cooking methods, from sautéing to grilling, baking, and steaming. Try marinating it before cooking to enhance its lean, mild flavor. You should see more fresh halibut now in supermarkets thanks to an extension of the fishing seasons.

Chef Robert McGowan, of the Old Ebbitt Grill in Washington, D.C., has an easy way to cook halibut for entertaining: Sauté one side of the halibut until lightly browned, place the halibut browned side up on a lightly oiled baking sheet, and finish cooking in a 425° oven. It's a snap.

Mahimahi

Fishermen from Spain to South America have enjoyed *mahimahi,* an explosive game fish for years. (In many regions, mahimahi [MA-hee MA-hee] is known as *dolphin fish,* although it is no relation to the mammal dolphin.) Hawaiian fishermen gave the fish its name, which means "strong-strong." Mahimahi is a lean fish with a sweet, moderately mild flavor. The meat is dense — somewhat less so than swordfish — and has a large, firm flake. Its translucent flesh ranges in color from pale pink to light beige when raw; cooking turns the meat creamy white. Grill, sauté, broil, deep fry, poach, steam, or smoke. Mahimahi usually is sold in fillets. You can substitute mahimahi for swordfish, tuna, salmon, grouper, and shark.

Look for a reddish line down the center and the sides of a mahimahi fillet. Like tuna, swordfish, and shark (also fast-moving, migratory fish), this specialized tissue fuels mahimahi's bursts of speed. If the line is brown, the fish is getting old, so choose something else.

Shark

The star of _Jaws_ is making a tasty transition from big, bad fish to lean, mean steak machine. Shark cooks up firm with a dense meat that loves spicy, hearty seasonings. Grill, broil, or sauté shark, or stir it into gumbos and soups. Cook with a watchful eye because shark can dry out. You may find shark in your store labeled simply "shark," or by type, as follows:

- **Mako shark:** Caught in the waters off the U.S. west coast and around Florida, mako is the most popular shark, with a mild flavor and dense meat, similar to swordfish. Its pinkish flesh turns off-white on cooking.

- **Thresher shark:** Thresher shark's pale pink meat has a stronger flavor and slightly softer texture than mako. California catches the most.

- **Blacktip shark:** From Gulf of Mexico and Florida waters, blacktip shark cooks up white to a firm, chewy texture.

Sharks have no scales and a skeleton made of soft cartilage — so you don't have any tricky bones to pick out. Check the smell when you buy shark — if you smell any ammonia odor, don't buy it: The fish was likely not iced properly.

Tilapia

If you're not used to eating fish, _tilapia_ (tuh-LAH-pee-uh) is a great place to start. A warm-water fish that's native to the Middle East and Africa, tilapia has been farm-raised for thousands of years. It has a delicate, sweet, mild taste, and the fillets are easy to work with. The meat ranges from white to a pinkish hue, and is low in fat. When you grill tilapia, the texture firms like snapper; when you bake the fish, the texture remains moist, like cod. It adapts well to a wide range of seasonings. Bake, broil, sauté, or deep fry tilapia, or add it to gumbo, curries, or soups. You can substitute tilapia for cod, snapper, flounder, or orange roughy.

You may find tilapia as whole fish or swimming in tanks in Asian markets; these are ideal steamed.

Tuna

After years of being relegated to tuna-salad sandwiches, tuna is now showing up whole as beautiful, boneless steaks. You can recognize raw tuna by its distinctive flesh color, which ranges from rosy pink to deep ruby red. (When exposed to air, tuna's surface color changes to a brownish-red.) Tuna is ideal for grilling, broiling, or sautéing, and cooks up meaty and tender like a steak. The meat turns beigy-tan on cooking. Like steak, you may prefer to cook tuna medium-rare. But tuna is low in fat compared to beef and cooks fast, so watch carefully to keep it from drying out.

You can find different types of fresh tuna, as shown in Table 9-1.

Table 9-1	Fresh Tuna Varieties
Type	*Characteristics*
Yellowfin (*ahi*)	Ruby red color, full-flavored Most common fresh tuna When canned, called "light"
Albacore	Creamy rose color, mildest taste Only tuna canned as "white meat"
Bigeye	Ruby red color, tastes stronger than yellowfin
Bluefin	Deep ruby red color, highest oil content, richest taste Revered by Japanese for raw sushi and sashimi; expensive
Skipjack (*bonito*)	Dark red color, strong, distinctive flavor Canned as "light" Dried in Japan (See "The other fish stock" sidebar, later in this chapter)
White tuna (not a true tuna)	When your sushi chef offers you "white tuna," it's likely escolar (See the "Escolar" section, later in this chapter.)

The other fish stock

In a longstanding tradition, the Japanese transform fresh skipjack tuna or bonito into a valuable seasoning ingredient. They dry, smoke, and cure the fish into chunks hard enough to grate or shave, much the way you may grate Parmesan cheese (see Chapter 2 for more on shaving fish).

Bonito is an essential flavoring for *dashi*, a basic Japanese soup stock, and it adds a smoky element to fish soups and stews. You can find dried, shaved bonito in Japanese or Asian markets — and it lasts forever.

You may see a dark red patch on a tuna steak. Tuna is a sleek, powerful fish that continually swims a broad swath of tropical and subtropical global waters, and this specialized tissue makes possible tuna's rapid bursts of speed. Because this tissue has a fishier, more bitter taste than the rest of the fish, you may want to trim it before cooking.

Don't hesitate to buy frozen tuna. For years, the Japanese have been buying frozen tuna (and other fish) to be used in raw preparations, such as sushi and sashimi. We first encountered whole frozen bluefins at Tokyo's Tsukiji market, where row upon row of these frosty giants line the hall (bluefin tuna may reach 10 feet and weigh up to 1,200 pounds). Buyers check the quality of the meat for color, sheen, and texture before bidding big bucks for the big ones.

U.S. Regional Favorites

When you grow up near the water, you always think that your local catch is the best. And though you may taste fabulous fish from places afar, those first fish memories keep you coming back. If you're a transplant far away from home, see Chapter 24 for a list of our favorite U.S. companies that fly fish to you overnight.

Mid-Atlantic to northeast (Virginia to Maine)

This is an eclectic array of fish. Some fish are pan size or good for oven-baking (ocean perch, hybrid striped bass, and black sea bass), while others are big and won't win a beauty contest (monkfish and ocean catfish). Shad, bluefish, and the wild striped bass migrate up and down the east coast — spring heralds the start of their annual run.

Black sea bass

If you see a whole, small black sea bass in your fish case, nab it. The fish range from 1½ pounds to 5 pounds, and the meaty, dense flesh bakes beautifully moist and succulent. Black sea bass feeds on crabs, shrimp, clams, and oysters, among other crunchy shellfish, and has a mild, salty-sweet taste. The white flesh turns snow white with cooking. Sea bass have big crab-like flakes, with a texture that's slightly softer than striped bass (which is not a relative). The whole fish also is ideal for steaming with Asian seasonings. Sauté or broil the fillets.

Bluefish

If you've eaten bluefish and it's been both terrific and terrible, your experience may be similar to Leslie's. In bluefish experience number one, a friend gave Leslie a bluefish that was freshly caught down on the eastern shore of the Chesapeake Bay, where the blues abound in the summer. The fish's flesh was clear and shining and colored grayish-blue with a deep red band running down the center of the fillet. (Cooking turns the flesh a lighter grayish-blue.) The bluefish, simply broiled with lemon, had a rich, full flavor, similar to mackerel, and a big, soft, slightly chewy flake.

On to bluefish experience number two, which was strong, fishy tasting, and had mushy flesh. Bluefish has a short shelf life, and this fish was past its prime. Bluefish are aggressive, voracious fish, and as with other highly predatory species, their digestive enzymes are powerful. Left ungutted, the flesh spoils quickly. If a bluefish is cleaned and iced fast, the flesh will be firmer, the taste milder, and the shelf-life longer.

When buying bluefish, check the color of the fillet's central red band. If the flesh has turned brown and spreads out like a bruise into the rest of the fish, this indicates improper icing. This blood-rich muscle may taste bitter or fishy, so remove it, if desired, before cooking. Small bluefish taste milder than large bluefish: The small, young fish feed mostly on tasty crustaceans and mollusks, while the older blues eat oilier, stronger-tasting fish such as menhaden. Bluefish also is called *snapper blue, blue, chopper, harbor blue, billet,* and *tailor.*

The fatty flesh of bluefish stands up well to high temperatures and to acids such as lemon, lime, tomato, white wine, and vinegar. Panfry or grill small whole bluefish (under 2 pounds); larger fish are better baked. Broil, grill, or bake fillets, leaving the skin on to hold the flesh together. Bluefish, like salmon and mackerel, smokes beautifully.

Monkfish

Monkfish won't win the prettiest fish award, but its taste makes up for its looks. Imagine a fish shaped like tadpole and the size of a baby grand piano (well, almost), with a big head, a bigger mouth, floppy fins, loose, mottled skin, and a small tail — and you can understand why American fisherman threw monkfish back into the sea for years. It wasn't until Julia Child presented a 25-pound monkfish to her astonished television audience back in the late 1970s that monkfish became popular in the United States. Monkfish meat (from the tail only) is dense with a mild, slightly rich taste; the white flesh turns whiter with cooking. Because the meat is solid and firm, monkfish doesn't flake, unlike most fish.

In spite of being listed in one reference book under "Miscellaneous Uncouth Fish," monkfish is revered in European kitchens where it is an essential ingredient in Spanish paella and French bouillabaisse. Simmering monkfish in soups, stews, and sauces turns the meat tender and moist (monkfish absorbs the flavors that it swims in while still staying-in-shape). Grill (great as kebabs), sauté, or bake monkfish, or cut the fish into fingers and deep-fry tempura-style. Monkfish partners well with simple seasonings or hearty Cajun, Caribbean, or Indian flavors. The French call this fish *lotte*.

A cellophane-like, gray membrane covers monkfish meat and makes the flesh tough to cut. Remove the membrane before cooking: Slip a sharp knife under the membrane, as you would the silverskin (tough outer white membrane) of beef tenderloin, and hold the membrane taut. Gently slide the knife the length of the fish and cut the membrane loose.

Ocean catfish

We probably shouldn't discuss our biases, but the French term *loup de mer* (sea wolf) for this delicious, underrated fish strikes us as significantly more palatable than the English names: *ocean catfish* and *wolffish*. That being said, try ocean catfish when you have the chance. The fish is another lucky shellfish-cruncher, dining on crabs, lobsters, clams, and more. The meat is sweetly flavored, white (both raw and cooked), and has a big, dense, moist flake, similar to halibut. Sauté, bake, or broil ocean catfish.

Ocean perch

This pretty, bright-red-skinned fish is the only Atlantic perch, unlike its cousin, the red Pacific rockfish, which has countless west coast relatives. Ocean perch range between 1 and 3 pounds, and have small fillets that you usually find skin-on. The fish has a mild taste and white flesh that turns brighter white when cooked, with a firm, but tender meat and fine flake. For a quick meal, sauté, bake, or broil ocean perch, or grill it on a grill topper. Or stir the perch into soups, chowders, or stews for equally tasty bites. Also called *redfish, rosefish,* and *red perch.*

Shad

Shad stocks are rebounding along with the wild striped bass, and springtime heralds the annual shad migration on the U.S. eastern coast from the Atlantic to freshwater rivers where the fish spawn. The largest member of the American herring family, *shad* (pronounced SHAD) averages 3 to 5 pounds and is prized for its roe (fish eggs). Shad roe are clustered in two large oval sacs and encased in a paper-thin, transparent, edible membrane. They are a deep rosy-brown and have a rich, nutty taste. Sauté the roe in butter (or even better, bacon drippings) until lightly crisped. Leave the center slightly pink to avoid overcooking to a dry, granular texture. Shad has rich flesh, but it's brimming with bones and impossible to successfully fillet at home. You can find boneless fillets and they work well baked or grilled. Shad's beigy-tan flesh stays the same color when cooked, with a moderately firm texture.

Shad fishing is an important link to the past. Decimated shad stocks are recovering, thanks to successful restoration efforts. Now the fish are swimming in abundance up the Susquehanna River, a tributary of the Chesapeake Bay, and further north in the Hudson River Valley. For an old-fashioned shad planking festival, see Chapter 19.

Skate

With a flat, diamond-shaped body and whip-like tail, a *skate* looks much like a kite in full sail. The portion you eat is the meat from the ribbed, triangular side wings. Skate has a shiny, light pinky-white flesh when raw that turns white and firm when cooked. The meat tastes mild, somewhat sweet like crab, and is delicately nutty. Skate is silky tender, with easy-to-eat meat: Simply pull the meat in slender shreds away from the ribs or rays. Skate is a long-standing favorite of the French, who poach skate, skin on, and serve it with a lemon, brown butter, and caper sauce. Sauté, steam, or grill skate as well.

Chef Bob Kinkead, of Kinkead's restaurant in Washington, D.C. is the skate master — he often has skate on his menu. For one of his dishes, Chef Kinkead serves skate, walnut crusted with a jewel-like sherry beet sauce; a tender cauliflower flan; and a medley of sautéed spinach, carrots, and shiitake mushrooms. He suggests a light red wine, such as a Pinot Noir or Chinon to suit these seasonings. For more traditional lemon-butter preparations, try a Riesling wine that picks up the sweet, crab-like flavor of the skate.

Here are Chef Kinkead's skate-master tips:

- ✔ Skate is extremely perishable and should be cooked the day you buy it.
- ✔ Skate (like shark) acquires an ammonia smell quickly, so it is easy to tell if your fish is not fresh.
- ✔ Skinning skate is a real chore, so let your fish seller do it, and then you can cook skate as you would any flatfish, such as flounder and sole.

Striped bass

Striped bass is a classy-looking fish, with glistening silver skin streaked with dramatic black stripes. It's also a glorious eating fish, with a mildly sweet flavor and moist, meaty, but tender flesh. The *wild stripers* or *rockfish* (as they are regionally known) migrate from Florida to Maine in warm months. They

Restoring the striped bass legacy

When Captain John Smith of the Jamestown Colony sailed into the James River at the southern end of the Chesapeake Bay in the early 1600s, he reported catching literally tons of striped bass in a single tide. The stripers reigned in these territorial northeast waters until the 1980s, when wild stocks were on the verge of collapse. Coastal states, including Connecticut, Delaware, Maryland, New York, Rhode Island, and Virginia, closed their striped bass fishing at various times between 1985 and 1989. Striped bass populations rebounded through the 1990s, and states cautiously opened commercial and recreational fisheries. Today, the stripers are back in record numbers, with anglers on the Hudson River recording fish up to 40-pounds. So the news is good: Overfished stocks can rebound, when you give them a chance.

cruise the northeastern U.S. coast, migrating from the Chesapeake Bay north to southern Canada, then back in the fall. *Hybrid striped bass* (a naturally occurring match in the 1930s between the wild ones and freshwater bass) is now farm-raised.

Both wild and hybrid striped bass have translucent pinky-gray flesh (wild stripers have a central red line down the center of the fillet). The meat turns white when cooked. As with many farmed fish, the hybrids have a milder taste and a bit softer texture than the wild. The hybrids grow to plate-size, (1½ to 2 pounds), so their flake is smaller compared to the big, silky flake of wild fish. But nothing beats a whole baked striped bass, whether wild or farm-raised. Sauté or broil striped bass (on a plank, as is Chesapeake Bay tradition) for equally delicious results. The hybrids offer advantages: Grill, steam, or deep-fry the whole fish for a dramatic presentation.

Southeast and Gulf Coasts (from the Carolinas to Texas)

The warm waters of North and South Carolina, Georgia, Florida, Louisiana, and Texas breed a group of regional fish that give you more superb eating. You find a variety of firm, meaty, distinctive white fish, from grouper and snapper to drum, sheepshead, and pompano (which is considered the filet mignon of fish). Toss cobia, amberjack, and escolar into the mix to round out the group. Gulf-caught tuna, mahimahi, and swordfish are popular and broadly available, so we include them with other fish on the national scene.

Amberjack

In the U.S. tropical Gulf and Atlantic waters, *amberjack* is the most common member of the diverse, global *jack* family. Also known as *greater amberjack*, the fish has a moderately strong flavor. Its rosy pinky-amber flesh cooks to white, and has a firm texture like mahimahi. When amberjack is cut into steaks, there is a dark red strip of flesh toward the center. As with tuna, you may want to trim this flesh for milder tastes. Grill, sauté, or broil amberjack.

Cobia

If you have the chance to try cobia, seize the opportunity. Cobia (COH-bee-ah) rarely finds its way into other regions, but every time we serve the fish, friends rave. *Cobia* (also called *lemon fish*) is a cross between swordfish and mahimahi in taste and texture, with a mild, sweet, rich flavor (this tropical game fish feeds on shrimp and crab) and a moist, dense meat. The light beige meat remains the same color when cooked. Grill, broil, sauté, or smoke.

Drum

The famed redfish of Cajun cooking is really a *red drum*. And although wild, red drum have not been caught commercially since the late 1980s, the fish is now being farm-raised in the south. Black drum and red drum are interchangeable in recipes; both have a sweet, mild flavor. The raw white flesh, sometimes with a red tint, stays white when cooked; the thick fillets have a tender, soft flake. Sauté, blacken, grill, or broil drum, or add to chowders and soups.

Escolar

Escolar (EHS-coh-lar) has a moist, snow-white meat and luxurious richness that New Orleans (and more recently, national) chefs love. With its firm, flaky, silky-textured flesh, this Gulf fish is similar to Chilean sea bass and Pacific sablefish. Grill, broil, or sauté. Because of its high fat content, escolar is nicknamed *oilfish* (and sometimes, *escolax*), for its purgative qualities if you eat too much. A Florida seafood wholesaler, who sells Gulf fish to over 700 national chefs, recommends a 6-ounce portion if you have a hearty system; otherwise 4-ounces is the sensible way to go. If your local sushi chef offers you white tuna, it is likely escolar.

Grouper

Grouper, like cod, comes from a huge family, but unlike cold-water cod, groupers swim in tropical waters worldwide. Groupers range in size, but generally have a heavy-set body, which gives you great eating from meaty fillets. The raw ivory to white flesh cooks up even whiter, with a firm, heavy flake. Grill, broil, sauté, or bake (but watch carefully because grouper is lean and can dry out), or add grouper to chowders and soup.

Paula Sexton of Sexton's Seafood in Birmingham, Alabama, has been cutting fish for over 30 years. Paula sells only Gulf fish (except for farm-raised Atlantic salmon), and could write the book on grouper. Paula tells us that *scamp* is the Cadillac of groupers, and the one she prefers. Scamp is one of the smaller groupers with a fine, small flake. *Black* or *gag grouper* taste just about as good. *Yellowedge,* a bigger fish, has a larger flake and coarser texture, that comes with increased size. Paula buys over 20 kinds of grouper for the fish market, including strawberry, warsaw, and snowy groupers. An amazing array of Gulf fish!

Pompano

Pompano (PAHM-puh-noh) has a relatively flat, slender body, weighs between 1 to 2 pounds, and is ideal for baking whole. It's always a surprise to pick up a pompano, because the fish seems heavy for its size. The fillets are thin, with an oyster-white flesh that turns off-white when cooked. And the meat is a dream — a dense, firm texture with a small, chewy flake and sweet, rich, nutty taste. Grill, sauté, plank, poach, or bake pompano in packets. As one friend says, this fish is the filet mignon of the sea, with a price tag to match its taste.

Sheepshead

Much of this small fish is caught in the Gulf of Mexico off the coast of Louisiana, where the fish is a familiar staple. *Sheepshead* is excellent eating and is similar to snapper (see the following section). A sheepshead crunches its way through a tasty diet of crab, oysters, shrimp, and barnacles. The fish has a mild, well-rounded flavor and is lean. Its translucent, bright-white flesh cooks up snowy white with a moderately firm flake. Broil, bake, or sauté fillets; panfry, grill, or bake whole small fish.

Sheepshead is a member of the *porgy* family, a group of fish known around the world as *sea bream.* Red and yellow sea bream are beloved in Japan, while *dorade* is the name of this family's highly respected cousin that lives in the Mediterranean. In the United States, porgies populate Atlantic coastal waters: In the mid-Atlantic, this popular panfish is known as *scup,* a name originally derived from Native Americans.

Snapper

Snappers are superb to eat, with firm, white meat, and mild flavor. Snappers have more names to describe their colorful skin than there are colors in the rainbow*: red snapper, yellowtail, silk, vermilion* or *mangrove,* and more. The raw flesh ranges from translucent pink- or red-tinged to beigy-gray to white. Whatever the raw color, all snapper turn white when cooked. The meat runs from dense and firm with large flakes to snappers with more delicate, tender flesh and smaller flakes. Snapper is wonderful when cooked whole or cut into chunks and deep-fried. Grill, broil, bake, or sauté fillets, with the skin on (scales removed) to keep the flesh from falling apart.

Red snapper is the finest eating — and the most costly — of all snappers, with its dense, flaky meat. Although it's really impossible to distinguish red snapper fillets from similar snappers, look for skin-on fillets that have a cherry red skin and ask your fish seller if it's true red snapper. Skin-off fillets are a dead giveaway that the fish is not red snapper, so don't pay red snapper prices for a look-alike.

If you live on the west coast, Pacific rockfish legally may be labeled as "Pacific snapper" or "red snapper" within certain geographic areas — but technically, rockfish is not a snapper.

Inland lakes — great and small

You don't need to feel so sorry for your land-locked (or nearly so) friends in the U.S. Midwest, far removed from the ocean's bounty. A fairly well-kept secret is the succulent freshwater catch that Midwesterners enjoy from the Great Lakes and inland Canadian lakes. For Marcie's dad, an Iowa farmer, "going up north fishing" was his beloved, albeit infrequent, escape from the rigors of tending his livestock and land. The welcome-home suppers she remembers of pan-fried walleyes remain unmatched by any exotic seafood Marcie has subsequently tasted around the globe.

Thanks to Tere Drenth, our midwestern editor, we rediscovered just how great-tasting freshwater fish can be. To make sure we didn't overlook Tere's favorite — Great Lakes whitefish — we connected on the Web with Captain Jack Donlan, a walking encyclopedia of all things freshwater. If you're a displaced Midwesterner with a nostalgic craving for walleye, whitefish, lake trout, and yellow perch, turn to Chapter 24 to find out how to order these specialties.

Lake trout

Once the star of the Door County fish boil (see the "Door County fish boil" sidebar, later in this chapter), lake trout were the dominant commercially harvested fish in the Great Lakes. One or more unique strains have been found in each lake. The sea lamprey and overfishing reduced the availability of this fine-tasting fish, which is much fatter and firmer than whitefish.

The difference a space makes

"Attention: Will the true whitefish please rise to the surface and flap your caudal fin?"

"No, not you saltwater whiting, cod, hake, cusk. Go back underwater. The winner is *coregonus clupeaformis* — lake whitefish."

Don't be confused. Be aware such whitefish wannabes are often sold as "whitefish" simply because their flesh is white. A more accurate label would be "white fish" (with a space). Although lake whitefish cooks up to be quite white, Captain Jack Donlan points out, raw whitefish is often tinged with pink. Whitefish is named for its silvery, white exterior appearance.

Door County fish boil

Good friends Lynn Nelson, and Barb and Jim Bunning made sure we knew that the Packers aren't the only thing that northern Wisconsin is noted for. Head farther north from Green Bay to Door County, where their famous fish boils generate almost as much hoopla as Brett Favre does. The quarterbacks for this event preside over a cauldron that sits askew above a wood fire. First they add tiny, red-skinned potatoes, and sometimes onions, to cook briefly in very, very salty boiling water. Then they gently lower chunky lake whitefish steaks into the pot. When the fish are nearly cooked, it's time for the spectacular *overboil.* Stand back — kerosene is thrown on the fire to create intense, leaping flames that cause the pot to boil over on its tipped side. The bubbling liquid's high salt content causes impurities and fish oils to float to the top. These spew off, dousing the flames. Relish this hearty meal with lots of melted, made-in-Wisconsin butter and coleslaw. Save room for the grand finale — Door County cherry pie. Visit the Door County Web site at http://doorcountyvacations.com or call them at 920-743-4456.

To emulate this festive event at home, do as Barb does: Eliminate the kerosene and simply skim the boiling broth. Just don't forgo the cherry pie.

Look for trout where the flesh is pale yellow to almost orange. Avoid trout with very pale flesh — a probable sign that a *sea lamprey* (a parasitic eel-like fish) latched onto the trout as its unhappy host for an extended stay. Trout from Canadian lakes tend to be lean with good flavor. Make sure your fish-seller doesn't try to sell you a *siscoette* or *humpy,* a bloated cousin of the trout that will shrivel up in the skillet, oozing more grease than the fattiest sausage you've ever fried.

Lake whitefish

Succulent, sweet, and delicately nutty-flavored, this king of the freshwater fish is caught commercially in the deep Great Lakes and from cold, inland Canadian lakes. Taking Mom out for a wonderful, melt-in-your-mouth, broiled or baked whitefish dinner is a Mother's Day tradition in the Midwest. (Read the "The difference a space makes" sidebar, earlier in this chapter, to find out how the real whitefish got its name.) Marketed up to 8 pounds — sometimes bigger — whitefish has enough fat content to be smoked. It's also ground to make a premium gelfilte fish. When broiled or grilled, we like to give this delicate fish some extra support (see the Broiled or Grilled Whitefish in Foil Boats recipe in Chapter 12). Golden, smoked chubs — the quintessential Milwaukee fish — are small, young cousins of lake whitefish. You peel back the skin and flake off the tender, white meat.

Gefilte fish is a traditional Jewish holiday dish that consists of ground whitefish, carp, or pike mixed with eggs, matzo meal, onions, and seasonings. The mixture is formed into oval-shaped patties and poached in a vegetable broth. Serve gefilte fish cold with horseradish.

Walleye

Called "the sole of freshwater fish," *walleye* is highly prized for its delicate flavor and fine texture. Named for its bulging, marble-sized eyes, this lean fish is usually sold with its attractive, yellow-flecked skin left on. Locals prefer the flavor of walleyes caught in the winter. During summer, walleyes often feed in shallow, weedy areas where the algae-laden water and their diet impart an undesirable weedy or mossy flavor. Sometimes called *yellow pike, yellow pickerel,* or *walleyed pike,* walleyes are caught in gillnets on the Canadian side of Lake Erie until the build up of ice on the north shore curtails the fishing activity. Then the harvest switches to inland Canadian lakes where walleyes are netted through the ice primarily by Native American fishermen who travel in small seaplanes to remote, government-owned sites. The catch is sorted at a central facility in Winnipeg, Manitoba. Sauté, panfry, poach, steam, broil, or pickle.

Yellow perch

This little prize (full-grown fish range from only 6 ounces to 1 pound) carries a big price tag. Many say this firm, flaky, sweet meat makes the best pan-fried fish they have ever eaten — bar none. Sadly, Great Lakes stocks are low. Perch from other parts of the world are filling in the gap, but none approaches the delicacy of the true yellow perch as remembered by its Lake Erie fans.

Because our friend and colleague Lynn Nelson can't easily obtain the classic seafoods to create an authentic bouillabaisse for her French cooking classes in Huron, Ohio, she does precisely as the resourceful French would do: Make the most of the freshest foods of the region. A medley of the Great Lakes fish that we describe in this section goes into her soup kettle. Her students stir the saffron-scented, steaming soup in her century-old farmhouse. From the windows of her cooking school, The Provincial Kitchen, students gaze at a breathtaking view of Lake Erie, the source of the perch in the soup. The overall ambience isn't quite the same as the Riviera at Antibes, but it's still enchanting.

Netting smelt

The lure and the lore of smelts — and smelting — are also part of the Great Lakes heritage. *Smelt,* a small silvery 6-inch- to 8-inch fish that was inadvertently or intentionally introduced to the Great Lakes in the early part of the century, gathers in schools in the spring along the shallow shores to spawn. Dip-netting smelt from the lake or stream bank is a popular, nocturnal Great Lakes social activity. Read about the excitement of smelts in Chapter 19 (in the "Port Washington Smelt Fry," section).

Wine with Hawaiian fish

Hawaii Chef George Mavrothalassitis (we just call him "Mavro") has a passionate interest in pairing wine with food, so much so that on the menu of his Honolulu restaurant, Chef Mavro suggests a wine by the glass with every item. When he contemplates pairings, he points out that it is important to think not only of the fish, but of the sauce and/or garnish that will be served with it. For light preparations of opaka-paka, with its mild, delicate flavor, Mavro's top choice is a dry, non-oaky white wine, such as a Pinot Grigio from Italy, with a Sonoma Sauvignon Blanc his second. But if the fish

has a stronger sauce — say with garlic or tomato — he suggests a light, fruity red such as Pinot Noir. Chef Mavro also suggests Pinot Noir for opah, an easy choice for this fish's more pronounced flavor and texture.

"Avoid Cabernet Sauvignon with any fish," Mavro notes, explaining that its long-lasting flavor on the palate overwhelms the flavors of fish. If you're a big fan of those oaky Chardonnays, Chef Mavro says go ahead and sip it alongside opah — the fish stands up better than most to the woody tones of these wines.

West coast

The waters from California to Alaska, and over in Hawaii, too, produce an abundance of amazing fish. With sophisticated air transportation, mainland Americans and others can now enjoy fish the Hawaiians have raved about for years. Pacific rockfish (or *snapper*, as it's locally known) is a big player in this region, as is wild-caught Pacific salmon. Sturgeon used to be, and we honor its heritage. And although Pacific halibut is a big catch in this region, we feature it with the other new fish on the block earlier in this chapter because it is hugely popular.

Opah

One of the most distinctive-looking fish to come from the sea, Hawaii's *opah* (*OH-pah*) offers brilliant colors both inside and out. The huge, round fish, also called *moonfish,* has silvery blue-gray skin with lots of white dots, framed by bright-red fins. The color of the flesh in each fish ranges from pale orange-red to light pink, though it all cooks up to paler ivory-white color. Opah meat has a rich, moist character and full flavor that's delicious broiled, grilled, steamed, or sautéed.

Opakapaka

This lilting name is long, but it is oh-so pronounceable: (oh-pah-kah-PAH-kah). Considered by many to be the best among Hawaii's many snappers, the *opakapaka* (also knows as *crimson snapper* or *pink snapper*) has been one of the most popular fish in Hawaii for decades. Not quite as crimson as its name suggests, the skin is a light reddish-brown. Opakapaka's pale pink flesh cooks up white and firm, with a delicate flavor. It is great steamed or baked (whole or fillets), as well as panfried, sautéed, or broiled. Other snappers or rockfish are generally good substitutes for opakapaka.

Pacific rockfish

You can find dozens of varieties of rockfish available on the Pacific coast and into the Gulf of Alaska. Among the most familiar and most popular is the *yellow-eye rockfish,* with brilliant orange skin and its namesake bright yellow eyes. Other common varieties include *yellowtail, quillback,* and *canary.* Sometimes Pacific rockfish are labeled as "snapper" or "red snapper," though they aren't related to the true red snapper from the eastern United States. The lean flesh of rockfish is a pinkish-white to white, which cooks up white and very flaky. Small whole rockfish are ideal for steaming; fillets are best panfried, steamed, or broiled to keep the delicate flesh from falling apart. See the "Ocean perch" section (rockfish's cousin), earlier in this chapter, for related tidbits.

Pacific salmon

In Alaska and the Pacific northwest, salmon is revered not only for its flavor but for its significance to the native people, and to the history of the region. There are five primary species of Pacific salmon, which range in flesh color from a soft rosy-pink to deep orange-red. (Flip to Chapter 6 for an abundance of salmon tips and recipes.) Their flavors likewise range from mild to full and pronounced. Often, the flavor profile is directly related to the salmon's fat content, which varies from species to species (and within species, from different waters or at different times of the year). In general, Pacific salmon lend themselves to grilling and to smoking, which Pacific northwesterners perfected long ago.

Sablefish

Sablefish takes its name from its almost black, velvety-feeling skin. It is commonly known as *black cod,* although it is not a member of the cod family. Sablefish has a pearly white flesh, both raw and cooked, and a rich, mild flavor. The meat is firm with a dense, tender flake. Sablefish, like Chilean sea bass, stays moist and succulent when cooked because of its oil-rich flesh (sablefish is also called *butterfish*). Grill, sauté, broil, bake, or smoke. Smoked sablefish is often called smoked sable. Sablefish range from the coast of California to the Bering Sea.

The Japanese have a traditional preparation for sablefish, called *kasu cod,* that also is popular in the Pacific northwest. Black cod is marinated in a thick paste made with the fermented mash (*sake kasu*) from the sake wine-making process. When grilled or broiled, the fish turns golden and slightly crusty around the edges, and has a tangy taste from the rice wine mash.

Sturgeon

Sturgeon is one of the most unlikely looking fish imaginable, a throwback to the prehistoric era with knobby, bony plates covering its long slender body. It is also the largest of all freshwater fish, with some recorded at over 1,000 pounds. The ivory-white flesh is a delicacy in the Pacific northwest (and beyond), both fresh and smoked. Because of short seasons and limited supply, wild sturgeon isn't widely available but is definitely worth enjoying when you find it on a menu or at a fish market. Sturgeon is also being farmed, primarily in California. The firm, delicately flavored fish (similar in texture to swordfish) is delicious cooked simply: grill, panfry, or steam.

Sturgeon is acclaimed as the source of caviar. For the insider scoop on caviar and other fish eggs, see Chapter 10.

On the Fringes of the Mainstream

The fringe fish listed in this section are an eclectic crew from exotic to everyday. Some are exotics from afar — such as John Dory and its Mediterranean companions. You often see these newcomers first in a fine restaurant, before they slowly meander into better fish markets. Steelhead and char have wild home-grown roots, but now are also farm-raised. Orange roughy appears now and again in your supermarket, and is generally available frozen or thawed.

Arctic char

Arctic char is closely related to salmon and trout and has many characteristics of both, with a flavor that falls between the two. The flesh of char is a soft rosy-orange pink and cooks up to a pale pink with lightly flaky texture, a bit more tender than salmon. You can use Arctic char in virtually any recipe that calls for salmon. It's delicious baked, broiled, grilled, poached, panfried, or smoked. Char grows wild in the icy waters of northern Canada and Europe; most char is a freshwater fish, but some fish swim to saltwater, as do salmon. The char you see at your fish counter is most likely farm-raised, either from Iceland or Canada's north.

Who could imagine that a feed of wild Arctic char would crown Leslie's final day kayaking Baffin Island's majestic fiords far up in the Canadian Arctic? With the char running in full swing, her friends bartered the beauties from local fishermen, and fried the regal fish in a cast iron skillet sizzling with hoarded butter in the light of the midnight sun.

John Dory and its Mediterranean companions

John Dory, rouget, and *dorade* are small fish that are outstanding cooked whole, grilled, or baked. The three fish are landed in Mediterranean waters, with John Dory also swimming in the far-away waters of New Zealand and Australia.

- **John Dory** is a slender, oval fish with a distinctive black spot or thumbprint on its side. The meat is white and sweet, with a firm texture; after it's cooked, the bones are easily removed from whole fish. Bake, steam, or grill. John Dory is also known as *St. Pierre's* or *St. Peter's fish.* Legend has it that St. Peter left the mark of his thumb on the side of the fish when he kindly threw it back into the ocean to survive.

- **Rouget** is a rosy skinned, small fish with dense white flesh, and a small, tight flake. Highly prized since ancient times, it's also called *red mullet.*

- **Dorade**, or *sea bream,* has slightly rosy flesh that turns white on cooking, with a sweet, moist, firm texture that's similar to snapper. Dorade is related to porgy and to sheepshead.

Orange roughy

Orange roughy hails from deep down under — and way up north. The fish is caught off the coasts of New Zealand, Australia, Africa, and Iceland at depths of over 3,000 feet, and is generally flash-frozen. The fish has a mild, moist white flesh that cooks up bright white with a texture slightly firmer than cod. Sauté, broil, or fry. Because orange roughy lives in the dark, it feeds on shrimp, squid, and fish it can see — the ones that literally light up.

Steelhead

Its pinky-orange flesh looks like salmon, so some fish sellers call it *salmon trout* — it's also known as *steelhead trout.* Known well by sportfishers who relish the fighting spirit and flavor of wild steelhead, this fish is often an enigma: Is it a trout or is it a salmon? The simple answer is that it's a trout — rainbow trout to be exact. But what's different is that steelhead don't live exclusively in freshwater the way that other trout do, but instead make a trip out to salt water before returning to freshwater, as do salmon. Steelhead are now being farmed-raised on the west coast, making them even more like their larger cousins in flavor, size, and color. Cook steelhead as you would salmon or trout.

Chapter 10

Out of the Mainstream

We're hooked on seafood — and we know that we've gone overboard when friends begin to equate gift-giving with fish. We've received more than enough fishy t-shirts, but smoked salmon and caviar are always welcome. So here's a brief look at fish out of the mainstream.

In this chapter, we offer tips for working with calamari (which we're *not* suggesting for gift-giving), for "smoking out" salmon, and for savoring caviar and its eye-popping cousins. See recipes in Chapter 11 for calamari and Chapter 13 for caviar. For a listing of companies that send smoked seafood overnight, flip to Chapter 24.

We leave the sea cucumber, gooseneck barnacles, seaweed, and fish songs for another time and place.

Call Me Calamari

Forget about calamari's less-than-designer look, and focus on the fun. Friends who've never worked with *calamari* — squid in plain old English — are surprised at how easy it is. (Figure 10-1 shows you how to clean it.) And calamari is even quicker now, because you may be able to find it already cleaned in your supermarket. Calamari freezes well, so check out the frozen food section as well.

The name calamari takes its roots from the Italian *calamaro,* but calamari is also popular in nearby Mediterranean countries (such as Spain) throughout Asia, and along coastal Mexico (don't miss the calamari tostados). Calamari lends itself to a range of seasonings, from soy and ginger to garlic, tomatoes, and chiles. Cook calamari almost any way: fry for crispy tastes; simmer for tender bites; stir into soups; or stuff, grill, or marinate with onions and serve, as we enjoy, martini-style.

When buying calamari, look for whole, unbroken bodies with tentacles intact. Cleaned calamari should be just that: White, clean whole bodies or rings that are free of the speckled membrane and have a firm, shiny flesh. (Refer to Figure 10-1 for what to do when the chick-pea size beak remains with the tentacles.) Much of the calamari you see will likely have been frozen and thawed. You can refrigerate whole, uncleaned calamari for 1 to 2 days; cleaned calamari, 2 to 3 days, in a tightly closed container.

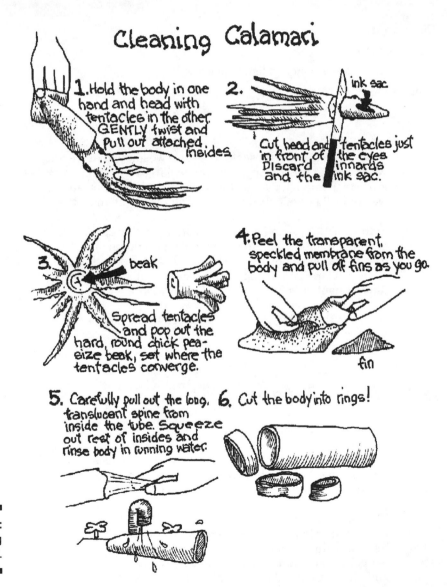

Figure 10-1:
Cleaning
calamari.

Cooking turns calamari's flesh firm. Whether the meat stays tender or toughens to springy rubber bands depends on how you cook it. Cook squid quickly — 1 to 2 minutes — so that it doesn't toughen in the first place, or simmer, 20 to 30 minutes, to bring it back to tender. Either way, calamari's white flesh stays white.

Where There's Smoke — and Salt

From frosty northern coasts to steamy Asian shores, countries have preserved fish for centuries through salting, drying, smoking, pickling, or fermenting into pungent fish sauces. Today we use the techniques almost exclusively for the glorious tastes they offer.

Smoked fish: In starring or supporting roles

You can find a wide range of smoked fish and shellfish, from salmon and trout to scallops, mussels, and shrimp. Think of bacon or ham, and extend their uses to smoked fish. Look for handy snack-size, vacuum-packed smoked fish, including salmon, bluefish, mackerel, and sablefish; whole fish, such as trout and whitefish; and sides of wild and farmed salmon.

Almost anything that swims can be smoked, but fish that are high in oil, such as salmon or mackerel, work best: They absorb smoke faster and have a better texture than lean fish, which tend to dry out with smoking. In the case of salmon, Atlantic salmon and Pacific kings are the traditional choice, but chum and pink salmon offer delicious, affordable tastes.

Smoked salmon and hearts-of-palm pinwheels

These pretty, easy roll-ups win big praise. For 3 dozen pinwheels, you need ½ pound cold-smoked salmon slices, one 14-ounce can hearts of palm, and 40 large capers. Cut the salmon slices in half lengthwise and crosswise into ½-inch strips. Cut hearts of palm into ½-inch wide pieces. Wrap the salmon around the hearts of palm, secure with toothpick, and slip a caper on one end of the toothpick.

Savoring wine with smoked salmon

We asked two well-respected fish smokers for their thoughts about wines that work well with smoked salmon.

✔ For cold-smoked salmon with its buttery texture, try a Semillon for a slightly less traditional pairing, suggests Des FitzGerald, owner of Ducktrap River Fish Farm in Maine. For a classic, festive pairing, choose Champagne or other sparkling wine.

✔ Because hot-smoked salmon has more pronounced flavor than cold-smoked, try a wine that's full bodied, but still relatively dry. Sauvignon Blanc, Pinot Gris, Sancerre, and Gewürztraminer, are the recommendations from Dominique and Chouchou Place, who own Gerard & Dominique Seafoods near Seattle.

Prior to smoking, seafood is salted, either with salt applied directly to the fish or with a salt and water solution. Salting removes some moisture from the flesh and leaves it receptive to absorbing flavors. Herbs and spices, sugar, spirits, and *woods* (the woods used in the smoking process) contribute to the personality of the fish.

Just as single-malt scotch lovers or wine lovers debate the flavors that different woods impart to their beverage of choice, devoted fish smokers debate the merits of different types of hardwoods. Some prefer oak, maple, hickory, juniper, and alder; others believe that cherry, apple, pear, button-wood, or sea grape produce even more flavorful smoke. Still others blend woods for their signature seafood. Whichever wood is chosen, it's burned as dust, chips, or logs.

You can find two types of smoked seafood: cold smoked and hot smoked.

✔ **Cold-smoked** seafood is smoked gently and slowly, so it isn't actually cooked during smoking. Cold smoking gives fish and shellfish a delicately smoky flavor and transforms the flesh to a silky, smooth texture. It is often sold sliced. Scottish-, Norwegian-, and European-style smoked salmon are generally cold-smoked. Their flavors vary because of the spices, smoking woods, and techniques used.

✔ **Hot-smoked** seafood is smoked over a higher heat, for a shorter time, and cooks as it smokes. Hot smoking gives fish and shellfish a firm, moist, and chewy (but tender) texture, and rich, rounded smoky flavor. The top surface of the fish is burnished golden brown. Hot-smoked fish flakes into nice big chunks, but also slices well with a serrated or electric knife. Salmon may be referred to as northwest- or Alaskan-style, or in the United States as *kippered* (even though a true European kippered fish is cold-smoked).

CLOCKWISE FROM UPPER LEFT: Kiwifruit "Fuzzy Logic" Salsa, Fiesta Shrimp Salsa, Sablefish with Strawberry Balsamic Sauce, Roasted Red-Pepper Velvet, Sunshine Salsa

CLOCKWISE FROM LOWER LEFT: **Costa Rican Tilapia, Cantonese Whole Steamed Fish, Big Fish Swallows the Little Fish, Macho Nachos, Asian Noodle Bowl with Salmon**

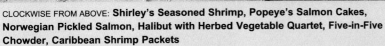

CLOCKWISE FROM ABOVE: **Shirley's Seasoned Shrimp, Popeye's Salmon Cakes, Norwegian Pickled Salmon, Halibut with Herbed Vegetable Quartet, Five-in-Five Chowder, Caribbean Shrimp Packets**

ABOVE: **Rosemary's Christmas Calamari; Shrimp with Lemon, Sun-Dried Tomato, and Goat Cheese Dip; Creamy Oyster Shooters; Layered Southwestern Dip with Surimi; Decadent "Retro" Crab Spread; Mussels Royale**

FAR LEFT, TOP TO BOTTOM: **Cool Summer White Bean Soup with Shrimp Sunburst, Smoked Salmon Pinwheels with Two Surprises, Cornmeal-Coated Snapper with Fresh Corn Salsa**
RIGHT, TOP TO BOTTOM: **Black Olive Tapenade-Topped Salmon, Steamed Salmon Pockets with Emerald Sauce, Sautéed Scallops with Grapefruit and Arugula**

CLOCKWISE FROM LOWER LEFT: **Tarragon Salmon Kebabs, Grilled Jerk Tuna on Focaccia, Volcano Salmon and Couscous Salad, Middle Eastern Grilled Catfish Fingers, Grilled or Broiled Whitefish in Foil Boats, Grilled Lobster with Tropical Vinaigrette, Texas-Style Bacon-Wrapped Barbecue Shrimp**

Backyard Lobster and Clam Bake

Smoked seafood needs to be refrigerated, like any other perishable seafood, because modern smoking techniques alone don't preserve fish. If you buy smoked fish that's vacuum packed, you can refrigerate the package, unopened, for 10 to 12 days (or until the "best by" date on a package). After it's opened, the fish keeps for about 5 days, as does smoked fish that you buy unpackaged from the deli or prepared-food case.

Smoked seafood can be the star of your meals, whether you cast it in the lead or a supporting role.

- **The lead role:** Present smoked fish simply, on a large platter, surrounded with plain crackers or mini breads. Add lemon wedges, a dish of capers, sour cream, plain or spiked with horseradish, and a Scandinavian-style mustard dill sauce.

- **The big supporter:** Stretch the tastes of smoked seafood by pairing it with other foods.

  - Tacos, quesadillas, or fajitas

  - Soups and chowders — creamy, tomato, or corn

  - Sour cream, crème fraiche, yogurt, or cream cheese

  - Crisp potato hash

  - Hearts-of-palm or asparagus roll-ups

  - Pasta, salads, and bagels

If you have a side of smoked salmon that you're not eating in one frenzy, here's what we suggest: Divide the salmon into 3 or 4 big portions and store each in a resealable plastic bag. Rather than hauling out a whole side every time you want a snack, individual packages are easy to handle and stay cold. If you freeze smoked fish as soon as you bring it home (wrapping it well), you can keep it about 2 months. We suggest that you eat it sooner, because the taste and texture will be nicer.

It's a box, it's a pouch, it's a can!

Have you ever seen smoked salmon in a decorative box or in a foil pouch? It's sold at room temperature and not refrigerated. Think of the thin, foil pouch as a can in disguise. The salmon is cooked in the *retort* pouch just like seafood is cooked in a can, and like a can, it may be safely held at room temperature. Before you purchase foil-packed fish, check the package for tight, firm seals with no cracks or pinpricks. After it's opened, refrigerate as you do other smoked seafoods.

Well-preserved relations

What's the difference between lox and nova? Gravlax and jerky? It's a question of mastering the art of salting, smoking, seasoning — and of science. Table 10-1 shows you how.

Table 10-1 Who's Who in World of Smoked and Cured Salmon	
Name	**Description**
Lox (an Americanization of German *lachs* or Scandinavian *lax*, salmon)	Traditionally, lox was never smoked. Salmon was salted in barrels and shipped from the Pacific northwest to New York for the deli trade. Today, lox has come to mean almost any lightly smoked, mild-cured salmon.
Nova	Nova is salmon that's cold-smoked, and traditionally made with Atlantic salmon from Nova Scotia, hence the name *Nova*.
Gravlax (GRAHV-lahks)	A Scandinavian specialty that's cured, not smoked. Raw salmon is buried in salt, sugar, pepper, and fresh dill for 48 hours. Translates from Swedish as "salmon from the grave."
Salmon jerky (Indian cure salmon)	Heavily salted salmon that traditionally is cold-smoked for up to two weeks until chewy and rubbery. Popular with backpackers.

When you want to bring a hint of smoked flavor to dips, chowders, or casseroles, try liquid smoke. *Liquid smoke* is a condensate of natural smoke. Be sure to check the bottle label before purchasing — it should contain simply water and natural wood smoke concentrate — period. To use, sparingly add a drop or two of liquid smoke, mix, and let stand a few minutes to blend flavors before tasting.

Saucy fish

Think of fish sauce as the saucy way to preserve extra fish and their parts. Fish sauce is a thin brown liquid with a pungent aroma, one that you'll likely know as *nam pla* from Thailand or *nuoc mam* from Vietnam. It is made by packing small fish, including anchovies, in salt, fermenting them for 3 months or so, and drawing off the liquid.

Fish sauce is the heart and soul of southeast Asian cuisine, and is used the way Americans use salt, to add flavor and intensify the tastes of other ingredients. Use fish sauce judiciously. It may take you a while to grow accustomed to its taste.

Fish sauce isn't limited to the Far East. The Egyptians, Greeks, and Romans all developed similar fish sauces. The Romans were particularly thrifty, and made their fish sauce, called *garum*, with fish guts, rather than whole fish.

Fantastical Fish Eggs

What do peanuts, popcorn, and caviar have in common? They're all salty — and they're great with beer. (At the turn of the century, saloons in the western United States served American caviar free to promote the sale of beer.) Generically, caviar refers to fish eggs (or *roe*) that are salted. Both freshwater and saltwater fish are used to make caviar, with sturgeon caviar the most expensive and lumpfish (the red and black caviar packed in tiny jars) among the least costly.

Salting it away

Salting the eggs preserves them, draws out moisture, and develops flavor. In general, caviar should have whole, uncrushed eggs (some liken the size of caviar to grains, such as couscous), be shiny and glistening, and have no fish odor.

Will the true caviar please stand up?

For centuries, the Soviet Union and Iran set the world standard for caviar quality with Caspian Sea sturgeon. (The break-up of the Soviet Union has put Russian sturgeon fisheries and future of Caspian caviar in question with the lack of strict central oversight of the industry.) Three species of sturgeon may be called true caviar: beluga, osetra, and sevruga. The color of the eggs is generally not a quality-determining factor.

- **Beluga** (beh-LOO-ga): Glossy eggs or *grains* slightly larger than couscous ($\frac{1}{16}$ inch); creamy, rich mild taste; and delicate fine skin, that squishes like liquid butter, rather than "pops" when eaten. Silvery to charcoal gray.

- **Osetra** (o-SEH-tra): Nutty, mildly fruity taste; slightly chewy bite that pops. Brownish-gray. Also called ossetra and oscietra.

- **Sevruga** (seh-VROO-ga): Full sea-like flavor, with firm chewy pop; smallest of the three sturgeon.

When you see the word "caviar" used by itself in the United States, it refers to sturgeon roe. All other roe sold in the United States must include the name of the fish, such as "salmon caviar" or "whitefish caviar." Other caviars you find include lumpfish, flying fish, herring, trout, mullet, and paddlefish.

Caviar basics

All fish eggs are encased in a skein or sac. Most roe, such as sturgeon, salmon, and lumpfish, is separated from the sac before salting; some may be salted in the sac, including Pacific herring and mullet. To make caviar, the roe is rubbed over a screen to separate it from membranes, then washed, salted, and packed. Caviar made from fish other than sturgeon is usually pasteurized in jars. After opening, refrigerate and use within several days.

Sturgeon caviar is traditionally packed in small tins that are coated inside to avoid the transfer of any metallic flavor, and then vacuum sealed. (This is the reason you should break out your pearl spoons, rather than metal ones, for really good caviar.) Sturgeon caviar is not heat-processed or pasteurized, and must be kept cold. Stored in a sealed tin in the coldest part of the refrigerator (or on ice), the caviar will keep about 4 weeks. After it's opened, use within 48 hours.

If you see the word *malossal* on a caviar label it means "little salt" in Russian. This means the caviar has been lightly salted, and thus, is supposed to be high quality.

You can stretch the taste and cost of caviar by pairing it with:

- Waves of sour cream in a margarita glass
- Mini-potatoes or mushroom caps filled with crème fraîche
- Crab-stuffed avocado
- Steamed rice, mashed potatoes, pasta, or scrambled eggs
- The appetizer suggested in the "Smoked salmon and hearts-of-palm pinwheels" sidebar, earlier in this chapter

Made in America

In the last half of the 1800s, the United States had thriving caviar industries: white sturgeon in California and the Pacific northwest, Atlantic sturgeon on the east coast, and lake sturgeon in the Great Lakes region. Overfishing in the late 1800s wiped out most of the sturgeon. Currently the United States produces Great Lakes caviars from a variety of fish, salmon caviar, and regional sturgeon (and other fish) caviars.

- **Great Lakes caviar:** Whitefish roe is a pale-golden color and sparkles like sunshine, with a small delicate, crunchy egg. Herring and chub roes are pale melon-orange with a less crunchy texture. Trout roe is light melon-golden with a delicate taste and juicy bite.

- **Salmon caviar:** Salmon roe is the largest of all caviars, with each egg about ¼-inch diameter. Widely used in sushi bars, salmon roe (or *ikura*) is bright orange-colored, translucent, and has a juicy pop when you bite into it. The Japanese, who consume huge quantities of salmon caviar, say that chum salmon eggs make the best salmon caviar. Japan is the main market for United States and Canadian salmon caviar production. (The word *ikura* is derived from Russian and not from Japanese, as we had assumed.)

- **Regional caviars:** There is limited production of shovelnose sturgeon caviar (*hackleback*) from the Mississippi River system, of wild white sturgeon caviar in pockets along the east coast, and of farmed white sturgeon in California. You can also find caviar from two fish that are as primitive biologically as sturgeon, but unrelated: the bowfin (also called *choupique*) from Louisiana's bayous and the paddlefish (*spoonbill*) from the Tennessee River Basin and Midwest rivers.

Pressed caviar on a label refers to a process whereby broken caviar eggs are squeezed to a jam-like paste, and then packed in tins as caviar. Pressed caviar has an intense flavor. It's still expensive, but some view pressed caviar as a good value.

Roe-ing away

Other countries, including Iceland, Japan, Spain, and Italy, preserve fish eggs or roe, not only as separate eggs and whole sacs, but also by drying, pressing, or smoking.

Lumpfish caviar

Lumpfish roe is the popular black or bright red caviar that has a small, compact, chewy roe; fairly fishy taste; and firm, crunchy texture. Lumpfish are caught in the northern waters of Iceland, Canada, and Scandinavia.

Flying fish caviar

Widely used as a garnish in sushi bars, the tiny fluorescent-orange roe from the flying fish has a crispy, firm crunch. Flying fish roe (*tobiko* in Japanese) is naturally yellowish-white, so the color is artificial. Look for *tobiko* (toe-BEE-ko) in a range of colors from pale green (flavored with *wasabi*, Japanese horseradish) to bright red and spiced with chiles.

Kazunoko

Pacific herring roe is a pale golden-yellow, dense oval skein of eggs that runs in the 2-inch-long range. Kazunoko (ka-zoo-NO-ko) is popular as sushi. Also farmed on strips of seaweed; crunchy and briny for people who are into serious ocean tastes.

Sea urchin

Sea urchin, or *uni,* is a delicacy in Japan (and elsewhere), where it is usually eaten raw in sushi. Sea urchin is a 1- to 2-inch oval skein with a pumpkin-orange flesh, buttery rich texture, and iodiney, briny flavor with a fruity hint of mango. Although urchin is called sea urchin "roe," technically it's not fish eggs, but the reproductive organ of either a male or female urchin.

Mediterranean — and north

Fish roes of these regions include cod roe from Norway and the North Sea, and tuna and mullet roes (or *botargo*) from the Mediterranean, among others. The roes are salted, dried, smoked, or pressed as whole roe or into cakes. The preserved roes are hard and firm, and may be used in dishes, such as the creamy Greek dip *taramasalata,* sliced and served on buttered bread, or shaved (like Parmesan cheese) into pasta.

Part IV
Making the Most of Your Catch

The 5th Wave   By Rich Tennant

"Someone should tell Phil he's sautéing three of my lures in that pan of onions and garlic."

In this part . . .

We're passionate about cooking and eating fish, so we enthusiastically encourage you to fit fish into your menu — anywhere. In this part, we give you recipes for sensational seafood for noshing and nibbling. For the main event, take your choice of a multitude of fish and shellfish. In addition, savor seafood in casual salads, soups, and sandwiches, or top with one of the sassy sauces or salsas. Finally, in this part, we offer you recipes to get your kids enthused about fish.

Chapter 11

Starring Snacks and Appetizers

. . . .

In This Chapter

▶ Creating the party spirit

▶ Avoiding party frenzy with make-ahead recipes

▶ Whetting appetites with exotic seafood

. . . .

*W*hen your party begins with seafood appetizers, you're guaranteed happy guests and lip-smacking results. Take your pick from this bevy of seaworthy beginnings — whether you're dining solo, impressing a special someone, or hosting the entire office staff. Avoid party planning frenzy and make almost any of these dishes in advance.

Although the recipes in this chapter are intended as starters, we confess that some of our best parties both start and end right here. We're big on the casual approach to nibbling and noshing, often inviting our guests to help us cook. If you prefer a more conventional approach to entertaining, we hope you delight in our make-ahead recipes and those you create without any cooking whatsoever.

Recipes in This Chapter

▶ Beer-Spiked Shrimp Peel

▶ Rich's Grilled Clams

▶ Texas-Style Bacon-Wrapped Barbecue Shrimp

▶ Layered Southwestern Dip with Surimi

▶ Chunky Tuna and Corn Cakes

▶ Swordfish Escovitch

▶ Smoked Salmon Pinwheels with Two Surprises

▶ Marinated Artichoke, Herring, and Olive Antipasto

▶ Creamy Oyster Shooters

▶ Decadent "Retro" Crab Spread

▶ Calamari Martini with Pickled Onions

▶ Mussels Royale

▶ Rosemary's Christmas Calamari

Letting Off Steam

Get everyone into the party spirit and gather 'round the pot. For our Beer-Spiked Shrimp Peel, enlist a guest to do the honors and preside over the steaming brew that cooks shrimp to perfection in no time flat. When weather permits, move the group outside to the picnic table and fire up the grill for a clam feast. The second recipe in this section features an innovative, two-step, clam-steaming technique. Don't be surprised if your guests pluck the clams directly from the pan.

Beer-Spiked Shrimp Peel

In upstate New York, peel 'n' eat shrimp parties are a popular pastime. Roll up your shirt sleeves and dig in. Spread newspapers on the kitchen table, grab a tall stack of paper napkins, and start the party. The perfect host steams the shrimp in small batches and rightfully expects eaters to interrupt their slurping long enough to cheer the chef each time a platter of replenishments comes to the table. Sufficiently flavorful by themselves for most eaters, these shrimp don't require further enhancements. Embellishments for insatiable flavor cravers would be a splash of malt vinegar, a squeeze of lemon, or a dash of Old Bay Seasoning or chili powder.

Preparation time: *10 minutes*

Cooking time: *5 minutes*

Steeping time: *3 to 5 minutes*

Yield: *2 to 4 servings*

24 ounces full-flavored beer	*½ teaspoon white pepper*
1 tablespoon minced garlic	*1 teaspoon fennel seeds (optional)*
1 teaspoon red pepper flakes	*1 pound raw, shell-on, medium (41/50 per pound) or large shrimp (31/35 count)*
¾ teaspoon kosher salt	

1 In a large pot, bring the beer, garlic, red pepper flakes, salt, white pepper, and fennel seeds to a boil, stirring to reduce foam. Cover, reduce heat to medium, and simmer for 3 minutes to blend the flavors. If you have time, slit the shrimp shell down the back, leaving the shell intact, so the shrimp absorb more flavor from the cooking liquid.

2 Stir the shrimp into the beer and cook, uncovered, for 1 to 2 minutes. Remove the pan from the heat, cover, and let stand 3 to 5 minutes until the center of the shrimp has turned white. Drain shrimp and place in a serving bowl. Pass lots of napkins.

Vary It! When Saint Patrick's Day rolls around, go for the green. Cook your shrimp in Irish beer and serve with three green sauces presented in green pepper cups. Need ideas for sauces? See Chapter 15 for the Tangy Cilantro Topper, Tomatillo Salsa, and Dill Pesto with Asian Notes; Chapter 5 for a Remoulade Sauce.

Easy to peel shrimp, which still have the shell on but are slit down the back, make quick work of this recipe. For subsequent batches, simply reuse the broth, adding additional beer or water as necessary.

Rich's Grilled Clams

This sure-fire recipe is a favorite of our friends Rich Catanzaro (the Director of Seafood Marketing for HEB Grocery Company in Texas) and Chad Ballard and Tim Parsons (the guys who grow the clams at Cherrystone Aqua Farms in Virginia). In this two-part method, jumpstart the cooking by placing the clams directly on the grill. Finish cooking the clams in garlic-studded liquid to keep them moist and tender.

Preparation time: *15 minutes*

Cooking time: *5 to 15 minutes*

Yield: *6 to 8 servings*

6 dozen littleneck clams, 6 to 7 pounds (of uniform size)

4 to 5 cups water

2 teaspoons kosher salt

4 teaspoons minced garlic

2 teaspoons olive oil

1 teaspoon red pepper flakes

2 lemons, cut into wedges

Crusty Italian bread

1 Quickly rinse clams under cold running water and check that shells are tightly closed. (Check out Chapter 8 for information about checking shellfish.) Prepare a hot fire in a charcoal or gas grill.

2 As the grill heats, make the seasoning liquid in a large, heavy, metal pan: Mix 4 cups of the water, salt, garlic, oil, and red pepper flakes. Place the pan on grill and heat until the liquid is hot, then move pan to one side of the grill, freeing the main area for grilling clams.

3 For ease of handling, grill clams 18 at a time. Place clams in a single layer directly on grill. Cook until shells begin to open and juices bubble out, 1 to 2 minutes. With tongs, lift clams carefully to minimize spilling juices and place them in the metal pan to finish cooking. Clams steam more evenly in a single layer.

4 Grill the remaining clams and keep adding to the pan. The clams are cooked when the shells fully open; it takes from 5 to 15 minutes to steam the clams, depending on the heat distribution. If the seasoning liquid evaporates, add a bit of water. If the pan becomes too crowded, remove some clams with juice and keep warm. (Or offer to your hungry guests who are likely hovering around the grill!) Serve the clams and juice in bowls. Pass the lemon wedges and crusty bread.

Avoid pan-demonium when all your pans are shiny bright. Nest two disposable foil pans for a sturdy substitute, or mold a big piece of heavy-duty foil to cover the bottom of a pan that you don't want stained with grill flare-ups.

Warm Up Your Party with Chiles

Chiles are hot these days, and we offer you recipes to warm up your next party. You decide the degree of heat.

- **Jalapeños and Texas-style shrimp:** Your party will be a sizzling success when you grill shrimp with a zesty surprise inside. Tuck a narrow ribbon of jalapeño inside each shrimp before wrapping in a luscious bacon spiral. An unbeatable combination! Have no fear: The chile provides a pleasant zip, but the overall effect is definitely not mouth-scorching.

- **Mild green chiles and southwest surimi dip:** We add crab-flavored surimi to create a seafood version of this familiar dip. Ribboned layers of Tex-Mex flavors stack up to a special make-ahead, no-cooking-required, party appetizer. When you're not throwing the party, offer to bring this crowd-pleasing dish to a friend's.

- **Smoky chipotle chiles and tuna cakes:** Discover the rich, fragrant tastes of *chipotle chiles* (jalapeños that are dried and smoked) in pretty, corn-speckled cakes.

- **Habaneros and swordfish escovitch:** Bring a tropical beat to your party with the Caribbean's signature chile. The habanero is guaranteed to fire up your party goers' spirits.

While handling chiles, don't touch your face or eyes (or other sensitive body parts) until you've washed your hands thoroughly to remove fiery volatile oils. They can sometimes cause a nasty sting. If you have sensitive skin, wear food-safe, disposable gloves while preparing chiles. Discard the gloves before moving on to other prep steps.

Texas-Style Bacon-Wrapped Barbecue Shrimp

Texans Shirley and Harley Goerlitz travel the national barbecue circuit beating competitors from coast to coast with their succulent barbecued ribs and pork. Their Texas-style shrimp are a sure winner, too. Make lots. Your guests will devour these decadent tastes in a flash. Use a big shrimp for this recipe because the bacon needs time to crisp without overcooking the shrimp. Check out Figure 11-1 or the photo of the shrimp on the grill in the color section near the center of the book — both can help you wrap this dish up in a flash.

Preparation time: 40 minutes

Cooking time: 5 minutes

Yield: 6 to 8 servings

1 pound raw, shell-on, extra-large shrimp (26/30 per pound)

5 fresh hot chiles, such as jalapeños

13 to 15 strips thin-sliced bacon (about ¾ pound)

3 to 4 tablespoons barbecue seasoning, barbecue rub, or chili powder

2 lemons, halved

1 Brush the grill grid with oil and prepare a medium-hot fire in a charcoal or gas grill. As the grill heats, peel shrimp and butterfly. Core, seed, and devein hot chiles and cut lengthwise into ¼-inch wide strips.

2 Cut each strip of bacon in half crosswise. You need ½ piece of bacon for each shrimp. (To reduce fat, you may want to trim and discard excess fat from outer edges of bacon strips.)

3 Place the shrimp butterflied side up and sprinkle with about ⅛ to ¼ teaspoon barbecue seasoning. Place a strip of hot chile down the center of the shrimp and close shrimp over chile. Start at one end of the shrimp and wrap bacon around the length of the shrimp. (You don't have to secure the bacon with a toothpick; as the bacon cooks, it seals the shrimp together.) Repeat with the rest of the shrimp.

4 Just before cooking, squeeze the juice from 1 lemon over shrimp. Add shrimp to the grill, close the grill cover, and grill shrimp, until crispy brown, about 3 minutes. Turn shrimp, drizzle with juice from the second lemon and grill until browned and shrimp are cooked through, about 2 minutes. Serve hot.

Texas-Style, Bacon-Wrapped BBQ Shrimp

Peel, devein and butterfly the shrimp.

Place shrimp butterflied side up, sprinkle with seasoning + place a ¼" strip of jalapeño down the center.

Close shrimp.

Start at one end and wrap the bacon around the length of the shrimp!

Ready to grill!

Figure 11-1: Wrapping shrimp with bacon.

If you prefer to flip all of the shrimp at once, try our friend Margie Norris's trick. Place the shrimp in a flat wire fish or hot dog basket, grill and turn — easy does it. Or if you're more comfortable grilling seafood with a grill topper, that works fine as well.

Surimi is a shellfish look-alike that's made from finfish, usually white-fleshed Alaskan pollock. The fish is minced and mixed with egg whites, spices, and sometimes a bit of crab. Surimi (or imitation crab) is formed into crab-like flakes or chunks. The meat is white with red streaks, and is tender and slightly chewy. Use surimi in fajitas, tacos, salads, pasta, or sushi as an inexpensive shellfish option, but add it at the end of the cooking time to keep it from toughening. Surimi is a staple in Japanese cuisine.

Layered Southwestern Dip with Surimi

The profusion of layers in this hearty recipe stacks up to one tall success. There are lots of variations on this colorful theme, but the addition of surimi takes it to a new dimension. Take a peek at this layered look in the color photo section near the middle of this book. Try blue corn tortilla chips and watch your friends dive into — and discover — the tastes of the southwestern United States.

Preparation time: *30 minutes*

Yield: *8 servings*

1 can (16 ounces) nonfat refried beans	*½ teaspoon chili powder*
1 can (4 ounces) chopped mild green chiles, undrained	*½ teaspoon kosher salt*
2 tablespoons sour cream	*½ teaspoon minced fresh garlic*
1 tablespoon plus 1 teaspoon taco seasoning mix or chili powder	*1 can (2¼ ounces) sliced black olives, drained*
6 to 8 ounces surimi, divided	*½ cup seeded, chopped tomato*
1 ripe avocado	*½ cup cooked corn or thawed, frozen corn*
1 tablespoon fresh lime juice	*¼ to ½ cup shredded cheddar cheese*
1 tablespoon mayonnaise	*2 tablespoons thinly sliced green onion tops*
½ teaspoon Worcestershire sauce	*Tortilla chips*

1 In a medium bowl, mix together the beans, green chilies, sour cream, and taco seasoning. For the base layer, spread bean mixture in an 8-inch circle on a serving platter. Shred surimi with fingers. Sprinkle half the surimi over the beans.

2 Peel, pit, and coarsely chop the avocado into a small bowl. Add the lime juice, mayonnaise, Worcestershire sauce, chili powder, salt, and garlic; mash with a fork until almost smooth. Spread avocado mixture over surimi.

3 Sprinkle ⅔ of the remaining surimi over the avocado layer; reserve remainder to garnish dip. Top surimi with the olives, tomato, corn, cheese, onion tops, and reserved surimi.

4 Cover dip and refrigerate until ready to serve, up to 2 hours. Bring to room temperature, about 15 minutes before serving. To serve, dip in or spoon onto tortilla chips.

Vary It! Crabmeat or cooked salad shrimp are tasty substitutes for the surimi. Add extra spicy taste and serve the dip with Chipotle Aïoli Sauce in Chapter 15.

Look for ready-made guacamole in the refrigerated case or freezer section of your supermarket (you need about ½ cup of guacamole to replace 1 avocado).

Chunky Tuna and Corn Cakes

Chock full of our favorite smoky chipotle chiles, these hearty cakes make a lip-smacking snack, appetizer, or first course (in our warped way, we like them as leftovers for breakfast, too, because they reheat beautifully in the microwave). Double dip the cakes in a dynamic duo of sauces, such as Roasted Red-Pepper Velvet and Tomatillo Salsa, both in Chapter 15.

Preparation time: *40 minutes*

Cooking time: *6 minutes*

Yield: *8 snack or first course servings (eight 2-inch cakes)*

½ cup sour cream

½ cup cooked corn or thawed, frozen corn

½ cup minced fresh cilantro or parsley leaves (1 small bunch)

¼ cup finely chopped red bell pepper

2 teaspoons chili powder

½ teaspoon kosher salt

1 chipotle chile (canned in adobo sauce), undrained and minced

1 pound tuna steak or loin

¼ cup dry bread crumbs

1 to 2 tablespoons vegetable oil

1 In a medium bowl, mix sour cream, corn, cilantro, red pepper, chili powder, salt, and chipotle chile. Let stand to blend flavors while dicing tuna.

(continued)

2 To more easily dice tuna: Cut the steaks into ¼-inch thick slices, lengthwise into ¼-inch strips, and then across into ¼-inch dice.

3 Stir tuna and bread crumbs into sour cream mixture until well mixed. Moisten hands with water or spray with corn oil; form tuna mixture into eight 2-inch cakes, about ½-inch thick. Refrigerate for 30 minutes to let bread crumbs absorb moisture and cakes firm.

4 Preheat oven to 200°. Cook cakes in two batches to prevent overcrowding. Add 1 tablespoon oil to a large, heavy skillet and heat over medium high heat until a drop of water sizzles when added to the oil, about 4 minutes. Add tuna cakes to skillet, reduce heat to medium, and cook 3 minutes until the bottom is browned; loosen cakes part way through cooking. Turn cakes and cook 3 more minutes until cakes are firm but slightly springy and browned on the bottom. Keep warm in a single layer in the oven. Scrape browned bits from skillet before cooking remaining cakes.

5 Serve with your favorite sauce.

Vary It! You can easily transform the cakes into a first course. On each plate, fan several avocado and tomato slices, place a tuna cake at the base of the fan, and top the cake with mixed greens. Drizzle with the Toasted Pine Nut and Shallot Vinaigrette in Chapter 15. Instead of tuna, try swordfish, salmon, mahimahi, grouper, or shark.

Not sure just where chipotles fit into the chile clan? Refer to the Avocado Chipotle-Glazed Salmon recipe, in Chapter 6. ***Hint:*** It's a value-added jalapeño.

Swordfish Escovitch

In many of our recipes, we identify where preparations "may be made ahead to this point," but you certainly don't have to. Here, however, is a recipe that definitely does taste best when you make it a day ahead. Get a head-start on your next party with our Caribbean-inspired swordfish pickled with peppers and onions. It's great for a picnic, your buffet table, or a first course. Instead of marinating raw fish, you pour a hot marinade over almost-cooked swordfish to pickle it and finish the cooking. If you're not planning a party, don't despair. Pickling makes this recipe an especially good keeper so you can nibble on great tastes for several days.

Preparation time: *45 minutes*

Cooking time: *20 minutes*

Yield: *8 first course servings*

1½ pounds swordfish steaks

½ pound cucumbers

½ cup white wine vinegar

½ cup dry sherry

¾ teaspoon kosher salt

¾ teaspoon freshly ground black pepper

1 tablespoon whole allspice

1 tablespoon minced fresh thyme or 1 teaspoon dried thyme leaves

1 to 1½ teaspoons minced fresh hot chiles, or ½ teaspoon habanero, pequin, or red pepper flakes

12 queen size pimento-stuffed olives, sliced

8 quarter-size slices ginger, unpeeled

⅓ cup flour

1 tablespoon plus 1 teaspoon olive oil

1 medium onion, halved and thinly sliced

1 red bell pepper, cored, seeded, and thinly sliced

1 orange or green bell pepper, cored, seeded, and thinly sliced

4 large garlic cloves, minced

1 Rinse the swordfish with cold water and pat dry with paper towels. Remove skin and cut into 8 portions; set aside.

2 Peel the cucumbers, leaving four thin strips of skin for color contrast. Halve cucumbers lengthwise and scoop out the seeds; slice on the diagonal into ⅛-inch thick half moons.

3 Combine the pickling solution ingredients: In a small bowl, stir together the vinegar, sherry, ½ teaspoon each salt and pepper, allspice, thyme, chiles, olives, and ginger.

4 Mix the flour and remaining ¼ teaspoon each salt and pepper on a dinner plate. In a large, heavy skillet, heat 1 tablespoon oil on medium heat until hot, 3 to 4 minutes. While the oil heats, lightly coat the fish on both sides with flour, carefully shaking fish to remove excess flour. Sauté the swordfish until golden brown, about 4 minutes, shaking pan to prevent sticking. Turn fish and sauté until the flesh just turns opaque, about 2 minutes, but is still slightly underdone (if desired, cut a slit into the side of swordfish to check doneness). Place the swordfish in a shallow dish; cover to keep warm. (If your skillet is small, cook the swordfish in two batches.) Scrape the skillet and wipe dry with paper towels.

5 In the same skillet, heat the remaining 1 teaspoon oil on medium-high heat. Add the onions and sauté, partly covered, until lightly colored and softened, about 3 minutes, stirring. Add the cucumbers, peppers, and garlic; sauté partly covered until softened, about 5 minutes, stirring. Reduce heat to medium-low and pour the vinegar mixture over the vegetables. Cover and cook until marinade is hot and to blend flavors, about 5 minutes.

6 Pour the hot marinade over the fish and cover; refrigerate overnight. Serve the swordfish room temperature or warmed. (Discard ginger before serving and remind guests that whole allspice berries, like whole peppercorns, are too pungent to eat.)

Vary It! Try Spanish mackerel, mahimahi, tuna, or shark instead of swordfish.

Kitchen Artistry: No Cooking Required

To overcome any residual fears that you may have about ruining seafood by overcooking, just don't cook it at all! Roll, mix, and stir three more delicious appetizers into your party repertoire. Create your edible art in advance, and energize your party spirit.

Smoked Salmon Pinwheels with Two Surprises

Traditional cold-smoked salmon may be familiar as lox, but hot-smoked salmon can be a surprising new taste treat. Hot-smoked salmon has a firm, flaky texture (similar to canned salmon) and a hearty, smoky taste. Combine its robust personality with silky cream cheese for seductive spreads and dips. Double the surprise and add crunchy red lumpfish caviar to the spread. Our testers tell us that for a party you should probably double the recipe: After four minutes, the pinwheels vanished. You can find more smoky information in Chapter 10 — and you can find an enticing photo of these pinwheels in the color photo section near the middle of this book.

Preparation time: *30 minutes*

Yield: *6 servings*

3 ounces plain or seasoned hot-smoked salmon

½ cup cream cheese, softened

2 tablespoons plain, nonfat yogurt

3 to 5 teaspoons red lumpfish caviar, divided

Tabasco sauce to taste

Four 8- to 10-inch spinach, jalapeño, or sun-dried tomato and basil tortillas

2 to 3 ounces fresh spinach, stems removed, or baby mixed greens

1 On a cutting board, mash half the salmon with a fork; break remaining salmon into chunks. In a small bowl, stir cream cheese and yogurt together until the consistency of heavy mayonnaise. Stir in the mashed salmon, 1 tablespoon caviar, and Tabasco sauce. Add salmon chunks and carefully blend.

2 Spread about 3 tablespoons of the smoked salmon mixture in a thin layer over tortilla to within ½-inch of the edge. Cover tortilla with ¼ of the spinach leaves and press leaves lightly onto spread (keep leaves about 2-inches from the edge you roll towards so they won't spurt out as you roll). Roll tortilla jellyroll style and press edge to seal; scrape extra spread that may squeeze out when rolled. Repeat with remaining tortillas, smoked salmon spread, and spinach to make 4 rolls.

3 Wrap tortilla rolls (seam side down) tightly in plastic wrap and refrigerate 2 hours or overnight. To serve, slice rolls on the diagonal with a serrated knife into ¾-inch wide pieces. You'll get about 7 slices from an 8-inch tortilla (save the jagged end pieces for a snack). Serve the pinwheels at room temperature with the cut side up. Top each pinwheel with a bit of the remaining caviar, if desired.

Vary It! When hot-smoked salmon isn't readily available, canned red salmon and liquid smoke are more than acceptable "stand-ins." Substitute ½ can (7½ ounces) red salmon, drained, and ½ teaspoon liquid smoke. For either version, wasabi-flavored flying fish roe is dynamite stirred into this spread. For super zing, replace spinach leaves with arugula.

Serve the smoked salmon mixture (Step 1) in a colorful bowl and pass water wafers or melba toast rounds. Or for an easy lunch, cut a tortilla in half, spoon on salmon mixture, add greens, and wrap into a cone.

Marinated Artichoke, Herring, and Olive Antipasto

This kaleidoscope of colors and flavors is convincing evidence, even to hardnosed math geniuses, that the whole is sometimes greater than the sum of its parts. Expect rave reviews from unexpected corners with this one. Ours came from grown-ups who unflinchingly claimed to dislike herring in any shape or form, and, equally surprisingly, from Leslie's 7- and 10-year-old nieces, Liza and Nora Bloom. Go figure kids' tastes!

Preparation time: 30 minutes

Yield: 10 servings (3 cups)

1 jar (6 ounces) marinated artichokes

1 jar (12 ounces) herring bits in wine

⅓ cup finely chopped red onion

⅓ cup finely diced green bell pepper

⅓ cup finely diced red bell pepper

1 can (4 ounces) chopped black olives, drained

1 cup bottled chili sauce

1½ tablespoons fresh lemon juice

2 teaspoons dried oregano leaves

½ teaspoon Worcestershire sauce

4 to 6 dashes Tabasco sauce (optional)

Baguette toasts, melba toast rounds, or Belgian endive leaves

(continued)

1 For the antipasto, drain artichokes and finely chop. Drain herring and discard liquid and onions. Trim and discard skinny edges of herring bits. Cut herring into ¼- by ½-inch rectangles. In a medium bowl, combine the artichokes, herring, onion, green and red peppers, and black olives.

2 For the chili herb sauce, in a medium bowl, combine the chili sauce, lemon juice, oregano, Worcestershire sauce, and Tabasco sauce. Stir the antipasto ingredients into the sauce. You can refrigerate the antipasto 1 to 2 days before using.

3 To serve, spoon antipasto onto toasts or into Belgian endive leaves.

Creamy Oyster Shooters

Slurp oysters from a shot glass, topped with a sensuous Creole mustard cream. If you're so inclined, add a splash of pepper-spiked vodka and let the good times roll. Our friends Ti Martin and Lally Brennan introduced us to these seductive snacks at one of their family restaurants, the Palace Café in New Orleans. Imagine you're in the Big Easy, and embrace the city's love affair with wretched excess. Don't miss the photo of this and other party dishes in the color photo section near the center of this book.

Preparation time: *10 minutes*

Standing time: *1 hour*

Yield: *2 to 3 servings*

½ cup mayonnaise

2 tablespoons Creole mustard or course-ground mustard

2 tablespoons red wine vinegar

1 tablespoon minced shallot

½ to 1 teaspoon kosher salt

1 teaspoon freshly ground black pepper

8 to 9 oysters, shucked, drained

Dash of Tabasco sauce

French bread (optional)

Whisk together the mayonnaise, mustard, vinegar, shallot, salt, and pepper. Refrigerate the mustard cream for 1 hour to blend flavors. Put each oyster into a shot glass (or on the oyster shell) and add about 1½ tablespoons of mustard cream. Top with a dash of Tabasco sauce. Slurp, enjoy, and sop up the extra sauce with French bread.

A Seafood "Retro"-spective . . .

Containing menus and venues galore, *Cocktail Parties For Dummies,* by Jaymz Bee (IDG Books Worldwide, Inc.) confirms that the cocktail party (with or without alcoholic beverages) is making a comeback. Unabashedly, we suggest you bring back one of the most rich-tasting, calorie-laden appetizers that has ever touched our lips. For this indulgence, don't even think about not using the real things: real crab (not surimi) and real full-fat cream cheese.

Dive into the martini resurgence — but don't sip this one. Instead, serve our calamari martini (complete with pickled onions) in a classic martini glass and savor it in style. We realize that the '80s aren't really retro, but we offer you this signature recipe from Leslie's catering days. We never cease to be amazed at the bargain prices that mussels sell for — Mussels Royale are slimming, both on your party budget and on your guests' waistlines.

Finally, enhance your holiday customs and adopt Italian traditions from Christmas past — and present. Rosemary's Christmas Calamari nicely rounds out your appetizer offerings.

Decadent "Retro" Crab Spread

If you vaguely remember Mom and Dad's cocktail parties, you may have snitched a bit of this ladies' magazine classic that soared to fame and acclaim in the '60s. Mom's may not have included vermouth or Old Bay Seasoning, ingredients that have a special affinity for crab. Double the recipe for your holiday open house. Any fresh, pasteurized, or canned crabmeat works well. Leftovers (wishful thinking!) reheat beautifully in the microwave. Be sure to check out this classic dish showcased in the color photo section near the middle of the book.

Preparation time: *25 minutes*

Cooking time: *25 to 35 minutes*

Yield: *6 to 8 servings (2½ cups)*

½ pound crabmeat

¼ medium onion

12 ounces cream cheese, softened

2 tablespoons dry white vermouth

1 to 2 teaspoons Old Bay Seasoning

2 to 3 tablespoons sliced almonds (optional)

Sturdy crackers such as water wafers or Italian crostini

(continued)

1 Preheat oven to 350°. Pick through crabmeat, discarding any bits of shells. Grate onion on medium-size grater (⅜-inch holes) to make 2 tablespoons. In a large bowl, blend the cream cheese, onion, vermouth, and Old Bay Seasoning until smooth. With a spatula or large spoon, gently fold in the crab to blend well.

2 Spoon mixture into a shallow ovenproof dish or pie plate (a shallow dish gives you more browned topping and heats faster). Top with almonds, if using. Bake until the top is bubbly and lightly brown, 25 to 35 minutes. Serve warm with a spoon or elegant spreader.

For this recipe, don't go to the expense of buying deluxe lump crabmeat, because those tender hunks of crab break apart anyway when you stir the dip together. The easiest way to inspect crab for bits of shell is to gently rub the small portions between your fingers, placing cleaned crabmeat in a separate dish. See Chapter 7 for more information about crabs.

Crab is often packaged in 12-ounce containers. For that amount, combine two 8-ounce packages cream cheese, 2 tablespoons sour cream (so that you don't have to buy a third package of cream cheese), 2 to 3 teaspoons Old Bay, and 3 tablespoons vermouth. Bake as directed in Step 2.

Calamari Martini with Pickled Onions

If you love calamari (squid), you're probably always looking for an excuse to eat it. Surprise your friends and offer a calamari cocktail as a first course. Serve the marinated calamari in a martini or margarita glass, atop martini pickled onions and shredded lettuce. For a buffet, serve calamari, onions, and greens in a shallow dish and set toasted baguette slices nearby.

Preparation time: *30 minutes*

Cooking time: *30 seconds*

Yield: *4 servings*

½ cup cider vinegar

6 tablespoons water

2 tablespoons gin

½ teaspoon dry white vermouth

1 teaspoon kosher salt

1 medium white onion, peeled, halved, and sliced

Mustard Duet (see Marinated Shrimp in a Mustard Duet recipe in Chapter 5)

2 teaspoons kosher salt

1 pound cleaned calamari, including tentacles, or 1½ pounds whole calamari, cleaned (see Chapter 10 for cleaning instructions)

2 to 3 cups finely shredded iceberg lettuce

1 In a small pot, bring the vinegar, water, gin, vermouth, and 1 teaspoon of salt to a boil. Stir the onion into the vinegar mixture and remove the pot from the heat. Let stand 15 minutes to soften onion and lightly pickle; drain and set onions aside.

2 While the onion is marinating, make the Mustard Duet.

3 In a covered 4- or 5-quart pot, bring 3 quarts of water and 2 teaspoons of salt to a boil. To prepare the calamari, cut the calamari tubes into ⅛-inch rings and the triangular side flaps (trimmed from the cleaned tubes) into ¼-inch wide strips; combine with tentacles and set aside.

4 Add the calamari to the boiling water, stir, and cook until firm, but still tender, about 30 seconds. Immediately drain calamari and add warm to Mustard Duet Marinade. The marinated calamari may be made ahead to this point and refrigerated up to 8 hours. Remove calamari from the refrigerator 15 minutes before serving to brighten flavors.

5 To serve, in the following order, divide lettuce, onion, and marinated calamari among four martini glasses.

Mussels Royale

Even friends who claim they don't like mussels devour this popular appetizer from Leslie's catering days. The mussels are steamed and served on the half shell, topped with a creamy vinaigrette (called Sauce Royale) made from the steaming liquid. Check out the photo spread near the center of the book to see how to arrange the mussels. The dish is named for Leslie's fish supplier, Tom Royale, who always stayed for tastes after he delivered the mussels.

Preparation time: *45 minutes*

Cooking time: *5 minutes*

Yield: *about 40 mussels, 8 servings*

¾ cup dry sherry or white wine

¾ cup water

6 large shallots, peeled and quartered

2 pounds medium mussels, cleaned and debearded (see Chapter 8 for cleaning instructions)

Sauce Royale (see the following recipe)

1 small head escarole or iceberg lettuce, shredded (optional)

(continued)

1 To steam the mussels, combine wine, water, and shallots in a 4- to 5-quart pot. Place a vegetable steamer rack in pot, cover, and on medium-high heat bring to a boil. Place mussels on rack, cover, and steam until shells open and mussels are firm, but juicy tender, 3 to 5 minutes, shaking pot occasionally; discard any unopened mussels and transfer the cooked mussels to a bowl.

2 For each mussel, twist off one half of mussel shell and discard. Loosen mussel from the remaining half shell and leave mussel in shell. Set mussels aside while making the sauce.

3 Remove the steamer rack, discard the shallots, and keep the cooking liquid in the pot. Boil the cooking liquid on high heat, uncovered, until reduced to 6 tablespoons, about 6 minutes. Pour reduced liquid into a measuring cup, leaving any sediment in the pot; cover the cup with plastic wrap to keep the liquid warm (you get a better sauce emulsion with warm liquid). Use the reduced liquid to make the Sauce Royale (recipe follows).

4 To serve, prepare the Sauce Royale (see the following recipe). Spoon about 1 teaspoon of sauce over each mussel. Place a layer of escarole on a serving platter and arrange mussels in concentric circles around the tray (nestling the mussels on lettuce keeps them from tipping over). Serve at room temperature.

Sauce Royale

It's easier to make the sauce if you assemble the ingredients before you steam the mussels — the sauce uses the mussel-steaming liquid.

1 tablespoon red wine vinegar

1 tablespoon fresh lemon juice

1 teaspoon Dijon mustard

¾ teaspoon freshly ground black pepper

2 large shallots, peeled and quartered

2 garlic cloves, peeled

½ cup olive oil

3 tablespoons fine dry bread crumbs

5 tablespoons minced fresh parsley

1 In a measuring cup, stir together the vinegar, lemon juice, mustard, and pepper; set aside.

2 In a food processor or blender, pulse the shallots and garlic until minced. With the machine running, add the vinegar mixture, scraping the cup to get all the pepper; add the reduced mussel liquid from cooking the mussels, and pulse to blend. With the machine still running, slowly drizzle in the olive oil until lightly emulsified. Add the bread crumbs and pulse to blend. Pour the sauce into a bowl and let stand 20 minutes to allow bread crumbs to absorb liquid and sauce to thicken slightly; taste and adjust seasonings. You can make the sauce ahead to this point and refrigerate overnight. Stir the parsley into the sauce just before serving.

Vary It! The Toasted Pine Nut and Shallot Vinaigrette in Chapter 15 also makes a scrumptious topping for the mussels.

For party planning, divide the recipe into two do-ahead steps: Steam the mussels the day before your party and arrange mussels on the half shell in a single layer on a jellyroll pan; cover tightly with plastic wrap both lengthwise and crosswise. Make the sauce and refrigerate.

Rosemary's Christmas Calamari

For thousands of Italians, it simply wouldn't be Christmas Eve without calamari. Typically, the calamari is deep-fried, and unless the cook stays in the kitchen during the celebration, the dish often suffers from reheating. Creative cook Rosemary DeLuca perfected this sautéing technique that reheats beautifully for her holiday open house — she cooks up ten pounds of calamari for her appreciative family and guests. Her signature recipe adds an unexpected ingredient: *pepperoncini* slivers (Italian pickled chiles) for a zesty surprise.

Preparation time: *55 to 60 minutes*

Cooking time: *8 minutes*

Yield: *6 to 8 servings*

1 pound cleaned calamari tubes and tentacles

10 to 12 medium pepperoncini

¼ cup extra virgin olive oil

2 tablespoons minced fresh parsley

Egg Mixture

2 eggs, well-beaten

1 tablespoon grated Parmesan cheese

1 teaspoon dried parsley

2 tablespoons minced fresh basil (optional)

4 to 5 teaspoons fresh lemon juice

Kosher salt and freshly ground black pepper to taste

⅛ teaspoon kosher salt

⅛ teaspoon freshly ground black pepper

(continued)

Crumb Mixture

1 cup seasoned, fine Italian bread crumbs

¼ cup grated Parmesan cheese

1 tablespoon dried parsley

½ teaspoon kosher salt

⅛ teaspoon freshly ground black pepper

1 In a large bowl, stir 2 tablespoons salt into 1 quart cold water. Add calamari and let it soak for 20 minutes. Drain and rinse under cold running water. Refer to Chapter 10 for cleaning instructions.

2 While calamari is soaking, heat 1 quart water to a boil in a large pan. Remove pan from heat and immediately add calamari. Blanch for 30 seconds, then transfer calamari to a colander and quickly chill under cold running water. Drain well and pat dry with paper towels. Cut calamari tubes into ½- to ¾-inch rings. Halve the larger tentacles.

3 Remove stems from pepperoncini, halve lengthwise, and remove and discard seeds. Slice pepperoncini into thin, narrow strips.

4 In a bowl, combine all ingredients for egg mixture. In a shallow pie plate, combine crumb mixture. Dip each piece of calamari into egg mixture, drain briefly, then coat with crumb mixture, shaking off excess. Arrange in a single layer on waxed paper until all are coated with crumbs.

5 In a 12-inch or larger nonstick skillet, heat oil on medium-high heat. Add calamari and sauté until golden brown, stirring occasionally, about 4 to 5 minutes. Sprinkle with the fresh parsley, basil, pepperoncini, and lemon juice; stir gently to combine.

6 Remove from heat. Taste and adjust seasonings (salt and pepper). Keep warm on buffet table. Serve with cocktail forks.

Vary It! To add red holiday accents to this dish (as we did for the color photo near the middle of this book), substitute pickled, hot, red cherry peppers for half of the pepperoncini.

 Nothing rivals Rosemary's freshly made calamari, but the recipe reheats surprisingly well. Transfer cooked calamari in a single layer to a large shallow dish; refrigerate uncovered until chilled. When cold, tightly cover container and refrigerate up to 24 hours before serving. To serve, reheat, uncovered, in a preheated 350° oven for 10 to 15 minutes.

Chapter 12

The Main Event with Finfish

· ·

In This Chapter

▶ Boosting your grilling savvy

▶ Lovin' the oven for main-dish casseroles

▶ Rubbing it in: Stockpiling seafood seasonings

▶ Preventing pan-demonium — enjoying stove-top success

▶ Solving soggy problems with no-fail, crispy coatings

· ·

A lmost faster than you can phone for pizza delivery, we show you how to have a show-stopping, appetizing, nutritious fish dish on the table. Jump right in. Slather, smear, and rub the seasonings in. Worldly flavors beyond the oh-so-familiar are waiting for you. Have fun. Be flexible. And most of all, don't fret, because in this chapter, we lead you from the grill to the stovetop.

Finfish is the star of these delicious recipes, and we hope that it's the headliner on your menus at least twice a week, too. That's the target recommended by health and nutrition advocates. For a "fish"iona-dos who crave — and consume — fish more often, that's great. For frenzied cooks, who find the twice-a-week target more of a challenge, this chapter is designed to inspire you!

Grate Af"fin"ity: Fish on the Grill

Grilling tops the list of our favorite ways to prepare seafood. So make a splash with your friends and cook fish on the grill. Grilling is fast, easy, and takes the mess and fuss out of your kitchen. At an outdoor party, we believe that nothing beats the smoky succulence of grilled fish. For more fireside know-how, flip to Chapters 2 and 4.

Grill searing — sizzling success

Cooking seafood directly on the grill gives you crispy, caramelized tastes from the searing heat of the grill racks. In the first recipe, the grouper dons a creamy marinade that guarantees the fish won't dry out from intense grill heat, plus this meaty fish flips easily. (If you feel more secure using a grill topper, you still get delicious results.) The recipe for catfish fingers has its own flipper — a sturdy chopstick, slipped through the fish, maintains the shape and helps you turn it.

Grilled Grouper with Louisiana Cream

Moe Cheramie, a friend and seafood guru who hails from New Orleans, inspired this double-duty Louisiana cream. Part of the cream acts as a marinade, part as a serving sauce when mixed with sour cream. The blend of herbs evokes familiar Louisiana flavors. During grilling, the magic of mayonnaise in the base seals in the grouper's moisture and makes a crispy coating. Quick-cooking couscous and peas are tasty accompaniments for this weeknight dish.

Preparation time: *20 minutes*

Marinating time: *60 minutes*

Cooking time: *7 to 9 minutes*

Yield: *4 servings*

4 green onions, including tops, cut into 1-inch chunks

1 cup mayonnaise

1 tablespoon plus 1 teaspoon fresh lemon juice

4 fresh basil leaves or 1 teaspoon dried basil leaves

2 teaspoons Worcestershire sauce

2 teaspoons Creole mustard or coarse-ground mustard

2 teaspoons fresh oregano leaves or ½ teaspoon dried oregano leaves

1½ teaspoons fresh rosemary leaves or ½ teaspoon dried rosemary leaves

1 teaspoon paprika

1 teaspoon freshly ground black pepper

¾ teaspoon kosher salt

⅛ to ¼ teaspoon cayenne pepper

4 skinless grouper fillets, 6 to 7 ounces each

3 to 4 tablespoons sour cream

1 For the Louisiana cream base, in a food processor or blender, pulse the green onions until finely chopped. Add the mayonnaise, lemon juice, basil, Worcestershire sauce, mustard, oregano, rosemary, paprika, pepper, salt, and cayenne, and process until blended. Makes about 1½ cups.

2 Place the grouper in a shallow dish and spoon ¾ to 1 cup Louisiana cream on top (reserve remaining mixture for the serving sauce base); turn fillets to evenly coat. Refrigerate grouper, covered, to marinate for at least 1 hour or overnight. While the fish marinates, make the serving sauce. Into the reserved Louisiana cream, stir 3 to 4 tablespoons of sour cream to taste; set aside.

3 Brush grill grid with oil and prepare a medium-hot fire in a charcoal or gas grill, just before adding fish. Grill grouper, with grill lid closed, until golden brown and a bit crispy, 7 to 9 minutes, turning every 3 minutes. Serve grouper with the serving sauce.

Discard the cream that you used to marinate the grouper because it contains raw seafood juices.

From our messy experience, don't be tempted to substitute lowfat mayonnaise for regular mayonnaise, because the fish will stick to the grill.

Middle Eastern Grilled Catfish Fingers

Gail Forman, a fellow food writer, first served this catfish to Leslie at a summer barbecue. Grilling adds a rich, smoky flavor to the refreshing tastes of the Middle Eastern marinade. Try Gail's unique presentation: Slip a chopstick through the catfish for easy turning and to keep the fish flat. Check out the platter of these fingers in the color photo section near the center of this book.

Preparation time: *30 minutes*

Cooking time: *7 to 8 minutes*

Yield: *4 servings*

(continued)

⅓ cup olive oil

3 tablespoons fresh lemon juice

1 bunch fresh cilantro, leaves picked, washed, and dried

1 small onion, peeled, quartered

2 cloves garlic, peeled

1 tablespoon paprika

2 teaspoons ground cumin

1 teaspoon kosher salt

½ teaspoon freshly ground black pepper

¼ teaspoon cayenne pepper

1½ pounds catfish fillets

8 disposable wooden chopsticks or bamboo skewers, soaked 1 hour

1 For the marinade, in a food processor or blender, process the olive oil, lemon juice, cilantro, onion, garlic, paprika, cumin, salt, pepper, and cayenne until thick and blended.

2 Rinse catfish and pat dry. For easy handling, cut catfish fillets into fingers, about 4 inches long by 1 inch wide (see Figure 12-1) or 1-inch cubes for kebabs. Place catfish in a shallow pan and pour marinade over; turn fish to evenly coat. Refrigerate catfish, covered, to marinate for at least 1 hour or overnight.

3 Brush grill grid with oil and prepare a medium-hot fire in a charcoal or gas grill. While the grill is heating, slip chopsticks through catfish fingers or skewer cubes on bamboo skewers. Discard used marinade. Grill catfish, with grill lid closed, until golden brown and a bit crispy, 7 to 8 minutes, turning every 3 minutes. Serve with hot steaming couscous, if desired.

Vary It! Monkfish, swordfish, tuna, or grouper work well instead of catfish.

 Because grouper flakes more easily during cooking than catfish, use bamboo skewers rather than the chopsticks.

Creating Catfish Fingers

Figure 12-1: Chopsticks make for easy turning.

4" — 1" — Cut the catfish fillet into fingers, about 1" wide + 4" long. ☆ If the fillet is HUGE, first cut it down the center! meeeOW! Stick a chopstick through each marinated fish finger!

A kinder, gentler grilling

Most tender, delicate fish, such as freshwater whitefish, sole, and haddock, may fizzle rather than sizzle when you attempt to grill them over direct heat. To grill these fish successfully, place them in a container. Disposable foil broiler pans sold in most supermarkets work well. You can also create a handcrafted foil boat, described in the following recipe. With the hood down and vents closed, you create a cozy, oven-like environment, with the heat source still directly below the pan. The pan buffers the grill's intense, drying heat and holds tasty juices intact. Gain the advantage of the smoky aromas permeating the fish, plus keep your kitchen cool during hot summer weather.

Grilled or Broiled Whitefish in Foil Boats

Delicacies are often delicate, and freshwater whitefish is oh-so-tender and delicate. A grill grid is not this fish's friend. Put whitefish directly on the grill rack and it dries out and falls through the cracks. Instead, cradle the fillets in foil boats so the fish cooks gently, stays juicy, but still picks up the smoky notes from grilling. To get a clearer picture of the foil boats, check out the color photo section near the center of this book. Adapt this recipe for any fragile fish.

Preparation time: 10 minutes

Cooking time: 8 to 10 minutes

Yield: 2 to 3 servings

1 to 1½ pounds freshwater whitefish fillet, skin on

1 tablespoon melted butter

1 green onion, including some tops, finely chopped

1 tablespoon minced fresh parsley or dill (or 2 teaspoons Ann's Award-Winning Herbs for Fish — see the recipe later in this chapter)

1 tablespoon fresh lemon juice

½ teaspoon sugar (optional)

½ teaspoon kosher salt

¼ teaspoon freshly ground pepper, preferably white

Lemon slices for garnish

1 Prepare a medium-hot fire in a charcoal or gas grill. While grill is heating, rinse fish under cold water, drain, and pat dry with paper towel.

2 Following the outline of the fish fillets, shape heavy-duty foil into a shallow boat or tray with ½-inch sides, about 1 inch wider than each fillet.

3 Place each fillet skin-side down into its boat. In a small bowl, combine the butter, onions, parsley, lemon juice, sugar (if using), salt, and pepper. Spoon or drizzle over fish.

(continued)

4 Place foil boats on grill and cook with grill lid closed for 8 minutes or until the fish just begins to flake at a nudge of a fork. No turning is needed.

5 To serve, cut into portions and gently slide a spatula under the cooked fish, leaving the skin (or most of it) on the foil. Garnish with lemon slices.

Vary It! Broil whitefish with surface of fish 6 inches from heat source. This distance allows the fish to cook through without turning. Any closer and the top may dry out or burn before the bottom is sufficiently cooked. If your oven has an enhancement allowing the broiler and oven heating elements to operate simultaneously (providing heat from above and below), using both will give the most uniform cooking for this recipe.

Worry-Free Baking

Don't overlook the appeal of oven-baked casseroles, even if you think you've outgrown your taste for the classic, cornflake-topped tuna casserole. Our updated fish casseroles feature tilapia, snapper, and swordfish. These recipes are sophisticated enough for an elegant dinner party or simple enough for weekday fare. Take advantage of their great flavors and the bonus of an easy all-in-one meal. Preheat the oven and put in the casserole, and the meal cooks superbly. Thanks to the evenness of the controlled temperature, you're assured of great results without having to hover or stir.

Costa Rican Tilapia

Catch the tropical flavors of the sunny Caribbean with tilapia, a small, perch-like fish. Tilapia (tuh-LAH-pee-uh) has a mild taste, a small snapper-like flake, and firm, white flesh. Tilapia traces its wild origins to the Nile River in Egypt and is currently farm-raised in warm waters around the world. Frank Simon, a friend who farm-raises tilapia in Costa Rica, shares this classic dish, brimming with beans and rice. To up the "wow" factor when you serve this dish, garnish the top with extra orange wheels as shown in the color photo section near the center of this book.

Preparation time: *30 minutes*

Marinating time: *15 minutes*

Cooking time: *30 minutes*

Yield: *6 servings*

3 tablespoons fresh lime juice

3 tablespoons olive oil, divided

4 tablespoons finely chopped fresh cilantro or parsley, divided

4 teaspoons minced garlic, divided

1½ teaspoons kosher salt, divided

¼ teaspoon sugar

6 tilapia fillets, about 5 ounces each

¾ cup long-grain rice

1 cup chopped onions

2 oranges, peeled, seeded, coarsely chopped

1 can (28 ounces) diced tomatoes, undrained

1 can (15 ounces) black or pinto beans, drained, rinsed

1 teaspoon dried oregano leaves

½ teaspoon freshly ground black pepper

¼ teaspoon cayenne pepper

1 For the tilapia marinade, combine lime juice, 1 tablespoon olive oil, 2 tablespoons cilantro, 1 teaspoon garlic, ½ teaspoon salt, and sugar in a shallow dish. Add tilapia and marinate 15 minutes, turning once.

2 To prepare the bean and rice mixture, cook the rice according to package directions and keep warm while the tilapia is marinating. Preheat oven to 400°. In a large, high-sided skillet or saucepan, heat 2 tablespoons olive oil on medium heat. Add remaining garlic and onions; sauté until translucent, about 5 minutes, stirring. Add 2 tablespoons cilantro, oranges, tomatoes, beans, oregano, 1 teaspoon salt, pepper, and cayenne. Cook, uncovered, until hot, 7 to 8 minutes, stirring occasionally.

3 Transfer hot rice to a 9- by 13-inch or 2½- to 3-quart baking dish. Spoon the bean mixture on top of rice and gently blend. Slightly overlap tilapia fillets on top and scrape marinade over fillets. Bake until the flesh of the tilapia just begins to flake at the nudge of a fork, 16 to 20 minutes.

Vary It! Snapper, striped bass, whitefish, cod, flounder, halibut, and haddock are tasty substitutes for tilapia.

A chopstick works well when you need to stir tender mixtures of rice or couscous to prevent the grains from breaking up.

Use leftover cooked rice (2 cups), if desired, and reheat in the microwave for 2 to 3 minutes.

Dixie's Swedish Fish with Spinach

Relatives in Sweden served our friend Dixie Blake this pretty dish when she visited earlier this year. In Sweden, salmon is the fish of choice, but we wanted to suggest other fish you could use just as easily. At first glance, the garlic topping the fish may seem excessive. We can only tell you that our neighbor's three-year-old daughter, Bianca, kept asking her mother for more fish.

Preparation time: *15 minutes*

Cooking time: *20 minutes*

Yield: *4 servings*

12 ounces fresh spinach

¾ cup heavy cream

1 teaspoon kosher salt

¾ teaspoon white pepper or freshly ground black pepper

¾ teaspoon freshly ground nutmeg or pinch ground nutmeg

3 tablespoons minced garlic

1 tablespoon olive oil

4 teaspoons minced fresh dill

1½ lemons

4 skinless snapper fillets, 6 to 7 ounces each

1 Preheat oven to 425°. Wash spinach, remove stems, and tear leaves in half; set aside. In a measuring cup, mix the cream, salt, pepper, and nutmeg. In a small dish, combine the garlic, olive oil, and dill. Cut whole lemon into wedges to serve with the snapper; reserve lemon half to squeeze over fish.

2 Lay the spinach in the bottom of a 9- by 13-inch baking dish (the pan needs to be large enough to hold the spinach and let juices evaporate as spinach cooks). Stir cream and pour over the spinach. Arrange snapper on top of spinach down the center of the dish. If the fish has a thin tail-end, tuck it under the fillet for more even cooking. Spread the garlic mixture on top of each fillet to evenly coat. Plan to serve the snapper from the baking dish.

3 Bake snapper for 18 to 20 minutes, until the flesh of the snapper just begins to flake at the nudge of a fork.

4 To serve, squeeze the juice from the reserved lemon half on top of each fillet. Carefully lift snapper and spinach onto each dinner plate. Spoon sauce over fish (there is about 1 tablespoon rich, silky cream sauce per person) and serve with lemon wedges.

Vary It! Salmon, striped bass, Pacific rockfish, mahimahi, grouper, black sea bass, or Chilean sea bass work well instead of snapper. If you're cooking salmon, and prefer it medium rare, start checking doneness after 14 to 15 minutes of cooking.

Don't be tempted to use light cream or half-and-half rather than heavy cream. The fat content in heavy cream keeps the cream from curdling when it interacts with the oxalic acid in spinach. Lower-fat cream contains a higher percentage of milk solids, which may have a tendency to separate or curdle at high temperatures when the cream and spinach combine.

Sicilian-Style Swordfish with Capers

Bursting with fresh herbs, this swordfish dish is inspired by one which Anna Tasca Lanza served Leslie at her family home at Regaleali, Sicily. Oregano, thyme, rosemary, and mint thrive in Sicily's hot, dry climate, and swordfish abound in nearby Mediterranean waters. Serve the swordfish with linguine tossed with olive oil and sautéed zucchini medallions splashed with lemon.

Preparation time: *45 minutes*

Cooking time: *12 to 14 minutes*

Yield: *4 servings*

1½ pounds swordfish steaks

¾ cup dry white vermouth, white wine, or clam juice

⅓ cup drained capers

¼ cup minced fresh flat leaf or curly parsley

2 tablespoons finely chopped mixed fresh herbs (any combination of oregano, thyme, mint, and rosemary), or 1 to 2 teaspoons dried Italian herbs

10 oil-cured black olives, pitted, slivered

½ teaspoon kosher salt (optional)

1 teaspoon freshly ground black pepper

1 tablespoon olive oil

2 teaspoons unsalted butter

3 cups sliced leeks or white onions

4 teaspoons minced garlic

1 pound medium white mushrooms, wiped clean, quartered

1 Cut swordfish into 4 portions and place in a single layer in a lightly oiled baking dish. Preheat oven to 450°.

2 In a bowl, stir together the vermouth, capers, parsley, mixed herbs, olives, salt, and pepper; set aside. In a large, heavy skillet, heat oil and butter over medium heat until butter starts to foam, about 3 minutes. Add leeks and garlic; sauté partly covered until tender, about 8 minutes, stirring occasionally (don't worry if the leeks brown a bit — the vermouth mixture will loosen them).

(continued)

3 Add mushrooms and increase heat to medium-high. Cook, covered, until mushrooms soften slightly, about 4 minutes. Stir in the vermouth mixture, reduce heat to low, and simmer the sauce, uncovered, for 2 minutes, stirring.

4 Spoon the sauce over the swordfish and bake, uncovered, until the flesh of the swordfish just begins to flake with the nudge of a fork, 12 to 14 minutes. Transfer a portion of swordfish onto each plate and spoon sauce on top.

Vary It! Halibut, mahimahi, mackerel, bluefish, striped bass, shark, or salmon work well instead of swordfish.

A leek looks like a giant green onion and can be quite sandy. To clean leeks, trim the root end and most of the tough green top. Cut leeks in half lengthwise and hold under running water, pulling back layers to remove sand; pat dry. Place leek cut-side up and slice crosswise into half-moons.

Creative Fish in a Flash

Cooks around the globe — from the Orient and India to the Middle East, Europe, the Caribbean, Mexico, and South America — imaginatively enhance seafood with herbs and spices. Seasonings and seafood are perfect partners. You can enhance fish for creative, quick cooking with our easy flavored butters, seasoning rubs, and herb blends.

Add spark with a drizzle of flavored butter — a little goes a long way. In our five flavored butters, fresh ingredients, such as ginger or herbs, give you the liveliest flavors. But dried herbs infuse butter beautifully, especially when you blend the flavors for at least 6 hours.

If you're on a salt-restricted diet or when you just want great taste, let our savory rubs and herb mixtures chase salt out of your kitchen. Rubs and herb mixtures are blends of herbs and spices that flavor the surface of seafood during cooking. The flavors of rubs and blends are highly concentrated because you rub or sprinkle them in a thin layer onto fish or shellfish. We adore fresh herbs, but high quality dried herbs and spices are the key for our rubs and herb blends.

Rubs richly enhance the following fish because they are meaty, firm, or contain some fat:

- Catfish
- Chilean sea bass
- Grouper
- Mahimahi
- Salmon
- Snapper
- Swordfish
- Tilapia
- Tuna

Rubs and herb blends add the best flavor when you sauté, grill, or broil fish. The intense direct heat jump-starts the fragrant oils and flavors of herbs and spices into action. Baking seafood with herb blends also works nicely. Seafood's natural moisture releases more aromatic flavors.

For rubs and blends to curry more favor from your dinner guests, check out Chapter 7 for Chesapeake Bay-Style Seasoning and Louisiana Crab and Shrimp Boil. When you want to orchestrate a tropical beat, don't miss our Jamaican jerk mixture in the Grilled Jerk Tuna on Foccacia recipe in Chapter 14.

Spicy notes and herbal hints

Here are some tips for concocting the fullest flavored seasonings.

- Choose dried herbs and spices that have bright, unfaded color; hearty fragrance; and clear, intense flavor.

- Smell the herbs. Bring out their incredible aroma by placing the herbs in the palm of one hand and rubbing the herbs with the heel of your other hand. Sniff. The heat and friction from the rubbing coax the volatile oils and the fragrance out into the open. If there is little or no aroma, the herbs are probably old and likely will have a faded or bitter taste.

- Retain the freshness of your rubs and herb blends by storing in a tightly sealed opaque or light-resistant container. Store in a dark, cool place away from the heat of the stove or the light of a window. Light, air, and heat are the major enemies of dried herbs and spices: their aromas diminish, flavors turn stale, colors fade, and volatile oils turn rancid. If desired, refrigerate or freeze rubs, but seal tightly. Repeated movement in and out of the cold may cause condensation on the inside of the container. Quality herbs and spices should retain their aroma for six months.

Five Flavored Butters

When you want to showcase the intrinsic flavors of fish or shellfish, transform basic butter with magical herbs and seasonings. Sharon Tyler Herbst, a friend of ours and author of *Cooking Smart,* shares her masterful mixtures. Use this method for making flavored butters, unless otherwise noted in the recipe.

1 In a food processor, mini-processor, or with an electric mixer, process the butter until smooth. Add the remaining ingredients (see the suggested recipes that follow) and pulse to blend.

2 Pack butter into a custard cup or small crock, or form into a goat-cheese like log. See Figure 12-2.

3 To best blend the flavors of the seasonings with the butter, refrigerate flavored butter for at least 6 hours. Before using, let butter stand at room temperature for 20 to 30 minutes to soften slightly. You may refrigerate the butter up to a week, or wrap tightly and freeze up to 3 months.

Steps for Making Flavored Butters

Figure 12-2:
Concocting magical butters.

Put the butter in a bowl and let it get soft... but DON'T MELT IT!

Use a fork, mixer, or processor to blend seasonings.

Turn butter out, onto a piece of waxed paper and roll into a uniform cylinder.

Refrigerate or freeze and cut off pats as you need them.

You may also use the butter, melted, to drizzle over fish before cooking or as a finishing touch to add luscious flavor to seafood. To melt, place butter in a microwave-safe measuring cup. Cover loosely with plastic wrap and microwave on high, for 1 to 2 minutes, depending on the power of your microwave oven and the quantity of butter. Or melt the butter in a small saucepan over low heat for 3 to 4 minutes.

Toasted Sesame Butter

Yield: *1 cup*

10 tablespoons (1¼ sticks) butter, softened

½ cup toasted sesame seeds, finely ground

2 teaspoons Asian toasted sesame oil (optional)

¼ teaspoon kosher salt (optional)

Ginger-Chive Butter

Yield: ¾ *cup*

8 tablespoons (1 stick) butter, softened

2 teaspoons peeled and minced fresh ginger

1 tablespoon minced chives

Kosher salt and freshly ground black pepper to taste

Mustard-Tarragon Butter

Yield: ¾ *cup*

8 tablespoons (1 stick) butter, softened

¼ cup Dijon mustard

2 tablespoons finely chopped fresh tarragon or 2 teaspoons dried tarragon

⅛ teaspoon kosher salt

⅛ teaspoon freshly ground pepper

Herb Butter

Yield: ½ *cup*

8 tablespoons (1 stick) butter, softened

¼ cup finely chopped fresh herbs, such as basil, dill, fennel, oregano, rosemary, thyme, or tarragon, or 1½ tablespoons dried herbs

Kosher salt and freshly ground pepper to taste

Lemon-Dill Butter

Yield: ¾ *cup*

8 tablespoons (1 stick) butter, softened

3 tablespoons finely chopped fresh dill

¼ teaspoon kosher salt

1 tablespoon fresh lemon juice

For this butter, combine butter, dill, and salt. Gradually add lemon juice, beating constantly, until incorporated.

Ann's Award-Winning Herbs for Fish

As a former teacher and avid home cook, our friend Ann Wilder became distraught when she bought dried herbs and spices lacking the oomph and aroma she expected. Curious, she explored the problem and ended up launching her own company, Vanns Spices. Now many top chefs won't cook without her spices, and fine food stores that stake their reputation on impeccable quality carry the Vanns line or insist she source and package their private-label spices and herbs. Among her award-winning products is Herbs for Fish, a favorite of ours. In case it's not sold where you shop, Ann willingly scaled down her secret recipe for you do-it-yourselfers.

Preparation time: *5 minutes*

Yield: *Generous ¼ cup*

1 tablespoon whole fennel seeds

1 tablespoon plus 1 teaspoon dried basil leaves

2½ teaspoons dried granulated garlic

2 teaspoons lemon pepper

1½ teaspoons dried minced onion

1 teaspoon dried parsley

½ teaspoon dried chervil

In a glass container with a tightly fitting lid, gently combine all ingredients. Store in a dry, dark area. Use within 6 months for top quality. Sprinkle 1 to 2 teaspoons on a pound of fish before baking or broiling. A drizzle of melted butter or high quality olive oil is the only additional flavoring you need.

Brandied Pepper Rub

Leslie first got hooked on the Brandied Pepper Rub when Ann Wilder (owner of Vanns Spices) shared her signature recipe for Leslie's *Chicken on the Run* cookbook. The rub's even better on seafood. Pat the chunky mixture onto salmon, Chilean sea bass, sablefish, tuna, swordfish, or jumbo sea scallops.

Preparation time: *5 minutes*

Yield: *about ¼ cup*

¼ cup coarsely ground or cracked black pepper

3 tablespoons good brandy

¼ to ½ teaspoon minced garlic

¼ to ½ teaspoon minced shallot

½ teaspoon drained, chopped canned green peppercorns (optional)

1 Stir the pepper and brandy together. Add the garlic, shallot, and green peppercorns, if using. Let stand for 30 minutes before using. As a guide; one serving of fish needs ½ teaspoon brandied pepper to season each side.

2 Pat the blend onto the seafood of your choice. Great for sautéing, grilling, or broiling. Store pepper mixture tightly covered and refrigerate up to 1 month. Add a bit of brandy if mixture dries out.

Vary It! Here are some of our favorite ways to enjoy Brandied Pepper beyond seafood: Stir into a vinaigrette or creamy salad dressing, toss with green beans, mix into a flavored butter or goat cheese mousse, or blend into Pam's Sting Ray Bloody Marys in Chapter 8.

Preventing Pan-demonium: Stovetop Success

If you're a cook who insists on quick meals, the stovetop is your answer! Finfish is Mother Nature's ultimate fast food. And it naturally comes that way. Finfish cooks faster than any other meat or protein. In techno-talk, all that's needed to cook fish is to elevate its internal temperature high enough to coagulate (or firm) the proteins. And coagulation happens almost 30 degrees lower for fish than for chicken, pork, or beef.

As long as you don't cook finfish too long, high heat by itself won't toughen the fish. If the finfish you bought is ½ inch thick or less, you can have it cooked and ready for the plate in about five minutes. If you have a stash of our flavored butters on hand (see the "Creative Fish in a Flash" section, earlier in this chapter), add a dollop, and announce "Dinner's ready!"

Because fish cooks quickly, we include recipes with the bonus of add-ins to embellish your special catch: luscious strawberry sauce, snappy corn salsa, and a sensuous sherry sauce.

Beat the challenge of creating a crisp, golden crust when you pan-sear fish by trying our searing paste. You don't need extra fat in the skillet, so you can say good-bye to messy spatters.

Searing Paste

Here's one of our solutions for a golden brown crust on finfish without overcooking its delicate flesh and without deep-frying. We spread this paste on the surface right before adding the fish to the hot skillet. When you use this paste instead of adding fat or oil directly to the skillet, you eliminate excess fat and spattering. You may want to double the recipe and keep your stash at the ready in the refrigerator. Leave it at room temperature long enough to reach a spreadable consistency (or quickly zap it in the microwave, just a couple seconds on medium-high power).

Preparation time: *5 minutes*

Yield: *¼ cup (enough for 3 to 4 pounds fish)*

2 tablespoons melted unsalted butter

2 tablespoons all-purpose flour

½ teaspoon salt

½ teaspoon sugar

½ teaspoon freshly ground black pepper, finely ground

Stir together all ingredients in a small container to form a smooth paste. Store leftovers, covered, in refrigerator. Use a flexible spatula to spread a thin coating on top and bottom surfaces of fish before pan-searing. Before applying the searing paste, dry fish with a paper towel so the paste will adhere.

Sablefish with Strawberry Balsamic Sauce

Combine the jewel-tones of ripe strawberries and ruby balsamic vinegar, add an accent note of black pepper, and you've composed a symphony of flavors that harmonize perfectly with elegant sablefish. "Pretty as a picture" is what we hope you'll say when you inspect this dish in the color photo section near the center of this book. If sablefish (also known as black cod) isn't available, don't postpone your culinary concert. Less noble, but equally delicious stand-ins are halibut, orange roughy, or Chilean sea bass.

Preparation time: *20 minutes*

Cooking time: *10 minutes*

Yield: *4 servings*

1½ pounds sablefish fillet, about 1-inch thick

4 teaspoons Searing Paste (see the previous recipe)

1 teaspoon toasted unhulled sesame seeds (optional)

½ cup Strawberry Balsamic Sauce (see the following recipe)

4 strawberries, stemmed and thinly sliced

Fresh flat leaf parsley or mint sprigs for garnish

1 Rinse fish and pat dry. Divide fish into 2 portions, then carefully cut portions horizontally into ½-inch thickness, creating 4 portions. (**Note:** We prefer the flavor of these thinner portions. If, instead, you wish to cook inch-thick portions, increase top-of-stove cooking time or finish cooking in a preheated 425° oven.)

2 Use a small, flexible spatula to spread a thin coating of Searing Paste on the top and bottom surfaces of the fish (about ½ teaspoon of the Searing Paste for each surface).

3 Preheat a large, heavy skillet or nonstick griddle on medium-high heat. Add fish; gently press each portion to assure good contact with the heating surface. Cook until golden brown, about 2 minutes, turn with a slotted flat spatula, and cook second side until golden brown, about 2 minutes.

4 Place fish on warm dinner plates and sprinkle each with sesame seeds. Spoon a tablespoon of warm Strawberry Balsamic Sauce on each. Garnish with sliced berries and parsley. Pass additional sauce.

Strawberry Balsamic Sauce

Yield: ½ cup

½ cup finely chopped strawberries

2 tablespoons finely diced red onions

2 tablespoons balsamic vinegar (preferably aged)

1 tablespoon water

¼ teaspoon freshly ground black pepper

1 to 2 teaspoons sugar

¼ teaspoon kosher salt

1 In a 2-cup glass measuring pitcher or other microwaveable container, combine the strawberries, onion, vinegar, water, and pepper. Heat, uncovered, on high power for 2 minutes. Stir, and heat for an additional 1 to 2 minutes until onions are softened.

2 Using a fork, stir sauce and press fork tines against larger pieces of berries and onions to crush them. Stir in sugar and salt. Sauce may be made ahead and reheated before serving. Serve slightly warm, but not hot.

(continued)

Refrigerate leftover Strawberry Balsamic Sauce for up to one week or freeze for up to one month. This sauce is also delicious served with grilled halibut, grilled salmon, boneless chicken breasts, or pork tenderloin. You may want to follow our recipe testers' recommendation and make a triple batch of the sauce to have on hand and to use the rest of a pint of berries.

Cornmeal-Coated Snapper with Fresh Corn Salsa

Do you like a crispy, cornmeal crust? This triple-dipping technique — first flour, then milk, finally cornmeal — makes a crisp, sturdy crust that works best with fish fillets that are ½ inch thick or thicker, such as catfish, striped bass, grouper, whitefish, cod, and haddock. It's important to chill the coated fish before cooking to ensure the crust will stick to the fish (and not end up in the skillet). The warm salsa with tomatoes and corn nicely complements the cornmeal's flavor. Check out the color photo section near the center of this book for an example of this dish.

Preparation time: *30 minutes*

Cooking time: *9 minutes*

Yield: *4 servings*

½ cup all-purpose flour

½ teaspoon kosher salt, divided

½ teaspoon freshly ground black pepper, divided

½ cup milk

¾ cup plus 1 tablespoon yellow cornmeal, divided

Pinch cayenne pepper

4 skinless snapper fillets, about 6 ounces each

2 tablespoons olive oil

Fresh Corn Salsa (see the following recipe)

1 Combine the flour with half the salt and pepper on a plate; stir to mix. Put the milk in a shallow bowl. Combine ¾ cup of the cornmeal and cayenne pepper with the remaining salt and pepper on another plate and stir to mix. Coat one snapper fillet in the flour mixture, shaking gently to remove excess; quickly dip the fillet in the milk, allowing excess to drip off, then finally coat the fish evenly in the cornmeal mixture. Set aside on a plate sprinkled with the remaining cornmeal, repeating with the remaining fish pieces. When all the snapper is coated, cover the plate and refrigerate for 30 minutes.

2 After the fish is chilled, heat olive oil in a large skillet, preferably nonstick, over medium heat, about 3 minutes. Add the fillets and cook until lightly browned and firm on the bottom, about 4 minutes. Carefully turn the fillets and continue cooking until the fish is browned on the second side and the flesh of the snapper just begins to flake with the nudge of a fork, 4 to 5 minutes longer. Carefully transfer the fish to a plate and cover with foil to keep warm. (Depending on the size of your skillet and the fillets you're using, you may need to cook the fish in two batches.) Use the same skillet to immediately prepare the Fresh Corn Salsa.

Fresh Corn Salsa

1 tablespoon olive oil

1 medium tomato, cored and finely diced (about 1 cup)

1 cup cooked corn or thawed, frozen corn

¼ cup finely chopped green onions

½ to 1 jalapeño or serrano chile, seeded and minced (optional)

Kosher salt and freshly ground black pepper to taste

2 tablespoons fresh lime juice

After the snapper is removed from the skillet, lightly wipe out the skillet, add the olive oil, and heat on medium-high heat. Add the tomato, corn, green onions, chile, and salt and pepper to taste; cook until warm and aromatic, about 2 minutes. Remove skillet from the heat and stir in the lime juice. Place the snapper on individual plates, spoon the salsa over, and serve right away.

Panfried Sole with Sherry

Simple one-pan recipes, such as this one, make fast work of whipping together a sauce to spoon over this lightly coated fish (the recipe doubles easily to serve four). Tasty alternatives for the sherry include vermouth or white wine, as well as fresh lemon or lime juice. Feel free to use whatever fresh herbs you prefer: Chives, chervil, basil, cilantro, or tarragon are all delicious. This panfrying technique is best with thin fish fillets, including flounder, tilapia, pompano, and pickerel.

Preparation time: *20 minutes*

Cooking time: *5 to 6 minutes*

Yield: *2 servings*

(continued)

¼ cup flour

¼ teaspoon kosher salt, divided

½ teaspoon freshly ground black pepper, divided

2 sole fillets, 5 to 6 ounces each

1 tablespoon butter

½ cup dry sherry

1 tablespoon minced fresh parsley

1 Combine the flour with half the salt and pepper on a plate; stir to evenly mix. Coat the fish fillets with the flour mixture, shaking gently to remove excess (preferably over a sink, because the flour flies everywhere). Set fish aside on waxed paper.

2 Heat the butter in a large skillet, preferably nonstick, over medium heat until butter begins to bubble, 2 to 3 minutes. Add the fish fillets and cook until lightly browned, 2 to 3 minutes. Carefully turn the fillets and cook until lightly browned on the second side and the flesh of the fish just begins to flake with the nudge of a fork, 2 to 3 minutes longer. Transfer the fish fillets to a plate and cover with foil to keep warm.

3 Add the sherry to the skillet, increase the heat to high, and bring to a boil, stirring to loosen any bits stuck to the bottom of the skillet. Boil until slightly thickened, 1 to 2 minutes. Season to taste with remaining salt and pepper. Stir in the parsley, and remove the skillet from the heat. Arrange the fillets on individual plates, drizzle with the sherry sauce, and serve.

Sesame-Seared Tuna with Bok Choy

Tuna coated with sesame seeds and paired with Asian seasonings is a magical combination. And if you use both white and black sesame seeds, the color contrast is enticing. For an authentic Japanese taste, look for the pepper mix, *togarashi*, to use instead of the salt and pepper. For a fancier presentation, cut the cooked tuna steaks into thick slices and serve them fanned out, with the bok choy alongside.

Preparation time: *30 minutes*

Cooking time: *4 to 5 minutes*

Yield: *4 servings*

4 tuna steaks, about 6 ounces each, 1-inch thick

1½ teaspoons Asian toasted sesame oil, divided

½ teaspoon kosher salt

¾ teaspoon freshly ground black pepper

2 tablespoons sesame seeds

1 tablespoon vegetable oil

4 baby bok choy, thinly sliced (about 4 cups)

6 ounces shiitake or white mushrooms, stems trimmed, thinly sliced

1 tablespoon soy sauce

1 Rub the tuna steaks with 1 teaspoon of the sesame oil and season with salt and pepper. Sprinkle both sides of the tuna steaks with the sesame seeds and pat seeds to ensure that they stick to the tuna (if you like tuna cooked on the rare side, refrigerate tuna to chill slightly, about 30 minutes).

2 Heat the vegetable oil in a large skillet or in a wok over high heat. Add the bok choy and mushrooms and stir-fry until the vegetables are tender, 3 to 5 minutes. Stir in the soy sauce with the remaining ½ teaspoon sesame oil. Remove skillet with vegetables from heat and set aside while cooking the tuna.

3 Heat a large, heavy skillet, preferably cast iron, over medium-high heat. When the skillet is very hot, add the tuna pieces and cook undisturbed until nicely browned on the bottom, about 1 minute for rare, 2 minutes for medium-rare to medium. Carefully loosen tuna with a spatula, turn the tuna pieces, and continue cooking to taste, 1 to 2 minutes longer. If you prefer your tuna more well done, take the pan from the heat, cover, and let sit for another minute or two.

4 Quickly reheat the bok choy mixture over high heat. Set the tuna pieces on individual plates, spoon the bok choy mixture alongside, and serve immediately.

Vary It! Swordfish, salmon, mahimahi, sablefish, Chilean sea bass, or shark work well instead of tuna.

With its slender, snow-white stalks and small, dark-green leaves, baby bok choy makes a pretty color contrast to the tuna. Larger bok choy also works well, but you may need to halve or quarter the head first before slicing. Napa cabbage would be a tasty substitute for the bok choy (although you won't have the dramatic color contrast).

Grouper and Zucchini Skillet Cakes

Golden brown and tender moist, these pancake-like cakes are ideal for brunch or a light supper. The cakes also reheat beautifully in the microwave for a snack. You can easily make the batter two to three hours ahead of time. If you use the batter directly from the refrigerator, you'll need to add a minute or two extra of cooking time. For faster results, bring the batter to room temperature before cooking the skillet cakes.

Preparation time: *45 minutes*

Cooking time: *8 minutes*

Yield: *4 servings (12 to 16 cakes)*

2 eggs

2 tablespoons milk

2 tablespoons minced shallots or onions

4 teaspoons minced fresh thyme or dill

½ teaspoon kosher salt

½ teaspoon white pepper

½ teaspoon freshly ground nutmeg or pinch ground nutmeg

¼ teaspoon cayenne pepper

1 medium zucchini, shredded or grated

¾ pound grouper, skinless, bones removed, chopped ¼- to ½- inch dice

¼ cup grated Parmesan cheese

½ cup flour

½ teaspoon baking powder

2 to 3 teaspoons corn oil

2 teaspoons unsalted butter

Spray vegetable oil (optional)

1 In a medium bowl, beat eggs with a fork until blended. Stir in milk, shallots, thyme, salt, pepper, nutmeg, and cayenne. Add zucchini and grouper; stir until mixture is blended.

2 In a small bowl, stir together cheese, flour, and baking powder. Sprinkle flour mixture over grouper and vegetables; stir to mix well. Let stand for 15 minutes for flour to absorb liquid.

3 Preheat oven to 200°. Cook skillet cakes in two batches to prevent overcrowding. Add 2 teaspoons oil to a large, heavy skillet and heat on medium-high heat for about 4 minutes, until a drop of water sizzles when added to the oil. Add 1 teaspoon butter and swirl pan to melt. Use about 2 tablespoons of batter for each cake. Spoon batter into skillet and pat tops of skillet cakes lightly with a wet fork to flatten, if desired. Reduce heat to medium and cook cakes 2 minutes until browned; flip cakes and cook 2 more minutes until skillet cakes are firm but slightly springy and golden on the bottom.

4 Keep cooked cakes warm in a single layer in the oven while you cook the remaining cakes, adding remaining oil and butter to skillet as needed. Serve warm with your favorite sauce, such as the Roasted Red-Pepper Velvet in Chapter 15, or extra Parmesan cheese and lemon wedges.

Vary It! Try shrimp, catfish, halibut, shark, or mahimahi instead of grouper.

More Stovetop Success: Under Cover

There's good reason to put the lid on finfish. Undercover cooking captures the natural moisture of fish securely in the pan, rather than letting the juices evaporate away. When you cook halibut and snapper on a bed of seasoned vegetables, the flavors of the fish and the juices nicely marry together. This undercover cooking is really a self-steam without adding water.

For a more traditional steam, cook seasoned whole fish over water. Steam surrounds the fish for moist undercover cooking. Poaching fish surrounded with liquid, and covered, to boot, gives you the moistest undercover cook. You get succulent, tender fish every time.

Halibut with Herbed Vegetable Quartet

Colorful and chunky, this pretty vegetable medley is the perfect partner for almost any fish or shellfish. Take a look at its color photo near the center of this book to see why the photographer rated this recipe as a ten for visual appeal. Keep in mind that a thicker fish needs an extra minute or two to cook. Serve with crisp baked potatoes.

Preparation time: *40 minutes*

Cooking time: *16 minutes*

Yield: *4 servings*

1½ pounds halibut steaks or fillet, about 1-inch thick

6 ounces arugula or spinach washed, stemmed

¾ pound baby carrots, halved crosswise

1 tablespoon olive oil

2 cups finely chopped leeks

4 ribs celery, finely chopped

2 tablespoons chopped garlic

1 teaspoon kosher salt, divided

¾ teaspoon white or freshly ground black pepper, divided

2 tablespoons minced fresh thyme or parsley, divided

1 cup vegetable broth or clam juice

¼ teaspoon paprika

(continued)

1 Cut halibut into 4 portions, removing skin, if desired.

2 Stack arugula leaves and slice crosswise into ⅛ inch strips; reserve. In a food processor with the motor running, add carrots through the feed tube and coarsely chop, 10 to 15 seconds.

3 In a large, heavy skillet, heat oil over medium-high heat. Add carrots, leeks, and celery; sauté until tender-crisp, about 8 minutes, stirring. Add arugula, garlic, and half the salt, pepper, and thyme; sauté until vegetables soften, 2 minutes, stirring.

4 Add the vegetable broth and set halibut on top of vegetables. Season the halibut with paprika and the remaining salt, pepper, and thyme. Cover and simmer until the flesh of the halibut just begins to flake at the nudge of a fork, 6 to 8 minutes. Spoon vegetables and fish onto warm dinner plates and serve.

Vary It! Salmon, whitefish, tilapia, snapper, mahimahi, and shrimp are tasty substitutes for halibut. Or place cleaned clams or mussels on top of the vegetable quartet, cover, and steam until they open. Serve in soup bowls with crusty bread.

Snapper with Caribbean Sofrito

Sofrito derives its name from the Spanish verb *sofreir*, which means to fry lightly. In Spain, onions, leeks, and smoked ham are slowly cooked in olive oil to produce classic sofrito, the base for much of the country's regional cooking. Caribbean Island versions of sofrito add to this blend native tomatoes, chiles, salt pork, and achiote (ah-chee-OH-tay) seeds. The seeds lend the characteristic golden color to sofrito. Finding achiote seeds can be a challenge, so see the shortcut at the end of the recipe for creating paprika oil.

Preparation time: *35 minutes*

Cooking time: *40 minutes*

Yield: *4 servings*

1 tablespoon achiote or paprika oil

6 cups thinly sliced onions, about 1¾ pounds

1 can (28 ounces) peeled, diced tomatoes, drained

3 tablespoons minced garlic

1 to 1½ teaspoons freshly ground black pepper

1 teaspoon dried basil leaves

½ to 1 teaspoon minced habanero or 1½ teaspoons minced jalapeño or serrano chiles

½ to 1 teaspoon kosher salt

¼ cup drained capers

4 skinless snapper fillets, about 6 ounces each

¼ cup minced fresh cilantro or parsley

1 In a large, heavy, high-sided skillet or saucepan, heat achiote oil on medium heat until hot. Add the onions, toss well to coat (watch them turn pumpkin gold), and cook partly covered until softened, about 5 minutes, stirring. Add the tomatoes, garlic, 1 teaspoon pepper, basil, chiles, and ½ teaspoon salt.

2 Cook, partly covered, until the onions are extremely tender, about 20 minutes, stirring often. Uncover and cook until moisture evaporates and the sofrito is thick, 8 to 10 minutes, stirring often to keep onions from sticking too much. Stir the capers into the sofrito. Remove 1 cup sofrito and refrigerate (great for a quick dinner for two later in the week).

3 Arrange the snapper on top of the sofrito in the skillet. Season the snapper with the cilantro and the remaining salt and pepper to taste. Cover and continue to cook on medium heat until the flesh of the snapper just begins to flake with the nudge of a fork, 6 to 7 minutes.

4 With a wide spatula, remove snapper and place on a plate. Spoon the sofrito into a warm, shallow serving dish and place snapper on top. Serve with rice or beans.

Vary It! Try tilapia, pompano, catfish, flounder, or shrimp instead of snapper.

Achiote seed is the rusty-red seed of the annatto tree. The triangular seed is slightly smaller than a peppercorn and has a mild, musky flavor. In Caribbean and Spanish cooking, achiote is used primarily to color rice and other foods a bright saffron yellow. Commercially, achiote colors margarine, butter, and cheese. (The label on Leslie's jar of seeds notes that achiote — or annatto seeds — are used by "particular people in their cooking.")

To make achiote oil: In a small pot, heat ½ cup vegetable oil on medium-low heat until hot. Stir in 2 tablespoons achiote seeds and remove from the heat as soon as the oil turns crimson, 1 to 2 minutes. Cool oil, strain, and refrigerate indefinitely. Use achiote oil when you want to add its distinctive yellow-red color to seafood sautés or to marinades.

If achiote seeds aren't available, stir 2 tablespoons each paprika and turmeric into ½ cup hot oil and remove from heat; cool, strain through paper towels, and refrigerate up to a month.

Golden Poached Mahimahi
with Shrimp

Mahimahi is one of Leslie's favorite fish — the sweet taste and firm, lean flesh lends itself beautifully to poaching. Sautéing mahimahi golden brown on one side before poaching adds flavor to the poaching broth and burnished color when you present the dish. If you worry about overcooking fish, poaching is a forgiving, worry-free cooking technique. The Fennel Pepper Sauté with capers and arugula is a big-flavored side dish that you can make ahead before you cook the fish.

Preparation time: *45 minutes*

Cooking time: *30 minutes*

Yield: *6 servings*

Fennel Pepper Sauté (see the following recipe)

6 skinned mahimahi fillets, 5 to 6 ounces each, 1 to 1½ inches thick

¾ teaspoon kosher salt

1 teaspoon white pepper, divided

1 tablespoon plus 1 teaspoon olive or garlic oil

3¾ cups clam juice

1½ cups dry white vermouth or white wine

4 garlic cloves, peeled

½ lemon, sliced

Pinch red pepper flakes

½ pound raw, peeled, extra-large shrimp (30/35 per pound), deveined

Lemon wedges (optional)

1 Pat fish dry with paper towels; season top with salt and ½ teaspoon pepper. Heat 1 tablespoon oil in a large, heavy skillet over medium-high heat until hot, 3 minutes. Add 3 fillets to skillet, seasoned side down, and cook 2 minutes; loosen with spatula and cook on the same side until browned, 2 minutes more. Transfer to plate. Repeat with remaining 1 teaspoon oil and 3 fillets.

2 Combine the clam juice, vermouth, garlic cloves, lemon slices, red pepper flakes, and remaining ½ teaspoon white pepper in a heavy, 10-inch saucepan. (This size allows the liquid to just cover fish.) Bring liquid to a boil. Reduce heat to low, cover and simmer to blend flavors, 10 minutes.

3 Place mahimahi, browned side up, in poaching liquid and add any juices that have accumulated on the plate. Cover and poach gently on low until still slightly springy and almost white in the center, about 10 minutes. Using a slotted spoon, transfer fish to a warm plate. Tent with foil. Add shrimp to broth and poach, uncovered, until tender and pink, 1½ to 2 minutes. Using a slotted spoon, transfer shrimp to the plate with the mahimahi.

4 Reduce poaching liquid to make a sauce to serve with fish, if desired, or serve fish with lemon wedges. To reduce liquid, remove lemon slices and garlic from poaching liquid and discard. Bring liquid to a boil and cook until reduced to about ¾ cup, 20 minutes, stirring. Add any juices that have accumulated on the plate from the mahimahi and the shrimp, and boil 1 minute more.

5 Divide the Fennel Pepper Sauté among six dinner plates and top with fish and shrimp. Spoon cooking liquid over, if using.

Fennel Pepper Sauté

For a casual presentation, serve the mahimahi, shrimp, and fennel trio family style. Mound the vegetables in the center of a large platter, set the mahimahi fillets in a sunburst around the vegetables, and top with shrimp. Pour the reduced poaching liquid over the seafood and vegetables, and serve.

Preparation time: *15 minutes*

Cooking time: *5 minutes*

Yield: *6 servings*

2 medium fennel bulbs with stalks (about 10 ounces each) or 1 large fennel bulb (about 1 pound)

2 teaspoons olive oil

1 leek, washed, halved lengthwise, white part thinly sliced

½ orange bell pepper, diced ¼-inch

2 tablespoons drained capers

2 tablespoons slivered, oil-cured black olives

¼ teaspoon white pepper

1¼ cups finely chopped arugula (about 4 ounces) or watercress

1 Pull feathery dill-like fronds off fennel stalks and reserve to garnish dish. Cut the tough stalks from the bulb and discard. Slice fennel bulb vertically into quarters; discard the core. Place fennel cut side down and thinly slice on the diagonal, starting where the stalks were removed. You need about 3 cups sliced fennel.

2 Heat oil in a large, heavy skillet over medium-high heat until hot, 1 to 2 minutes. Add fennel, leek, bell pepper, capers, olives, and white pepper; sauté until crisp-tender, about 3 minutes, stirring often. Add arugula and sauté until wilted, 1 minute. Serve with reserve fennel fronds as garnish.

Vary It! Try halibut, swordfish, or salmon instead of mahimahi.

Thick, center-cut mahimahi fillets make the prettiest presentation, but poaching works particularly well for fillets which vary in thickness. If the fillets you find run in the ¾-inch thick range, simply reduce the poaching time to about 8 minutes. You can freeze the strained poaching liquid to use another time in soups or stews.

Cantonese Whole Steamed Fish

Forget the floral centerpiece! Reserve the space in the center of the table to proudly present and serve your succulent masterpiece family style. After the oohs and aahs, grab your chopsticks, and let everybody savor each delicious morsel. Check out the color photo section near the center of this book to see our steamer set-up using a platter in a wok, as well as the green onion brushes suggested to garnish this dish.

Preparation time: *20 minutes*

Cooking time: *15 to 20 minutes*

Yield: *4 to 6 servings*

1 whole, cleaned firm-fleshed fish (2½ to 3 pounds), such as red snapper, striped bass, rockfish, or sea bass

5 to 6 green onions

2 tablespoons soy sauce

2 tablespoons hoisin sauce

2 tablespoons sherry or mirin (Japanese rice wine)

1 tablespoon peeled and finely diced fresh ginger

1 teaspoon Asian toasted sesame oil

1 teaspoon fermented black beans (optional)

1 Arrange empty tuna can rims (both ends removed) or other supports to elevate a heatproof, rimmed platter that can fit inside a large cooking pot and allow the lid to fit tightly. Add 1-inch water to pan. Flip to Chapter 4 for ideas and inspirations for improvising a steaming set-up big enough to hold a heatproof serving platter. Make sure there's a big enough gap for steam to circulate between the dish and the outer edges of the cooking pan.

2 Check fish to make sure all scales are removed. Preferably leave head and tail on fish. Rinse fish inside and out under cold water and pat dry. Measure fish at thickest part to calculate total steaming time (10 minutes per inch). Slash fish with three shallow, parallel, diagonal cuts on each side.

3 Mince one green onion, including the tender green parts. Make green onion brushes for garnishes from the remaining onions.

4 In a small bowl, combine minced onions and the remaining ingredients. Coat the inside surfaces of the fish with about ⅓ of this seasoning mixture.

5 Position fish on the platter and place dish in steamer. Pour remaining seasoning mixture across top of fish. Turn heat to high. As soon as water boils, cover pan, reduce heat to medium-high or just hot enough to maintain full steam and begin timing, allowing 10 minutes for each 1-inch thickness.

6 Turn off heat, remove cover, making sure hot steam doesn't hit your face. Test for doneness with a nudge of a fork (the flesh should look opaque). Use heatproof mitts to carefully lift platter from steamer. Garnish platter with green onion brushes and serve.

Sculpt green onion brushes by fringing both ends of 5- to 6-inch segments of green onions (white and some green parts). Using the point of a paring knife, make inch-long parallel slits, spaced about ⅛-inch apart, at both ends of the onion. Plunge these into ice water and watch the fringed ends open to form a frilly garnish.

Chapter 13

The Main Event with Shellfish

In This Chapter

▶ Reeling in the compliments with crusty shellfish

▶ Popping the secrets of close-mouthed shellfish

▶ Creating economical weekday meals

Mention lobsters, scallops, or shrimp to your guests, and they shower you with accolades — before you even turn on the stove or fire up the grill.

The recipes in this chapter offer you a selection of slam-dunk shellfish solutions for your next party extravaganza, award-winning dinner, or thrifty weekday meal. Perfect your techniques for crisp-frying oysters, cooking shellfish in the shell — both grilling and stove-top steaming, and for quick-cooking calamari.

Shellfish gets lots more coverage in Chapters 5, 7, and 8. Plus, you can discover where calamari hides its slender, cellophane-like shell in Chapter 10.

Cracking the Code of Crusty Shellfish

You don't have to stick with tradition and steam or boil lobsters, crabs, and shrimp. Instead, when warm weather beckons, we suggest that you take shellfish into the great outdoors and fire up the grill. Both lobsters and soft-shell crabs lend themselves to the smoky flavors grilling imparts. Or when you're ready for hands-on fajita fun, sauté shrimp with zesty flavors, and then wrap in tortillas with a crispy slaw. Our step-by-step clues help you solve the mystery of cutting and cleaning this group of crusty shellfish.

Grilled Lobster with Tropical Vinaigrette

One taste of this golden mango sauce and you'll be transported to the sunny, bleached shores of Martinique. Flecked with peppers and crunchy cucumbers, this silky sauce complements rich-tasting lobster. Whether you grill lobster tails or whole east coast lobsters (see Sue Barber's tip at the end of the recipe), this simple, succulent seafood will be an instant hit with your guests. Check out the photo of this dish in the color photo section near the center of the book.

Preparation time: *20 minutes*

Cooking time: *8 to 10 minutes*

Yield: *4 servings*

Four 8-ounce lobster tails

1 to 2 tablespoons olive oil

Kosher salt and freshly ground black pepper to taste

Tropical Vinaigrette (see the following recipe)

Grilled garlic bread (optional)

1 If frozen, thaw lobster tails in the refrigerator overnight.

2 Brush grill grid with oil and prepare a medium-hot fire in a charcoal or gas grill. As the grill heats, prepare lobster tails (see Figure 13-1). Use about 1 teaspoon olive oil for each lobster tail; rub onto the cut surfaces of the lobster meat, and season to taste with salt and pepper.

3 Place lobster tails on the grill, meat-side up. Grill lobster, with grill lid closed, until the meat is opaque, 8 to 10 minutes, turning once. Serve with Tropical Vinaigrette and grilled garlic bread, if you like.

Lobster Tails as an Open Book

Figure 13-1: Cutting a lobster tail for moist tastes.

Set each lobster tail on a cutting board with translucent membrane down, curved shell facing up.

With kitchen shears or heavy knife, cut through the curved shell + meat, leaving membrane intact.

Open tail gently like a book so it's hinged in the center.

meat

shell

Tropical Vinaigrette

Preparation time: *25 minutes*

Yield: *about 2 cups*

½ pound cucumber

One 1-pound mango, pureed

¼ cup plus 2 tablespoons fresh orange juice

¼ cup vegetable oil

2 tablespoons rum (optional)

2 teaspoons peeled and minced or grated fresh ginger

2 teaspoons grated orange zest

2 teaspoons minced fresh thyme or ½ teaspoon dried thyme leaves

1½ teaspoons minced garlic

¾ teaspoon kosher salt

½ to 1 teaspoon pequin chile flakes or red pepper flakes, or 1½ teaspoons minced fresh hot chiles

1 Peel the cucumber, leaving four thin strips of skin for color contrast. Halve cucumber lengthwise and scoop out the seeds; cut flesh into ⅛-inch dice (about 1 cup).

2 In a medium bowl, whisk the mango puree, orange juice, oil, rum (if using), ginger, orange zest, thyme, garlic, salt, and chile flakes together; stir in cucumber. Taste the vinaigrette and adjust seasonings.

Don't feel that you have to tango with a mango when you try to cut it up. See Chapter 14 for tips on how to cube a mango. To puree a mango, place mango cubes in a food processor, blender, or mini-processor, and blend until smooth. A 1-pound mango yields about 1 cup puree. Don't worry if you puree a larger mango; simply refrigerate the extra puree up to a week or freeze up to a month. Great in salad dressings or marinades, such as the Mustard Duet in Chapter 5.

You can also grill whole lobsters. Count on one 1½ pound lobster per person. For easy handling, our friend Sue Barber of the Maine Lobster Promotion Council, suggests boiling lobster first for 4 minutes. Drain lobster and cool slightly. Turn lobster belly side up and cut the lobster lengthwise completely through the meat and shell to yield two halves per lobster. Discard the dark stomach (a gritty sac) that's located behind the eyes, and the soft, green *tomalley* (liver). Rub olive oil into the meat as in the Grilled Lobster with Tropical Vinaigrette recipe (Step 2).

Sue likes to start the lobster meat side down on grill, and then grill 8 to 10 minutes, turning once. As an alternative to the Tropical Vinaigrette, try Sue's tangy citrus sauce: Combine the juice of 1 lemon and 1 lime with 1 stick melted butter and ¼ cup minced cilantro. Reserve half as a serving sauce and half to baste lobster meat while cooking. For do-ahead preparation, boil lobsters in the morning, split, cover, and refrigerate. Remove lobsters from the refrigerator about 10 minutes before grilling.

Asian Shrimp Fajitas with Napa Ginger Toss

Toss sautéed curly shrimp with our zesty Dill Pesto from Chapter 15 (or when you're on the run, prepared basil pesto). Then, wrap shrimp with napa cabbage and pickled ginger slaw in a flavored tortilla for invigorating, hands-on tastes. Drizzle on the Indonesian Peanut Sauce (also in Chapter 15) for an extra layer of vibrant flavor.

Preparation time: *45 minutes*

Cooking time: *3 minutes*

Warming time: *10 to 12 minutes*

Yield: *4 servings (makes 8 fajitas)*

1½ pounds raw, extra-large (26/30 per pound) or large shrimp (31/35 count) peeled and deveined

Eight 7-inch curry, garlic herb, or cilantro pesto tortillas

2 tablespoons peanut oil

2 tablespoons plus 2 teaspoons Dill Pesto (see Chapter 15)

Napa Ginger Toss (see the following recipe)

Indonesian Peanut Sauce (see Chapter 15)

1 Slit shrimp to make them curl and catch more sauce: Cut through the body of the shrimp to split it in two from the head to within ½-inch of the tail end. This leaves the end of the shrimp intact with the split body attached. (See Chapter 5 for help making curly shrimp.)

2 Preheat oven to 300°. Use two large sheets of foil to wrap tortillas and place in oven to warm, 10 to 12 minutes. Place shrimp in a bowl and drizzle with 1 tablespoon oil; gently toss with a rubber spatula to coat.

3 Heat remaining tablespoon of oil in a large, heavy skillet on medium-high heat. Add shrimp and cook until shrimp are still a bit translucent in the center, about 2½ to 3 minutes. (The shrimp will finish cooking upon standing.)

4 Place shrimp in a bowl, add pesto, and gently mix until well coated.

5 To serve, pass warm tortillas, Napa Ginger Toss, and shrimp. Let guests assemble their own fajitas: Top tortilla with about ¼ cup Napa Ginger Toss and shrimp. Roll tortilla to enclose filling; halve crosswise, if desired. Serve with Indonesian Peanut Sauce, if desired.

Napa Ginger Toss

A pale green salad highlighted with shreds of bright orange carrot, pink, pickled ginger, and black sesame seeds. No calorie-laden salad dressing here. The ginger juice moistens the light, crisp toss.

Yield: *4 cups*

One 12-ounce head napa or Chinese cabbage

1 cup julienned carrots

¼ cup pickled ginger, drained, slivered

1 tablespoon black or toasted sesame seeds, or black caraway seeds

1 Cut cabbage in half lengthwise, leaving core intact. Shred cabbage crosswise and put into medium bowl.

2 Toss cabbage with carrots, ginger, and black sesame seeds. Assemble up to 3 hours before serving.

Grilled Louisiana Soft-Shell Crabs

Our friend (and fish expert extraordinaire) Chef Jamie Shannon, of Commander's Palace in New Orleans, teams local soft-shells with the bounty of the season: meaty beefsteak tomatoes (known as Creole tomatoes in Louisiana) and crisp, seasonal greens.

Preparation time: *45 minutes*

Cooking time: *6 to 8 minutes*

Yield: *4 servings*

1 Vidalia or other sweet onion

¼ cup plus 2 tablespoons sugarcane vinegar or cider vinegar

¾ teaspoon sugar (optional)

4 fresh, large soft-shell crabs (about 4 ounces each)

2 tablespoons vegetable oil

3 tablespoons Creole or barbecue seasoning, or chili powder, divided

4 Creole or beefsteak tomatoes

8 ounces mixed baby salad greens or watercress, rinsed and dried

⅓ cup slivered fresh basil (10 to 12 large leaves)

Kosher salt and pepper to taste

Commander's Ravigote Sauce (see the following recipe)

(continued)

1 Peel onion, slice paper thin, and place in a large bowl. Add the cane vinegar, toss, and set aside. (If you use cider vinegar, dissolve sugar in vinegar before adding to onion.)

2 Clean the soft-shell crabs (see Figure 13-2) or ask your fish seller to do it for you. Pat crabs dry with paper towels. Place crabs in a small pan, drizzle with oil, and gently rub oil into both sides to coat. Sprinkle a total of 2 tablespoons of Creole seasoning onto both sides of the crabs. (Don't try to rub seasonings in; they stick to your fingers.)

3 Slice tomatoes into 2 thick slices each; reserve tomato ends for another use. Sprinkle both sides of the slices with 2 to 3 teaspoons Creole seasonings.

4 Brush grill grid with oil and prepare a medium-hot fire in a charcoal or gas grill. As the grill heats, add the greens and basil to the onions and vinegar. Season with salt and pepper and toss.

5 Transfer crabs to the grill with a spatula to keep them intact. Grill crabs with grill lid closed until crabs turn a deep red-brown and legs are crispy, 6 to 8 minutes, turning once. (Tongs work well for turning because the meat has firmed.)

6 To serve, spoon a tablespoon of Commander's Ravigote Sauce onto each plate. Place 2 tomato slices on sauce and top tomatoes with a crab. Place the greens on top of the crab, and spoon about 1 tablespoon of sauce over each serving. Pass remaining sauce.

Cleaning Soft-Shell Crabs is NOT for the Squeamish!

Figure 13-2: Cleaning soft-shell crabs.

First, you need to snip off the eyes and mouth with a pair of scissors.

Remove the gills just under the top shell on either side of the crab...

and then pull off the little flap (the apron) at the back of the crab.

Commander's Ravigote Sauce

Yield: 1¾ cups

1 cup mayonnaise

½ cup Creole mustard or coarse-ground mustard

1½ green onions, including tops, finely chopped

1 tablespoon capers, drained and coarsely chopped

1 hard-cooked egg, finely diced

1 to 2 teaspoons horseradish

¼ teaspoon freshly ground black pepper

In a bowl, combine all ingredients. Taste and adjust seasonings. Makes about 2 cups. You can refrigerate the sauce up to a week.

Choose a buttery Chardonnay to complement the crabs.

When you buy live soft-shell crabs, look for movement, particularly around the eyes and mouth to make sure that the crab is alive. The crab should have a plump, springy body with a translucent, gray-blue soft shell. For freshest flavor, clean soft-shells within two hours of cooking. (If necessary, you may refrigerate cleaned soft-shell crabs overnight.)

Shellfish to Suit Your Mood

Let your cravings be your guide: rich, luxurious scallops paired with grapefruit and arugula for refreshing tastes; luscious, tender oysters fried to decadent perfection; or simply cooked clams and mussels, steamed in the coastal tradition. Break out the bread, the napkins — and the kids — when you're ready for hands-on fun.

Sautéed Scallops with Grapefruit and Arugula

This light, warm-weather supper is pictured in the color photo section near the center of this book. The zingy flavor of pink grapefruit is a surprisingly refreshing complement to sweet sea scallops, especially when served on crisp, slightly peppery arugula.

Preparation time: *35 minutes*

Cooking time: *5 to 6 minutes*

Yield: *4 servings*

3 pink grapefruit, divided

2 teaspoons sugar

¾ pound arugula with stems trimmed, or 8 ounces mixed baby greens

1¼ pound sea scallops, rinsed, patted dry with paper towels

½ teaspoon kosher salt

½ teaspoon freshly ground black pepper

2 tablespoons olive oil

1 tablespoon minced chives

¾ teaspoon poppy seeds or toasted mustard seeds (optional)

(continued)

1 Cut both ends from one of the grapefruit just to the flesh with a serrated or small sharp knife. Set the grapefruit upright on a cutting board and use the knife to cut away the peel and skin, following the curve of the fruit. Working over a bowl to catch the sections and juice, hold the peeled grapefruit in your hand and slide the knife blade down one side of a section, cutting the section from the membrane. Cut down the other side of the section and let it fall into the bowl. Continue for the remaining sections, turning back the flaps of membrane like the pages of a book. Squeeze the grapefruit membrane into the bowl to extract additional juice; repeat with second grapefruit.

2 Cut the third grapefruit in half crosswise and squeeze the juice into the bowl. You need about ¾ cup total of grapefruit juice. Taste juice for tartness and stir in sugar as needed. Rinse and dry arugula.

3 On the side of each scallop, pull off the small tab-like, tough muscle (see Chapter 8). Season the scallops with salt and pepper and cook in two batches for best browning. Heat the oil in a large skillet, preferably nonstick, over medium-high heat for 3 to 4 minutes until hot. Add the scallops and cook until nicely browned but still translucent in the center, about 2 minutes on each side. Transfer the scallops to a plate and set aside.

4 In the same skillet, add the grapefruit juice from the bowl, holding the grapefruit sections to the side. Bring the juice to a boil, add the grapefruit sections and scallops, shake to evenly distribute, and remove pan from the heat. (You don't want to overcook the scallops, or they'll become rubbery.) Stir in the chives; taste and adjust seasonings.

5 Arrange the arugula on individual plates and spoon the scallops, grapefruit, and sauce on top. Sprinkle with poppy seeds, if using. Serve at once.

Vary It! For a special luncheon, serve the scallops with a lemon pepper linguine. And for equally delicious results, try large shrimp instead of scallops.

Substitute ready-to-eat fresh grapefruit sections (you need 1½ cups) and grapefruit juice (¾ cup) when you don't have time to peel and juice whole grapefruit.

Barbara's Grand Slam Fried Oysters

Picture a submarine sandwich, piled high with crisp, fried oysters, and you've got the famous New Orleans po'boy sandwich. When Gulf oysters were plentiful and cheap, you could buy an inexpensive meal of oysters stuffed into a loaf of French bread, hence the name, poor boy, which is shortened to "po'boy." Barbara Howard, our friend and a talented cook, shares her recipe for fried oysters. Flip to Chapter 5 for our jazzy Remoulade Sauce.

Preparation time: 25 minutes

Cooking time: 10 minutes

Yield: 4 servings

1 pint oysters, about 24 oysters	*1 cup peanut oil or corn oil*
32 saltine crackers	*½ to ¾ cup tartar sauce or Remoulade Sauce*
1 teaspoon Old Bay Seasoning (optional)	
Four 6-inch baguettes	*1⅓ cups shredded iceberg lettuce*
1 egg	*Freshly ground black pepper to taste*
1 tablespoon cold water	

1 Place oysters in a strainer and drain liquid; reserve liquid for soup, if desired. Place saltines in a resealable plastic bag and crush to make crumbs slightly coarser than dried bread crumbs and a uniform size, for most even frying. Mix in Old Bay Seasoning, if using. Place half the crumbs in small bowl (the sides of the bowl hold the crumbs better than a plate when coating the oysters); reserve remaining crumbs.

2 Cut baguettes in half lengthwise and scoop centers of the top halves, leaving a ½-inch rim.

3 In a small bowl, with a fork, beat the egg with water until well mixed. Place half the oysters into the egg mixture and with a fork place 2 to 3 oysters at a time on top of the cracker crumbs. Toss crumbs onto the oysters with the fork (it keeps your fingers from getting coated); then, with fingers, pat crumbs in place. Turn oysters and pat crumbs in place, as needed.

4 Place coated oysters on a plate large enough to hold all the oysters in a single layer. In batches, coat remaining egg-washed oysters and place in a single layer on the plate. Discard the used crumbs (they're too wet to use) and add dry crumbs to bowl. Coat remaining oysters in batches as in Step 1.

5 For draining the hot, cooked oysters, set a wire cake rack inside a rimmed baking sheet. Heat oil in a medium skillet over medium-high heat until oil shimmers but does not smoke, about 5 minutes.

6 Preheat oven to 300° and place an ovenproof platter in to heat. Place baguettes on a cookie sheet, lightly cover with foil, and heat until warm. Cook oysters in two batches. Lift oysters with a spoon or your fingers and gently place into oil in a single layer. The oil comes about half way up the oysters and sizzles when you add the oysters. Cook oysters until golden brown on the bottom, 1 minute. Carefully turn oysters with a slotted spoon, and cook until browned, 1 minute longer.

(continued)

7 Remove oysters with a slotted spoon and drain on wire rack; transfer oysters to the warm platter and return platter to oven. Cook remaining oysters (the second batch may brown faster than the first because the skillet is hot) and drain.

8 Spread the cut surfaces of each baguette with about 1 tablespoon of tartar sauce or the Remoulade Sauce in Chpater 5. Divide the oysters evenly among the baguettes and top oysters with shredded lettuce. Season with pepper to taste, add baguette tops, and serve.

If you cook two pints of oysters to double this recipe, plan to use clean oil for the second pint. As the oysters cook, crumbs fall into the oil. The crumbs may burn and darken the oil. Have a heatproof container on hand in which to pour the used oil; wipe skillet with a paper towel and heat new oil for the next batch.

Serve Barbara's Grand Slam Oysters po'boy style, or score big with three more tastes: for an appetizer, dip oysters into Chipotle Aïoli Sauce (see Chapter 15); top a juicy grilled steak with the crispy fried oysters; or for a divine eggs Benedict (as one of our friends recalls with mouth-watering glee eating in a restaurant in North Carolina), place fried oysters on poached eggs, and then ladle on the Hollandaise. Sounds wickedly good to us.

Classic Steamed Clams

Sometimes it's hard to beat utter simplicity. A steaming bowl of clams and some crusty bread are about as simple — and as sumptuous — as it gets. A true classic that never goes out of style. Offer a large bowl into which guests can discard empty shells.

Preparation time: *15 minutes for 2 dozen clams*

Cooking time: *15 minutes*

Yield: *2 to 4 dozen clams*

24 to 48 littleneck or other small, hardshell clams	*1 teaspoon roasted garlic (homemade or prepared)*
12 ounces beer	*¼ teaspoon salt*
1 cup water	*¼ teaspoon freshly ground black pepper*
¼ cup chopped onion	*Melted butter*
1 to 2 tablespoons fresh lemon juice	

1 Quickly wash clams and check that shells are tightly closed. (Refer to Chapter 4 for tips on checking shellfish.)

2 In a large pot, combine the beer, water, onion, 1 tablespoon lemon juice, garlic, salt, and pepper. Add clams to pot and bring to a boil over high heat. Reduce heat to medium.

3 Set a timer for 5 minutes (the minimum time clams need to steam). Using a large spoon, stir clams gently; cover pan tightly, and steam 5 to 8 minutes, or until all clams are open. Remove pot from heat.

4 Using a slotted spoon, divide clams among wide, individual serving bowls. Leave any unopened clams in pot, cover pot tightly, and continue cooking for 2 to 3 more minutes to see if clams open. Discard any clams that remain unopened.

5 Taste cooking liquid for saltiness and adjust seasonings if needed. (You can alleviate any excessive saltiness by adding more lemon juice.)

6 Check broth for gritty sandiness in bottom of pot. If necessary, strain broth before pouring into individual serving cups for dunking clams or sipping. Offer melted butter to top off clam broth or serve butter in separate individual containers for double dunking.

Freeze extra broth in ice cube trays. Pop frozen cubes into a plastic freezer bag and use to poach fish or to enhance soups and sauces.

Classic Steamed Mussels

While clams have sturdy flavors that are complemented by steaming in beer, mussels possess a delicacy that's best embellished with wine. Otherwise, our classic, simple approach is much the same as Classic Steamed Clams (see previous recipe). A steaming bowl of mussels and some crusty bread are simple and delicious.

Preparation time: *15 minutes*

Cooking time: *12 minutes*

Yield: *2 main course or 4 appetizer servings*

(continued)

2 pounds cultured (farm-raised) mussels

½ cup dry white wine

⅓ cup water

2 tablespoons diced Vidalia or other sweet onion

1 tablespoon chopped fresh herbs such as basil or parsley, or 2 teaspoons dried basil leaves

1 teaspoon minced garlic

2 to 3 teaspoons butter or extra virgin olive oil (optional)

Freshly ground black pepper

1 Gently scrub the mussels under cold running water and pull and discard the hairy beard from the side of the mussel. Discard mussels with broken shells. Squeeze the sides of mussels with shells that are open (or *gaping*). If they don't firmly close, discard these gapers as well. (Refer to Chapter 8 for the scoop on checking shellfish.)

2 In a large pot, combine the wine, water, onion, herbs, and garlic. Add mussels to pot and bring to a boil over high heat. Reduce heat to medium.

3 Set a timer for 3 minutes (the minimum time mussels need to steam). Using a large spoon, stir mussels gently, cover pan tightly, and steam until all the shells open, about 3 to 5 minutes. Remove pot from heat.

4 Using a slotted spoon, divide mussels among individual, rimmed soup plates. Leave any unopened mussels in pot, cover pot tightly, and continue cooking for 1 to 2 more minutes to see if mussels open. Discard any mussels that remain unopened at this point.

5 Return heat to high and vigorously boil mussel broth for 1 minute to concentrate the flavors. Enrich broth with butter or olive oil, if desired. Add pepper to taste. Ladle the broth equally over the mussels. Serve with crusty bread for dipping.

No Shell in Sight

Slip ready-to-eat surimi or cleaned calamari into our Italian-inspired recipes for easy weeknight suppers.

If you've never cooked calamari or surimi (and you don't have an Italian grandmother to guide you), this section shows you how.

Surimi and Potato Frittata

Just as you may prefer your own potato salad or barbecue sauce recipe, so Italian cooks embrace their personal way to make a filled omelet, known as a *frittata*. To make a frittata, you start by sautéing a filling (often a variety of thinly sliced vegetables) on top of the stove, pouring the eggs on top, and cooking until the eggs are partly set. We like to finish our frittata under the broiler instead of the oven, because broiling makes the top turn golden brown and slightly crispy while the inside stays moist and creamy.

Combine eggs with almost any filling for a pretty, tasty, and economical dish. A 10-inch skillet is a good size for four servings, but if your pan is smaller — and, hence, the frittata thicker — simply let the frittata finish cooking in the residual heat after you turn off the broiler. Serve the frittata with crunchy coleslaw.

Preparation time: *20 minutes*

Cooking time: *6 to 10 minutes*

Yield: *4 servings*

7 large eggs	*1 tablespoon olive oil*
1 tablespoon water	*1 cup thinly sliced zucchini (1 small zucchini)*
1½ teaspoons dried tarragon or basil leaves	*½ cup thinly sliced green onions*
½ cup grated sharp cheddar cheese, crumbled, or blue cheese	*2 teaspoons minced garlic*
½ teaspoon kosher salt	*¾ pound surimi or cooked, peeled small shrimp*
1 teaspoon freshly ground black or white pepper	*¼ cup roasted red bell pepper, cut into ¼- by 2-inch strips*
1 medium potato, red or russet (6 ounces)	

1 Before you turn on the broiler, set the rack so the top of the skillet will be about 2 inches from the broiler; preheat the broiler. In a medium bowl, whisk together the eggs, water, and tarragon, and then stir in half each of the cheese, salt, and pepper. Cut the potato in half and then into ⅟₁₆-inch thick slices.

2 In a 10-inch, ovenproof skillet, heat the oil over medium-high heat. Add the potatoes, zucchini, onions, garlic, and remaining salt and pepper. Cook, partly covered, until the vegetables are tender and lightly browned, about 5 minutes, loosening them with a metal spatula. Stir in surimi (coarsely chopped, if necessary) or cooked shrimp to evenly distribute.

3 Pour the egg mixture into skillet and gently lift the edges of the vegetables with the spatula to distribute eggs. Decorate the top with the roasted pepper strips and sprinkle on remaining cheese. Cook until the bottom of the frittata is set, 3 to 4 minutes.

(continued)

4 Place the skillet 2 inches from broiler and broil until the eggs are fully set and the top is golden brown and lightly puffed, 3 to 4 minutes. (If the top is browned but the eggs are not fully set, turn off the boiler, shut the broiler door, and let the frittata cook 2 to 3 minutes longer.)

5 With a sharp knife, cut the frittata into 4 wedges and loosen the outside edge; let frittata stand for 2 minutes before serving.

You can remove the first piece of the frittata whole — without having it fall to pieces! Slip the end of a metal spatula under one cut side edge of a wedge to loosen; repeat with the second edge. Hold a dinner plate next to skillet, lift the wedge — holding your breath — and slip the frittata onto the plate.

You may also substitute 1 pound of peeled, raw, small shrimp for the surimi. Stir the shrimp into the lightly browned vegetables (see Step 2), and cook 1 minute, stirring.

Seven-Minute Calamari with Tomato Sauce

Joyce Goldstein, cookbook author and highly respected chef whose services as a restaurant consultant are much in demand, knows menu logistics. Her experiences and research show that when calamari is listed on the menu, more is ordered than when the menu simply calls it "squid." Because this is an Italian-inspired recipe, using the term "calamari" (which is Italian) is especially fitting.

Quick-cook or slow-simmer the tomato-based calamari sauce, as you prefer. Our testers recommend adding all of the options (feta, olives, and red pepper flakes) to accentuate the sunny Mediterranean flavors.

Experienced seafood cooks use two methods to cook calamari in order to avoid any resemblance to springy rubber-bands. Either cook the calamari quickly, so that it doesn't toughen in the first place, or cook it for an extended period of time, to tenderize it. Pressure cooking is a quick way to achieve the same effect as long cooking. Without a pressure cooker, Seven-Minute Calamari becomes Half-Hour Calamari. Simply simmer the ingredients in a large, covered saucepan for 30 minutes or until the rings are tender.

Preparation time: *10 minutes*

Cooking time: *7 minutes*

Yield: *4 to 6 servings*

8 ounces cleaned calamari rings

1 can (28 ounces) diced tomatoes, undrained

1 cup chopped celery

½ cup chopped onion

1 teaspoon dried basil leaves

Salt and pepper to taste

4 to 5 tablespoons crumbled feta cheese (optional)

4 to 5 tablespoons sliced ripe olives (optional)

Red pepper flakes (optional)

Minced fresh parsley or basil for garnish

Cooked ridged tubular pasta (such as rigatoni or mostaccioli) or brown rice

1 If calamari is frozen, place in a bowl of cold water until rings are separated and nearly thawed (about 5 minutes). If frozen calamari rings are unavailable, buy cleaned calamari tubes and cut into ½-inch rings (or see Chapter 10 for cleaning calamari instructions). You can use calamari tentacles, but for this recipe, we prefer rings only.

2 Combine calamari, tomatoes, celery, onions, and basil in pressure cooker. Attach cover according to manufacturer's directions and heat on medium-high heat. Begin timing when the regulator gizmo indicates that pressure cooking has begun (about 2 to 3 minutes). Cook under pressure for 4 minutes and remove from heat. After about a minute, place cooker under cold running water to release pressure.

3 Season to taste with salt and pepper. Stir in feta, olives, and red pepper flakes, if desired. Garnish with parsley or basil and serve over pasta or rice.

Chapter 14

Salads, Soups, and Sandwiches

. . . .

In This Chapter

▶ Crafting one-dish seafood salads

▶ Stepping up to the seafood salad bar

▶ Marrying seafood flavors in make-ahead soups

▶ Netting seafood for soup

▶ Building seafood sandwiches

. . . .

*1*f seafood had a middle name, it would be "versatile." Toss seafood into salads, swirl into soups, and slip into sandwiches for stylish tastes. Discover wilt-free salads that are ideal for causal summer buffets, make-ahead soups with flavors that marry nicely when refrigerated overnight, and sandwiches that are as flexible as the seafood they house. We cover the waterfront in this chapter, with recipes that partner the familiar with the exotic.

> ### Recipes in This Chapter
>
> ▶ Good Luck Black-Eyed Peas with Crab
>
> ▶ Mussels with Fennel and Black Beans
>
> ▶ Smoked Trout with Thyme Potatoes
>
> ▶ Swordfish Salad with Pesto Vinaigrette
>
> ▶ Chunky Cioppino
>
> ▶ Catfish, Oyster, and Black Bean Gumbo
>
> ▶ Five-in-Five Chowder
>
> ▶ Winter-Warming Walleye, Wild Rice, and Not-So-Wild Mushroom Soup
>
> ▶ Cool Summer White Bean Soup with Shrimp Sunburst
>
> ▶ Tropical Mahimahi Pita Pockets
>
> ▶ Juan's Grilled Fish Wrap with Creamy Salsa Verde
>
> ▶ Grilled Jerk Tuna on Foccacia
>
>

Salad — Not Just Rabbit Food

Some people scornfully call salads "rabbit food," but consider this: Middle-aged rabbits don't have a paunch, do have their own teeth, and haven't lost their romantic zeal. Add great tasting, nutritious seafood to boost salads' stellar benefits even higher. Grill or broil your favorite seafood, and then toss with greens and grains galore. Choose firm- and moderately firm-fleshed seafood, such as salmon, tuna, swordfish, mussels, or shrimp. These fish and shellfish stand up better to tossing than do tender, delicate fish, such as flounder or orange roughy. We're sure you'll agree this selection of enhanced "rabbit food" beats the same old thing.

Good Luck Black-Eyed Peas with Crab

In the southern United States, black-eyed peas are one of several "good luck omens," essential to be eaten on January 1. We hope you agree; this salad is much too good to be limited to one day of the year. Cooks are in luck anytime, because this recipe is quick, easy, and can be made a day ahead (except for adding the seafood). Use any bean combination in place of the black-eyed peas for equally delicious tastes.

Preparation time: *20 minutes*

Yield: *6 servings (10 cups)*

2 cans (14 ounces each) black-eyed peas, drained, rinsed

2 cups cooked corn or thawed, frozen corn

2 cans (4 ounces each) chopped, mild, green chiles, undrained

1 cup finely chopped mixed fresh herbs: basil, parsley, oregano, mint, or cilantro

1 red bell pepper, finely chopped

½ cup finely chopped green onions

½ cup fresh lime juice

2 tablespoons sugar

2 to 3 teaspoons kosher salt

2 serrano chiles, minced or ½ to 1 teaspoon cayenne pepper

1 pound crabmeat

3 tablespoons olive oil

1 In a large bowl, mix the black-eyed peas, corn, chiles, herbs, red bell pepper, and green onions.

2 For the dressing, in a small bowl stir together the lime juice, sugar, salt, and serrano chiles until sugar and salt are dissolved. Spoon the dressing over the salad and toss. *Note:* The salad may be made ahead to this point and refrigerated overnight.

3 Pick through crabmeat and discard any shell fragments. Gently stir crab into salad; drizzle oil over salad and mix well. Taste and adjust seasonings before serving.

Mussels with Fennel and Black Beans

Licoricey fresh fennel and robust black beans make a tempting backdrop for sweet, tender mussels. Ideal for a summer buffet, the personality of this pretty salad blossoms, especially when made in advance. Bring salad to room temperature about 20 minutes before serving to brighten the flavors. Look for more tips about working with fresh mussels in Chapter 8.

Preparation time: *30 minutes*

Cooking time: *15 minutes*

Yield: *6 servings (10 cups)*

1 medium fennel bulb with stalks (about 10 ounces) or 1 small fennel bulb (about 5 ounces)

1 yellow bell pepper, cored and quartered

3 ounces fresh spinach (about 4 cups loosely packed)

2 cans (15 ounces each) black beans, drained and rinsed

¾ cup water

4 shallots, peeled and quartered

8 whole garlic cloves, peeled

4 pounds small to medium mussels, cleaned and debearded

⅓ cup sherry vinegar or white wine vinegar

4 teaspoons Dijon mustard

½ to 1 teaspoon kosher salt

1 teaspoon freshly ground black pepper

¼ to ½ teaspoon cayenne pepper (optional)

¼ cup olive oil

1 Pull feathery dill-like fronds off fennel stalks and coarsely chop; set aside. Cut the tough stalks from the bulb and discard. Slice fennel bulb vertically into quarters; discard the core. Place fennel cut-side down and thinly slice on the diagonal, starting where the stalks were removed.

2 Slice pepper crosswise into matchstick-size pieces. Wash and dry spinach and cut crosswise into thin ribbons. In a large bowl, combine the fennel bulb and fronds, yellow pepper, spinach, and beans. **Note:** If making a day ahead, add spinach just before serving.

3 In a 10-inch pot, combine the water, shallots, and garlic. Place a vegetable steamer rack in pot, cover, and bring to a boil on high heat. Place mussels on rack, cover, and steam for 3 to 5 minutes; discard any unopened mussels. Transfer the mussels to a bowl and set aside.

(continued)

4 Remove the steamer rack and scoop out the shallots and garlic with a slotted spoon. To make the base for the salad dressing, boil the cooking liquid uncovered until reduced to ¼ cup; finely chop the shallots and garlic and put in a medium bowl. Add reduced mussel liquid to shallot mixture along with the vinegar, mustard, salt, pepper, and cayenne, if using. Whisk in olive oil.

5 Reserve eight mussels in their shells to decorate the salad and remove the rest of the mussels from their shells. Add mussel meats to fennel mixture. Pour dressing over salad and toss. Taste and adjust seasonings. Spoon salad into a large, shallow serving bowl. Top salad with reserved mussels on the half shell and serve.

If you substitute cooked fish or shellfish (shrimp, crab, clams, or crawfish) for the mussels, you need broth in order to make the salad dressing liquid. To make a quick broth, in a medium pot, bring one 10-ounce can clam juice (1¼ cups), 4 shallots, and 8 cloves garlic to a boil. Boil uncovered until the vegetables are soft and the liquid is reduced to ¼ cup, about 10 minutes. Finish the dressing as in the recipe by chopping the shallots and garlic, and adding the vinegar, mustard, and other ingredients.

High-quality Spanish sherry vinegar is a kitchen staple prized by many experienced cooks. You can make a tasty substitute with 2 parts red wine vinegar (that's at least 6 percent acidity) and 1 part dry- or medium-dry sherry.

Smoked Trout with Thyme Potatoes

Looking for an elegant recipe for a bridal shower luncheon — or a simple solution for a one-dish summer supper? This salad showcasing smoked trout stands out in either venue. It's best to use fresh herbs — in this recipe, dried herbs simply don't have the fragrance and freshness that this salad needs. If you don't have fresh thyme, fresh tarragon, fresh basil, or flat leaf parsley are worthy stand-ins.

Preparation time: *30 minutes*

Cooking time: *10 minutes*

Yield: *4 servings*

1¼ pounds small red potatoes, skin-on

¾ pound snow peas or sugar snap peas, cleaned

2 tablespoons olive, garlic, or herb-flavored oil

3 heads Belgian endive or one 10-ounce head iceberg lettuce

2 tablespoons drained capers

¼ cup minced fresh thyme leaves

¼ cup balsamic vinegar

2 tablespoons finely chopped chives or green onion tops

1 teaspoon white pepper

¼ teaspoon kosher salt

¾ pound boneless smoked trout fillet or other smoked fish or shellfish

1 Put the potatoes in a large pan with cold, salted water. Bring to a boil and simmer until just tender when pierced with the point of a knife, about 10 minutes. Drain the potatoes, let cool slightly, and cut into quarters. While the potatoes are cooking, in a medium pot, bring 2 inches of water to a boil under a vegetable steamer rack, add the snow peas, and steam for 1 minute. Run the peas under cold water to stop cooking and pat dry.

2 In a large bowl, combine the potatoes and the snow peas. Add the olive oil and toss to coat. Sliver the endive on the diagonal and add to the potato mixture along with the capers, thyme, balsamic vinegar, chives, pepper, and salt; toss to coat. Flake the trout into bite-size pieces (about 2½ cups); discard any skin and bones. Add trout to the salad and gently mix. Taste, adjust seasonings, and serve.

If you buy a whole, head-on trout, you need 2 trout, about 8 ounces each.

Swordfish Salad with Pesto Vinaigrette

A refreshing, satisfying salad for balmy summer evenings. Grill corn on the cob while you're grilling the swordfish and dinner's ready!

Preparation time: *40 minutes*

Cooking time: *8 to 10 minutes*

Yield: *4 servings*

(continued)

½ pound frisée, escarole, or mixed baby greens

¾ pound cucumbers

1 can (14 ounces) hearts of palm, drained

16 cherry tomatoes, quartered

2 tablespoons minced shallots

1 pound skin-on swordfish steak, about 1-inch thick

2 teaspoons olive oil

1 to 1½ teaspoons kosher salt

1 to 1½ teaspoons freshly ground black pepper

¼ cup raspberry or red wine vinegar

½ cup homemade or purchased pesto

1 Brush grill grid with oil and prepare a medium-hot fire in a charcoal or gas grill. As the grill heats, rinse frisée, dry well, and tear into bite-size pieces. Place frisée in a large bowl. Peel cucumbers, leaving four thin lengthwise strips of skin for color contrast. Halve cucumber lengthwise and scoop out the seeds; thinly slice cucumber on the diagonal into half moons. Slice hearts of palm on the diagonal into ¼-inch thick ovals. Add the cucumbers, hearts of palm, tomatoes, and shallots to the frisée.

2 Rub both sides of swordfish with oil and season each side with ¼ teaspoon salt and pepper. Grill swordfish, with grill lid closed, for 3 minutes. Gently flip swordfish, cover the grill, and cook 3 minutes more. Turn swordfish again and cook about 2 minutes, or until the flesh of the swordfish turns just opaque. Remove swordfish from grill and let stand 1 to 2 minutes to slightly cool.

3 In a small bowl, stir the vinegar into the pesto to mix. Discard the swordfish skin and cut or break fish into ¾-inch chunks. Add swordfish to salad, and spoon pesto vinaigrette on top. Gently toss salad and season to taste with remaining salt and pepper.

Vary It! Instead of basil pesto, try the Dill Pesto with Asian Notes recipe in Chapter 15.

To compose your own seafood salads, check out Table 14-1, which suggests fish for you to cook at home, and smoked and marinated prepared seafood to track down at your seafood market.

Table 14-1	Stepping Up to the Seafood Salad Bar	
Seafood Salads in This Book	*Your Home-Cooked Seafood*	*Short-Cuts from Your Seafood Counter*
Good-Luck Black-Eyed Peas with Crab	Salmon, shrimp, catfish, rockfish, bluefish	Smoked seafood: trout, mussels, salmon, white-fish; crawfish, shrimp, surimi; marinated mussels or calamari rings
Smoked Trout with Thyme Potatoes	Mahimahi, striped bass, swordfish, salmon	Smoked seafood: mussels, mackerel, bluefish, salmon; canned salmon, tuna; crab, surimi, crawfish
Swordfish Salad with Pesto Vinaigrette	Tuna, shrimp, Chilean sea bass, grouper, shark	Smoked trout, mussels, salmon; shrimp, surimi
Mussels with Fennel and Black Beans	Clams, scallops, shrimp, tilapia	Marinated mussels or calamari rings; shrimp, crab, crawfish; canned salmon, tuna

Soup's On

Nothing beats a bowl of steaming seafood soup to banish chilly blasts. Whether you say soup, stew, chowder, or bisque, these dishes reflect the great culinary heritage in the United States. Soups often feature the local catch of the day, so take advantage of featured seafood specials when you shop — choose seafood that will retain its shape and not flake apart. In this section, we offer soups to fit your everyday and entertaining needs: do-ahead soups, fast-fixin' soup, and a pretty cool soup for switching seasons.

Chunky Cioppino

With the arrival of the crisp days of autumn, nothing cuts the chill like a bowl of thick, steaming, seafood stew. Serve this quick and easy version of cioppino (chuh-PEE-noh) with crusty sourdough bread and a fennel salad dressed with a warm bacon vinaigrette, or over penne pasta to serve more people.

Preparation time: *30 minutes*

Cooking time: *15 minutes*

Yield: *4 servings (7 cups)*

2 tablespoons olive oil

1 cup minced green onions, including tops

2 tablespoons minced or pureed garlic

3 cups homemade or 2 containers (15 ounces each) ready-to-use marinara sauce (plain or flavored)

1½ cups dry red wine

1 teaspoon dried basil leaves

1½ teaspoons kosher salt, divided

¼ teaspoon freshly ground black pepper

Pinch cayenne pepper

1 pound Pacific rockfish, grouper, monkfish, striped bass, or snapper, skinned, or a combination of any fish, cut into ¾ inch cubes

¼ pound raw, large shrimp (31/35 per pound), peeled, deveined

¼ pound shucked, drained oysters (optional)

1 In a heavy 4- to 5-quart pot, heat oil on medium heat. Sauté onions and garlic until softened, stirring, about 5 minutes. Add marinara sauce, wine, basil, 1 teaspoon salt, pepper, and cayenne. Bring stew base to a boil and reduce heat to medium low. Cook base, partly covered, about 5 minutes, stirring. (Partly covering lets some liquid evaporate but keeps the tomato sauce from popping out of the pot.)

2 Stir fish and shrimp into stew, partly cover, and cook until fish is almost opaque, 3 to 4 minutes. Add oysters and cook until edges curl, about 1 minute. Ladle stew into bowls and serve.

If you use small shrimp or rock shrimp (discussed in the Appendix), add them with the oysters to avoid overcooking. When unexpected guests drop in, you can easily extend the cioppino to serve more people. Cook ravioli or penne, and serve the cioppino over the pasta. Use any of the following seafood instead of the seafood that the recipe suggests: calamari rings, scallops, or a pound of live, scrubbed clams or mussels.

Quick fish stock

When you don't have time to make stock from scratch, try this quick alternative. Begin with bottled or canned clam juice. To each cup of clam juice, add ½ cup water, ¼ cup dry white wine, 1 small sliced onion, and 2 peppercorns.

Simmer, covered, 10 minutes and strain. If you want flavor options beyond clam juice, start the stock with vegetable broth, tomato or vegetable juice, or chicken stock.

Catfish, Oyster, and Black Bean Gumbo

Although the ingredient list is long, this hearty gumbo is easy to assemble, and the gumbo flavors develop nicely when refrigerated overnight before serving. We include directions for reheating the gumbo and adding the seafood before serving. If okra isn't one of your favorite vegetables, this soup will still be delicious if you replace the okra with steamed green beans. Round out the meal with a salad and cornbread.

Preparation time: *40 minutes*

Cooking time: *25 minutes*

Yield: *6 to 8 main course servings (about 10 cups)*

2 tablespoons olive oil

1 red bell pepper finely diced

¾ cup finely chopped celery

1½ cups minced shallots or sweet onions, such as Vidalia

3 tablespoons minced garlic

20 fresh okra cut into ½-inch coins

24 ounces full-flavored beer

1 cup clam juice, fish stock, or chicken broth, fat skimmed

8 ounces shucked oysters, drained and liquid reserved if desired

½ cup minced fresh parsley

¼ cup Worcestershire sauce

1 teaspoon dried basil leaves

1 teaspoon kosher salt

1 teaspoon freshly ground black pepper

½ to 1 teaspoon red pepper flakes

½ teaspoon dried oregano leaves

1 can (6 ounces) tomato paste

2 cans (14 ounces each) black beans, drained, rinsed

1½ cups long-grain rice

1 pound catfish fillets, cut into ¾-inch pieces

1 pound raw, small shrimp (51/60 count), peeled and deveined, or ½ pound peeled rock shrimp

(continued)

1 In a heavy, 5-quart pot, heat oil on medium heat until hot. Add the red bell pepper, celery, shallots, and garlic, and sauté until partly softened, 5 minutes, stirring. Add okra and sauté until tender, 5 minutes, stirring. Don't worry if the mixture sticks or browns; the caramelized bits will loosen as the gumbo cooks, enhancing the flavor.

2 Stir in the beer, clam juice, oyster liquid (if using), parsley, Worcestershire sauce, basil, salt, pepper, red pepper flakes, and oregano. Whisk in tomato paste until well blended. Add beans and simmer uncovered on medium heat for 15 minutes, stirring. The gumbo may be made ahead to this point and refrigerated overnight. Reheat soup before adding seafood.

3 Shortly before serving, cook rice according to package directions.

4 Stir in the catfish and simmer 2 to 3 minutes; stir in the shrimp and oysters and simmer until shrimp turn opaque and oyster edges curl, 1 to 2 minutes. Do not overcook, because the seafood continues to cook in the hot soup when taken from the heat. Spoon rice into individual soup bowls and ladle the gumbo on top.

 You may substitute frozen okra for fresh. Remove frozen okra from package, separate under cold running water and drain. Proceed as with fresh okra.

Five-in-Five Chowder

Nacho cheese is the subject of one-liners. *(What do you call cheese that isn't yours? Nacho cheese.)* Granted, it doesn't have the status of Brie, but it can be a tasty time-saver. Reach for this key ingredient and create our creamy chowder with five ingredients that cooks in five minutes. Many fish work in this recipe. Our top recommendations: walleye, haddock, halibut, or salmon. You may want to serve this casual soup with fish-shaped crackers as shown in the color photo section near the center of the book.

Preparation time: *5 minutes*

Cooking time: *5 minutes*

Yield: *4 servings (makes 4½ cups)*

1 cup chicken broth

1 cup cooked corn or thawed, frozen corn

1 cup milk

1 cup bottled nacho cheese sauce (sometimes labeled cheese and salsa, preferably mild)

1 cup bite-size cubes of raw fish, skin off (about 6 ounces)

Cooked bacon crumbles (optional)

Minced fresh parsley to garnish

1 In a blender or food processor, pulse broth and ½ cup corn until fairly smooth. (While this step is desirable for a creamy chowder, it's not essential if you're pressed for time or don't have a blender or food processor.)

2 In a large saucepan on medium-high heat, combine broth-corn mixture, remaining corn, milk, and cheese sauce. Stir chowder to blend well and heat until hot, about 3 minutes, stirring frequently. Reduce heat to medium and add fish. Simmer chowder until fish is barely opaque, 1 to 2 minutes. Promptly remove from heat, because the fish continues to cook in the hot chowder when removed from the heat.

3 Top each serving with bacon crumbles (about a tablespoon per serving) and parsley.

Ready-to-eat bacon strips are a mess-free shortcut for this recipe. Simply reheat bacon on layers of paper towel in microwave, crumble, and add to chowder. Because the chowder calls for equal amounts of ingredients, this recipe is easy to scale up or down.

Winter-Warming Walleye, Wild Rice, and Not-So-Wild Mushroom Soup

Rent the video of *Grumpy Old Men* and sip this hearty soup while you chuckle over the antics of those wild and wooly north country ice fishermen on and off the frozen lakes. When your favorite fisherman comes home empty-handed, you can still enjoy authentic freshwater fish flown to you from icy northern waters — check out our Web site recommendations in Chapter 24. Or net yourself any of these satisfying saltwater substitutes from your local fishmonger: haddock, perch, orange roughy, or snapper.

Preparation time: *10 minutes*

Cooking time: *12 minutes*

Yield: *4 servings (makes 5 cups)*

2 cups well-seasoned chicken or vegetable broth

1⅓ cups cooked wild rice (½ cup uncooked, prepared according to package directions)

1 cup chopped onions

1 cup chopped celery

1 cup chopped cremini (brown) or portabella mushrooms

1 cup ¾-inch cubes walleye, skin discarded (about 6 ounces)

1 teaspoon dried tarragon leaves, crumbled

1 teaspoon Worcestershire sauce

½ teaspoon salt, preferably seasoned salt, such as Lawry's

4 to 5 tablespoons half-and-half or light cream (optional)

(continued)

1 In a large saucepan or Dutch oven, combine broth, wild rice, onions, celery, and mushrooms. Cover and cook over medium-high heat for 6 to 8 minutes or until onions and celery are nearly softened.

2 Reduce heat to low and stir in fish, tarragon, Worcestershire sauce, and salt. Simmer until fish is opaque, 3 to 4 minutes.

3 For a creamy soup, stir in half-and-half and continue to cook until soup is hot, about 1 minute. Serve warm.

Before the cream is added, this soup freezes successfully. Make a double batch, cool it quickly, and then package in serving-size containers. Thaw overnight in the refrigerator or use the defrost setting on your microwave.

Cool Summer White Bean Soup with Shrimp Sunburst

When you're ready for a change of season, savor the tastes of summer with this tangy white bean soup enriched with tomatoes, cucumbers, and fresh basil. Float shrimp on top and serve with hot toasted cheese bread and a watercress and endive salad. The food processor makes quick work of pureeing the vegetables.

Preparation time: 30 minutes

Chilling time: 3 to 4 hours

Cooking time: 2 minutes

Yield: 4 main course or 6 first course servings (makes 6 cups)

1 pound raw, shell-on, large (31/35 per pound) or extra-large shrimp (26/30 count)

1½ pounds ripe tomatoes, peeled, cored, seeded, divided

1 cucumber (8 ounces), peeled, halved, and seeded; divided

4 garlic cloves, peeled

4 shallots, peeled, quartered

2 cans (15 ounces each) cannellini or other white beans, rinsed, drained, and divided

½ cup chopped, roasted red bell pepper

¼ cup balsamic vinegar

2 tablespoons olive oil

1 tablespoon kosher salt

1 teaspoon sugar

1 teaspoon freshly ground black pepper

½ cup finely chopped fresh basil plus basil sprigs to garnish

1 To cook the shrimp, bring a large pot of water to a boil. Place a large bowl with water and ice in sink, as illustrated in Chapter 5. Add shrimp to boiling water and cook just until center of shrimp almost turns white, 2 to 2½ minutes. Drain shrimp and plunge into ice water to stop cooking; peel shrimp, halve lengthwise to help shrimp float (and go twice as far), and set aside.

2 For the soup, separate ⅓ each of the tomatoes and cucumbers; cut into ¼-inch dice and set aside. Coarsely chop remaining ⅔ of tomatoes and cucumbers.

3 With the food processor running, add the garlic and mince; add the shallots, mince, and scrape workbowl. Add 1 cup beans and puree, scraping bowl as needed.

4 Add coarsely chopped tomatoes, cucumber, and roasted peppers to the workbowl and puree, about 30 seconds. With the machine running, add the vinegar, oil, salt, sugar, and pepper to blend.

5 Pour soup into a large bowl and stir in reserved tomatoes and cucumbers, remaining beans, and chopped basil. Cover and chill soup for 3 to 4 hours before serving. If desired, make soup one day in advance, but reserve diced tomatoes and cucumbers to add shortly before serving.

6 For the prettiest presentation, serve soup in shallow soup dishes. For each serving, arrange 5 to 7 shrimp halves, cut side down, in a sunburst on top of soup (place shrimp tails at the middle of the sunburst). Pinch basil leaves from stalks and put several leaves at the sunburst center, as shown in the color photo section near the center of this book. Place remaining shrimp in a bowl, garnish with basil, and let guests stir shrimp into their own soup.

Saluting Seafood Sandwiches

Sandwiches offer flexibility at your fingertips. And as our friend Gail Bellamy, food editor of *Restaurant Hospitality,* so aptly notes, "Sandwiches today speak many languages." Mexican tortillas, Middle Eastern pitas and flatbreads, Indian naan, and Italian focaccias are redefining our concepts of this familiar finger food. We are wrapping, rolling, stuffing, and topping these breads from afar with seafood galore. In this chapter, we share flavorful fillings and innovative sauces for you to assemble and enjoy. Today's sandwiches are still pick-up food, but now they're filling and fun.

Tropical Mahimahi Pita Pockets

Messy, but fun, these pita pockets are brimming with tangy onion sprouts and the tropical beat of mango, mahimahi, cilantro, and ginger. Nectarines, papaya, or peaches are a sweet substitute for mangoes. Those who like the tropics hotter may want to add a splash of their favorite zesty bottled hot sauce. For mango-peeling tips, see Figure 14-1.

Preparation time: *40 minutes*

Cooking time: *6 to 8 minutes*

Yield: *4 servings (2 pockets per person)*

⅓ cup honey mustard

2 tablespoons cider vinegar

2 tablespoons plain, nonfat yogurt

2 tablespoons grated or minced fresh ginger

1 teaspoon kosher salt

1 pound skin-on, mahimahi fillet, about ¾-inch thick

¾ pound cucumbers

2 mangoes (10 ounces each), peeled and diced ½-inch square

2 cups thinly sliced radishes

1 cup minced fresh cilantro or parsley

4 large pita breads, halved crosswise and warmed

3 ounces onion sprouts or other spicy sprouts, washed, drained, and well-dried

1 Preheat broiler. For the dressing, in a small bowl, mix honey mustard, vinegar, yogurt, ginger, and salt until smooth. Place mahimahi skin-side-down on broiler rack and spread 2 tablespoons mustard dressing on top; reserve remaining dressing for salad.

2 Broil the mahimahi 4 to 5 inches from broiler until the fish just begins to flake when nudged with a fork, 6 to 10 minutes. Remove mahimahi from oven and let stand on the rack while preparing the salad.

3 Peel cucumbers, leaving four thin strips of skin for color contrast. Halve cucumbers lengthwise and scoop out the seeds; thinly slice cucumbers on the diagonal into half moons. In a large bowl, toss cucumbers, mangoes, radishes, and cilantro.

4 Gently lift the mahimahi from the skin and break fish into chunks. Add mahimahi to salad, pour dressing on top, and gently mix. Taste and adjust seasonings. Pass pita pockets and let guests spoon sprouts into pita pockets and top with the mahimahi salad.

Vary It! Try bluefish, mackerel, tuna, salmon, striped bass, grouper, Chilean sea bass, or rock shrimp instead of mahimahi.

Pare pita prep by starting with precooked seafood instead of fresh mahimahi. Smoked fish, such as bluefish, mackerel, trout, or whitefish pair successfully with these tropical flavors.

How to Cut a Mango

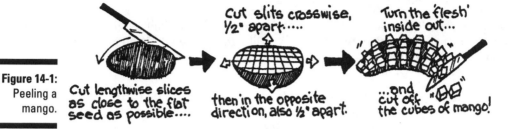

Figure 14-1:
Peeling a mango.

Cut lengthwise slices as close to the flat seed as possible....

Cut slits crosswise, 1/2" apart..... then in the opposite direction, also 1/2" apart.

Turn the 'flesh' inside out... ...and cut off the cubes of mango!

Juan's Grilled Fish Wrap with Creamy Salsa Verde

This pretty, fresh-tasting dish is a mainstay of casual San Diego eateries. And former restaurateur John Blake concocts his version of the popular wrapped fish for kids — and adults — galore. Heat a soft corn tortilla lightly on the grill so that it folds nicely around the fish, and then top with shredded cabbage, red salsa, creamy salsa verde, and a squeeze of lime. Make the creamy salsa verde at least a day before using for the best flavor.

Preparation time: *35 minutes*

Cooking time: *5 to 6 minutes*

Yield: *4 servings*

¼ cup fresh lime juice

¼ cup olive oil

1 tablespoon minced garlic

4 to 6 fresh or pickled jalapeño peppers, seeded, minced

1 teaspoon kosher salt

1½ pounds skinless grouper fillet

Twelve 6-inch tortillas, preferably yellow corn

1 small head (¾ pound) cabbage, cored and finely shredded

1 cup tomato salsa

Creamy Salsa Verde (see the following recipe)

2 limes, quartered

(continued)

1 In a medium bowl, stir together the lime juice, oil, garlic, jalapeños, and salt. Cut the grouper into small pieces, about 2-inches by 1-inch that will wrap nicely in the corn tortilla (6 to 8 pieces per person). Add the grouper to the bowl and refrigerate to marinate 1 hour.

2 Prepare a medium-hot fire in a charcoal or gas grill; heat a lightly oiled grill topper (see Chapter 2) at the same time. You need a grill topper to keep the small pieces of grouper from falling through the grill racks and for easy turning. Place grouper on topper and spoon marinade onto the grouper.

3 Grill grouper, with grill lid closed, until golden brown and a bit crispy, 5 to 6 minutes, turning once. Use a long-handled spatula to turn 3 or 4 pieces of fish at a time (using tongs to turn individual pieces takes too much time). Remove fish to a warm plate and loosely cover to keep warm. Scrape grill to clean before heating tortillas.

4 Place tortillas on the grill to heat through, uncovered, and get a few grill marks (it is not necessary to brush the tortillas with oil). Have a large piece of tin foil handy and place tortillas on foil as you remove them from the grill. Wrap tortillas to keep warm.

5 Let everyone wrap his or her own soft taco, topping the corn tortilla with 2 to 3 pieces of grouper, shredded cabbage, tomato salsa, Creamy Salsa Verde, and a squeeze of lime.

Vary It! Mahimahi, swordfish, tuna, salmon, catfish, or cod also wrap well.

Creamy Salsa Verde

Preparation time: *10 minutes*

Yield: *1½ cups*

½ cup sour cream	*⅓ cup dried parsley flakes*
½ cup mayonnaise	*1½ teaspoons fresh lemon juice*
⅓ cup salsa verde (green chile salsa)	*¾ teaspoon seasoned salt, such as Lawry's*

Combine the sour cream, mayonnaise, salsa verde, parsley, lemon juice, and seasoned salt until smooth and well blended. Make the sauce a day ahead, if possible, to let the parsley rehydrate fully.

If you want to use the sauce shortly after making it, use fresh parsley instead of the dried.

Grilled Jerk Tuna on Foccacia

Capture the beat of the festive island lifestyle with lusty Jamaican jerk, a favorite cooking method that seasons pork, chicken, seafood, or beef with a traditional, highly spiced seasoning blend before grilling over a slow, hot fire. Spicy, sweet and seductive, jerk is a dry blend that keeps well. It's easy to transform this dish into a party appetizer: Slice the cooked tuna, lay the tuna on top of the foccacia, and cut into individual bites.

Preparation time: *40 minutes*

Cooking time: *3 to 4 minutes*

Yield: *4 servings*

4 tuna steaks, ¾-inch thick
(about 1¼ pounds total)

1 to 2 tablespoons olive oil

8 teaspoons whole allspice, ground or 8 teaspoons ground allspice

2 tablespoons dry mustard

4 teaspoons dried thyme leaves

4 teaspoons paprika

2 teaspoons granulated onion

2 teaspoons lemon pepper

1 teaspoon white pepper or freshly ground black pepper

1 teaspoon red pepper flakes

½ teaspoon granulated garlic

½ teaspoon cayenne pepper

½ teaspoon cinnamon

½ teaspoon kosher salt

Foccacia

1 Rinse the tuna with cold water and pat dry with paper towels. Rub each portion of tuna with ¼ to ½ teaspoon oil per side.

2 In a small bowl combine the allspice, mustard, thyme, paprika, onion, lemon pepper, white pepper, red pepper flakes, garlic, cayenne, cinnamon, and salt. Makes about ½ cup of jerk.

3 Sprinkle one side of each portion of fish with 1½ teaspoons jerk; pat the seasoning onto the fish, turn, and repeat with second side. Refrigerate for 1½ hours until jerk is moistened, turning once. Store the extra jerk blend in a cool dark place up to 6 months.

4 Brush grill grid with oil and prepare a medium-hot fire in a charcoal or gas grill. Grill tuna, with grill lid closed, turning once, until tuna is springy and medium-rare, 2 to 3 minutes per side. For tuna that's more rare, grill tuna 1 to 2 minutes less. Do not overcook — tuna continues to cook after removing from the fire.

5 Grill foccacia until lightly toasted on both sides. Top foccacia with grilled tuna (as shown in the color photo section near the center of this book) and serve with your favorite sauce, such as the Chipotle Aïoli or Tomatillo Salsa, in Chapter 15.

Vary It! Swordfish, cobia, and mahimahi are good alternatives for the tuna.

A Granny Smith apple, orange, and sweet onion salad is a refreshing side dish.

The more finely ground a seasoning is, the more bitter it can be, so look for granulated garlic and onion rather than powders or salts.

Don't stop with our seafood sandwich recipes. Design your own sandwiches. Go beyond sliced bread and rolls for your sandwich base with widely available ethnic flat breads, such as lavash, crusty foccacia, and flavored wraps. Choose your favorites and transform them into your signature sandwich.

Table 14-2 shows you some of our favorite combinations. Note our suggestions to convert our salad recipes into dynamite sandwiches. Flip to Chapter 15 for the recipes for the saucy toppers. (We know that topping grilled portabellas with seafood fillings isn't a true open-faced sandwich, but the flavor combination of mushroom, fish, greens, and sauce is a winner.)

Table 14-2	**Building Seafood Sandwiches**		
Seafood Fillings	*Breads, Wrappers, and Handy Holders*	*Crunchy Sandwich Stuffers*	*Saucy Toppers*
Grilled shrimp, tuna, grouper, swordfish, salmon, mahimahi, scallops	Flavored tortillas, grilled focaccia, portabella mushrooms	Shredded cabbage, mixed salad greens	Chipotle Aïoli, Indonesian Peanut Sauce
Fried oysters, clams, soft-shell crabs	French baguettes, sesame seed buns	Sprouts, shredded spinach	Remoulade Sauce
Crabmeat or surimi	Lavash, pita	Bacon, lettuce, tomato, avocado	Chipotle Aïoli
Smoked salmon, mackerel, bluefish	Indian naan	Slivered red pepper or fennel	Cool as a Cucumber
Good-Luck Black Eyed Peas with Crab	Jalapeño or cilantro tortillas, pita		Roasted Red-Pepper Velvet
Smoked Trout with Thyme Potatoes	Corn tortillas, pita		Tangy Cilantro Topper

Seafood Fillings	Breads, Wrappers, and Handy Holders	Crunchy Sandwich Stuffers	Saucy Toppers
Swordfish Salad with Pesto Vinaigrette	Grilled portabella mushrooms, focaccia, herb tortillas		
Mussel Salad with Fennel and Black Beans	Curry tortillas, pita		Catalan Romesco Sauce
Tuna, salmon, or lobster salad	Lavash, corn tortillas	Spicy sprouts	Cool as a Cucumber, Tangy Cilantro Topper

Chapter 15

Sassy Sauces and Salsas

In This Chapter

▶ Stirring up sensational sauces

▶ Mastering *safe* mayonnaise

▶ Adding a magical beat with salsas

Seafood partners perfectly with a rainbow of condiments, from savory sauces and salsas to vinaigrettes, barbecue sauces, and spiked-up mayonnaise. You can prepare many of the sauces ahead and keep them on hand for easy entertaining or quick weekday meals. Or stir up a quick stove-top sauce for a cool weather supper. Add spice, elegance, or pizazz to your seafood cooking. All these sauces and salsas have a natural affinity for seafood.

Sinful Sauces

Cooks around the world serve their favored regional sauces with seafood. In your travels, you can find sauces that simply accompany seafood (such as aïoli, the pungent garlic mayonnaise from southern France), sauces that contain morsels of succulent shellfish (creamy Nantua crawfish sauce, inspired by the famous catch of this French town northeast of Lyons), and other sauces that use salted, fermented fish and shellfish, including anchovies and shrimp, as their base. These aromatic fish sauces are as familiar a condiment in southeast Asia as ketchup is in the United States. We love a variety of sauces with fish, and in this section, we offer you our favorite ethnic tastes to enhance your seafood cooking.

Indonesian Peanut Sauce

Twenty-five years ago, Dutch relatives in Aruba introduced Marcie to this "exotic" foreign condiment. They served the sauce with satay — the now familiar marinated and grilled shrimp, chicken, or pork on bamboo skewers. These days, you can find a variety of bottled peanut sauces on supermarket shelves around the world. This homemade sauce is cheaper and better than bottled — even with shortcuts and twists on authentic ingredients. Serve the sauce with grilled or broiled seafood for rave reviews.

Preparation time: *6 minutes*

Cooking time: *1 minute*

Yield: *1 cup*

⅓ cup crunchy or plain peanut butter

1 tablespoon peeled and grated fresh ginger

1 tablespoon fresh lime or lemon juice

1 tablespoon citrus marmalade, lemon curd, or apricot jelly

1 tablespoon hoisin sauce

1 tablespoon soy sauce

3 tablespoons coconut milk or half-and-half

1 to 2 tablespoons water

Asian toasted sesame oil (optional)

Tabasco sauce or tiny hot chile, minced (optional)

1 Add peanut butter, ginger, lime juice, marmalade, hoisin sauce, and soy sauce to a two-cup or larger glass measuring pitcher or other microwaveable container. Heat on high for 20 to 30 seconds to warm and soften peanut butter sufficiently to make it easier to blend ingredients; mix thoroughly. Or warm ingredients in a saucepan over low heat, stirring until smooth.

2 Stir in coconut milk or half-and-half. Slowly add just enough water to thin sauce to the consistency of mayonnaise. Add up to ¼ teaspoon of sesame oil for a toasty note. If you like heat, add Tabasco sauce or minced chile. Serve at room temperature. If sauce becomes too thick, warm briefly in the microwave or dilute with additional water or coconut milk. Serve with grilled seafood.

Vary It! Create a hearty sesame noodle salad: Heat peanut sauce and stir in additional coconut milk, half-and-half, or water until sauce is thin enough to toss with cooked soba (buckwheat) noodles. Stir in bite-sized cooked seafood, shredded fresh carrots, and chopped scallions. Garnish with toasted sesame seeds and serve at room temperature.

Store leftover peanut sauce tightly covered and refrigerated for up to two weeks. Reheat in microwave on medium for 30 seconds, and then stir thoroughly.

Tangy Cilantro Topper

"Peas, peas, glorious peas. . ." Rather than rolling and rambling 'round the plate, peas add colorful character to this sassy sauce. Team the topper with grilled seafood such as salmon, halibut, or swordfish, or with steamed clams, mussels, or shrimp. You can guarantee a thick sauce by checking out the tips with the Steamed Salmon Pockets with Emerald Sauce recipe in Chapter 6.

Preparation time: *20 minutes*

Cooking time: *2 minutes*

Yield: *2 cups*

1 teaspoon vegetable oil

2 tablespoons coarsely chopped shallots

½ teaspoon chili powder

¼ teaspoon ground cumin

1 cup frozen green peas, thawed

½ cup packed fresh cilantro or parsley leaves, washed, and well dried (1 small bunch)

½ to 1 chipotle chile (canned in adobo sauce), undrained

½ cup sour cream

½ cup plain, nonfat yogurt

2 tablespoons fresh lime juice

½ teaspoon kosher salt

1 In a glass measuring cup, stir together oil, shallots, chili powder, and cumin. Cover with plastic wrap, and microwave on high for 1 to 1½ minutes until shallots are tender, stirring once. Or heat oil in a small skillet over medium-low heat. Add shallots, chili powder, and cumin. Sauté, partly covered, stirring occasionally, until shallots are tender, about 5 minutes.

2 In a blender or food processor, place peas, cilantro, shallots, and chipotle; pulse until finely chopped and blended. Add sour cream, yogurt, lime juice, and salt. Process until blended. Taste and adjust seasonings. Serve sauce slightly chilled. You can refrigerate the sauce for several days.

For the spicy scoop about chipotle chiles, refer to the Avocado Chipotle-Glazed Salmon recipe in Chapter 6.

Dill Pesto with Asian Notes

A rich, vibrant, green sauce. And just like Italian basil pesto, a little dill pesto goes a long way. Create a creamy sauce to accompany seafood by stirring 1 tablespoon pesto into 6 tablespoons of yogurt or sour cream; slip pesto under the shell of big shrimp for a dazzling Grilled Pesto Shrimp; stir into honey mustard to serve with smoked salmon; spread onto tortillas for wraps; or use instead of Emerald Sauce in Steamed Emerald Salmon in Chapter 6.

Preparation time: *25 minutes*

Yield: *1 cup*

2 bunches (3 ounces each) fresh dill or cilantro

⅓ cup coarsely chopped green onions, including tops

6 garlic cloves, peeled or 1 tablespoon roasted garlic puree

2 tablespoons fresh chocolate mint or peppermint leaves

4 teaspoons sugar

2 teaspoons ground Asian chili paste, such as sambal oelek, or ½ teaspoon red pepper flakes

2 teaspoons kosher salt

1 teaspoon curry powder

½ cup peanut oil

1 Pick dill fronds, wash, and dry well because excess moisture will thin the pesto. You should have about 2 cups well-packed fronds. If you are short, add mint to make up the difference.

2 In a food processor, place the dill, onions, garlic, mint, sugar, chili paste, salt, and curry powder. Process until mixture is minced. With the machine running, drizzle in the oil and process until the pesto is well blended and thick, 1 to 1½ minutes. You can refrigerate the pesto up to 5 days. We like to freeze half the batch to have on hand. To keep the top of the pesto from discoloring due to exposure to the air, press plastic wrap onto the surface before sealing the container.

For more fiery information about sambal oelek, refer to the Volcano Salmon and Couscous Salad recipe in Chapter 6.

To make Grilled Pesto Shrimp, choose big shrimp — from U-15 to 26/30 per pound. Slit the shrimp shell down the back and devein. Carefully pry open shells — without removing them — and slip pesto between the shells and shrimp flesh, and then press shells to close around shrimp. Grill shrimp over a hot fire until firm, but slightly springy, and lightly browned (the heat caramelizes the sugar in the pesto). Pass lots of napkins.

Cool as a Cucumber

Refreshing and brimming with fragrant fresh dill and crunchy cucumbers. Partner the creamy cucumber sauce with seafood fajitas, tacos, wraps, and pita pockets; spoon onto any grilled seafood or poached salmon; and serve with seafood burgers and cakes.

Preparation time: *10 minutes*

Yield: *2 cups*

2 cucumbers (8 ounces each)

1½ cups plain, nonfat yogurt (drained, if desired)

½ cup minced fresh dill or fennel fronds

½ cup finely chopped chives or green onions

1 teaspoon kosher salt

1 teaspoon sugar

1 teaspoon freshly ground black pepper

Pinch cayenne pepper (optional)

1 Peel cucumbers, leaving 4 lengthwise strips of skin for color contrast. Halve cucumbers lengthwise and seed. Coarsely shred cucumbers on a grater and squeeze in your hand to remove as much excess moisture as possible.

2 In a small bowl, mix cucumbers, yogurt, dill, chives, salt, sugar, pepper, and cayenne. Cover and refrigerate. If desired, make sauce up to 1 day before using. Serve slightly chilled.

Wildcat Mustard Sauce

Great for dipping stone crab claws, king crab legs, crawfish, and shrimp, and for saucing the Coastal Fondue Party seafood in Chapter 17.

Preparation time: *10 minutes*

Yield: *1 cup*

½ cup plus 2 tablespoons mayonnaise

¼ cup plus 2 tablespoons Dijon mustard

½ to 1 teaspoon Tabasco sauce

½ teaspoon Worcestershire sauce

Kosher salt and freshly ground pepper to taste

Whisk the mayonnaise, mustard, Tabasco sauce, and Worcestershire sauce together. Let the sauce stand for 30 minutes to develop flavors; taste and adjust seasonings. You can refrigerate the sauce up to a week.

Catalan Romesco Sauce

In the Catalonia region of Spain, this rustic, bold sauce is as popular as tartar sauce is in the United States. Like tartar sauce, every cook has a special version. Sweet red peppers and finely ground nuts are the basic ingredients. From there, the add-ins vary widely — bread crumbs, tomatoes, garlic, and onions. Marcie's treasured version stems from a list of ingredients handwritten in Spanish by the owner of a tiny, open-air, seaside café where she dined one moonlit evening in Tossa de Mar on the Costa Brava. Serve this bright — and healthy — sauce at room temperature with your favorite broiled, poached, or grilled seafood.

Preparation time: *20 minutes*

Yield: *½ cup*

½ cup skin-on, salted, smoked whole almonds

½ cup coarsely chopped and drained roasted red peppers

1 tablespoon red wine vinegar

¼ teaspoon sweet Spanish or Hungarian paprika

¼ to ½ teaspoon hot paprika or chili powder

2 tablespoons extra virgin olive oil

1 Use a food processor with a steel blade to finely grind the almonds, stopping to scrape down the sides of bowl as needed. Add red peppers, vinegar, and both the sweet and hot paprika. Pulse to process until quite smooth.

2 With the processor running, dribble in the oil through the feedtube until the sauce is smooth. Taste and adjust seasonings as desired.

3 Serve at room temperature. May be made 1 to 2 days ahead and refrigerated. Sauce keeps up to a week when refrigerated.

Carol's Tequila Salsa Cream

When you want to warm things up, try this quick and easy stove-top sauce. Leslie's friend Carol Young (a skillful cook who whips up Ron's eclectic catches) devised the recipe after tasting a sauce served with swordfish at the Buffalo Roam restaurant. The chef shared his secret ingredient — tomato salsa — and here's Carol's interpretation. Our splash of tequila highlights the sauce's sweet notes. This chunky, creamy sauce complements a variety of fish from cod, halibut, snapper, and whitefish to swordfish, shark, mussels, and shrimp.

Preparation time: 5 minutes

Cooking time: 7 minutes

Yield: 4 servings (about 1¼ cups)

1 teaspoon butter	2 tablespoons tequila
1 cup tomato salsa	¼ cup heavy cream

1 In a large, heavy skillet, melt butter on medium-high until the butter sizzles, about 3 minutes.

2 Carefully add the salsa and tequila to avoid splashing, and heat until bubbling hot, 1 to 2 minutes, stirring occasionally.

3 Stir in the cream, and heat until slightly thickened, 1 to 2 minutes. Serve the sauce warm over your favorite fish. Leftover sauce reheats beautifully in the microwave.

Don't be tempted to substitute light cream for heavy cream. The recipe needs the fat in the heavy cream to keep the sauce from separating.

Mom's Cajun Barbecue Sauce

We make this robust basting sauce by the gallon and keep it on hand for the entire grilling season. Familiar Cajun seasonings simmer to a seductive blend and jazz up fish without blasting it to oblivion. The sauce partners beautifully with salmon, shrimp, scallops, halibut, Chilean sea bass, orange roughy — just about any seafood. Don't hesitate to make the sauce with dried herbs. When Leslie grew up in northern Ontario, she grilled all winter long (after they swept the snow off the grill) and there certainly were no fresh herbs available then.

Preparation time: 10 minutes

Cooking time: 5 minutes

Yield: 4 cups

(continued)

Mom's Basic Barbecus Sauce (see the following recipe)

2 tablespoons minced fresh basil or 1 teaspoon dried basil leaves

2 tablespoons paprika

2 tablespoons freshly ground black pepper

2 tablespoons fresh lemon juice

4 teaspoons minced garlic

4 teaspoons minced fresh oregano or 1 teaspoon dried oregano leaves

2 teaspoons minced fresh rosemary or 2 teaspoons crushed, dried rosemary leaves

4 bay leaves

½ to 1 teaspoon kosher salt (optional)

½ to 1 teaspoon cayenne pepper

1 In a large saucepan, combine 4 cups Mom's Basic Barbecue Sauce with basil, paprika, pepper, lemon juice, garlic, oregano, rosemary, bay leaves, salt, and ½ teaspoon cayenne pepper. Bring to a boil and simmer covered for 5 minutes to blend flavors, or microwave on high for 2 to 3 minutes. Remove from heat and whisk in the reserved oil. Taste and adjust cayenne. You can refrigerate the sauce up to 2 months.

2 The basting sauce coats seafood more evenly if you heat it before using. To use the sauce, grill seafood of your choice over a medium hot fire for 2 minutes per side to sear. Baste seafood with warm Cajun sauce and turn every 2 to 3 minutes.

Dish out and heat only the amount of sauce you need to avoid contaminating the entire batch of sauce with raw seafood juices.

Mom's Basic Barbecue Sauce

Preparation time: *10 minutes*

Yield: *4 cups*

½ cup packed brown sugar

½ cup Worcestershire sauce

½ cup espresso or double-strength regular coffee

6 tablespoons cider vinegar

1½ cups ketchup

½ cup corn oil

In a large saucepan off the heat, mix the brown sugar, cider vinegar, Worcestershire sauce, and coffee. Whisk in the ketchup. Whisk oil into the completed Cajun Barbecue Sauce.

Count on ¼ cup barbecue sauce per person to baste about 6 ounces of fish.

Vinaigrette: Beyond Oil and Vinegar

Some cooks adore baking, while others prefer grilling. Leslie, on the other hand, delights in stirring up exotic vinaigrettes and sauces. Just as salads have evolved beyond simple greens, vinaigrettes have outgrown their narrow definition of an oil and vinegar dressing.

Toasted Pine Nut and Shallot Vinaigrette

Golden, toasted pine nuts add sensuous flavor to this chunky vinaigrette. Walnuts, pecans, or almonds also add nutty nuances, when pine nuts aren't available. If you use olive oil, use a mild-tasting oil. Extra virgin olive oil may be too strongly flavored for this vinaigrette.

Preparation time: *15 minutes*

Cooking time: *5 minutes*

Yield: *1¼ cups*

½ cup hazelnut or olive oil, divided

½ cup minced shallots

3 tablespoons plus 1 teaspoon raspberry vinegar

2 tablespoons medium sweet sherry

2 teaspoons Dijon mustard

2 teaspoons freshly ground black pepper

1 teaspoon kosher salt

¼ cup pine nuts, toasted

¼ cup minced fresh parsley

1 In a small skillet, heat 2 tablespoons oil over medium-low heat until hot. Add shallots and sauté until softened and translucent, about 5 minutes, stirring.

2 In a small bowl, whisk together the vinegar, sherry, mustard, pepper, and salt. Gradually whisk in the remaining oil, cooked shallots with oil, and pine nuts. Stir in parsley just before serving (the acid from the vinegar turns parsley yellowish). Serve dressing room temperature and stir well before using.

Follow these steps to toast pine nuts: In a dry skillet, toast pine nuts over medium-low heat until golden brown and fragrant, 6 to 7 minutes. Don't be tempted to crank up the heat to toast the pine nuts faster. We've done that more times than you'd want to count, and can guarantee that pine nuts burn easily and fast.

Add spark to a beautifully grilled piece of fish and drizzle with this vinaigrette. Or toss grilled fish and the vinaigrette with greens, hearty fare, and magical extras to create your signature seafood splash. See Table 15-1 for salad tossing ideas.

Table 15-1	Toasted Pine Nut and Shallot Vinaigrette Salad Tosses		
Toss with Seafood	*Plus Greens*	*Plus Hearty Fare*	*Add Extras*
Grilled tuna	Arugula	Cannellini beans	Goat cheese
Grilled swordfish	Red and green curly leaf lettuce	Corn	Roasted red peppers
Shrimp	Julienned zucchini	Rice	Black olives
Halibut, grouper	Watercress	Couscous	Capers
Mahimahi	Spinach	Chickpeas	Preserved lemons
Salmon	Flat leaf parsley	Lentils	Gorgonzola
Seared scallops	Pea shoots, spicy sprouts	Polenta	Shaved Romano cheese
Fried oysters	Mixed greens	Croutons	Lemon zest
Steamed clams	Fresh fennel	Red potatoes	Orange zest

Masterful Mayonnaise

Transform classic, creamy mayonnaise into a tantalizing sauce for fish and shellfish by swirling in piquant tastes:

- Tapenade or chopped black or green olives
- Roasted garlic
- Sun-dried tomatoes
- Japanese wasabi
- Pickled capers or caperberries
- Indian coriander or mint chutney

Roasted Red-Pepper Velvet

Creamy and thick, this sensational sauce is bursting with roasted red peppers. Any fish will love it! To see that it's lovely to look at, too, check the color photo section near the middle of the book. Serve with any grilled, poached, or steamed seafood, from shrimp and mussels to salmon, cod, or snapper. When we were looking for a technique to make homemade mayonnaise that used an alternative to raw eggs (which could contain salmonella), a talented friend of ours, Sharon Tyler Herbst, came to the rescue. Sharon is the award-winning author of numerous acclaimed culinary reference books, including *Food Lover's Companion*.

Preparation time: *15 minutes*

Yield: *2 cups*

¾ *cup roasted red bell peppers*

¼ *cup pasteurized liquid eggs, such as Egg Beaters*

1½ tablespoons Dijon mustard

1 tablespoon fresh lemon juice

1 teaspoon kosher salt

1 teaspoon dried tarragon leaves

½ teaspoon freshly ground pepper

½ cup corn oil

½ cup olive oil

10 to 12 dashes Tabasco sauce

1 Slit peppers and pat dry with paper towels to remove excess moisture; coarsely chop. Set aside.

2 In a food processor, place the pasteurized eggs, mustard, lemon juice, salt, tarragon, and pepper. Process until blended, 5 to 10 seconds.

3 With the machine running, slowly drizzle in the corn oil and olive oil until sauce thickens to form mayonnaise.

4 Add the roasted peppers and Tabasco sauce. Pulse until peppers are chopped but not pureed. Taste and adjust seasonings. You can refrigerate the sauce up to a week. (Frankly, we can't keep this luscious sauce in our houses that long; it's too tempting to spoon it out and eat on anything.)

Chipotle Aïoli

When we first tasted this sauce at La Tache World Bistro and Wine Bar in Phoenix, its spicy, smoky character wowed us. The heat scale of the aïoli rises as the chipotle infuses the sauce, so you may want to start with 1½ chiles and taste along the way.

Preparation time: *20 minutes*

Standing time: *1 hour*

Yield: *2½ cups*

2 cups sour cream

½ cup mayonnaise

⅓ cup fresh basil or cilantro leaves, washed, well dried, and coarsely chopped

1 to 2 tablespoons fresh lime juice, divided

1 tablespoon roasted garlic puree

1½ to 2 chipotle chiles (canned in adobo sauce), undrained and minced

¾ teaspoon chili powder

¾ teaspoon ground cumin

½ teaspoon kosher salt

⅛ teaspoon cayenne pepper

In a food processor, combine sour cream, mayonnaise, basil, 1 tablespoon lime juice, roasted garlic puree, chipotle chiles, chili powder, cumin, salt, and cayenne pepper; pulse until well blended. Let aïoli stand, refrigerated, for 1 hour or overnight, to develop chipotle heat. Taste and adjust lime juice and seasonings.

To roast garlic, cut the top quarter off a head of garlic, set on a piece of foil, and drizzle with 1 teaspoon oil. Fold the foil to enclose garlic and bake in a preheated 425° oven for 35 minutes; loosen foil and bake 5 minutes. Pop out cloves and mash into a puree. See Figure 15-1.

How to Trim and Roast garlic

Figure 15-1: Roasting pungent garlic to subtle tastes.

Trim one quarter off the top end of the head of garlic.

Pull off the papery, outside layer.

Set on foil, drizzle oil over top of cloves, wrap up foil, and bake.

After roasting, pull off the cloves and squeeze one end to pop out tender garlic.

If you don't have time to roast garlic, look for prepared flavored mayonnaise, such as roasted garlic or roasted onion, to replace the mayonnaise.

Chipotle Aïoli partners perfectly with any grilled seafood, such as tuna, swordfish, mahimahi, grouper, shrimp, or scallops; works as a dipping sauce for stone crab claws, king crab legs, or crawfish; and is ideal to serve with the Southwestern Seafood Dip in Chapter 11.

Salsas with a Beat

According to Mark Miller in his evocative cookbook, *Coyote Café,* "Salsas are like a mini-fiesta for the taste buds, at once sharp and sweet, hot and cool." *Salsa* is the Mexican word for sauce — a dish of salsa or relish is as common to the Mexican table as salt and pepper is to Americans. Wake up simple fish and shellfish dishes with exuberant tastes from the Caribbean and the American southwest.

Sunshine Salsa

This kaleidoscope of juicy, sweet fruit, zesty mint, and crunchy pine nuts partners perfectly with any grilled seafood, especially the Grilled Jerk Tuna on Foccacia in Chapter 14. You can see both the salsa and the jerk tuna in the color photo section near the center of this book. The recipe calls for equal amounts (about ½ cup each) of the nectarine, mango, and red bell pepper, so mix 'n' match your favorite fruits and peppers in season: apricots, melons, peaches, or pineapple, and green, orange, or chocolate-brown peppers.

Preparation time: *20 minutes*

Yield: *2 cups*

½ Granny Smith apple (skin on), cored, cut in ¼-inch dice (½ cup)

2 tablespoons fresh lemon juice

1 teaspoon sugar

½ teaspoon kosher salt

1 nectarine, skin on, cut in ¼-inch dice

½ mango, cut in ½-inch dice

⅓ large red bell pepper, cored and cut in ¼-inch dice

2 tablespoons minced green onion, including tops

2 tablespoons finely chopped fresh mint

1 to 2 tablespoons toasted pine nuts or pecans

½ to 1 teaspoon minced serrano or other hot chile

(continued)

1 In a medium bowl, toss apple, lemon juice, sugar, and salt together as soon as apple is cut to prevent browning.

2 Stir in nectarine, mango, red pepper, green onion, mint, pine nuts, and chile. Taste and adjust sugar, if necessary.

3 If desired, make the salsa up to a day in advance, reserving the mint and pine nuts to add several hours before serving. Serve salsa slightly chilled.

> *Vary It!* If you prefer to use the whole mango and apple, the recipe doubles easily.

 Chef John Ash, culinary director of Fetzer Vineyards and award-winning cookbook author, grills fresh pineapple for a fruit salsa he serves with grilled shrimp. Simply brush pineapple slices with olive oil and grill them until lightly browned. Grilling fruit adds a rich caramel note to any dish.

Kiwifruit "Fuzzy Logic" Salsa

A kiwi's plain brown, fuzzy wrapper belies its sparkling attributes. The kiwi bursts with refreshing, sweet-tart flavor and dazzling emerald color, accented with crunchy, tiny black seeds. This sublime, simple salsa is a bright — and logical — way to perk up seafood of your choice. Flip to the color photo section near the center of this book for a close-up look at this sprightly salsa.

Preparation time: 8 minutes

Yield: 1 cup

2 large kiwi, peeled and cut into ¼-inch dice (1 cup)

2 tablespoons finely chopped red onion

1 serrano or jalapeño chile, seeded and minced

1 tablespoon minced fresh cilantro

1 to 2 teaspoons maple syrup or honey

Kosher salt to taste

In a small bowl, combine the kiwi, onion, chile, and cilantro. Because kiwis vary in sweetness, taste before adding enough maple syrup to soften any harsh tartness without becoming cloyingly sweet. Add salt to taste. Serve at room temperature or chilled.

Tomatillo Salsa

Tart-tasting tomatillos (often from Mexico) look like small green tomatoes wrapped in crackling, papery husks. Try this refreshing, zesty salsa with firm-textured fish including tuna, swordfish, and mahimahi or rich-tasting fish such as bluefish, mackerel, Chilean sea bass, sablefish, and escolar. It also makes a great topping for clams on the half shell.

Preparation time: 15 minutes

Standing time: 10 minutes

Yield: 1 cup

4 to 5 fresh tomatillos (about 6 ounces)

¼ cup thinly sliced green onions, including tops

2 tablespoons finely diced red bell pepper

1 to 2 tablespoons fresh lime juice

1 to 2 tablespoons chopped mixed fresh herbs: cilantro, basil, or oregano, to taste

1 jalapeño pepper, seeded and minced

2 teaspoons peanut oil

1 teaspoon brown sugar

½ to 1 teaspoon kosher salt

½ teaspoon freshly ground black pepper

Pull husks from tomatillos and discard (see Figure 15-2). Wash tomatillos and cut into ½-inch cubes; set aside. Stir tomatillo, onions, red bell pepper, lime juice, herbs, jalapeño pepper, oil, brown sugar, salt, and black pepper together. Let salsa stand at room temperature for about 10 minutes to blend flavors. Taste and adjust seasonings.

Vary It! If you can't find tomatillos, substitute tomatoes, but use green bell peppers instead of red for color contrast. Don't use canned tomatillos for this salsa — they lack the fresh, tart flavor that you want.

Figure 15-2:
Peeling a tomatillo is like husking an ear of sweet corn.

tomatillos

Pull off the papery husk and rinse sticky skin with water!

Chapter 16

Kids' Fare

What's the best way to hook kids on eating fish? When they catch it themselves.

Just ask ten people age ten and older to name the best fish they ever ate. More than half will likely tell you it was the very first fish they ever caught. Be prepared to be regaled with infinite details of their first fish story — from the moment they felt the first tug on their line to the first crispy bite, served directly from Mom's, Dad's, or Grandpa's sizzling cast-iron skillet.

Do your kids have their own fish story to tell? If they don't, stop reading and go fishin'. . . .

It's Catching

Lug along that old cast-iron skillet, pack some cornmeal, and don't skimp on the bacon *grease*. This memory-making moment is no time for a nonstick skillet and a measly spritz of spray oil.

Anne Sterling, a friend of ours who specializes in cooking classes for kids, shares this story of how her daughter learned to like fish. When ten-year-old Elizabeth Alsina (who prefers to be called Emma) was five, she refused to even taste fish until, you guessed it, she and her grandpa went fishing. Did she eat the fish she caught? You betcha. Did she like it? You betcha. Does she continue to eat fish and like it? Yes. Especially when she helps cook it just the way she and her grandpa fixed her never-to-be-forgotten first catch. Her grandpa used butter, not bacon grease, and that's delicious, too.

Crispy Fishy

So you have to settle for second best when your catch comes from the supermarket, and the electric range in your kitchen, not a campfire, is your heat source. Emma Alsina's technique is nonetheless yummy. She coats the fish with flour, but lets her mom cook the fish in the hot fat, which can spatter.

Preparation time: *5 minutes*

Cooking time: *5 minutes*

Yield: *4 servings*

1½ pounds thin skinless fish fillets, any kind

½ cup flour

1 teaspoon wheat germ (optional)

⅛ to ¼ teaspoon garlic powder (optional)

Kosher salt and pepper

2 tablespoons unsalted butter

2 tablespoons olive oil

1 lemon, cut into wedges

1 Rinse fish under cold running water and pat dry. Cut it into serving-size portions.

2 Pour the flour and the seasonings into a large resealable plastic bag. Seal the bag and shake it to blend the seasonings. If you don't want to measure, you can simply add a pinch of each seasoning you choose.

3 Unseal the bag, add one piece of fish at a time, close the bag, and shake. Open the bag, gently tap the fish to knock off excess flour. Set the floured pieces on a piece of waxed paper or a plate. Repeat with other pieces.

4 Using a large, heavy skillet over medium-high heat, melt butter and add oil. Panfry fish until golden brown on each side, about 1 minute per side for thin fillets (such as flounder) and 2 to 3 minutes per side for thicker pieces.

5 Serve with lemon wedges.

April fools!

Do you know what the French watch out for on April Fool's Day? A fish on their backs! Yes, in France they celebrate April Fish or *Poisson d'Avril*. That's the day that the new year used to begin until Pope Gregory XIII adopted a different calendar in 1582. Some people didn't accept the new calendar and still celebrated the new year on April 1. They were labeled *April Fools* or *April Fish*.

An April Fish joke in France is to try to sneak up on someone and stick a construction paper fish (with a piece of double-faced tape on one side) on his or her back without getting caught. Even better, French candy stores sell all sorts of fish-shaped candy at this time of year. (We're still saving our life-size, dark chocolate fish, filled with *friture:* tiny chocolate sea creatures and praline truffle eggs. It's too beautiful to fillet.)

Just Don't Get Caught Foolin' Around

These lighthearted, kid-friendly recipes are for the young at heart of any age. Cutting up in the kitchen is the ultimate way for your whole family to have fun — and eat well at the same time.

Big Fish Swallows the Little Fish is a two-fold French inspiration. For a whale of a good time, cook *en papillote* (see Chapter 2 for more details). Design your own version of the French *Poisson d'Avril* — or April Fish (see the "April fools!" sidebar).

Makin' Waves can either be a family affair or a night when grown-ups are only supervising — not cooking — in the kitchen. For older children, rent the video *Jaws* for another thematic evening when you make and bake Shark Bites.

Big Fish Swallows the Little Fish

Using parchment to cook fish not only seals in the flavor but makes clean-up a breeze. Kids can have fun cutting the parchment to resemble a whale. Even preschoolers love to add fishy designs with nontoxic markers to the whale shapes. That's the big fish. Then, put the little fish inside, arranging vegetable fish "scales" on the fish that will cook inside the whale. Crimp the parchment edges together to seal. Microwave the packets one at a time or bake them all at once in the oven.

(continued)

For the best whale watching, see a photo of this dish in the color photo section near the center of the book. Use whatever fish fillets the kids like best. Serve with seashell-shaped pasta for a whale of a meal.

Preparation time: *20 minutes*

Cooking time: *12 minutes*

Yield: *4 servings*

4 serving-size fillets of skinless salmon, flounder, tilapia, or catfish (about 1½ pounds total)

2 tablespoons olive oil or melted butter (or olive oil spray)

Kosher salt and pepper to taste

4 sheets parchment paper, about 12- by 18-inches each

2 medium zucchini or 4 small red-skinned potatoes

1 to 2 tablespoons finely chopped fresh herb of your choice (optional)

1 Rinse fillets under cold water and pat dry. Brush a little oil on both sides of the fish. Season with salt and pepper.

2 Fold each piece of parchment in half, forming a rectangle 12- by 9-inches. Use a soft pencil to outline a heart-shape, but instead of forming the point, flare the design upward at the end to form the whale's tail. Cut around the outside edges, leaving the folded edge intact. (If you have difficulty imagining the shape, look at the photo of this dish in the color photo section, near the center of this book.) Use nontoxic markers to decorate one side with whale features or nautical designs.

3 Open the parchment and lightly brush the inside with oil. Place a single serving of fish on the undecorated side of the whale. Cut thin rounds of zucchini or potatoes and overlap the vegetable "scales" on the fish, starting at one end. Brush or spray with a little oil. Sprinkle with fresh herbs, if desired. Fill the remaining whales in the same manner.

4 Fold the other side of the whale over the fish. Crimp and fold the edges, forming as tight a seal as possible. Microwave each packet, one at a time, for 2 minutes on high if fillets are thin (such as flounder) or for 3 minutes if thick (like salmon). Packets will be hot. Open carefully to allow steam to escape away from your face or hands.

Vary It! Preheat oven to 400° and bake all four whales at the same time. Arrange them on two baking sheets and bake for 10 minutes for thinner fillets and 12 minutes if pieces are thicker. When opened, fish should just start to flake at the nudge of a fork.

Shark Bites

Maybe your kids would rather prepare Shark Bites for your April Fish dinner. Our colleague Kate Heyhoe shares this easy recipe. You can find other kid-friendly recipes, including Crunchy Fish Kisses, in her book *Cooking with Kids For Dummies* (IDG Books Worldwide, Inc.), and more tips and techniques at http://www.cookingwithkids.com.

Sharks aren't always mean, but they are lean. Kids old enough to use a knife can slice firm, easy-to-handle shark into thick strips, and mince the ginger, garlic, and green onion. Little ones can mix the marinade.

Shark gives a good boost of protein to growing bodies without being too strong in flavor for tender palates. Shark meat dries out quickly if cooked too long — so be careful not to overcook shark, or you'll give your jaws a workout!

Preparation time: *35 minutes*

Marinating time: *1½ hours*

Cooking time: *8 to 10 minutes*

Yield: *4 servings*

1½ pounds shark steaks, about 1-inch thick	1 teaspoon minced garlic
3 tablespoons fresh lemon juice	Dash of hot red pepper flakes (optional)
2 tablespoons soy sauce	2 teaspoons honey
2 teaspoons pineapple juice, Japanese mirin, or dry sherry	2 tablespoons sesame seeds
2 teaspoons Asian toasted sesame oil	2 green onions, minced
1 teaspoon peeled and grated or minced fresh ginger	3 pineapple slices, halved (optional)

1 Cut shark into long strips measuring 1-inch across.

2 Mix together the lemon juice, soy sauce, pineapple juice, sesame oil, ginger, garlic, and a small dash of red pepper flakes in a non-reactive baking dish or resealable plastic bag; reserve 2 tablespoons of the mixture to baste shark.

3 Place the shark strips in the marinade, turn to evenly coat, cover, and refrigerate 1½ hours or as long as overnight.

4 Preheat broiler.

5 Drain shark, discarding the used marinade, and place shark on a broiler pan lined with foil for easy clean-up.

(continued)

6 Broil shark 4 inches from heat for 5 minutes.

7 Remove pan from broiler, baste shark with reserved marinade and flip shark over, and then baste again.

8 Drizzle thin streaks of honey over shark. Sprinkle sesame seeds on top.

9 Return pan to broiler and broil 3 to 4 minutes more. Cut into one shark strip to see if it's cooked inside; the inside should be just barely opaque and white. If not, turn broiler off and let shark sit under hot broiler for another minute or so, until inside flesh is baked through.

10 When the shark is fully cooked, remove from the broiler pan and place on dinner plates. Pour the juices from the pan over shark. Garnish with green onions and pineapple slices, if desired.

Vary It! Swordfish, salmon, tilapia, catfish, or tuna all work well instead of shark.

 Peas and rice tossed with sautéed green pepper and onions are easy accompaniments.

 Avoid those all-too-familiar cries of "When do we eat?" by enlisting the kids to prepare the following nautical meal. To carry out the wavy theme with mashed potatoes ripples, you need a pastry bag or a heavy plastic bag and a large tip that has "jaggies" along the edge. Edible art is the most fun!

Makin' Waves

Kids can make dinner for the whole family with this quick-and-easy recipe made with flounder fillets and strips of zucchini. After a quick plunge in the microwave, the fish slides off the skewer all wavy and can ride along on a wave of mashed potatoes or swim in a sea of tomato sauce.

Preparation time: *15 minutes*

Cooking time: *6 minutes*

Yield: *4 servings (9 waves)*

1½ pounds flounder fillets

2 long, straight zucchini (about the same length as fish)

2 tablespoons olive oil

¼ teaspoon garlic powder

¼ teaspoon salt

Freshly ground black pepper

9 long wooden skewers

2 cups warm mashed potatoes or 1 cup warm spaghetti sauce

1 Cut each flounder fillet lengthwise into 3 uniform strips. Use a vegetable peeler to make wide, thin strips of zucchini. Don't peel the zucchini. The little stripes of green peel along the edges will accentuate the waves. You should have about 18 nice-looking zucchini strips about the size of the strips of fish. Chop the remaining zucchini and add to the mashed potatoes or to the spaghetti sauce.

2 Pour the olive oil into a small bowl and mix in the garlic powder, salt, and pepper to taste. Brush the fish and zucchini strips with this seasoned oil. Make "sandwiches" of fish with one strip of zucchini on top and one on the bottom. Weave the fish/zucchini onto wooden skewers making even "waves."

3 Microwave three skewers at a time on a microwaveable plate for 2 minutes at high power. When you stop microwaving the fish, the center of the fish will be slightly underdone (still a bit translucent); it will reach proper doneness out of the microwave. Cover to retain heat.

4 To make wavy mashed potatoes, insert a large, jagged-edge tip into a pastry bag or a heavy plastic bag with a corner snipped off. Squeeze potatoes into a squiggly pattern across each dinner plate. Reheat each plate in the microwave briefly to warm the potatoes. Then carefully slide a hot fish wave off its skewer onto the plate. Or spoon hot spaghetti sauce on the plate and arrange the fish waves on top.

Vary It! To bake "waves," arrange skewers on a baking sheet, preferably nonstick, so they don't touch. Bake at 400° for 8 minutes or until fish just begins to flake at a nudge of a fork.

Clam-moring for More

Who says clams are only a grown-up taste? Not us. We still recall with amazement the summer afternoon we let four boys, all under age 10, start eating steamed clams (see Chapter 13) before the adults gathered 'round. Within nano-seconds, the young ones were trying to see who could build the highest stack of empty shells. Fortunately, we had steamed 200 clams for eight adults and the four children. The last adult to show up was nearly out of luck, or more precisely, clams.

Mary's Clam Chowder is another proven kids' favorite. They'll be happy as clams when they smell the wonderful aroma of this chowder. This recipe and the ones that follow rank high with kids of all ages. Advanced junior chefs can tackle some of the prep steps in each of the following recipes, but don't count on them to prepare the entire recipe. Count them in, for sure, on the rave reviews for the cook.

Mary's Clam Chowder

Which comes first — a child's preferred tastes or a parent's favorite recipe? Either way, our friend and cook extraordinaire, Mary Landsman, raised her three kids on this chowder. As Amanda, Melissa, and Caitlin grew, Mary fine-tuned her chowder. And as young adults, the "kids" still love the chowder. For a colorful contrast, combine both russet and red-skinned potatoes. Mary prefers to use fresh clams, but canned or frozen clams also work well.

Preparation time: *45 minutes*

Cooking time: *55 minutes*

Yield: *4 servings*

3 dozen small fresh clams, scrubbed

3 slices bacon

⅔ cup coarsely chopped onion (about 1 medium)

2 to 3 teaspoons minced garlic

2 tablespoons flour

3 cups milk

1 teaspoon minced fresh thyme leaves or ¼ teaspoon dried thyme leaves

1 teaspoon Worcestershire sauce

½ teaspoon freshly ground black pepper

2 dashes Tabasco sauce

4 medium russet or red-skinned potatoes, skin on, cut into ½-inch cubes

⅓ cup minced fresh parsley, divided

1 teaspoon kosher salt (optional)

1 Quickly wash clams under cold running water and check that shells are tightly closed. (Refer to Chapter 8 for information about checking shellfish.)

2 Place a steamer rack in a 4- to 5-quart pot. Add ½ cup water, cover, and over medium-high heat bring to a boil. Place clams on rack, cover, and steam until shells open, 3 to 5 minutes, shaking pot occasionally. Discard any unopened clams.

3 Transfer the cooked clams to a bowl and reserve 1 cup cooking liquid for the chowder base, straining the liquid if sandy. In a small bowl, set aside 1 clam in the shell per serving to decorate the soup; cover. Remove the remaining clams from their shells and coarsely chop. Set aside.

4 In a large, heavy pot, sauté the bacon until crisp. Remove bacon and leave the drippings in the pan. Cool the bacon, crumble, and set aside. Add the onions to the bacon drippings and sauté over medium heat until translucent, about 5 minutes. Stir in the garlic and cook until softened, about 2 minutes.

5 Sprinkle the flour over the onion mixture, reduce heat to medium-low, and cook until the mixture is slightly thickened and light tan in color, about 3 minutes. Remove the pan from the heat and whisk in the reserved clam juice until smooth. Stir in the milk, thyme, Worcestershire sauce, pepper, and Tabasco sauce.

6 Return the pan to the heat, and cook the chowder base until hot and thickened, about 15 minutes (the mixture needs to be hot enough to both cook the potatoes and heat the chopped clams). Add the potatoes and cook 15 minutes. Stir in the chopped clams and ¼ cup parsley, and cook until the potatoes are tender, about 5 minutes more, stirring. (Don't worry about breaking up the potatoes; you need some to thicken the chowder.) Taste and add salt to taste.

7 Ladle the chowder into bowls and top with clams in the shell. Sprinkle with reserved bacon and parsley. Serve with bite-sized oyster crackers or homemade Irish soda bread, as Mary often does.

To use chopped, canned clams instead of live clams, you need 3 cans (6½ ounces each). This gives you about 1 cup clam meat and 1½ cups clam juice.

Tacos with Fresh Tuna and Black Beans

Teenagers love these hearty tacos for supper. And the filling reheats well in the microwave for a quick snack. Tart-tasting tomatillos (often from Mexico) look like small green tomatoes wrapped in crackling, papery husks. Substitute tomatoes if you can't find tomatillos.

Preparation time: *30 minutes*

Cooking time: *12 minutes*

Yield: *4 servings (8 tacos)*

(continued)

8 to 9 fresh tomatillos (¾ pound)

¾ pound tuna steak, 1-inch thick

4 teaspoons olive oil, divided

2 to 3 teaspoons chili powder

1 teaspoon kosher salt, divided

¼ cup minced fresh cilantro or parsley, divided

4 green onions, including tops, minced

4 teaspoons minced garlic

¾ cup finely diced red bell pepper

1 can (15 ounces) black beans, drained, rinsed

2 to 4 fresh or pickled jalapeño peppers, seeded and minced

2 tablespoons fresh lime juice

1 teaspoon sugar (optional)

8 to 10 taco shells, warmed

1 cup sour cream or plain, nonfat yogurt

1 Prepare a medium-hot fire in a charcoal or gas grill. As the grill heats, pull husks from tomatillos and discard. (See Chapter 15 for an illustration of tomatillos.) Wash tomatillos and cut into ½-inch cubes; set aside.

2 Rub both sides of tuna with 2 teaspoons olive oil and sprinkle with chili powder; season with ½ teaspoon salt just before cooking. Grill tuna, with grill lid closed (or broil about 2 inches from heat), turning once, until tuna is springy and medium-rare, about 2 minutes per side. Break tuna into flakes and toss with half the cilantro; cover and keep warm.

3 In a large, heavy skillet, heat remaining 2 teaspoons oil on medium heat. Add onions and garlic and sauté, stirring, until softened, about 4 minutes. Increase heat to medium high. Add tomatillos and red pepper and stir until warm, about 2 minutes more.

4 Add black beans, jalapeños, lime juice, sugar (if desired), remaining ½ teaspoon salt and 2 tablespoons cilantro; stir until warm, about 2 minutes (do not overcook or tomatillos will become soupy).

5 Place tomatillo mixture into a shallow serving dish and sprinkle tuna on top. Spoon filling into taco shells. Pass sour cream separately.

Vary It! Your family will love the tuna mixture wrapped in tortillas, too! Instead of tuna, try monkfish, catfish, swordfish, scallops, shrimp, or salmon.

Trick or Treat Surimi-Stuffed Spuds

Twice-baked potatoes are ideal for supper before the kids head out on Halloween. Our friend Becky Weikel (whose family taste-tested the potatoes) was positive that her kids would prefer the potatoes stuffed with shrimp rather than surimi. Was she surprised when they liked the taste of the surimi better! Add a crunchy bite by sprinkling bacon bits on top, if desired. Your kids won't be spooked by seafood after you serve these hot spuds.

Preparation time: *30 minutes*

Cooking time: *1 to 1¼ hours*

Yield: *4 servings*

4 large baking potatoes (each about 6 inches long)

10 to 12 ounces crab-flavored surimi, divided

1 cup shredded sharp cheddar cheese, divided

¾ cup sour cream

¼ cup melted butter

3 to 4 tablespoons milk

1 to 2 teaspoons Old Bay Seasoning

½ teaspoon onion powder

½ teaspoon freshly ground black pepper

¼ teaspoon paprika

1 Pierce potatoes with a fork and bake at 425° until soft, 45 minutes to 1 hour. While the potatoes are baking, coarsely chop the surimi; reserve ¼ cup surimi to top the potatoes.

2 After the potatoes are baked (and cool enough to handle), cut a thin horizontal slice from the top of each potato. Carefully scoop out the pulp and put it in a large bowl, leaving about a ¼-inch shell intact. Set shells aside. Increase the oven heat to 450° for the double baking.

3 Add ¾ cup cheese, sour cream, butter, milk, Old Bay Seasoning, onion powder, and pepper to the potato pulp. Beat with an electric mixer until smooth. Stir the surimi into the potato mixture and spoon into potato shells. Top each potato with reserved surimi and cheese, and sprinkle with paprika. Bake until hot, about 15 minutes.

 Microwave the potatoes on high for 8 minutes for a quick start. Slit potatoes, stuff, and bake at 450° until hot, about 15 minutes. (Be careful when you slit and stuff the microwaved potatoes — the skins are more fragile than on an oven-baked potato.)

Sesame Fish Dippers

Kids love these sesame-crusted coins, slipped onto skewers and dipped into Indonesian Peanut Sauce (see Chapter 15). Keep the crunchy dippers warm in the oven or make ahead and reheat in the microwave. The recipe is a breeze with the food processor, but if your hands are your essential kitchen tool, simply mince the vegetables, chop the fish, and mix. Also a great appetizer.

Preparation time: *45 minutes*

Cooking time: *6 to 8 minutes*

Yield: *4 servings (24 1½-inch dippers)*

½ ounce dried shiitake mushrooms, softened in warm water (10 to 14 mushrooms), or ¼ pound fresh shiitake mushrooms

2 tablespoons soy sauce

2 teaspoons rice or cider vinegar

2 teaspoons Asian toasted sesame oil

1 teaspoon ground Asian chili paste, such as sambal oelek (optional)

1-inch knob fresh ginger, peeled, quartered

4 green onions, including some tops, cut into 1-inch pieces

20 mini carrots, halved or 2 large carrots, peeled, coarsely chopped

1 pound monkfish, membrane removed, cut into 1-inch cubes

6 tablespoons dry bread crumbs

6 tablespoons untoasted sesame seeds

1 to 2 tablespoons peanut or vegetable oil

Spray vegetable oil (optional)

1 Remove mushroom stems and discard; halve mushrooms and set aside. In a small bowl, mix the soy sauce, vinegar, sesame oil, and chili paste.

2 In a food processor with the motor running, add ginger and mince. Repeat with green onions, scraping the workbowl as needed. Scrape the mixture into a medium bowl. With the food processor running, add carrots and mince; add mushrooms and mince. Add the mixture to the green onions. Remove mixture from food processor and place in a separate bowl. Put the monkfish in the processor and pulse until coarsely ground.

3 Add the monkfish to the carrot mixture. Stir in the soy mixture until blended, and then stir in the bread crumbs. To simplify making the dippers, divide the monkfish mixture into quarters. Moisten your hands with water or spray with vegetable oil. Form one quarter of the mixture into 6 small coins and place on a plate. Sprinkle tops with 2 teaspoons sesame seeds; turn coins and sprinkle with 2 more teaspoons sesame seeds. Repeat with remaining monkfish mixture and sesame seeds.

4 Preheat the oven to 200°. Cook the coins in batches to prevent overcrowding. Add 2 teaspoons of oil to a large skillet, preferably nonstick, and heat on medium-high heat for about 4 minutes, until a drop of water sizzles when added to the oil. Add 8 to 12 coins to skillet, reduce heat to medium, and cook 3 minutes until browned, loosening coins part way through cooking. Turn coins and cook 3 more minutes until browned; flip and cook 2 more minutes until hot all the way through. Drain on paper towels. Keep coins warm in a single layer in the oven while you cook the remainder.

5 If desired, slip coins onto bamboo skewers before serving with your favorite sauce.

Vary It! Try catfish, grouper, tilapia, or salmon instead of monkfish.

Monkfish is encased with a tough, silvery membrane that resembles plastic wrap. It's similar to the silverskin on pork tenderloins. Remove the membrane before cooking or it will shrink and toughen the meat. To remove it, hold one end of the membrane taut and gently slide a knife underneath to loosen.

Part V
Serving Seafood from A to Z

The 5th Wave   By Rich Tennant

Who ordered the Shrimp alla Diavola?

In this part . . .

In this part, we help you create winning combinations for entertaining friends with ease. We offer you recipes to launch the party and ideas for rounding out your menu. Not only does this chapter show you how to plan a step-by-step backyard lobster bash and a big-dipping seafood fondue, but it also steers you to regional melting-pot menus around the country.

We're also crazy about Japanese cuisine. In this part, we show you how to create a fun-filled sushi party at home — without any raw fish. And we help you tackle a few Japanese sushi bar menu basics.

Chapter 17

Festive Fish Menus

● ●

In This Chapter

▶ Throwing a melting pot theme party

▶ Lobster-and-clam-baking a backyard splash

▶ Fondue-ing with a fish

▶ Nibbling 'n' noshing

● ●

> ### Recipes in This Chapter
>
> ▶ Backyard Lobster-and-Clam Bake
> ▶ A Coastal Fondue
>
> ❧❦❧

*S*eafood makes a great party, and what better way to entertain friends, celebrate a special occasion, or throw a backyard splash than with a festive fish menu.

In this chapter, we offer you party menus that celebrate the bounty of the sea. Think of these recipes as your launching point. Use the menus to chart your course to a successful party. Then, sail to pirate's gold with your signature dishes.

You can find three sets of festive menus:

✔ Our first set, called Melting Pot Menus, takes inspiration from the lively cauldrons of the southwest U.S., Louisiana, and the Caribbean. Each party menu combines recipes found in this book (marked in bold) along with our suggestions for dishes to round out the party. Look in the index to locate the recipes in this book.

Wondering why we didn't include all of these recipes in the book? Because we had to limit the total number of recipes, we chose to feature primarily seafood recipes, and let you browse through your own files or other favorite cookbooks, including ...*For Dummies* cookbooks, for non-fishy side dishes, desserts, and beverages.

✔ Our second set, Blow-Out Seafood Bashes, features recipes for you and your friends to dive into together. The Backyard Lobster-and-Clam Bake and A Coastal Fondue are for enthusiastic team players.

✔ And our third set, Nibbles to Nosh, offers you two parties: a casual Super Bowl Bash and a slightly more upscale New Year's fling.

So catch your fish, gather friends, and set sail for a successful party with these festive fish menus.

Melting Pot Menus

Mix transplanted ethnic ingredients with plenty of local fare, and our culinary melting pots emerge. (We almost subtitled this book "with chiles, garlic, and cilantro galore.") Each region reflects a powerful, historic drive for territory — and for treasure. And we reap the benefits. From barbecue and salsa to gumbo and jerk, take your pick of a kaleidoscope of tastes for your next party.

Southwest seafood fiesta

We clearly adore the tastes of the U.S. southwest and its unique regional personality that mixes Old World and New World styles. The culinary influences of the early Spanish explorers combine with those of the Aztecs, Incas, and Pueblos to season this distinctive American melting pot. We hope the layers of flavors keep you, like us, coming back for more.

Macho Nachos   Fiesta Shrimp Salsa
Texas-Style Bacon-Wrapped Barbecue Shrimp
Layered Southwest Dip with Surimi

* * *

Tomatillo Salsa   Tortilla Chips

* * *

Tacos with Fresh Tuna and Black Beans
Juan's Grilled Fish Wrap with Creamy Salsa Verde

* * *

Good Luck Black-Eyed Peas with Crab

* * *

Locally Brewed Beer   Margaritas

* * *

Fiesta Brownie Sundaes with Nutty Caramel Sauce

Mardi Gras home-style

Southern Louisiana's culinary melting pot reveals Spanish, Native American, and French influences. And no one elevates food to party status better than the New Orleans crowd. Mardi Gras — the celebration of plenty on Shrove Tuesday before the advent of Lent — translates literally as *fat Tuesday* from French. So live by the local credo and "let the good times roll."

Creamy Oyster Shooters   **Mardi Gras Shrimp**

* * *

Catfish, Oyster, and Black Bean Gumbo
Chicken Jambalaya

* * *

Pickled Onions and Carrots   Rice Pilaf with Orzo

* * *

Gewürztraminer   Zinfandel

* * *

Pecan Ice Cream with Bourbon Street Hot Fudge Sauce

Caribbean beach party

Catch island fever with Caribbean cooking, an exuberant stew of eclectic, ethnic heritage. Almost everyone stirred the pot, from South American Arawak Indians (who brought grilling seafood — and the occasional iguana — to the islands) to Spanish, French, English, and Dutch adventurers to Africans, East Indians, and Chinese. Their island-hopping migrations stirred the eclectic compote into the explosive mosaic that we call Caribbean cuisine. Dance to the infectious rhythms of island cuisine with our lively menu.

Crab Empanadas   **Swordfish Escovitch**
Shrimp Satay with **Indonesian Peanut Sauce**

* * *

Grilled Jerk Tuna
Grilled Lobster with Tropical Vinaigrette

* * *

(continued)

Snapper with Sofrito   *Red Beans and Rice*   *Fried Plantains*

* * *

Hearts-of-Palm Salad with Chayote and Oranges

* * *

Coconut Island Punch   *Reggae Sunsplash Cocktail*

* * *

Rum Orange Tart   *Pina Colada Bread Pudding*

Blow-Out Seafood Bashes

When you're ready to throw a seafood extravaganza, our Backyard Lobster-and-Clam Bake and A Coastal Fondue fill the bill. Gather friends who are passionate about cooking and invite them for a day of gustatory camaraderie. Dive in together.

Backyard lobster-and-clam bake

Nothing's more fun than gathering friends for an old-fashioned New England clam bake — deluxe-style with whole Maine lobsters. But when driving to the beach takes 6 hours or longer, and digging a pit in your backyard isn't quite what you had in mind, try this grilled, steamed version. Only hard-working friends are welcome; no slackers allowed.

✔ Heavy-duty disposable roaster pans work well to steam this bounty on the grill — unless you're lucky enough to borrow a traditional seafood steamer. To improvise a steamer, you need four disposable pans (about 14 by 17 inches) for the bake: two for the bases to hold the seafood and two for high-topped lids to hold in the steam.

Gas grills are quick and clean for the bake, but if you have a charcoal grill and are using a traditional steamer, try this easy clean-up trick: Heavily coat the outside lower third and bottom of the steamer with liquid detergent and place on several layers of heavy-duty foil. Pot scrubbing is no longer the chore of bakes past.

✔ A grill that's 24 inches wide by 18 inches deep can accommodate the pans. If your grill is smaller, borrow an extra grill from a friend or steam the second pan on top of your stove.

✔ The lobster and clam bake is great fun, but messy! Protect your table with a disposable tablecloth set atop newspapers. For easy cleanup, set paper grocery bags lined with plastic bags around the table to throw shells into, and have lots of paper towels on hand. If you only have a few small sauce dishes, 4-ounce disposable cups work well. Offer melted butter mixed with an optional splash of fresh lemon juice for dipping seafood. For a zestier taste for the clams and mussels, also offer the Fire 'n' Brimstone Onion Garlic Sauce, later in this chapter. Break out the lobster crackers and picks, crack the shells, dip, and enjoy!

Backyard Lobster-and-Clam Bake

Preparation time: *With friends, about 1 hour*

Cooking time: *30 to 40 minutes*

Yield: *Feeds 8 to 10 hard-working, hungry folks*

4 heads romaine lettuce or equivalent amount of seaweed

6 leeks

12 cups water

48 ounces (4 bottles) beer

12 cloves garlic, peeled and smashed

6 shallots, peeled and halved lengthwise

20 sprigs fresh thyme or 1 tablespoon plus 1 teaspoon dried thyme leaves

3 sweet potatoes (1½ pounds), scrubbed, peel on, each cut in six pieces

8 to 10 small red potatoes

Salt and pepper to taste

8 to 10 ears corn, silk removed, husk on

6 live Maine lobsters, 1¼ pounds each

24 cherrystone or other medium hardshell clams, scrubbed

18 mussels, scrubbed, beards removed

1 to 1½ cups melted butter

½ cup fresh lemon juice

Fire 'n' Brimstone Onion Garlic Sauce (optional — see the following recipe)

Crusty French baguettes

1 Cut romaine in half lengthwise, leaving core attached; wash and pull out tender inner leaves, reserving them for a salad. If using seaweed, rinse and divide into two batches. Trim stem end of leeks, cut in half lengthwise, and wash thoroughly under running water to remove sand.

2 Prepare a hot fire in a charcoal or gas grill (the coals should be ash white or the gas on high for the seafood to steam best). To speed cooking, boil half the water separately in a tea kettle on top of the stove. In a pot on the stove, bring beer, remaining 6 cups water, garlic, shallots, and thyme to a boil.

(continued)

3 Elect friends to take all ingredients out to the barbecue. Place two pans on the grill. Fill each with half the hot water and half the beer mixture. Cover the bottom of each pan with 4 romaine halves, cut sides down, reserving 4 halves to top the bake, or use one batch of seaweed. Arrange the leeks over the romaine to finish covering the bottom. Add sweet potatoes and red potatoes, distributing the ingredients evenly between the two pans. Season with salt and pepper to taste. Cover the pans with the remaining roaster pans and steam for 10 minutes.

4 Top the potatoes with the corn and the lobsters. Top with remaining romaine leaves or the additional seaweed, and top with roaster pans. If the seal of the pans is rather loose, ensure faster steaming by weighting the tops of pans with bricks or rocks, and lowering the lid of the grill.

5 Steam for 20 minutes. If lobsters have not turned red, steam an additional 10 minutes. Remove the lobsters. Break lobsters apart — over the kitchen sink is best, place on a platter; cover and keep warm. (If the pan seal has not been tight, lobsters will be cooked after 30 minutes but may not be full bright red.)

6 Add clams to one pan and mussels to the second. Cover and steam for 10 minutes. Remove fully opened mussels and clams; steam remainder until fully opened. Place clams and mussels in one serving dish; corn and potatoes in second serving dish; and lobsters in remaining two. Discard leeks and romaine or seaweed from the steaming pan. Reserve ½ cup of the broth for the Fire 'n' Brimstone Onion Garlic Sauce. If you're still not too full, serve the broth for a "souper" finale, or freeze the broth to use for a soup base.

7 Serve the seafood and vegetables with the melted butter (let guests add lemon juice to taste), the Fire 'n' Brimstone Onion Garlic Sauce, and plenty of crusty French bread.

Fire 'n' Brimstone Onion Garlic Sauce

1 cup minced white onion

1 cup Vietnamese fish sauce (nuoc nam) or 1 cup water plus 2 mashed anchovies

⅔ cup fresh lime juice

¼ cup minced garlic

2 tablespoons sugar

1 teaspoon ground Asian chili paste, such as sambal oelek, or ¼ teaspoon red pepper flakes

½ cup reserved broth from steaming seafood

Up to 8 hours ahead, mix the onion, fish sauce, lime juice, garlic, sugar, and chili paste, stirring to dissolve the sugar; refrigerate. The sauce will be strong-tasting. To serve, bring to room temperature and stir in the broth. Serve in individual sauce dishes.

A coastal fondue: The big dip

Everybody loves to fondue, but few people have dipped during the last decade or longer. Dust off the fondue pots and get out your forks: Fish fondue is here. If, however, your fondue pot has found a new home, an electric frying pan, a heat-proof bowl, or a wok on a portable burner work just fine.

In the pot, fondue-ing it

Fondue, pronounced fahn-DOO, derives from *fondre*, the French word for "melt," says Sharon Tyler Herbst in her *Food Lover's Companion*. Fondue has several culinary meanings:

- ✔ Fondue can refer to *fondue au fromage*, the classic cheese fondue, or *fondue bourguignonne*, where guests cook beef in a pot of hot oil and dip into savory sauces. Or fondue can refer to chocolate fondue, where melted chocolate, cream, and liqueur are the dip for fruit or cake.

- ✔ Our fun fish fondue is adapted from the traditional Mongolian hot pot, a kind of Chinese fondue. Instead of cooking a variety of meat, poultry, and fish in a communal pot of simmering stock, we exclusively feature seafood. Dip into a variety of condiments, and then sip the rich broth, if you like.

In the swim: Plan ahead

Fish fondue fits in nicely with today's busy lifestyles because all of the food can be prepared ahead of time. Invite friends for supper or for the big game and serve your favorite seafood. Expect to win big when you take time to dip with friends.

- ✔ You can prepare the Oriental Dipping Sauce 1 to 2 days ahead and refrigerate. And all the finfish can be cleaned and prepared one day in advance, tightly covered, and refrigerated.

- ✔ For a party of four or more, use two or three fondue pots to ease the strain of crossing fondue forks and lost morsels of food while cooking. If your fondue forks are long gone, sturdy bamboo skewers work well. (You may want to keep brightly colored magic markers on hand for guests to mark their skewers.)

- ✔ In addition to giving your guests dipping forks, give each a separate eating fork. (Different forks for cooking and eating keep the broth and sauces clear.) And have tongs on hand to remove clams and mussels from the pot.

- ✔ If your supply of small (½ cup) bowls for sauces is limited, 4-ounce disposable glasses work well. And, if you're using a fondue pot, have lots of liquid fuel on hand for the burner to keep broth bubbling hot.

When everyone's had their fill of fish, cook all of the leftovers and use them in a carefree seafood salad for tomorrow's lunch.

A Coastal Fondue

Preparation time: 1½ hours

Yield: 4 to 6 servings

½ pound scallops

½ pound peeled, deveined large shrimp (31/35 per pound) or rock shrimp

½ pound monkfish, catfish, tilapia, or grouper

½ pound swordfish, tuna, or mahimahi

6 littleneck or other small hardshell clams

12 mussels

1 pint shucked oysters (optional)

1 pound cleaned calamari, including tentacles or 1½ pounds whole calamari, cleaned (see Chapter 10 for cleaning instructions)

½ pound mushrooms

1 large white onion

2 small zucchini

½ pound broccoli florets

4 quarts chicken broth

Oriental Dipping Sauce (see the following recipe)

1 Rinse scallops and, if using sea scallops, remove the little tab-like, tough muscle on the side of the scallop (see Chapter 8). Cut fish into ¾-inch cubes. Arrange scallops, shrimp, and fish on a large platter; refrigerate.

2 Scrub clams and clean and debeard mussels, discarding any with open or broken shells. Place in a serving bowl. Drain oysters and reserve liquid for broth, if desired. Cut calamari into rings. Place oysters and calamari in separate serving bowls. Cover seafood and keep chilled up to one hour before serving.

3 Using a clean cutting board, wipe mushrooms with a damp cloth and cut into thirds or quarters. Slice onion horizontally into ½-inch circles and separate into rings. Cut zucchini into ¼-inch slices. Attractively arrange all vegetables, including broccoli, on a large platter; cover with plastic wrap until the party begins.

4 In a 6-quart or larger pot over medium heat, bring chicken broth to a boil. Include oyster liquid, if desired (the juice adds good flavor to the broth, but turns the broth cloudy when heated). Carefully ladle hot broth into two fondue pots, filling each two-thirds full. Place fondue pots on stands and keep broth very hot but not boiling. As the broth evaporates during cooking, add hot broth to the pot to keep fish cooking fast.

5 Invite your guests to the table and begin the fondue fun. Because vegetables take longer to cook than fish, skewer each on separate fondue forks or skewers.

6 Time seafood carefully to prevent overcooking: calamari takes about 30 seconds to cook; oysters, 1 to 2 minutes; fish, scallops, and shrimp, about 2 minutes. Mussels and clams take 2 to 3 minutes (place clams and mussels 2 or 3 at a time in broth and remove when shell pops open).

7 For the sauces, provide each guest with individual bowls of the Oriental Dipping Sauce and other thin sauces. Serve thick sauces in communal bowls and spoon sauce onto your plate for dipping.

Vary It! Try the Wildcat Mustard Sauce or the Indonesian Peanut Sauce, both in Chapter 15.

Simplify your game plan by choosing precut vegetables from the salad bar at your supermarket and prepared dipping sauces. Look in the Asian section for spicy plum, teriyaki, peanut, or barbecue sauces.

Oriental Dipping Sauce

1 cup soy sauce

¼ cup fresh lemon juice

¼ cup cider vinegar

1 teaspoon Asian toasted sesame oil

1 teaspoon ground Asian chili paste, such as sambal oelek, or ¼ teaspoon red pepper flakes (optional)

½ cup finely chopped green onions

1 tablespoon toasted sesame seeds

In a 2-cup measuring pitcher or bowl, stir together the soy sauce, lemon juice, vinegar, sesame oil, and chili paste, if using. ***Note:*** You can make the sauce to this point, cover, and refrigerate. To serve, pour sauce into small individual dipping bowls and stir in green onions and sesame seeds.

Nibbles to Nosh

Noshing on seafood nibbles is our favorite party pastime. We offer a dressy festive menu for greeting the new year and a fan-friendly one for kicking around with friends.

Nibbles for New Year's Day

Welcome the new year in style with our dynamite, do-ahead starters. No cooking permitted on the day of your party; assembly is allowed.

Smoked Salmon Pinwheels with Two Surprises
Mussels Royale

* * *

Decadent "Retro" Crab Spread
Calamari Martini with Pickled Onions

* * *

Shrimp with Lemon, Sun-Dried Tomato, and Goat Cheese Dip

* * *

Norwegian Pickled Salmon   *Mini Tarragon Salmon Kebabs*

* * *

Rosemary's Christmas Calamari

* * *

Champagne

* * *

Death by Chocolate Cookies

Super Bowl noshing

Score big with sports fans of all ages when you create this almost total-shrimp experience. Most of the recipes use small or medium shrimp to stretch your seafood budget. But we include clams to make everyone happy. Get ready, get set — for your cheers.

Beer-Spiked Shrimp Peel   *Macho Nachos*

* * *

Mediterranean Shrimp Pizza   *Rich's Grilled Clams*

* * *

Super Bowl Baguettes with Shrimp and Artichoke Melt

* * *

Shirley's Seasoned Shrimp with Remoulade Sauce

* * *

Dark, light, and nonalcoholic beers

Chapter 18

A Japanese Seafood Primer

Recipes in This Chapter

▶ Sushi Rice for the Party

*J*apan and its culinary specialties are near and dear to our hearts. Two of our treasured fishy experiences took place in Tokyo: the first, a 3:00 a.m. tour of the sprawling Tsukiji fish market. The market is bustling with buyers bidding at frenzied auctions on a plethora of seafood: live swimming fish; fresh, dried, and salted fish (an entire room is devoted to vibrant orange sea urchin roe, nestled in small wooden trays, row upon row, stack upon stack); and giant fresh and frozen sushi-quality tuna. The second experience: our breakfast at a tiny sushi bar around the corner from Tsukiji (the waiting line was short at 7:30 a.m.), with tastes of the best quality.

Japanese cooking — and sushi — are more than raw fish. And fish quality is the reason why we don't offer any raw fish recipes in this book. Seafood for making fish-based sushi and sashimi must be pristine quality (there are special grades of fish) and handled under carefully controlled temperatures. Japanese chefs study for years to practice and perfect their technique for choosing the highest quality fish, creating exquisite dishes, and perfectly executing sushi and sashimi cuts.

But you can create a casual — and safe — sushi party at home with hand-rolled sushi, using and lots of cooked fillings and condiments. Your guests will have a blast. This chapter also contains a guide for deciphering sushi when you next tackle a Japanese menu in a restaurant or if you want to supplement your party. Plus, we list Web sites for you to check out that are packed with information on different sushi shapes, types of sushi, and step-by-step instructions for making Japanese specialties.

So get ready to flex those fingers and roll you own sushi.

A Hands-On Sushi Party

Picture a waffle cone filled with ice cream and you have the basic shape of hand-wrapped sushi. You can wrap your own cone-shaped roll easier than you can order coffee at an upscale coffee bar. So pass on the chopsticks and wrap up seasoned Japanese rice, fillings, and condiments in a square of crisp green-black seaweed for the perfect finger food.

Here's a list of what you need for a party of four and how to get your guests in the swim:

- **The wrapper:** Toasted seaweed sheets (*nori*), cut into halves (4-bite rolls) or quarters (2-bite rolls). Count on three sheets per guest.

- **Non-fishy fillings:** Sushi rice (see the following recipe). Thinly sliced avocado, green onion, or mango; shredded carrots or Japanese white radish (*daikon*); slivered cucumbers or snow peas; cooked asparagus spears or green beans; watercress or Japanese sea beans. About 1½ cups each of 6 to 8 fillings.

- **Fishy fillings:** Cooked crab, shrimp, surimi, smoked salmon, flying fish roe. About 1 cup each of 2 to 3 fillings. Flip to Chapter 10 for information.

- **Condiments:** Wasabi, soy sauce, pickled ginger, shiso or mint leaves, toasted sesame seeds, lemon wedges, Japanese pickles, pickled plum paste, funky bright-pink, sweetened dried fish flakes, flavored mayonnaise. Our Indonesian Peanut Sauce (Chapter 15) and Oriental Dipping Sauce (Chapter 17) are great.

- **Sips:** Japanese beer, hot and chilled sakes, and tea.

- **Nonedible helpers:** Disposable chopsticks, plates, dipping cups, finger wipes, paper towels, and finger bowls of water (lemon slice obligatory).

Set out a big bowl of sushi rice on your table and surround it with small bowls of fillings, condiments, and nonedible helpers. To make the rolls, follow these instructions:

1. **Place a piece of seaweed in the palm of one hand.**

2. **At the lower corner of the seaweed (and with wet fingers of opposite hand) spread a tablespoon or more of rice.**

3. **Top with a dab of wasabi, a selection of fillings, and roll into a cone.**

4. **Dip into your own little dish of soy sauce mixed with wasabi. Enjoy!**

Sake is Japanese for both the beverage and for salmon. This makes sense, because the Japanese are the largest consumer group of both delicious items.

Sushi Rice for the Party

Short-grain rice is the soul of sushi. While long-grain rice cooks up as dry, separate grains, short-grain rice clings together nicely and has a slightly chewy texture. Seasoned rice vinegar and *konbu,* a Japanese seaweed, give sushi rice its savory characteristics.

Preparation time: *45 minutes*

Cooking time: *30 minutes*

Yield: *8 cups*

4 cups Japanese short-grain white rice

3-inch square konbu (dried kelp), optional

4 cups water

2 tablespoons sugar

2 teaspoons kosher salt

¼ cup plus 2 tablespoons seasoned rice vinegar

1 Place rice in a strainer and rinse under cold running water until the water runs clear, shaking strainer. Let rice sit in strainer for about 30 minutes.

2 Place rice, konbu (if using), and water in a 5- to 6-quart heavy-bottomed pot. Cover and bring to a boil over high heat; remove and discard konbu. Reduce the heat to low, cover, and cook for 15 minutes. Remove rice from the heat and let stand, covered, 5 minutes.

3 As the rice is cooking, stir the sugar and salt into vinegar until dissolved. To season and cool the rice, place rice in an extra-large non-reactive metal bowl or on a jellyroll pan.

4 Pour half the seasoned vinegar over the rice. To avoid mashing the rice to a paste, use a thin-bladed spatula, dipped in cold water to keep rice from sticking. Gently lift and toss the rice to incorporate the vinegar, while cooling the rice by fanning with a magazine to shoo away the steam. The rice gets shiny and sticks together nicely.

5 Add the remaining vinegar, continuing to lift, mix, and fan until rice is cooled. This takes 5 to 8 minutes. Cover bowl with a moist clean towel. You may keep sushi rice at room temperature up to two hours before using. (If you refrigerate the rice, it becomes hard and loses its sticking power. The salt and vinegar help to inhibit spoilage.)

Surfing sushi on the Web

For more sushi-making tips and photos, check out these Web sites:

✔ http://www.nephco.com/sushi.html

✔ http://www.marystreet.com/sushi/index.html#making

✔ http://www.stickyrice.com/html/sushi.shmtl

We know that Japanese purists feel it's heretical to reheat leftover rice in the microwave, but you can — in small quantities. Or make fried rice cakes and top with sushi tidbits.

Deciphering a Japanese Menu

What is sushi anyway? Many people think of sushi only as small mounds of hand-shaped rice, spread with wasabi, and topped with a slice of raw or cooked fish or shellfish. This popular form of sushi evolved in Tokyo in the early 1800s, when you could pick up sushi at street stalls (see the following bulleted list). But sushi's origins date back to preserving fish by fermenting with salt, vinegar, and rice. There are countless shapes of sushi to discover — and picking it up with your fingers still works just fine.

Here are a few Japanese sushi basics:

✔ **Nirigi-sushi:** *Nigiri* means grasped or squeezed, and refers to the way the sushi chef shapes the rice. Popular toppings include raw tuna (*maguro*) and salmon (*sake*), cooked shrimp (*ebi*) or eel (*unagi*), and flying fish roe (*tobiko*). *Nigiri* usually comes in pairs.

✔ **Maki-sushi:** *Maki* means roll, so sushi rice and fillings are rolled in crisp seaweed sheets (*nori*). Three types of rolls are sliced: *Hoso-maki* (*hoso* means small) are 1-inch slender rolls, with one or two fillings, such as crisp, cooked salmon skin or cucumber; *futo-maki* (*futo* means large) are the fat rolls with a rainbow of fillings; and California-*maki,* the American sushi roll, has a filling of avocado, crab or surimi, and cucumber. This inside-out roll features rice on the outside and seaweed inside. You also find *temaki* (*temaki* means "handroll"), the cone-shaped hand rolls.

✔ **Sashimi:** Thin slices of raw fish, such as tuna and yellowtail, are prettily fanned on a tray and served with wasabi and pickled ginger. Mix a bit of wasabi with soy in a dish and dip in the fish. Chopsticks work best here.

✔ **Wasabi:** Picture a knobby green carrot, and that's wasabi. You may only see prepared wasabi piled in tiny mounds with sushi or sashimi, but the plant is a pungent horseradish-related root. We first saw wasabi flourishing in irrigated fields as we sped from Tokyo to Osaka on the bullet train. True wasabi is expensive and rare in the United States — the pale-green wasabi powder that Americans find is horseradish with mustard added. To make wasabi paste, stir cold water into the powder shortly before using to develop the fire. Wasabi loses its heat on sitting and when cooked.

Part VI
The Part of Tens

"Yeah, I get it, Larry. 'See food'."

In this part . . .

Whet your appetite with our selection of restaurants that specialize "solely" in seafood (we couldn't resist the pun). Here are our favorite fine dining/special occasion restaurants, casual eateries, and slurping-good oyster bars.

In this part, we also point you in the right direction for regional seafood festivals that pay tribute to the traditions and history of the region, and send you surfing the Web for timely seafood information.

Finally, we recommend our favorite seafood companies who fly fabulous fish (fresh, frozen, or smoked) to you overnight.

Chapter 19
Ten Great Seafood Festivals

. . . .

In This Chapter

▶ Discovering the best festivals around the United States

▶ Pacing yourself to savor local seafood

. . . .

*W*hether you want to celebrate your local seafood industry or add seafood adventure to your travel plans, America's regional seafood festivals are a great way to go. Most seafood festivals have a distinct down-home quality about them and convey their community spirit. Seafood festivals pay tribute to local industries that contribute both to the economy and to the traditions and history of the region.

In this chapter, we list a few of our favorite festivals for you to choose from, but keep in mind that there are many others throughout the country. We list the festivals in chronological order, from the start of the festival season to the end.

World Catfish Festival

Second Saturday in April
For more information, call 800-408-4838

Belzoni, Mississippi, is called the "Catfish Capital of the World," and this classic seafood festival features such highlights as the coronation of the Catfish Queen and virtually all the catfish you could want to eat, served with hush puppies, fries, and coleslaw. Truly dedicated catfish lovers test their stamina in the catfish-eating contest. New Orleans-style street entertainers and other live performances add to the festive atmosphere.

Port Washington Smelt Fry

Friday and Saturday following Easter
For more information, call 414-284-9069

This fish fry in Port Washington, Wisconsin, is really more of a special event than a festival. But there is such an appreciation of smelt-ness here that people come from near and far and happily wait in line for their chance to get all they can eat of these small fish from nearby Lake Michigan. The smelt recipe is secret — carefully handed down among the American Legion volunteers who host the event. The fried smelt, folded to eat like a hotdog, are served on a slice of rye bread with a scoop of coleslaw. Mmm-mm, tasty.

Wakefield Shad Planking

Third Wednesday of April
For more information, call 804-834-2214

Politics and fish may seem odd bedfellows, but for over fifty years the two have shared the stage at the annual Wakefield Shad Planking in Wakefield, Virginia. Sponsored by the Wakefield Ruritan Club, this shad feast has also been a stumping ground for Virginia politicians since the festival began. A few thousand pounds of the bony fish are nailed to oak planks and cooked long and slow over glowing embers. The shad are served with a secret sauce, coleslaw, and beer. It's an event of great proportions, especially during an election year.

Breaux Bridge Crawfish Festival

First weekend of May
For more information, call 318-332-6655

Partner Cajun culture and music with this area's most famous seafood and you get a stompin' good time at the annual crawfish festival in Breaux Bridge, Lousiana. Some of the best Cajun musicians gather and provide the soundtrack for an ocean of activities — cook-offs for crawfish étouffée (the rich, spicy Cajun stew served over rice), crawfish races, Cajun dance contests, crawfish eating contests, and the chance to feast on crawfish cooked in every way imaginable.

Kodiak Crab Festival

Thursday before Memorial Day through Memorial Day Monday
For more information, call 907-486-5557

For five days, locals in Kodiak, Alaska, salute their important seafood industry with parades, races, carnival, and plenty of outstanding fish and shellfish from nearby waters. Get your fill of halibut, king crab legs, salmon, and plenty of other local seafood treats, and join in the underwater treasure hunt, parades, and more.

Monterey Squid Festival

Memorial Day weekend
For more information, call 831-649-6544 or visit http://www.montereysquid.com

This squid festival in Monterey, California, began in 1984 as a fundraiser for the local Kiwanis Club and now it's a local Memorial Day tradition. Thousands come to enjoy their fill of squid cooked every which way — barbecued, broiled, panfried, deep-fried, in tacos. Crowds gather round the oversized skillet perched over a fire and chant out the ingredients as each is added to the massive stir-fry. Local and national chefs join in the fun, offering squid cooking demonstrations and tastings. It's an all-out squid-ucation, with activities for kids, arts and crafts, and live music.

Maine Lobster Festival

Begins the Wednesday before the first full weekend in August, and continues through Sunday
For more information, call 800-LOBCLAW or visit
http://www.mainelobsterfestival.com

Join the 80,000 people who flock to Rockland, Maine, each August to revel in lobster fun. Throughout the five-day festival, you can eat your fill of freshly cooked Maine lobster, watch the blindfold rowboat races, join in the Great International Lobster Crate Race, and watch the seafood cook-off and the lobster-eating contest. There are plenty of maritime displays, activities for the kids, and nonstop entertainment. Make sure you catch the big parade on Saturday.

Washington State Seafood Festival

First full weekend of October
For more information, call 360-426-2021

The locals in Shelton, Washington, just call it "Oysterfest," this annual gathering of seafood lovers in the heart of Puget Sound oyster country. The serious business is the oyster shucking competition for professionals that leads to the crowning of the West Coast Oyster Shucking Champion at the end of the weekend. The extravaganza of seafood includes oysters — freshly picked from local cultured beds — prepared dozens of ways, with Pacific salmon, mussels, and other seafood galore. You can also find a seafood cook-off, a beer garden with local microbrews, and live music.

St. Mary's County Oyster Festival

Third weekend of October
For more information, call 301-863-5015

Whether you are a world-class oyster shucker, first-class oyster sucker, or topnotch oyster cooker, celebrate the opening of the fall oyster season in Leonardtown, Maryland, on the Chesapeake Bay. The region is famous for its seafood, and oysters are the most celebrated delicacy. Come hungry and get your fill of oysters any way — raw on the half shell, fried, steamed, or stewed. Steamed and fried clams, Chesapeake crab cakes, and chowder also are on the menu. Brush up on your best recipes if you'd like to join the oyster cook-off. And for oyster shucking tips, don't miss the pros (including the Washington State winner) who compete in the championship to find the country's best oyster shucker. The winner heads to Ireland for the world shucking challenge. Live music, activities for the kids, and educational displays from local watermen contribute to the festive atmosphere.

Florida Seafood Festival

First weekend of November
For more information, call 888-653-9419

Pay heed to King Retsyo ("oyster" spelled backwards) during this decades-old celebration of seafood in Apalachicola, Florida, near the state's largest seafood-producing estuary, Apalachicola Bay. You can feast on oysters, mullet, shrimp, crab, and more. Highlights include the Blessing of the Fleet, which bestows blessings on the fishermen and their boats for a safe and successful fishing season.

Chapter 20

Our Top Ten Upscale Seafood Restaurants

In This Chapter

▶ Dining in sublime style

▶ Indulging in the best

*C*all us seafood fanatics. Point the compass on our travel adventures toward the sea, the beach, or the port. Even before we book a flight, we research regional seafood — and the chefs who proudly present the freshest catch of the day.

Whet your appetite on the road, as we have, with fish or shellfish that you can't always find at home. Thanks to others who share our piscatorial passion, seafood restaurants are thriving in both coastal and inland locations. We salute these gifted chefs who serve seafood exclusively (or almost exclusively).

These restaurants, listed alphabetically, epitomize the high-end seafood dining experience, ideal for your special occasions. (Save your pennies: The experience is worth it.)

Aqua

252 California Street, San Francisco; 415-956-9662
http://www.nextcenturyrestaurants.com/aqua.htm

Aqua exemplifies fine dining and continues to attract crowds who are looking for sophisticated seafood cuisine. Located in the city's financial district, Aqua's sleek dining room reflects the elegance of Chef Michael Mina's cooking. Signature dishes include savory black mussel souffle and medallions of ahi tuna with seared foie gras and Pinot Noir sauce. Settle in for some sublime tastes.

AquaKnox

3214 Knox Street, Dallas, Texas; 214-219-2782

Star Texas Chef Stephen Pyles has fully embraced seafood with his splashy, sleek restaurant in Dallas. Flavors and presentations are big and bold, with Asian and Latin influences mingling with his southwestern foundation. Choosing among dishes is next to impossible, so go with friends and sample lots of seasonal tastes, from rock shrimp and lobster dumplings to sizzling whole catfish with black beans, garlic, and ginger to banana leaf-steamed red snapper in red curry. Sit at the handsome bar for impromptu casual bites, including sparkling salmon tartare, oysters on the half shell, sushi, and sashimi.

Crustacean

9646 Little Santa Monica Blvd., Beverly Hills, California; 310-205-8990
1475 Polk Street, San Francisco, California; 415-776-2722

It's a family affair at the two Crustacean restaurants — one in San Francisco; the second in Beverly Hills. Matriarch Helen An fled her war-torn homeland of Vietnam with only a handful of recipes. Now, with the help of her daughters and her mother-in-law, An oversees a dynamic dynasty of remarkable seafood cuisine. Don't miss the roasted crab, served in a garlicky butter sauce, perfect with the garlic noodles alongside. The newer Beverly Hills location is stunningly decorated, echoing An's past; the San Francisco location, a bit more informal.

Farallon

450 Post Street, San Francisco, California; 415-956-6969
http://www.farallonrestaurant.com

This is a powerhouse seafood restaurant, pairing the inimitable style of co-owner and restaurant designer Pat Kuleto with the distinguished cooking of chef and partner Mark Franz. The whimsically romantic seafood décor kicks off the adventure. Belly up to the jelly bar, slip onto octopus stools, and read by the light of the jellyfish. Local, seasonal, and regional seafoods abound — plucked from fresh and salt waters worldwide. Sea of Cortez scallops with giant squid risotto and saffron-poached sablefish make this an inspired dining experience. Even the house green salad comes embellished with fennel-cured salmon.

Kinkead's

2000 Pennsylvania Avenue NW, Washington, D.C.; 202-296-7700

Admittedly, Kinkead's is one of Leslie's favorite seafood restaurants. That being said, Bob Kinkead's panache with fish generally wows folks everywhere. Leslie's favorites include crispy fried clams with fried lemon slices and the best tartar sauce, grilled squid with creamy polenta, and cod cheeks swimming in parsley butter. Move beyond appetizers and revel in pepita-crusted salmon, skate wings, or roasted monkfish with chorizo. As you dine, feast your eyes on Kinkead's funky fish sculptures — Bob's art collection is as finely crafted as his robust personal cuisine. Oysters on the half shell also star here.

Le Bernardin

155 West 51st Street, New York, New York; 212-489-1515
http://www.le-bernardin.com

This is surely one of the best seafood restaurants in the country, if not *the* best. Chef Eric Ripert finely maintains the impeccable standards of the original chef/owner, the late Gilbert Le Coze. In partnership now with Gilbert's sister, Maguy Le Coze, Ripert's cuisine is full of finesse with thoughtful, understated invention. Raw seafood dishes — such as ceviche or carpaccio — are stunning signatures here, but you'll be entranced by everything. Le Bernardin is a once-in-a lifetime experience. Don't miss it.

Matsuhisa

129 North La Cienega Blvd., Los Angeles, California; 310-659-9639

Celebrated Chef Nobu Matsuhisa is acclaimed on both coasts since opening Nobu in New York City, but his Los Angeles restaurant still thrills diners as the first son of this masterful genius. Everything is stellar here, especially the sushi and sashimi. But look beyond familiar pairings to Nobu's free-form creations. Delight in the oyster salmon roll — smoked salmon is the base of the sushi roll, while fresh oysters, chopped shiso, grated horseradish, garlic, and ginger top the salmon and are then formed into a roll. Here you find familiar foods in perfectly balanced flavor melodies. Cooked dishes shine, too, from halibut cheeks with pepper sauce to ethereal deep-fried sea urchin. Or opt for the chefs choice menu and discover tantalizing tastes that are exquisitely presented.

Oceana

55 East 54th Street, New York, New York; 212-759-5941

This cozy dining room may have you believe that you're dining near the captain's table on a fine ocean liner. And that's just what this restaurant wants to convey — a blend of coziness and sophistication that's echoed on the menu. Chef Rick Moonen has made signatures of his salmon tartare wrapped with smoked salmon and east-coast bouillabaisse, but the fixed price menu (a set cost for a variety of dishes) will tempt you with plenty of seductive options.

Ray's Boathouse

6049 Seaview Avenue NW, Seattle, Washington; 206-789-3770
http://www.rays.com

Two large fires haven't hurt the momentum at the classic waterfront restaurant, perched on Puget Sound with a full view of the Olympic Mountains (weather permitting). Regional seafoods are featured — from sturgeon to king crab — all expertly prepared. The kasu black cod is a local favorite. Upstairs, the café offers more casual fare, such as Thai mussels and great fish and chips on the relaxing outdoor patio.

Sooke Harbour House

1528 Whiffen Spit Road, Sooke, B.C., Canada; 250-642-3421

It's an idyllic spot, perched above the Strait of Juan de Fuca on Vancouver Island. Owner Sinclair Philip regularly scuba dives in the waters near the inn for eclectic items to feature on the night's menu. Don't be surprised to see gooseneck barnacles, limpets, sea urchin, or sea vegetables. (We first ate barnacles here — wild-looking creatures with a shell-encrusted foot.) The inn's extensive gardens supply the chefs with herbs, flowers, vegetables, fruits, and myriad edible treasures. It's little wonder *Gourmet* magazine once recognized Sooke Harbour House as the best restaurant in the world for authentic, local cuisine. And here, that means outstanding seafood — the freshest you may ever have.

Chapter 21

Our Top Ten Laid-Back Eateries

. . . .

In This Chapter

▶ Savoring seafood in relaxed, nautical settings

▶ Catching local flavors

. . . .

Each of these restaurants, with its distinct personality, is securely anchored in its local environment. Longevity, a strong emphasis on local seafood, a unique regional character — or a combination of all three — contribute to their success.

Flying Fish

2234 1st Avenue, Seattle, Washington; 206-728-8595
http://www.flyingfishseattle.com

This restaurant is in the heart of Seattle's hip Belltown neighborhood. Chef Christine Keff's menu and presentations are dynamic and appealing, with such unusual offerings as the whole fried snapper, served on a vast platter in full swim. Keff features wood-grilled and wok preparations — the salt-and-pepper Dungeness crab is outstanding. It's a great place for a group, with most of the dishes intended for sharing.

Fulton's Crab House

Pleasure Island, Disney World, Orlando, Florida; 407-934-2628

It may be in the center of Florida on Disney World property, but this restaurant is every bit the kind of seafood house you find in New England or in the Pacific northwest. Fulton's flies in exceptional seafood from around the country: first-of-the-season wild salmon from Alaska, day-boat scallops from New England, and the season's best oysters to stock the raw bar in the Stone Crab

Lounge. To add to the festive air, you board an old riverboat that's stylishly converted into this big restaurant. And don't be surprised if you see Donald Duck dining here one day.

Joe's Stone Crab

Open mid-October through mid-May
11 Washington Avenue, Miami Beach, Florida; 305-673-0365
http://www.joesstonecrab.com

Don't run when you see the lines at Florida's famous stone crab Hall of Fame. Stone crab lovers flock here during the season, often waiting two hours for the pleasure of digging into mounds of plump, sweet, chilled crab claws — served with Joe's legendary mustard sauce. In fact, Joe's 2,000 guests each night consume about one ton of perfectly chilled claws. Order your favorite side dishes, including coleslaw and the addicting sweet potato fries.

Legal Sea Foods

20 east coast locations; for information call 800-477-LEGAL
http://www.legalseafoods.com

Legal's motto, "If it isn't fresh, it isn't Legal," sums up the success of this Boston landmark. Legal offers customers traditionally prepared, pristine quality fish, from boiled lobster to crumb-topped New England baked scrod (small cod). Don't miss the tuna meatballs with fish-shaped ravioli on the award-winning kids' menu. George Berkowitz opened the first family fish shack in 1968, next door to the market his father opened in 1904; son Roger is now at the helm of this esteemed restaurant group.

Ocean Star

145 N. Atlantic Boulevard, Monterey Park, California; 818-308-2128
http://www.oceanstarseafood.com

Amidst the glitz and glamour of Los Angeles, it's often the ethnic restaurants that get top honors for seafood. If you were so inclined, you could invite 800 or more of your closest friends to this massive Hong Kong-style seafood restaurant in an eastern suburb of Los Angeles. You'll observe a choreographed chaos of activity throughout your meal, while you dine on lobster, crab, or live fish plucked from the fresh tanks out front. Santa Barbara rock cod and local sheepshead are two fish you often find in the swim.

Red Fish Grill

115 Bourbon Street, New Orleans, Louisiana; 504-598-1200
http://www.redfishgrill.com

Sculpted metal, brightly colored fish, oyster-shell mirrors (complete with pearls), and blazing neon lure you into this funky, hot, fish spot where casual and laid back are the order of the day. Check out the bounty of local seafood, from crawfish, shrimp, crab, oysters, and catfish to Gulf tuna and trout. Hickory wood-grilled fish has the starring role, but don't miss the shrimp po'boy sandwiches, crawfish étouffée, oysters three ways, Louisiana crawfish cake, or Bourbon Street pecan-crusted shrimp. Ralph Brennan oversees Red Fish, the newest member of the Brennan restaurant legacy in New Orleans — joining the highly acclaimed Commander's Palace, Mr. B's, Bacco, and the Palace Café.

Roy's Restaurants

Multiple locations; for information call 808-396-9875
http://www.roys-restaurants.com

Seafood and Hawaii are virtually synonymous, and restaurants throughout the islands offer exceptional regional seafood dishes. But among the standouts are Roy Yamaguchi's restaurants. Roy is one of the founders of Hawaii Regional Cuisine, a movement to promote and celebrate the distinctive ingredients and personality of Hawaiian cooking. Sparkling local seafood reigns, including opah, swordfish, mahimahi, opakapaka, and ahi tuna, among other species. Add fresh local fruits, vegetables, and seaweed to the mix, and you have distinctive Hawaiian flavors. Look for Roy's restaurants on Oahu, Maui, Kauai, and the Big Island, with a few locations on the mainland, as well.

Shaw's Crab House and Blue Crab Lounge

21 East Hubbard Street, Chicago, Illinois; 312-527-2722
http://www.shaws-chicago.com

Chef Yves Roubaud, General Manager Steve LaHaie, and the folks at Shaw's are passionate about fish, from prized local smelt to heralded regional species. Look for seasonal Alaska and Pacific northwest salmon and halibut, Dungeness crabs, and Maryland blue crabs presented in this classic coastal fish house setting. Or if you're lucky, catch the music of The Fabulous Fishheads while you slurp oysters in the Blue Crab Lounge.

Tadich Grill

240 California Street, San Francisco, California; 415-391-2373

This venerable seafood restaurant, dating back to 1849, still holds its own in the competitive business of downtown San Francisco restaurants. Don't expect too many modern influences on the menu, but if a great cioppino, crab Louis, clam chowder, or lobster Newburg sounds about right, this is the place. Locals also go for whatever fish is fresh that day, grilled or panfried. Tadich Grill is a slice of California history that still appeals today.

The Daily Catch

323 Hanover Street, Boston, Massachusetts; 617-523-8567

This small, no-frills spot in Boston's North End Italian neighborhood is only a few steps off the city's famous Freedom Trail. Calamari is king on the chalkboard menu — fried, stuffed, in salad, ground into calamari meatballs, or served in a variety of pasta dishes. But there is other seafood as well, prepared in similar fashion. Don't be surprised if your dinner arrives in the skillet, straight from the stove. Enough to serve a crowd, and guaranteed to please.

Chapter 22

Our Top Ten Oyster Bars

*W*hen we travel, we try to track down the best oysters. One adventure in France took us to the wholesale fish market at Rungis in Paris. Our tour began in the wee hours of the morning, and our guide thoughtfully timed breakfast so that we'd arrive at one of her favorite oyster farmers. As we sat on wooden oyster crates in the grower's stall, he carefully shucked his Brittany-raised oysters. Big, briny exquisite tastes — no better way to start a day!

Getting Ready to Slurp

Oyster bars stake their reputation on the quality of their oysters — and their oyster shuckers. Our oyster guru, Jon Rowley (a restaurant consultant and dedicated oyster proponent), shares tips for identifying perfectly shucked oysters:

✔ The oysters should be plump and whole, with no nicks, no cuts, no loose bits of shell, and absolutely no mud.

✔ The oysters should be presented in the cupped oyster shell to hold the juices.

✔ The oysters should be ice cold and nestled on a bed of ice to keep the oysters from tipping and spilling their juices.

Oyster Bar Heaven

The oyster bars in Table 22-1 offer both wild and farm-raised oysters. Selections usually change each day based on the best oysters available.

Table 22-1	Ten Great Oyster Bars
Name	**Description**
Acme Oyster House 504-522-5973 724 Iberville Street New Orleans, LA	Since 1910; boisterous, French-Quarter classic; oyster po'boys and gumbos.
Blue Crab Lounge, Shaw's Crab House 312-527-2722 21 East Hubbard Street Chicago, IL	Gather 'round the big oyster bar and "Royster with the Oyster" during the annual fall oyster festival.
Emeril's New Orleans Fish House 702-891-7374 3799 Las Vegas Blvd. S. Las Vegas, NV	Catch the spirit of the Big Easy with Gulf oysters aplenty (British Columbia kin, too); crawfish, oyster, and shrimp po'boys.
Casamento's 504-895-9761 4330 Magazine Street New Orleans, LA	Over 80 years old; classic, deep-fried oyster loaf; seafood gumbo; sparkling white, ceramic-tile walls.
Old Ebbitt Grill 675 202-347-4801 15th Street Washington, D.C.	One of the best; Annual Oyster Riot with winning wines from Oyster and Wine competition.
Oyster Bar & Restaurant 212-490-6650 Grand Central Terminal New York, NY	Since 1913; big and busting; rich oyster and seafood panroasts with creamy tomato base.
Rodney's Oyster House 416-363-8105 209 Adelaide Street East Toronto, Canada	Great Malpeques from Prince Edward Island, among others. Rodney's is in Vancouver, British Columbia, too.
Swan Oyster Depot 415-673-1101 1517 Polk Street San Francisco, CA	Since 1912; counter seating, no tables; retail food shop.
The Brooklyn Seafood, Steak & Oyster House 206-224-7000 1212 Second Avenue Seattle, WA	Pair fabulous northwest oysters with local microbrews and wines.
Union Oyster House 617-227-2750 41 Union Street Boston, MA	Since 1826; Boston's oldest restaurant; sit at oval wooden oyster bar and absorb the history.

Chapter 23

Ten Must-"Sea" Web Sites

In This Chapter

▶ Netting the answers you seek

▶ Expanding your seafood horizons

▶ Filtering out "fishy-facts"

Given our lighthearted penchant for things both "fishy" and "funky," we surprise ourselves most of all by our serious approach in selecting Web sites to recommend to you. Although cyberspace is filled with "catchy" seafood sites with cute and clever content, we stick with the solidly scientific here.

Whatever our quest for new facts, we never cease to be amazed by the depth and breadth of information and invaluable data we amass from the Internet. But where we already have a pretty firm grasp of a subject, we are often distressed by the amount of misinformation we glean as well. And it's not always apparent to us at first glance.

Nowhere has misinformation been more apparent than as we've collected seafood research from the Web for this book. News that you think is news may already be old. Even with authentic sources, listing a date with the document is not required. Further, a source that appears to be a legitimate scientific organization may be a front for cause-marketing or an activist campaign that you wouldn't be so eager to support if you knew their science wasn't as sound as it sounds.

With the ebb and flow of the seafood business, you're bound to find some sites ebb — even disappear. We've done our best to list sites and links with longevity. If you don't like a site we picked, we hope that it at least links you to ones that you like and find fruitful. The astonishing number of seafood sites continues to grow exponentially. Happy surfing!

Bigger Is Better

Two giant Web sites have an awesome number of links. Both sites are excellent resources for getting the global picture of seafood today.

Gadus Associates

http://home.istar.ca/~gadus/

Nova Scotia-based Gadus Associates is a ten-year-old fisheries science consulting company owned by Dr. Trevor Kenchington. On this powerful site, they claim to offer the most extensive list of marine fisheries links on the Web to bring you information from all parts of the world. We believe their claim is solid. In case you wonder, *gadus morhua* is the scientific name for cod, a fish with historic and economic importance to the Nova Scotia area.

National Marine Fisheries Service

http://www.nmfs.gov

The National Marine Fisheries Service (NMFS) is part of the National Oceanic and Atmospheric Administration (NOAA). This agency provides services throughout the entire maze of fisheries operations, at home and internationally. Use their search engine to get pointed in the right direction.

From East to West

Check out the variety of organizations on the Web that are targeting a specific seafood or promoting all the seafood bounty found in a particular state. Some of these groups and their sites are state-supported; others are privately supported by a fisheries industry; still others are jointly funded by both their state and their industry. We share two — one from the Atlantic and one from the Pacific.

Although we don't spotlight the dynamic sites from other states and fisheries, they're jam-packed with resources and recipes, and we invite you to explore them.

Maine Lobster Promotion Council

http://www.mainelobsterpromo.com

Sue Barber, a friend and colleague, is the executive director of this council. If you're feeling cyber-challenged, you may prefer to receive their newsletter with announcements about lobster festivals, recipes, contests, and much more. Call 207-947-2966 for details.

California Seafood Council

http://www.ca-seafood.org

From barracuda to yellow tail, the California Seafood Council embraces the entire catch. Diane Pleschner, another friend and colleague, is the manager of this council. She, too, oversees the production of a fact-filled newsletter, an alternative if you're just figuring out how to surf the Web. Call 805-569-8050 for information.

And All the Rest

Here's an assortment of sites that we like, in no particular order. If you think that the "www" is missing from a Web site address, not so. You can access several of our top ten selections through updated Web addresses (called *URLs*) that no longer require the customary "www."

Sea Grant Institute: University of Wisconsin

http://www.seagrant.wisc.edu/

Sea Grant programs in many states conduct research, education, and advisory services to promote the understanding, development, wise use, and conservation of ocean and coastal resources. Find helpful, how-to publications here — click on Publications on the home-page menu. Subjects include storing, thawing, canning, and freezing fish. From this Wisconsin site, you can link to Sea Grant sites in other states, too.

National Fisheries Institute

http://www.nfi.org

Want more recipes? Species information? Nutritional data? This site is for you. NFI is the largest fisheries trade association in the United States. Some parts of this Web site are restricted to their members only.

Seafood.com, Inc.

http://www.seafood.com or http://www.seafood-link.com

The goal of this multifunction site is to bring seafood buyers, sellers, and consumers together on the Internet. Post your seafood questions on Ask the Experts and log on later to get your answers, or start a lively discussion.

Seafood Network Information Center

http://seafood.ucdavis.edu/

The Seafood Network Information Center is the site that we head to when we want seafood-safety information. But the site is much, much broader than just safety tips — recipes and seafood information on almost any topic that you're interested in are just a click away. Based at the University of California in Davis, this Web site is also home to a food safety news-group, an e-mail dialogue among seafood experts around the world. Look over some of the archived files to see the scope of the scientists' discussions.

Aquaculture Network Information Center

http://aquanic.org

Based at Purdue University in West Lafayette, Indiana, this site is a gateway to the world's electronic resources for aquaculture. Great place to look for publications; many full-text versions are available to download.

Finally, go fishing. . .

http://stone-crabs.com/

Click on "fishing trip" after you reach this site. Jump into the fishing boat and you're off to gather stone crabs and carefully remove a claw from one of them — it rapidly grows a replacement. With just a few quick clicks, you're back to home port — armed with a new appreciation for this rare treat. Research should always be this much fun!

Chapter 24

Ten Great Shore-to-Door Seafood Shippers

- -

In This Chapter
▶ Catching seafood across the miles
▶ Gift-giving with flying fish

- -

*W*hen you want to give a unique gift or try a regional fish that rarely swims to your seafood market, refer to this chapter for some of our favorite seafood companies — they fly seafood to your doorstep overnight.

The J.M. Clayton Company

Whether you're a transplanted Marylander or a recent convert who hungers for a taste of blue crab, this Chesapeake Bay company (established in 1890) can satisfy your cravings. Clayton ships fresh, steamed Maryland blue crabs, with or without traditional Bay seasoning, as well as fresh or pasteurized crabmeat. The firm, sweet meat is perfect for making crab cakes. Whole crabs and fresh crabmeat are in season from May until mid-November, and pasteurized crabmeat year 'round. Call 800-652-6931.

Ducktrap River Fish Farm

Des FitzGerald makes our favorite cold-smoked salmon: rich, red-orange, farmed Atlantic salmon (Kendall-Brook label) is glossy, without excess surface oils, and presliced. The flavor is delicately smoky; the texture, silky-smooth. Ducktrap makes an outstanding smoke-roasted, peppered Atlantic salmon: firm, moist, and chewy, slightly salty-sweet with a nice peppery after-taste that doesn't overwhelm. Look also for smoked, small Maine shrimp and luscious, peppered mackerel. Ducktrap offers a full, written guarantee for product replacement or your money back. Check out their online catalog at http://www.ducktrap.com; to order, call 800-828-3825.

Francesca's Favorites

Come mid-October, fabulous Florida stone crabs are back in season — owner Peter Jarvis brings you fresh, just-cooked stone-crab claws. Francesca's is also our favorite place to order fresh Florida shrimp, fresh Caribbean lobster tails, fresh Key West yellowtail snapper fillets, and fine-quality caviars from the Caspian Sea. Try an exotic new crab — the golden crab from way down deep (2,000 feet) in Florida waters. Crack golden cocktail claws for sweet, moist meat, similar to snow crabs.

For easy crab soups, salads, or crab cakes, order a container of picked crab-meat. Francesca's offers a full, written guarantee for product replacement or refund. Call 800-865-2722 or order from their e-commerce secure site at http://www.valueamerica.com.

FreshFish4U.com

To succeed in the retail fish business for more than fifty years, you have to be doing lots of things right. Enjoy the same fine freshwater fish and customer service that keep Captain Jack Donlan's loyal shoppers coming back to The Fish House in Grand Blanc, Michigan. His son-in-law, Bill Milne, created their Web site and oversees Internet orders for their fresh (not frozen) fish.

Check out the Discussion Forum where Capt. Jack answers fish-related questions. Order specialties from the Great Lakes and Canadian lakes — yellow perch, walleye, lake trout, and whitefish — by using this e-commerce secure site — http://www.FreshFish4U.com — or calling toll-free 877-474-FISH.

Mail order checklist

Check your schedule, plan to be around when your flying fish arrives, and double-check the following before ordering:

✔ **Check shipping time:** Seafood should be shipped by overnight carrier.

✔ **Check packaging:** Packages should be sent in well-insulated boxes or coolers, with frozen gel packs or dry ice. Look for key words on the box: perishable, fresh seafood, keep cold.

✔ **Check shipping costs:** Some companies include shipping costs in their product prices; others charge separately based on weight.

Gerard and Dominique Seafoods

The best hot-smoked, northwest-style salmon: rich, smoky-sweet with layers of subtle flavors and no excess salt; firm, moist, chewy flesh; and a tawny, burnished surface that's speckled with sesame seeds. French-chef owners Gerard Parrat and Dominique Place also offer European-style, cold-smoked salmon that is lightly smoked and silky textured, as well as other smoked seafoods. Atlantic salmon that's farm-raised in the Pacific northwest is their choice for both hot- and cold-smoking. Full written guarantee for product replacement or refund. Call 800-858-0449 or e-mail g-d_seafoods@msn.com.

Horton's

It's a difficult choice between the brandied pepper or the pastrami smoked salmon. Jean and Don Horton produce Atlantic salmon that's lightly cold-smoked, with a firm, tender texture. The brandied pepper is delicately edged with pepper that adds bright, spicy tastes that don't overpower the salmon. Ditto for the pastrami — elusive, fruity notes enhance the smoke. See their online catalog at http://www.hortons.com; to order, call 800-346-6066.

LeBlanc's Gourmet Lobster Stew

LeBlanc's lobster stew has so much lobster meat in it, you may think you've been whisked to a lobster house on the coast of Maine. Patti and Gerald LeBlanc make their sumptuous stew (in their restaurant, Winnie's Restaurant and Dairy Bar) with all-natural ingredients: milk, cream, butter, house-secret spices, and lobster — whole claws and big pieces, more than ½ pound per quart. Now, that's a food label we love to read. Call 800-552-0142 or e-mail leblanc@ainop.com.

Legal Sea Foods

Legal's trademark is exquisite quality, thanks to Roger Berkowitz, President and CEO of this family enterprise. Superb live New England lobsters, lobster-bakes and clambakes, fabulous fresh fish (ask about Cape scallops and tuna), dynamite jumbo shrimp (beautifully cooked and peeled), and chowders galore. In addition, this site contains the best consumer cooking information and recipes. Call 800-343-5804 or log on to this e-commerce secure site at http://www.legalseafoods.com.

Maine Lobster Direct

A lobster *can bake* is a neat twist on the traditional Maine lobster bake. Lobsters and soft-shell clams are nestled in lots of seaweed in a large, shiny, gold can.

Russell Turner, Lobster Direct's intrepid owner, traces the heritage of the can bake to the 1940s when Ed Meyers, of Salt Water Farms in Maine, shipped live lobsters cross-country by rail in this paint-style can. Look for the Damn Good Clam and Seafood Chowder — also tasty. Call 800-556-2783, e-mail them at lobsters@maine.com, or log on at http://www.maine.com/lobsters. One-hundred percent satisfaction guaranteed.

Seafood Direct

Mike and Sharon Chiddick offer signature wild Alaskan and Pacific northwestern seafood, as well as other hard-to-find fish. The best: the Alaska king crab claws are fist size, with sweet, firm meat. Bright red-orange Copper River king salmon steaks have moist, chewy flesh, and the snow-white Alaska halibut loin cooks up with big, firm flakes. They also have Alaska snow crab cocktail claws, tuna, mahimahi — and from way down under, Australian lobster tails. All seafood is carefully frozen and vacuum-packed. The canned Dungeness crab is caught off the Washington and Oregon coast and has no preservatives added. Call 800-732-1836.

Taylor Shellfish

If you're an oyster lover, send a gift to yourself from Taylor. Taylor farm-raises their exquisite-quality oysters in inspected, certified-clean Puget Sound waters. You can find tiny Olympia oysters, the northwest's native gem; mildly salt-sweet, firm European flats; plump, crunchy Kumamotos and briny deep-cupped Pacifics, both in the shell and conveniently shucked. Add to the list Mediterranean mussels with their big, succulent meats, and sweet, delicate Manila clams. Call 360-426-6178 and ask for the retail store, or check out their e-commerce secure online store at http://www.taylorshellfish.com.

Appendix

Who's Who in the World of Shrimp

· ·

*F*rom more than 350 types of commercially harvested shrimp in the world, the following are the most common. While the shell color can be an identifier for a particular type of shrimp, we also give you information about the shrimp's cooked appearance, size range, taste, and harvest location. (Note that the term "skin" refers to the colored surface of the meat.)

Flip to Chapter 5 for tips for cooking shrimp to perfection, and get ready for a standing ovation when you star our shrimp recipes in your everyday and party fare.

- ✔ **White shrimp:** Raw white shrimp have grayish-white shells; when cooked, the shells turn red, the meat is white, and the skin is pinky-red. This shrimp is one of our favorites because of its firm, sweet, crisp, juicy flesh. Sizes range from under 10 to 110 per pound. Sauté, stir-fry, or use in shrimp cocktail. White shrimp are harvested in waters around the world, from southeast United States, the Gulf of Mexico, the Pacific coast, Mexico, Central and South America, and the Caribbean to central Brazil, India, and Indonesia. The shrimp are caught wild or farm-raised, depending on the location.

- ✔ **Brown shrimp:** Raw brown shrimp have light brown or tan shells; the cooked shells turn bright coral, with white meat and coral skin. This shrimp is another one of our favorites — full-flavored, firm, and crisp, some with a briny, iodiney flavor from their kelp diet. Sizes range from under 10 to 110 per pound. Sauté or peel-and-eat. Harvested wild in the southeast U.S., the Gulf of Mexico, the Pacific coast, and Mexico.

- ✔ **Pink shrimp:** You can identify raw pink shrimp by their light pink shells, some with an iridescent dot. When cooked, the shells turn dark pink, the meat is pinkish-white, and the skin is pink. Another of our favorites, pink shrimp is sweet, plump, and crisp, making it a great peel-and-eat shrimp. Sizes range from under 10 to 60 per pound. Pink shrimp are found wild in the southeast U.S., the Gulf of Mexico, Central America, and the Caribbean.

- **Tiger shrimp or black tigers:** Raw, this species has black- or blue-striped shells; cooked, the shells turn cardinal red, the meat is white, and the skin is red. You'll find a mild taste and high moisture content, in sizes ranging from under 10 to 110 per pound. Sauté or grill. Farmed and wild harvested in Thailand, Indonesia, India, and Asia.

- **Cocktail, bay, or salad shrimp:** These have delicate pink to reddish shells when raw; when cooked, the shells range from pale pink to red, the meat is pinkish white, and the skin is pink to red. Almost always sold cooked, this shrimp is tender and sweet, ranging in size from 70 to 500 per pound (one of the tiniest bites around). To eat shell-on, squeeze the tail and pop the meat out of shell. Harvested from the wild in the Pacific northwest, north Atlantic, Norway, and Iceland.

- **Rock shrimp:** Rock shrimp are named for their hard, thick, lobster-like shells. When cooked, the shells turn bright red, with pinkish-white meat and red skin. Rock shrimp are sweet, plump, and slightly chewy. Because the armor-like shell is tough to crack at home, most rock shrimp are sold shell-off and range in size from 25 to 110 per pound. These quick-cooking shrimp are great stir-fried and deep-fried, and in pasta and soups. Wild-caught in Florida, California, and the Caribbean, rock shrimp are a deep-water cousin of pink, brown, and white shrimp.

- **Freshwater shrimp:** Raw freshwater shrimp have bluish-gray shells that cook up pale red. When cooked, the meat is white and the skin is pale pink. The soft, mild-tasting flesh cooks quickly and benefits from added flavors. You can find freshwater shrimp up to 1 pound each. Farmed and harvested wild in Thailand, India, Indonesia, and the Philippines, with an extremely limited amount in the U.S.

- **Spot prawn or spot shrimp:** These shrimp have two distinctive white spots behind the head; when cooked, the shells turn grayish-red, with white meat and pale pink skin. You'll find a tender, softer texture than whites, pinks, or brown. Sizes range from 6 to 12 per pound, and they often come head-on, with the roe attached. Steam, grill, deep fry, or sauté. Found wild in the Pacific northwest.

Index

• Y •

• Z •

YOUR ONLINE RESOURCE
WWW.DUMMIES.COM

Discover Dummies Online!

The Dummies Web Site is your fun and friendly online resource for the latest information about ...*For Dummies*® books and your favorite topics. The Web site is the place to communicate with us, exchange ideas with other ...*For Dummies* readers, chat with authors, and have fun!

Ten Fun and Useful Things You Can Do at www.dummies.com

1. Win free ...*For Dummies* books and more!
2. Register your book and be entered in a prize drawing.
3. Meet your favorite authors through the IDG Books Author Chat Series.
4. Exchange helpful information with other ...*For Dummies* readers.
5. Discover other great ...*For Dummies* books you must have!
6. Purchase Dummieswear™ exclusively from our Web site.
7. Buy ...*For Dummies* books online.
8. Talk to us. Make comments, ask questions, get answers!
9. Download free software.
10. Find additional useful resources from authors.

Link directly to these ten fun and useful things at
http://www.dummies.com/10useful

WWW.DUMMIES.COM

For other technology titles from IDG Books Worldwide, go to
www.idgbooks.com

Not on the Web yet? It's easy to get started with *Dummies 101*®: *The Internet For Windows*®*98* or *The Internet For Dummies*®, 6th Edition, at local retailers everywhere.

Find other ...*For Dummies* books on these topics:
Business • Career • Databases • Food & Beverage • Games • Gardening • Graphics • Hardware
Health & Fitness • Internet and the World Wide Web • Networking • Office Suites
Operating Systems • Personal Finance • Pets • Programming • Recreation • Sports
Spreadsheets • Teacher Resources • Test Prep • Word Processing

IDG BOOKS WORLDWIDE BOOK REGISTRATION

Register This Book and Win!

We want to hear from you!

Visit **http://my2cents.dummies.com** to register this book and tell us how you liked it!

- ✔ Get entered in our monthly prize giveaway.

- ✔ Give us feedback about this book — tell us what you like best, what you like least, or maybe what you'd like to ask the author and us to change!

- ✔ Let us know any other ...*For Dummies*® topics that interest you.

Your feedback helps us determine what books to publish, tells us what coverage to add as we revise our books, and lets us know whether we're meeting your needs as a ...*For Dummies* reader. You're our most valuable resource, and what you have to say is important to us!

Not on the Web yet? It's easy to get started with *Dummies 101*®*: The Internet For Windows*® *98* or *The Internet For Dummies*®, 6th Edition, at local retailers everywhere.

Or let us know what you think by sending us a letter at the following address:

...*For Dummies* Book Registration
Dummies Press
7260 Shadeland Station, Suite 100
Indianapolis, IN 46256-3945
Fax 317-596-5498

™
··FOR DUMMIES

BESTSELLING BOOK SERIES